CASS SERIES: STUDIES IN INTELLIGENCE
ISSN: 1368-9916

(Series Editors: Christopher Andrew, Michael I. Handel, Wesley K. Wark and Richard J. Aldrich)

THE NORWEGIAN
INTELLIGENCE SERVICE

1945–1970

Also in the Studies in Intelligence series

British Military Intelligence in the Palestine Campaign 1914–1918 by Yigal Sheffy

British Military Intelligence in the Crimean War, 1854–1856 by Stephen M. Harris

Signals Intelligence in World War II edited by David Alvarez

Knowing Your Friends: Intelligence Inside Alliances and Coalitions from 1914 to the Cold War edited by Martin S. Alexander

Eternal Vigilance? 50 Years of the CIA edited by Rhodri Jeffreys-Jones and Christopher Andrew

Nothing Sacred: Nazi Espionage Against the Vatican, 1939–1945 by David Alvarez and Revd. Robert A. Graham

Intelligence Investigations: How Ultra Changed History by Ralph Bennett

Intelligence Analysis and Assessment edited by David Charters, A. Stuart Farson and Glenn P. Hastedt

TET 1968: Understanding the Surprise by Ronnie E. Ford

Intelligence and Imperial Defence: British Intelligence and the Defence of the Indian Empire 1904–1924 by Richard J. Popplewell

Espionage: Past, Present, Future? edited by Wesley K. Wark

The Australian Security Intelligence Organization: An Unofficial History by Frank Cain

Policing Politics: Security Intelligence and the Liberal Democratic State by Peter Gill

From Information to Intrigue: Studies in Secret Service Based on the Swedish Experience 1939–45 by C. G. McKay

Dieppe Revisited: A Documentary Investigation by John Campbell

More Instructions from the Centre by Andrew Gordievsky

Controlling Intelligence edited by Glenn P. Hastedt

Spy Fiction, Spy Films and Real Intelligence edited by Wesley K. Wark

Security and Intelligence in a Changing World: New Perspectives for the 1990s edited by A. Stuart Farson, David Stafford and Wesley K. Wark

A Don at War by Sir David Hunt K.C.M.G., O.B.E. (reprint)

Intelligence and Military Operations edited by Michael I. Handel

Leaders and Intelligence edited by Michael I. Handel

War, Strategy and Intelligence by Michael I. Handel

Strategic and Operational Deception in the Second World War edited by Michael I. Handel

Codebreaker in the Far East by Alan Stripp

THE NORWEGIAN INTELLIGENCE SERVICE

1945–1970

OLAV RISTE

Institute for Defence Studies, Oslo

FRANK CASS
LONDON • PORTLAND, OR

First Published in 1999 in Great Britain by
FRANK CASS PUBLISHERS
Newbury House, 900 Eastern Avenue
London IG2 7HH

and in the United States of America by
FRANK CASS PUBLISHERS
c/o ISBS, 5804 N.E. Hassalo Street
Portland, Oregon 97213-3644

Website: www.frankcass.com

British Library Cataloguing in Publication Data

Riste, Olav
The Norwegian intelligence service, 1945–1970. – (Cass
series. Studies in intelligence)
1. Intelligence service – Norway – History
I. Title
327.1'2481

ISBN 0-7146-4900-7 (cloth)
ISBN 0-7146-4455-2 (paper)
ISSN 1368-9916

Library of Congress Cataloging-in-Publication Data

Riste, Olav
[Strengt hemmelig. English]
The Norwegian intelligence service, 1945–1970/Olav Riste.
    p.   cm. – (Cass series, studies in intelligence, ISSN
1368-9916)
    Translation of: Strengt hemmelig / Olav Riste og Arnfinn Moland.
    Moland not considered a co-author because he did not participate
in the revision that preceded the translation–Pref.
    Includes bibliographical references and index.
    ISBN 0-7146-4900-7 (cloth). – ISBN 0-7146-4455-2 (paper)
    1. Intelligence service–Norway. 2. Internal security–Norway.
I. Title II. Series.
HV8230.A2R5713 1999
327.12481–dc21
                                                            99-23373
                                                            CIP

Typeset by Vitaset, Paddock Wood, Kent
Printed in Great Britain by
MPG Books Ltd, Bodmin, Cornwall

Contents

	List of Illustrations	vi
	List of Maps	viii
	Preface	ix
	Abbreviations and Glossary	xiii
1	Beginnings	1
2	Into the Cold War: Intelligence and Security	13
3	Occupation Preparedness: 'Stay Behind'	34
4	Through the Iron Curtain: Humint and Photint	55
5	Comint: Communications Intelligence	84
6	Electronic Intelligence (1): The Air Force as Elint Pioneer	115
7	Electronic Intelligence (2): The Norwegian Intelligence Service Takes Over	146
8	Sound Waves in the Seas: BRIDGE/SOSUS/CANASTA	164
9	Monitoring of Nuclear Tests	191
10	Telemetry: Surveillance of Space, Missiles and Satellite Activity	212
11	'Sets of Professional Bargains': The Foreign Relations of the Norwegian Intelligence Service	225
12	A State Within the State? Controlling the Intelligence Service	235
13	The Uses of Intelligence	249
14	'Square Pegs in Round Holes': Organisation and Personnel	262
15	Final Act for Evang	273
	Conclusion	287
	Operations and Code-Names	297
	Maps	302
	Bibliography	307
	Index	311

Illustrations

Between pages 142 and 143

1. Vilhelm Andreas Wexelsen Evang.
2. Colonel Alfred R. Roscher Lund.
3. Colonel Johan Berg.
4. Jens Christian Hauge.
5. Three photographs taken by agents on Norwegian merchant ships in Soviet ports: (a) Golf I-class diesel submarine; (b) a Foxtrot-class diesel submarine; (c) a saw mill on fire in Siberia.
6. CIA HQ, Langley, Virginia, in the mid-1960s.
7. U-2 spy plane.
8. RB-47 aircraft in flight.
9. Helge Reiss-Andersen.
10. Knut Willy Kval.
11. Plan of ICBM launch site at Plesetsk.
12. Four founding members of the NIS: (a) Alf Martens Meyer; (b) Jon K. Brynildsen; (c) Dag Falchenberg; (d) Erling Hellerslien.
13. First land station for the underwater sound surveillance system at Andøya in north Norway.
14. BRIDGE underwater sound surveillance system.
15. Satellite image of Severodvinsk shipyard.
16. METRO Elint station, near Soviet border: (a) in its earliest stages; (b) as fully operational, from 1961.
17. Large Soviet aerial complex on Hill 220 near Luostari air base.
18. HEKLA Elint/Radint station at Vardø.
19. Interior of HEKLA.
20. Three vessels used by NIS for missions: (a) *Eger*; (b) *Marjata* I; (c) *Marjata* II.
21. The main Comint station, at Vadsø.

22. The Fauske II (CODHOOK) station.
23. BARHAUG Elint/Comint station at Viksjøfjell: (a) the first fixed installation; (b) the station as completed; (c) section of the aerial in the tower; (d) a Comint 'position' or table.

Illustrations 6, 7 and 8 are reproduced with permission of the American Society for Photogrammetry and Remote Sensing (ASPRS): taken from Robert A. McDonald, *Corona between the Sun and the Earth: The First NRO Reconnaissance Eye in Space* (Bethesda, MD: ASPRS, 1997). Illustrations 11 and 15 are courtesy of the Central Intelligence Agency. All other illustrations are courtesy of the NIS.

Maps

		page
1. Active Norwegian intelligence stations, 1945–72		302
2. The northern Soviet Union and adjoining areas		303
3. The Soviet–Norwegian border region		304
4. Some intelligence targets in the Kola inlet		305

Preface

This book is a thoroughly revised version of a work by Olav Riste and Arnfinn Moland entitled *'Strengt Hemmelig': Norsk etterretningsteneste 1945–1970*, published by Norwegian University Press in 1997. That book was the result of a research project commissioned by the Royal Norwegian Ministry of Defence. The terms of reference for that project, agreed between the Ministry and the present author as leader of the project, was as follows: 'The aim of the project is to produce a scholarly historical study of the activity of the Norwegian Intelligence Service from 1945 up to about 1970.' It was further stated that:

> Arrangements will be made for the historians to have access to and be able to utilise all archival material and all oral sources which may be of importance to their work. The historians will enjoy complete freedom to produce their account in accordance with scholarly criteria, and the aim is that the result should be published. The Ministry reserves the right to review the manuscript before publication. Such review will only be for the purpose of assuring the legal right to privacy of persons mentioned, and to prevent publication of particularly sensitive information that might prejudice national security.

Owing to various reports alleging that most of the archive material of the intelligence service had been destroyed, the project leader felt it necessary to undertake a preliminary survey of the state of the archives before signing the contract. The survey showed that the archive material, although scattered and badly organised, seemed sufficiently rich to make possible a scholarly satisfactory study.

The work on the book was carried out at the Norwegian Institute for Defence Studies, and the practical arrangement was that the authors first went through the files of the various sections of the intelligence service, making notes, and marking those documents of which they required copies. The Intelligence Staff then produced the copies, reviewed them for possible declassification, and delivered them to the authors. Similar procedures were used for material in the ministries, the Defence High Command, etc. A certain number of persons were also interviewed for the book, but the time-consuming character of such oral history meant that this could only be done on a limited basis within the three-year schedule of the assignment.

While the initiative for the project had something to do with a spate of rumours and news stories about alleged wrongdoings or illegal activities by the secret services, this book is in no way in the nature of an investigation. A parliamentary commission of investigation was already at work when our project started, focused on allegations of unlawful surveillance of Norwegian citizens by all the secret services. But our project was carried out quite independently of that investigation, as it had a purely scholarly purpose. We decided to deal with the intelligence service as one of several aspects of Norwegian postwar history, although a very special aspect in view of its secret character. Above all, we have tried to see the service in the context of Norwegian and international security policy in the period.

As the Intelligence Staff until 1965 also had responsibilities in the security field, with particular reference to the security of the military, we have also looked at that aspect. We did so in view also of the difficult relationship between the Chief of Intelligence, Vilhelm Evang, and the Chief of the Security Police, Asbjørn Bryhn – difficulties which eventually were to lead to the dismissal of both from their posts. But we emphasise that it is the intelligence service as such which is our field of study. An additional reason for treating the security aspect more cursorily was that two other historians were at the same time commissioned by the Ministry of Justice to write the history of security surveillance and counter-espionage in Norway.

A commissioned work such as the present one, based on classified sources, could only be done in co-operation with the Norwegian Intelligence Service as well as with other public authorities which in one way or another – such as control and oversight – dealt with the service, and which thereby possessed material or information of value. But none of those institutions has had insight into or influence on the process of research and writing, nor has any of them tried to limit our access to or use of the material. Only after the manuscript was finished was it submitted to the Ministry of Defence for declassification and release. The result of that process was a few minor deletions, totalling less than one manuscript page, concerning mostly details about 'sources and methods' which we accepted as being still of a sensitive nature. The only limitation which we imposed on ourselves during the work was not to seek or divulge names of what we would call 'agents' – in the trade usually referred to as sources – that is, persons who went on missions or gave information without holding appointments in the service. As usual in scholarly works, detailed references to the sources have been given in the footnotes. But we have had to accept that only those parts of the documents which we quote or summarise are declassified and released. The rest of the documentation, although generally downgraded to lower classifications in the process of being made available to us, will remain classified until they – hopefully soon – can be released in full.

The manuscript for the Norwegian version of the book was to a high degree a co-operative effort, for which the two authors were jointly responsible, even if the actual writing of the various chapters was for practical reasons split between the two, with Arnfinn Moland having initial responsibility for Chapters 7–11 and 14–15. However, since Arnfinn Moland was prevented by other pressing engagements from taking part in revising and rewriting the manuscript for this English edition, it is his wish that Olav Riste stands as sole responsible author of the present book.

Abbreviations and Glossary

ABM	Anti-Ballistic Missile
ACCG	Allied Clandestine Co-ordination Groups (NATO)
Acint	Acoustic Intelligence
Acoustint	Acoustic Intelligence
Adm.T.P.	Administrasjon av tysk personell (administration of German personnel)
AEDS	Atomic Energy Detection Systems
AFNORTH	Allied Forces Northern Europe
AFSA	Armed Forces Security Agency
AFTAC	Air Force Technical Applications Centre
ALFN	Allied (from October 1945 'British') Land Forces Norway
ARPA	Advanced Research Projects Agency
ASW	Anti -Submarine Warfare
BND	Bundesnachrichtendienst
CIA	Central Intelligence Agency (United States)
CIG	Central Intelligence Group (predecessor to CIA)
CINCNORTH	Commander-in-Chief Northern Europe
Comint	Communications Intelligence
COMSEC	Communications Security
CPC	Clandestine Planning Committee (NATO)
DKN	Distriktskommando Nord–Norge (Defence Command North Norway)
ECM	Electronic Countermeasures
EK	Elektronisk Krigføring (electronic warfare)
Elint	Electronic Intelligence
ERO	Elektronisk Romovervaking (electronic space surveillance)
ESRO	European Space Research Organisation

EW	Early Warning
FBI	Federal Bureau of Investigation
FBT	Forsvarets Bygningstjeneste (defence constructions agency)
FD/E	Forsvarsdepartementets E-kontor (Defence Ministry Intelligence Bureau)
FD	Forsvarsdepartementet (Defence Ministry)
FFI	Forsvarets Forskningsinstitutt (Norwegian Defence Research Establishment)
FFSK	Forsvarets forsøksstasjon Kirkenes (Defence Experimental Station Kirkenes)
FFSV	Forsvarets forsøksstasjon Vadsø (Defence Experimental Station Vadsø)
FL	Finnmark Landforsvar (Finnmark Army Command)
FO	Forsvarets Overkommando (Defence High Command)
FO/E	Forsvarets Overkommando/Etterretning (Intelligence Staff)
FO/O	Forsvarets Overkommando/Operasjonsstaben (Operations Staff)
FO/S	Forsvarets Overkommando/Sikkerhetsstaben (Security Staff)
FOK	Flyvåpnets Overkommando (Air Force High Command)
FRA	Försvarets Radioanstalt (Sweden) (Defence Radio Agency)
FSJ	Forsvarssjef (Chief of Defence)
FST	Forsvarsstaben (Defence Staff)
FST/E	Forsvarsstaben/ Etterretningsstaben (Defence Staff/Intelligence)
FSTF	Forsvarets stasjon Fauske (Defence Station Fauske)
FSTH	Forsvarets Stasjon Høybuktmoen (Defence Station Høybuktmoen)
FSTKA	Forsvarets stasjon Karasjok (Defence Station Karasjok)
FSTM	Forsvarets stasjon Moen (Defence Station Moen)
GCHQ	Government Communications Headquarters (Britain)
GRU	Soviet military intelligence
GSV	Garnison Sør-Varanger (army garrison southern Varanger)

H	Hemmelig (Secret)
HP	High Priority
HOK	Hærens Overkommando (Army High Command)
Humint	Human intelligence
HV	Heimevernet (Home Guard)
ICBM	Intercontinental Ballistic Missile
JIB	Joint Intelligence Board
JIC	Joint Intelligence Committee
JAAC	Joint Acoustic Analysis Centre
K&V	Kontroll og varsling (Control and Warning)
KGB	Soviet security and intelligence service
KK/KU	Koordieringskomiteen/Koordineringsutvalget (Co-ordination Committee for the secret services)
KDV	Kvinnenes Demokratiske Verdensforbund (World Federation of Democratic Women)
LG	Liaisongruppa (liaison group)
LKN	Luftforsvarskommando Nord (Air Command North Norway)
LKS	Luftforsvarskommando Sør (Air Command South Norway)
LOFAR	Low Frequency Analysing Recorder
LOK	Luftforsvarets Overkommando (Air Force High Command)
LPG	Langtidsplangruppa (Long-term Planning Group)
LSTH	Luftforsvarets Stasjon Høybuktmoen (Air Force Station Høybuktmoen)
LT	Legal Travellers
MI6	Military Intelligence 6 (British secret intelligence service)
MAAG	Military Assistance Advisory Group
MAAU	Maritime Acoustic Analysis Unit
MAD CAT	Mobile Automatic Digital Collection and Analysis Trailers
MDAP	Mutual Defence Assistance Programme
MER	Månedlig etterretningsrapport (monthly intelligence report series)
MKN	Marinekommando Nord (Naval Command North Norway)
MM	Martens Meyer

MOU	Memorandum of Understanding
MVD	Soviet Home Office
MWDP	Mutual Weapons Development Project
NADGE	NATO Air Defence Ground Environment
NDRE	Norwegian Defence Research Establishment
NIE	National Intelligence Estimate (United States)
NIS	Norwegian Intelligence Service
NSA	National Security Agency ('No Such Agency')
NSC	National Security Council
OB	Order of Battle
OCC	Operational Control Centre
OCS	Operations by the Clandestine Services (NATO)
ONI	Office of Naval Intelligence
OSS	Office of Strategic Services
Photint	Photographic Intelligence
POT	Politiets Overvåkingsteneste (Security Police)
PVO	Soviet Air Defence
Radint	Radar intelligence
RA	Riksarkivet (National Archives)
RAF	Royal Air Force (British)
RCM	Radio Countermeasures
RNoAF	Royal Norwegian Air Force
RR	Riksrevisjonen (Auditor General's Office)
RSU	Regjeringens Sikkerhetsutvalg (Cabinet Defence and Security Committee)
Photint	Photographic intelligence
SACEUR	Supreme Allied Commander Europe
SACLANT	Supreme Allied Commander Atlantic
SAN	Sivert A. Nielsen
SAS	Special Air Service
SB	Stay Behind
Seismint	Seismic intelligence
SG	Standing Group (NATO)
SH	Strengt hemmelig (Top Secret)
SHAPE	Supreme Headquarters Allied Powers Europe
Sigint	Signals intelligence
SJE	Sjef Etterretningsstaben (Chief of Intelligence Staff)
SJO	Sjef Operasjonsstaben (Chief of Operations Staff)

SKN	Sjøforsvarskommando Nord (Naval Command North Norway)
SLBM	Submarine Launched Ballistic Missile
SMK	Statsministerens kontor (Prime Minister's Office)
SOB	Special Operations Branch
SOE	Special Operations Executive
SOK	Sjøforsvarets Overkommando (Naval High Command)
SOSUS	Sound Surveillance System
SPB	Special Projects Branch (NATO)
SSS	Space Surveillance System
SSS	Sjøforsvarets Stasjon Stave (Navy Station Stave)
STSJ	Stabssjef (Chief of staff)
Telint	Telemetry intelligence
UD	Utenriksdepartementet (Ministry of Foreign Affairs)
UHF	Ultra High Frequency
UK	United Kingdom
USAF(E)	US Air Force (Europe)
USIB	United States Intelligence Board
USN	US Navy
VHF	Very High Frequency
ØKN	Øverstkommanderende Nord-Norge (Commander-in-Chief North Norway)

1

Beginnings

The Norwegian intelligence service (NIS) may be said to have had two or even three starting points: 1940, 1942 and 1946. Such a statement implies in the first instance that whatever intelligence activity existed before the Second World War, it never attained the breadth and level of organisation required for it to merit being called 'a Norwegian intelligence service'. It is also meant to convey that the postwar Norwegian intelligence service could only to a very limited degree build on what had been done during the war. In most respects it had to start anew.

The situation before the war was described as follows by the person generally seen as the founder of the NIS, Alfred Roscher Lund, in the introduction to his official report on the wartime service:[1]

> In the General Staff this activity was part of the section on foreign armies, which took care of liaison with military attachés. A few of the younger officers had as their task to keep abreast of military developments in certain foreign countries, and their sources were mainly newspapers and periodicals ... The navy had by the outbreak of war in 1939 established a bureau to receive and register reports from the various naval stations.

All this was of course in part a reflection of the parlous state in which the Norwegian armed forces found themselves after having been run down during the interwar period. The only positive development noted by Roscher Lund was that in 'the autumn of 1939 the Ministry of Defence instituted a so-called information bureau which in fact dealt with code-breaking as well as dabbling in the field of radio monitoring'. But this was on a very limited scale.

The build-up of what was to become a large and extensive NIS, run by the Government in its wartime exile in London, had two roots.[2] In the occupied country, individual persons and small groups began from the autumn of 1940 to send reports, via couriers, to the Norwegian Legation in Stockholm, on the activities and military dispositions of the occupying power. At the same time Foreign Minister Halvdan Koht initiated an intelligence bureau attached to the Foreign Ministry in London and co-operating with British Military Intelligence. Koht's motive was a combination of a desire to have the fullest possible knowledge of developments in occupied Norway, and the need to establish and maintain the closest possible contact between Norway in exile and the people on the home front: he was concerned lest the Government should lose touch with its own people.

From the end of 1940 these activities, and the co-operation with the British Secret Intelligence Service, was transferred to a newly established intelligence bureau under the Ministry of Defence – Forsvarsdeparte-mentets Etterretningskontor, or FD/E – led by Major Finn Nagell. The actual intelligence work – the collation and analysis of enemy military activity in Norway – was, however, for the most part run by the British. Major Nagell's FD/E had as its primary task to work with the British in recruiting, training and running NIS agents sent to operate clandestine radio transmitters on the coast of Norway, and to report on enemy shipping and naval movements.

A fully fledged Norwegian military intelligence service began to be built up from the winter of 1942, after the Norwegian Government in exile had set up a joint Defence High Command – Forsvarets Over-kommando, or FO – charged with planning and preparations for the liberation of Norway. Colonel Roscher Lund, the first chief of the service, described its primary task as being

> To provide the FO with an intelligence basis for its activity. It was plainly obvious that the FO could not approach the allied authorities with proposals for operations, or claim to participate in operational planning, without such a basis.
> To provide allied authorities with a corresponding fund of intelligence for any allied operations on Norwegian territory ... Through supplying the fullest possible intelligence on which to base all operations in occupied Norway one could ensure that the operations were successful and carried out with the least possible casualties.

This would also spare the Norwegian people from loss, suffering, and material damage.

Another overriding aim was 'to keep the intelligence service under Norwegian control to the fullest possible extent'.

The Second Bureau of the Defence High Command – FO II – subsequently merged with the Defence Ministry's FD/E Bureau – developed into a service of a considerable size. By the end of the war it had grown into the largest section of FO, with a personnel of 223 men and women (the latter being mostly British female clerks). Its work had resulted in a massive and detailed survey of all aspects of Norwegian society – administration, communications and industry – as well as the forces and installations of the occupying power. The main sources of information were reports from persons and organisations in Norway, and interrogation of persons arriving to join the Norwegian forces being built up in the United Kingdom. A considerable underground network of intelligence organisations had developed in the occupied territory, with a network bearing the code-name XU as the largest one. Colonel Roscher Lund's estimate of the number of agents working for the NIS in Norway during the war counted 200 agents trained in Britain and Sweden, and a further 1,800 persons classified as contacts, helpers and couriers. An intelligence section attached to the Norwegian military attaché's office in Stockholm played a central liaison role between headquarters in London and the agents in the field.

Apart from their intelligence activities both FD/E and FO II were charged with controlling security – preventing enemy infiltration and espionage – within the Norwegian armed forces and civilian exile communities in the United Kingdom and Sweden. Historical accounts record many instances which show that this was a new and unfamiliar field of concern for Norwegians. Among more security-minded Britons the Norwegians were seen as somewhat naïve and gullible in their handling of secret information. Literature on the resistance movement in occupied Norway also has many examples from the early period when irresponsible talk had extremely serious consequences.

One aspect of intelligence work with important implications for security was cryptography – the making and breaking of codes. Co-operation with the Allies depended on their having confidence in the security of Norwegian ciphers. Norwegian cryptographic work had to be rebuilt from scratch after the occupying power assumed control of

Norwegian institutions and offices which had used ciphers before and during the Norwegian campaign in 1940. This field was in a way Colonel Roscher Lund's own 'baby' from before the war, and his report claims that while the Germans during the war managed to break the ciphers of many countries, Norwegian codes remained unbroken. Norwegian ciphers were used in communication between the central administration in London and the resistance organisations, the large merchant navy which played such an essential part in Allied maritime transport, and in Norwegian diplomatic correspondence. Control was exercised by a cipher council with representatives from FO II and the Foreign Ministry.

Another important element of security was the secret so-called 'catalogue of suspects' – a list of Norwegian nationals with 'presumed un-national attitude'. From a number of 18,000 names in January 1943 the list had grown to include 47,000 persons in May 1945. A directive from October 1944 defined the catalogue as a register of 'all Norwegian citizens in Norway who have been named as having in one way or another put themselves outside the national solidarity – members of the nazi party, presumed members, persons with alleged strong nazi sympathies, people who have profited excessively from work for the German occupation authorities or who have volunteered to work for the Germans, etc.'. The purpose of the list was to provide the information necessary to protect resistance work from infiltration, and the directive stressed that it was in no way meant to serve as a basis for postwar judicial proceedings against collaborators.

DOWNSIZING – AND NEW PLANS

Considering the size and achievements of the intelligence service during the war, one might have expected it to have a flying start in the postwar period. There are several reasons why this did not happen. For one thing the intelligence effort during the war had had a very peculiar orientation, being organised from abroad and directed towards the home country under foreign occupation. A peacetime NIS would of necessity have to be turned 'inside out', organised on home territory and directed at foreign countries. Secondly, the intelligence effort up to 1945 sprang from a self-evident need produced by a state of war and the aim of making a contribution to the liberation of the country. A peacetime intelligence service would need to be justified through a demonstrable external threat to national security, which could not be perceived during the first postwar years. A detailed plan for an extensive peacetime intelligence service, put on paper by Colonel Roscher Lund in the spring of 1944, was therefore left to gather dust in the archives for the time being.[3]

Reports from FO II from the summer of 1945[4] onwards show an organisation mainly employed in tasks connected with clearing up after the German occupation. This concerned in particular a corps of controllers which became known by the initials 'Adm.T.P' – Administrasjon av Tysk Personell. Their job was to work with Allied counter-intelligence in investigating Germans who had been doing military, paramilitary or police service in Norway, and who were under suspicion of having committed war crimes. As many as 173 officers were engaged in those tasks by 1 September 1945. A report from FO II in January 1946, with the telling title 'Survey of FO II's current organisation. Possibilities for downsizing', complained that the majority of the officers in the service were doing 'Adm.T.P.' work, and that most of them had applied to leave as soon as suitable civilian employment could be found. The total size of FO II at the end of 1945 was about 80 officers. Roughly 60 of them worked with 'Adm.T.P.', whose chief was now Major Vilhelm Evang. Nine officers worked in the security section, which was led by Lieutenant Einar Jacobsen. A small counter-espionage section numbered four officers, with Captain Kaj Martens as head, and the Cipher Section consisted of Second Lieutenant Nils Stordahl and three other officers. Finally there was an administrative section with Captain Andreas Lerheim and three other officers.

Earlier that autumn there had been a section variously called 'Intelligence bureau', 'Section for operational intelligence and documentation', or 'Intelligence and documentation section'. Its task had initially been to issue monthly surveys based on reports from the armed services and information from Allied authorities. But in fact its most important task had been that of securing and reviewing German wartime documents, in co-operation with the documents section of Allied Land Forces Norway, the inter-Allied (from October 1945 British) headquarters of the liberation forces for Norway. But such tasks were by their nature strictly temporary. By 10 November only two officers were left in that section, and both had left by the end of the year. In January 1946 a documents office emerged as a sub-division of the 'Adm.T.P.' section.

In January 1946 Norway's wartime Foreign Minister, Trygve Lie, was elected as the first Secretary-General of the United Nations. He immediately invited Colonel Roscher Lund to come with him to New York as his military adviser. Roscher Lund's parting shot as Norwegian intelligence chief was to produce another plan for the build-up of a central military intelligence service.[5] The most interesting aspect of that plan was the proposal for a two-pronged service: a military/operational intelligence service under the Defence High Command, and a 'Department for defensive and special intelligence' within the Ministry of Defence. The latter would consist of about a hundred mostly civilian intelligence specialists, compared with only about a dozen officers in the military intelligence section. Of the personnel in the intelligence department of the ministry over half should work with ciphers and communications intelligence. There should also be a liaison office charged with 'establishing all contacts required for the collection of information and using special agents where possible and as required'.

It may be surmised that this dual organisation model reflected a traditional military scepticism towards a clandestine intelligence service. Roscher Lund justified his proposal by remarking that such a special intelligence service ought to be placed under a Cabinet minister, since its work would be of special interest to three ministries, i.e. the Ministries of Defence, Foreign Affairs and Justice. He referred to the precedents of the prewar information bureau in the Ministry of Defence, and the wartime FD/E bureau. There was also a linkage to a contemporary proposal from the national police chief which stressed the need for a high-level committee to co-ordinate all information concerning the security of the realm. Such a committee could serve as controllers for the special intelligence service.

It was in connection with this plan that Roscher Lund officially nominated Vilhelm Evang as his natural successor as intelligence chief, by naming him as his preferred candidate to run the special, secret and mainly civilian intelligence service. Vilhelm Evang was then 37 years old. He was a science graduate from the University of Oslo, and had to escape to Sweden in 1941 because of involvement in resistance activities. He was then called over to London and, although a civilian, was given a temporary officer's commission to serve in FD/E. His work there had mostly to do with security matters, but Roscher Lund, as head of FO II into which FD/E was merged in 1944, must have noted his leadership qualities.

We do not know why the plan to have an intelligence service under the Ministry of Defence got nowhere. Instead, FO II lived on as an intelligence bureau within the Defence High Command, and from mid-1946 within the Defence Staff after the Defence High Command had been disbanded. The proposed defence budget for 1946–47 described the intelligence bureau as having five sections, one each for administration, for technical services, for communications intelligence, for passport control (based then in London), and the perennial 'Adm.T.P.' section. A subsequent budget proposal from January 1947 proposed a Defence Staff with four sections, one for organisation and mobilisation – FST I, an intelligence and foreign liaison section – FST II, a section for operations – FST III, and a logistics section – FST IV. Major Vilhelm Evang figures officially as Section Chief from 1 August 1947, and from 1 October the intelligence service no longer exists as FO II but as the Second Bureau of the Defence Staff, or FST II. It was later to become known as FST/E, where the E stood for *etterretning* or intelligence, and its full name would in the years to come change back and forth between 'Intelligence and Foreign Liaison Staff' and 'Intelligence and Security Staff'. Here we shall for the sake of simplicity refer to it as the Intelligence Staff, while bearing in mind that its responsibilities up to 1965 also included military security.

NEW ACTIVITY

With regard to intelligence work as such, the most interesting part of the postwar FO II was the section which first appears in October 1945 under the name of 'Radio control section', dealing with locating radio transmitters and monitoring signals traffic. The section chief, Lieutenant Jon K. Brynildsen, had an ambitious programme approved by the Defence Minister which looked towards a staff of four officers and as many as 29 radio operators. One of the priorities was to locate and identify illegal radio transmitters. In Norwegian law radio transmitters could not operate without an official licence, and the right of diplomatic missions to send and receive coded messages was subject to the condition that the traffic went through official telegraph channels.

One of the first initiatives taken by the new section was to contact the Swedish defence staff about co-operation in the monitoring of illegal radio transmissions in both countries. The Swedish communications intelligence bureau – Försvarets Radioanstalt, or FRA – had an impressive record of achievements in monitoring and code-breaking during the war, and was willing to co-operate. Brynildsen had far-reaching plans for his section. In a report from December 1946[6] he wrote that the work should not be limited to controlling illegal transmissions. It ought to embrace more wide-ranging communications intelligence activity, working in close co-operation with the cipher section, including the monitoring and decrypting of the military and diplomatic radio, telephone and telegraph communications of foreign countries and agents.

Brynildsen's plans were clearly inspired by a visit he and his deputy, Lieutenant Diseth, had made to Sweden's FRA in the autumn of 1946. His report described the Swedish bureau as an extremely well-organised and highly developed organisation, with a staff of about 400 persons occupied with all aspects of communications intelligence and cryptography. They had also been shown the plans for a vast underground headquarters equipped with state-of-the-art technology.

Progressing from plans to practical work in the field, Brynildsen's section moved quickly in 1946 to establish a 'home station' in a military camp taken over from the German occupation forces in Oslo. Two local stations were established at the same time, one near Stavanger and the other one near Trondheim. Some mobile direction-finding equipment left behind by the German forces was also put to use. Of particular interest, however, were the initiatives aimed at the establishment of a listening station in the county of Finnmark, near the Arctic borders of the Soviet Union:

> A complete and effective coverage of Norway will require the establishment of a subsidiary listening post in Northern Norway, equipped with its own direction-finding equipment for the control of radio communications in the northern areas. To explore the possibilities in that field, and to carry out a general monitoring of certain frequencies, a three-man unit led by Lieutenant Diseth was sent north in July. They returned after a month with much important material for further analysis, and steps have been taken to get official approval for a listening station near Kirkenes.

The July 1946 mission to Finnmark, codenamed TORKEL, constituted the origin for the first operative signals intelligence station in northern Norway targeted towards Soviet military communications. A detailed expedition report from FO II in August 1946 opened up interesting perspectives. The initiative for TORKEL was there explained as the result of observations in the spring of 1946, indicating 'a noticeably increased intensity of radio activity in the Arctic ocean area'. Some reports also suggested the presence of illegal radio transmitters in North Norway. Disguised as a scientific expedition for ionospheric research, the real mission was – in order of priority – monitoring of the Soviet Northern Fleet and Soviet air forces, Soviet army units in the area with attached air and police forces, Soviet radio-telephony, and monitoring radio signals which might be connected with possible experiments with V-2 rockets. Rumours had suggested that the Russians were test-firing V-2 rockets from East Germany towards the White and Barents Seas.

The TORKEL station had been set up near the town of Vardø, and was active for ten days. Most of the signals monitored were radio traffic to and from Soviet naval vessels and aircraft, which would require further analysis. But the sheer amount of traffic strongly suggested a need for continuous monitoring. No illegal transmissions had been registered, but there were some indications of experiments with rockets which ought to be investigated further. FO II now proposed setting up a listening station in eastern Finnmark near Kirkenes, initially for a trial period of at least six months, and manned by a station chief and six radio operators. Together with the stations established in the Oslo, Stavanger and Trondheim areas this would ensure nearly complete coverage of radio traffic inside Norway. Monitoring from Finnmark would then provide a basis for estimating the size and location of the Soviet armed forces in the North, and make it possible eventually to identify units, aircraft and naval vessels.[7]

The next phase of operation TORKEL began at the end of March 1947, as a team of nine men set themselves up in two uninsulated Nissen huts in a military camp near Kirkenes. 'This was now April, and the freezing temperatures of Finnmark were still with us. As the huts were without insulation we were burning firewood until the stoves were red hot. Still it could happen that the men woke up in the morning with their hair frozen to the wall.'[8] In the summer a wooden barracks was set up as station headquarters. The collected intelligence material was carried on foot to Kirkenes three times a week, and from there went by coastal steamer to Oslo for analysis. The total budget for that 1947 operation was 22,000 kroner. To obtain the goodwill of the army in the area Evang sent a special letter to the Army Commander North Norway, General A.D. Dahl, with a survey of Soviet air and naval forces in the North, adding that the information about the navy was 'in part the result of the work of our section at Kirkenes'.[9]

Through those small steps FO II would seem to have been on its way to becoming a real intelligence service, albeit on a small scale, by the end of 1946. A clear sign of this is that Vilhelm Evang, who had now taken over as head, had won through with some modest expansion plans. In a letter to his former chief in November 1946 he wrote that

> we have scaled the first hurdle. The highest authority has approved the institution in principle, and accepted the proposals now on the table. This signifies a considerable expansion from the current state of affairs, and will provide a basic framework which can achieve at least something in the years to come. The matter must of course be approved in a larger forum, and much of my time is spent preparing for this. I do not expect serious difficulties here, and regard with equanimity the fact that for the time being we are still having to deal with all kinds of cuts and tightening of belts.[10]

At this time Evang also presented his first budget proposal to the Ministry of Defence, for the fiscal year 1947–48. It was exceedingly modest, amounting to only about one million kroner of a total defence budget of about 250 million. The real cost of the service was in fact difficult to estimate, since the salaries of the military personnel were camouflaged under various regular branches of the armed forces. Other costs were hidden under a special budget section which did not appear in the proposal to the Storting. But Evang took care to suggest that the use of such secret funds should be audited by a special control committee.[11]

Apart from operation TORKEL little information exists about any intelligence operations as such by the FO II in 1947. But there are several indications that Evang at this time sought to develop contacts with other countries' intelligence services. In January he sought approval for an official visit to Germany and the UK. His visit to Britain came at the behest of British intelligence, presumably MI6, which in Evang's words 'claimed to have information that certain foreign powers were intensifying their activity in Norway, in a way that our country may become a focal point for the espionage networks of those countries'.[12] On 5 February Evang could inform the Chief of Defence Staff, General Ole Berg, about an arrangement with Britain's Joint Intelligence Board for the exchange of topographical material, and an agreement of an unspecified nature with MI6. In his note of the conversation Evang also mentions giving the General information about the military situation in Germany which presumably came from British sources. Of more particular interest was some information concerning Svalbard, which at that time was a hot issue for the Norwegian Government since the Russians were pressing for negotiations about the status of the archipelago. At issue was whether to renew discussions with the Russians about their 1944 demands for a kind of condominium with joint military bases. Presumably reflecting British viewpoints, Evang said that no war was considered likely during the next two years, but that a Russian occupation of Svalbard would be regarded by the Western powers as a *casus belli*. It was also assumed that the Soviet Union was using Svalbard as a warning against an expansion of the American bases in Iceland.[13]

The NIS also established relations at this time with Denmark, and expanded on the contact with the United States which had been initiated the previous year, when Major Martens had been sent to New York, ostensibly as Passport Control Officer, but in reality to establish liaison with the developing US intelligence organisations. US intelligence was then in the melting pot after President Truman had disbanded the war-time Office of Strategic Services (OSS) and replaced it by the embryonic Central Intelligence Group, which in the autumn of 1947 developed into the Central Intelligence Agency (CIA). Evang himself visited the United States in November 1947.[14]

The available material suggests that security and counter-espionage were becoming an increasingly important part of the Intelligence Staff's work. Their radio specialists were called in to improve security against spies eavesdropping on discussions in the Storting building, as well as securing the offices of the Prime Minister and other government offices and residences. In June 1948 Lieutenant Falchenberg was sent to Moscow to search through the Norwegian embassy building. He found no less than 13 microphones hidden in the walls.[15]

NOTES

1. The wartime Defence High Command in exile (Forsvarets Overkommando, or FO) produced in 1945 a mimeographed report in several parts, of which a condensed report on the intelligence service was Part II. We quote here from a separately produced most secret complete version which is available in Norway's national archives Riksarkivet. On the intelligence situation before the German invasion see also O. Riste, *Weserübung: Det perfekte strategiske overfall?* (IFS, *Forsvarsstudier*, 4, 1990).
2. The King and the Government, with elements of the administration and of the

armed forces, moved into exile in the UK after the country had been overrun by the German invaders in June 1940. For brief, popular surveys of Norway's wartime history see J. Andenaes, M. Skodvin and O. Riste, *Norway and the Second World War* (TANO, Oslo, 1965 and subsequent editions), and O. Riste and B. Nøkleby, *Norway 1940–1945: The Resistance Movement* (TANO, Oslo, 1973 and later editions).

3. RA, 2B.071.21 FO II (Roscher Lund) to FO, 28 April 1944: 'Oppbygging av etterretningstjenesten i Norge'.

4. NHM, file 'Oversikt over FO IIs organisasjon. 1945, 1946 og avviklingsarbeider'.

5. UD 38.5/53, FO II to Defence Minister Jens Chr. Hauge, Justice Minister Oscar C. Gundersen, Commissioner of Police Andreas Aulie, Deputy Commissioner Olaf Svendsen, 20 March 1946.

6. NHM, J.K. Brynildsen's report, 16 Dec. 1946: 'F.O. IIs Radioavdelings virke 1945/46'.

7. FO/E, Evang papers, FO II report, Aug. 1946.

8. FO/E, mimeographed booklet 'Erindringer fra E-tjenesten i Sør-Varanger og tilbakeblikk i Moens 30-årige historie', p. 7.

9. FO/E, copy file H 1947, Evang to General Dahl, 16 July 1947.

10. FO/E, Evang papers, Evang to Roscher Lund, 21 Nov. 1946.

11. FO/E, copy file H 1946, FO II to FD, 6 Dec. 1946.

12. Ibid., copy file H 1947, Evang to Forsvarsstaben, 6 Jan.1947.

13. FO/E, Evang papers.

14. UD 38.5/53, telegram UD to Nor. Emb. Washington DC, 21 May 1946, and FST II to UD, 19 Jan. 1948; FO/E copy file H 1947, Evang to Hauge, 18 Sept. 1947. 'Passport Control Officer' was the normal cover for British intelligence officers before the Second World War.

15. FO/E, box 'Spesielle E-rapporter', file 'Spesialrapporter'. Diseth's report 27 Jan. 1947; Falchenberg to Permanent Under-Secretary Skylstad, UD, 3 July 1948.

2

Into the Cold War: Intelligence and Security

In his first budget proposal after being formally appointed chief of the Intelligence Staff – its full name now being the Foreign and Intelligence Staff of the Defence Staff, with initials FST II – Vilhelm Evang wrote to the Chief of Defence Staff that it was impossible in July 1947 to predict requirements for his field of activities so far into the future as the spring of 1949. He gave two reasons. First he had no experience to build on as regards the organisational framework within which his section was now supposed to work. But there was another reason which was tied to the developing national security situation. 'Signs are multiplying that the military situation in the world in 1948–49 will be of a nature to require an increasing activity in the field of intelligence and security.'[1]

Without crediting Evang with prophetic foresight, that was a prediction which would come true to an even greater extent than he could have expected. The deepening conflict between East and West during 1947 – with the Truman doctrine in March, the Communist takeover in Hungary in May, and the initiatives for the Marshall plan in June as milestones – culminated in the breakdown of the conference of foreign ministers of the great powers in London in December 1947. It was after the end of that conference that Ernest Bevin alerted his American colleague about the need for a security system for the Western democracies.

Within the Norwegian Government there was by the middle of January 1948 still no outward sign of alarm. A discussion in the Defence Council on 14 January, based on an update of the work in progress of the 1946 Royal Defence Commission, was summed up by Prime Minister Einar Gerhardsen, who said that 'we may expect a few years of reasonably undisturbed work, although there are of course no guarantees'.[2] Such complacency hardly reflected the innermost feelings of all the members of the Cabinet. Defence Minister Jens Christian Hauge, for one, expressed his concern for the future in a conversation with the US military attaché a few days later.[3] Then, on 22 January, British Foreign Secretary Ernest Bevin made his landmark speech in the House of Commons calling on the nations of Western Europe to unite against the growing Soviet threat.

In the Norwegian Government, and within the defence establishment, the situation during February began to be felt as a threat to national security – in part even as a direct military threat against Norway from the neighbouring Soviet Union. A clear indication of how serious the crisis was felt to be was Defence Minister Jens Christian Hauge's renewed approach to the US military attachés on 17 February, when he went so far as to enquire about what assistance could be expected in case of war, stressing Norway's exposed strategic position between East and West. The crisis in East–West relations took a turn for the worse shortly afterwards, when it also acquired a specifically Northern European dimension. The Communist takeover in Czechoslovakia on 25 February, and even more the Soviet offer to Finland two days later of a non-aggression treaty, made the crisis acute. Diplomatic reports received in Oslo were suggesting that Norway might be next on Stalin's list of invitations.[4] The Government now had to act.

The initial reactions of the Government – generally referred to as the 'February measures' – had special relevance for the intelligence service in three ways. First, Prime Minister Gerhardsen in a pivotal speech on 29 February called for vigilance against the internal threat represented by the Norwegian Communist Party. Internal security against communist subversion was, in Norway as in most other Western countries, mainly a police matter. But security against enemy infiltration of military installations and activities was a matter of concern for the security section of the Intelligence Staff, and the demarcation line between military and police jurisdiction in such matters was no clearer in Norway than elsewhere. A history of the NIS therefore has to devote some attention to domestic security issues, even though they were not intelligence matters as such and also played a diminishing part in the daily life of Evang and his staff. The situation in Norway was further complicated by the zealous activities of British and American counter-espionage agents and their Norwegian accomplices, many of whom distrusted the efficiency and reliability of the official Norwegian agencies.

The organisation of the Security Police, and the question of co-ordination between it and the intelligence service, were the subjects of high-level discussions from April 1947. With the Minister of Justice, O.C. Gundersen, demonstrating an oddly passive attitude, Defence Minister Hauge took the lead in calling for a strengthening of anti-communist surveillance. He also proposed setting up a central committee to oversee and co-ordinate the activities of the two secret services. This was to be chaired by the Secretary to the Defence Council, composed of high-level representatives of the ministries of defence, foreign affairs, and justice, and served by a permanent secretariat.[5] Such a committee, which came to be known as 'Koordineringsutvalget' – the Co-ordination Committee – came into existence in January 1948, but with a loose structure and without a secretariat to provide continuity. Its work would also gradually become bedevilled by the personal antagonism between the chief of the Security Police, Asbjørn Bryhn, and Vilhelm Evang.

The 'February measures' that were of direct relevance to the intelligence service came as part of massive extraordinary budget allocations for the strengthening of military preparedness, especially in North Norway. Apart from sending north practically the whole of the air force and all naval vessels, military measures gave priority to expanding Sigint or – as it was still called – 'radio control' activities, as well as increasing security and protection of military installations. Of particular interest was the opening which the 'February measures' provided for intelligence work in foreign countries. Notable among such activities was the use of officers in the large Norwegian merchant navy to observe, photograph and report on items of military interest in Soviet and Eastern European waters and ports – sometimes referred to as the DELFINUS operation. From modest beginnings in the late 1940s this was to grow into one of the most important collection efforts of the NIS, as we shall see. NIS agents also worked in Western Germany, in contact with other Western intelligence services. Intelligence officers were also to be attached to Norwegian embassies, in the first instance in Finland.[6]

On 22 May the Defence Staff communicated to the ministry their detailed proposals on how to spend the extra funds. Three of the proposed activities were of such particular secrecy that they were only identified by the code names SATURN, JUPITER and URANUS. Their nature was only revealed in a personal letter that day from Evang to the Defence Minister. Specially important among the three was SATURN, which aimed at establishing a preparedness in the event of Norway again coming under enemy occupation. The plan was to prepare a network with about

50 radio transmitters located at strategically important points throughout Norway:

> The transmitters will be securely stashed away, and will only be activated if parts of the country become occupied by a foreign power. In case of an internal coup d'état individual transmitters may be activated by special agreement with the Defence Staff ... Preparations for the establishment of this network are well in hand. As operators of the transmitters we intend to select suitable persons who did not during the last war engage in similar underground activities and who are not identified as radio operators.[7]

The central station for the network would be the Intelligence Staff's main radio station in the Oslo area, but a reserve location in the interior of the country would be needed and was being prepared.

It is not entirely clear how the planning for such a preparedness for enemy occupation – soon to become known as 'Stay Behind' or just 'SB' – started. But the idea as such would have come naturally to people who recently had endured five years of resistance against German occupiers. The Defence Minister himself had been appointed to his post in 1945 at the relatively tender age of thirty, largely on the basis of his experience as wartime leader of the military resistance organisation. In the first postwar plan for the reconstruction of the Norwegian armed forces, which he presented to the Storting in the autumn of 1946, he found reason to emphasise that 'in the light of our wartime experience, a determined will to *fight on* even after military defeat and occupation is an essential part of a small country's defence preparedness'.

The idea of a 'Stay Behind' preparedness had also been presented to Evang by an unnamed British interlocutor, probably during the intelligence chief's visit to the UK in February 1947. The man he had then met appeared to have close connection with centrally placed defence and military circles, and the gist of the conversation was that the best Norway could hope for in case of a major war with the Soviet Union was the retention of a defence bastion in the country's southwest corner. 'Those considerations', Evang noted, 'have led the English to take a strong interest in the build-up of a defence in countries under enemy occupation. It seems as if both the Netherlands, France, and Belgium are in the process of setting up a more or less fixed organisation for an underground army.'[8]

Although those British thoughts and Evang's SATURN plan had

preparedness for an occupation as a common denominator, it is important to note that while the British were thinking in terms of military or para-military actions behind enemy lines, Evang was at this juncture preparing an exclusively intelligence and communication network. Plans were still at an early stage, but received further impetus at a high-level meeting in London some time in 1948 between Norwegian, British and American intelligence officers. An intelligence service memorandum later recorded a decision of that meeting 'to establish an apparatus in Norway whose task would be in the event of a complete or partial enemy occupation to communicate intelligence reports by radio or other means to an allied headquarters inside or outside the country. Colonel Evang was able to inform our allies that an apparatus which could be made to serve such a purpose was practically ready and at his disposal.'[9]

The 'apparatus' which Evang referred to leads us to the operation codenamed JUPITER in his letter to the Defence Minister of 22 May 1948. The purpose of JUPITER was to establish a network for the protection of important Norwegian industrial firms and their factories against infiltration or sabotage – again building on precedents from the wartime resistance movement, when the purpose had been to prevent German wholesale destruction of Norway's industrial infrastructure in the closing stages of the war. The Intelligence Staff had come across certain private initiatives with similar aims during the winter 1947–48, and feared the prospect of a right-wing witch-hunt. As it was imperative to keep any such activities under the control of the official secret services, Evang had joined with the head of the Security Police to persuade the leaders to abandon their attempt to establish a large private security and counter-espionage organisation.

Evang then co-opted some of them to form a selected group of reliable industrialists who would work with the intelligence service. The initial purpose of the group was to guard against 'fifth-column (communist) subversive activities in certain industries'. In a report to the Defence Minster in October 1948 Evang praised the group as loyal and disciplined collaborators. And in January 1949 he provided them with a new directive which clearly shows that this was the 'apparatus' referred to in his statement at the London meeting as being ready to take on additional tasks of an intelligence nature:

A. The work carried on until now will continue, concentrated on identifying persons considered dangerous in relation to the work under B below, reporting also on matters of relevant interest in industry.

B. To organise on a regional basis an apparatus for the collection of military intelligence, intended to start operating under an occupation or in situations where regular contact with the legal national authorities has been broken. The actual work will not begin until expressly ordered, but the organisation must be completely established in peacetime. The onward transmission of the collected intelligence will be outside the purview of the apparatus.[10]

As the directive made clear that industrial intelligence was also to be collected, there is little reason to doubt that this new organisation, derived from Evang's JUPITER scheme, would henceforth be combined with or at least closely connected with Evang's SATURN set-up. The combination, it has to be said, was an odd one: a semi-private organisation, charged on the one hand with peacetime counter-espionage and the protection of industry, and on the other with wartime intelligence collection against an occupying power. But these were early days, and the shape of Norway's 'Stay Behind' preparedness was still changing. The next move came from the Defence Minister himself.

JENS CHRISTIAN HAUGE'S 'PARTISAN' SCHEME

On 25 October 1948 a top-secret letter and memorandum from Defence Minister Hauge asked the Chief of Defence Staff, Lieutenant-General Ole Berg, to establish forthwith what he called 'an FO 4 preparedness'.[11] The General could have no doubt about what Hauge meant. 'FO 4' had been a section of Norway's Defence High Command in exile charged with planning and carrying out sabotage and other underground activities in occupied territory. Hauge now asked that a planning section composed of experienced wartime leaders be set up, under the guidance of the Intelligence Staff. The plan which Hauge envisaged should aim at an apparatus for the following purpose:

Free Norwegian authorities must be able to organise sabotage and 'small war' activity against targets of military significance in areas of Norway that may temporarily be occupied by the enemy (communications, industrial plants, military stores, units, etc.). It will be necessary to carry out such measures *already as part of an armed struggle in Norway*. The apparatus must therefore have a high preparedness already in peacetime.

Hauge emphasised that the aim was not to create anything like a secret army. Guerrilla warfare in the enemy's rear would be a task for special commando units left behind by a retreating army, as well as units of the locally based Home Guard. Partisan activity, and not guerrilla warfare, would be the mission of the new 'FO 4' preparedness. He foresaw small action groups of two to four men, operating together and with access to pre-positioned depots of radio transmitters, arms and other supplies. The groups should be recruited from specially selected army and Home Guard NCOs with local knowledge of their area of operations. Veterans from the wartime military resistance should only be used as instructors – obviously because they would be too easy to identify and eliminate by an invading enemy and his local informers. Liaison among the action groups and to the central authorities would be maintained by way of an extensive but independent radio network.

The planning group proposed by Hauge made their report in January 1949. That document can no longer be found, but its main points are revealed in a progress report from September 1952 which also names the new organisation:

I. DEFINITION
ROCAMBOLE is a strictly top secret military organisation under the direct command of the Defence Chief (Chief of Defence Staff), whose task will be to perform isolated missions of particular military importance on occupied Norwegian territory. It is a condition that each single action will be on a direct order from the Defence Chief, and that the task can be performed by a few determined and hardy persons who have been organised, trained and equipped for such missions.
II. THE TASKS may be:
1. Destruction of material targets, by explosives or in other ways.
2. Protection of installations or communications on a temporary basis in connection with the liberation of a given area, or
3. Other missions, like the organisation of larger secret groups, reception of airlifted personnel and supplies, reconnaissance, special intelligence tasks, guerrilla actions, coups, assassinations, etc.[12]

We see that the organisation here proposed under the name of ROC – short for ROCAMBOLE – differed from Hauge's scheme in that guerrilla warfare was not excluded from its range of missions. Intelligence work was also now to form part of its tasks.

The chairman of the planning group was Hauge's close wartime collaborator Jens H. Nordlie, and he was also put in charge of building up the organisation. At a meeting he and other members of his staff had with British representatives – presumably from the Special Operations Branch of MI6 – in London in February 1949, plans were discussed. In the heightened tension caused by Soviet attempts to dissuade Norway from seeking membership of the Atlantic Pact, it was evidently decided to accelerate the build-up of ROC. The intention was now to establish 15 five-man groups before the end of the year. Only the leader and the radio operator for each group were to be recruited and trained in the first instance. The other group members would be nominated but not activated. Co-operation with the British was meant to provide the organisation with the necessary equipment, such as radio transmitters and explosives. Britain would also be the location of a wartime headquarters if the whole of Norway became occupied.

The results of the London meeting were reported to the Chief of Defence Staff and Defence Minister Hauge, and met with general approval. Hauge was, however, somewhat sceptical about the British emphasis on industrial sabotage, and there was some doubt about the wisdom of letting the British have the names of all ROC personnel.[13] In the meantime the Americans had begun to show an interest in co-operating on occupation preparedness – apparently after some doubt due to misgivings about Evang's radical past. With Hauge's approval the ROC leaders then met with an American official, Harold Stuart, who introduced himself as a representative of the US National Security Council. The Americans were now provided with details of the planning for ROC, and with lists of the special equipment being required.[14]

From the spring of 1949 ROC was mainly occupied with training security officers for the most important industrial firms. Training radio operators and obtaining suitable equipment for them also had high priority. A survey from the end of 1949 showed that training had been completed for nine group leaders and seven radio operators. The tripartite US–UK–Norwegian co-operation was expanding, and at a meeting in London in October financing arrangements had been agreed. Radio equipment would be provided free of charge by the United States and

Britain, whereas Norway would pay 50 per cent of all other equipment as well as all training expenses. The target was now set at about 40 groups, to cover the whole country including northern Norway.[15]

INTELLIGENCE WITH A NORTHERN FOCUS

The third of the special operations which Evang had referred to, URANUS, concerned a plan for an intelligence mission to Spitzbergen. An officer from the Intelligence Staff had spent the winter 1947–48 in the area, and Evang wished to have a permanent station there. Ever since the war it had been clear that the Soviet interest in the archipelago, while traditionally of an economic nature, also had strategic overtones. Norway therefore needed to keep tabs on Soviet activity there, for the obvious reason that this was Norwegian territory, but also in order better to understand Soviet intentions and actions in the larger area of the Barents Sea and northern Russia. Above all, there was an evident Western interest in the fullest possible intelligence about Soviet naval activities in an area which constituted their only direct access route to the Atlantic. As Evang stated to the Foreign Ministry in 1949, a listening post on Spitzbergen was 'an exceptionally well-suited observation point for us in our surveillance of Soviet maritime movements'.[16]

Suspicion that the Soviet mining settlement on Spitzbergen shielded activities of a military nature was behind an approach by the British Royal Air Force in April 1948, requesting Norwegian approval for an overflight of the area. Approval was given, and the after-action report revealed that in fact several flights had been made, partly to establish if the Russians were building an airfield there. Nothing was found, but lingering suspicions led to efforts by the Norwegian air force to mount photo reconnaissance flights in the summer of 1948.[17]

These modest intelligence efforts on Spitzbergen were soon to be overshadowed by an increasing activity in the province of Finnmark, spurred by the Government's 1948 'February measures' to increase vigilance and defence preparedness in the light of the sharpening international tension. With a mostly uninhabited border area towards the Soviet Union, intelligence activities would here go in parallel and sometimes hand in hand with the work of frontier security and counterespionage. In addition to the Comint work mentioned earlier, centred on the TORKEL station, Humint – human intelligence or agent operations – would soon follow.

The new 192-kilometre frontier towards the Soviet Union was identical to the previous border line towards the Finnish Petsamo corridor, and was mapped and marked by a joint commission in 1947. The Soviets lost no time in erecting fences and watchtowers, and the whole area gave a sombre impression, as recorded by a Norwegian intelligence officer who arrived there that year:

> The formerly Finnish crofts lay desolate and waste. Apart from the border guards little was seen of Soviet activity. They built watch-towers and barbed-wire fence barriers. Their border patrols were on alert, and took positions with their guns in readiness whenever they saw a Norwegian patrol. Little suggested wartime allies and a peaceful border between good neighbours.[18]

On the Norwegian side the border was guarded by units of army conscripts lodged in primitive huts, or tents in summer time. The effect of this was hardly more than symbolic, but Evang thought it futile to attempt a close frontier surveillance:

> In regard to what is possible, it is considered impossible both in economic and practical terms to attempt a hermetic sealing of the frontier. If the Russians wish to send persons illegally across the border they will be able to do this even if the Norwegian border guard should be very strongly reinforced.
>
> The main point must therefore be ... to keep tabs on the illegal border crossings and their purpose. In practice this means establishing co-operation between the police and the military for the main purpose of finding out what the persons illegally crossing the border are up to.[19]

From the intelligence point of view the problem was to gain knowledge of what was going on east of the barbed wire. Little could be seen from Norwegian territory, as Lieutenant Skau remembered:

> Of military activity we could observe that Luostari airfield had been put into operation. An infantry battalion was stationed at Kontiosalmi, and the border troops had their headquarters at Salmijärvi, with 10–12 observation posts spaced out from Grense Jakobselv to Grensefoss. There was also some military activity around Petsamo/Liinahamari and further east. But with our small binoculars we could only observe the areas near the border.[20]

As Army Command North Norway in the spring of 1947 requested observations of the traffic on the main north–south highway on the Russian side, a Norwegian officer and a soldier ventured across the border on skis. They went as far as the Arctic highway, and although hailed by soldiers aboard a column of Soviet military vehicles, who must have taken them for one of their own border patrols, got safely back to Norwegian territory.[21]

The first proposals to intensify intelligence and surveillance activities in the border districts were, not unexpectedly, put forward by the Army Commander North Norway, General Arne D. Dahl, in the spring of 1947. The increased strategic importance of the area, its proximity to one of the world's strongest military powers, and the greater mobility of modern armed forces, required greater vigilance. Hence a network of professional intelligence officers was required, to work in conjunction with local paid or unpaid surveillance agents. But it was not before well into 1948 that the three army commands in North Norway had their own specially trained intelligence and security officers. In November Evang transferred some modest secret funds to Army Command North Norway, with a request for intelligence collection specially targeted towards the Soviet land forces in the north. Priority was given to transport infrastructure and particularly road conditions on the Kola Peninsula, and photographs of Russian military personnel and their watchtowers.[22]

In the meantime the main source of intelligence about Soviet activities remained the TORKEL Comint listening post, whose intercepts of Soviet military radio signals provided information about naval and air movements as well as some intelligence about the order of battle of land forces in the area. For the analysis of such signals the Intelligence Staff had made efforts to build up a small cipher section with code-breaking as a priority task. From March 1948 onwards the gist of this information was circulated to the relevant military and civilian authorities through memoranda from the newly established Co-ordination Committee for the secret services. Items from one of the first memoranda based on material from TORKEL included information that seven MVD surveillance vessels were patrolling the Murmansk coast; that MVD troops had installed themselves in the Salla area near the Finnish border; and that one battleship, one cruiser, ten destroyers and seven submarines from the Soviet Northern Fleet had been identified.[23]

From the end of 1948 a greater variety of sources began to appear. In a category of its own was a special report from the British Joint Intelligence

Committee, addressed personally to Defence Minister Hauge, entitled 'Defence of Scandinavia'. Its transmission was the result of an agreement between Hauge and British Secretary of Defence A.V. Alexander about the provision of occasional intelligence reports of special relevance to the Norwegian Government. The security-conscious JIC had some doubts about the wisdom of such generosity to a foreign country, and took care to amend the report accordingly. Omitted from the list of persons to whom the report might be circulated was, oddly enough, the Norwegian Chief of Defence Staff. The probable reason was that the British military attaché, Colonel Treseder, had reported suspicions that General Berg was not to be trusted – suspicions that the ambassador, Sir Laurence Collier, promptly dismissed as 'first-class nonsense'.[24]

Of more immediate interest than such general British reports was the increasing flow of Humint information about the military situation in the vicinity of the Finnish and Norwegian borders. This came mainly from two sources. On the one hand the Finnish-speaking intelligence officer posted to Army Command Finnmark had established contact with several Finnish army officers. This information could in due course be checked against intelligence gathered by an officer from the Intelligence Staff attached to the Norwegian legation in Helsinki. Having been at war with the Soviet Union from 1941 to 1944 the Finnish military and their intelligence service had unparalleled knowledge of the Soviet armed forces.[25]

As Norway during February–March 1949 was preparing to become one of the founding members of the North Atlantic Pact, an increasing flow of intelligence reports made clear that tension was growing, and that there was considerable concern about what retaliatory action the Soviet Union might be contemplating. At a meeting of the Defence Council on 4 March Defence Minister Hauge reviewed the information at hand, and stated that the Government's policy would be guided by two main considerations: '(1) that all "internal" preparations would be accelerated, such as defence plans and mobilisation directives, but that (2) no drastic defence measures were to be undertaken which might suggest a fear of an immediate attack.'[26] The same wish not to provoke the Soviet Union became apparent when Hauge on 9 March put on paper a report based on a conversation with a person identified as 'B' who clearly had close contact with leading Finnish circles. From the conversation he concluded that the reported Soviet demonstrations of strength along the Finnish border were intended to frighten the Finns, possibly in preparation for demands for Soviet military bases in northern Finland. Hauge's own conclusion was that any such bases would seriously damage the chances of defending northern Norway. 'In our own interest we must therefore do everything we can to avoid giving the Russians an excuse for such demands on Finland.'[27]

Shortly afterwards Evang submitted an assessment suggesting the presence of five Russian divisions in the Murmansk–Petsamo region near Norwegian territory. One source of this information was the Finnish workers at a power station near the point where the borders of the three countries meet – a source which Evang later questioned since the information might have been planted by Russian co-workers. His other sources were radio intercepts by TORKEL and – for the first time – observations by a reliable officer on a Norwegian merchant vessel. To gain a clearer picture of the situation near the Norwegian border Evang now asked the Norwegian air force to undertake a programme of photo reconnaissance flights, concentrating on roads and airfields in the border area. In the late summer of 1949 the intelligence officers of Army Command North Norway hatched a daring plan to send agents on brief Humint missions across into Soviet territory. But Sub-Lieutenant Skau, who as intelligence officer for the border garrison would have had to organise the missions, turned down the idea since the likely results would not be worth the risks involved.[28]

Another indication of the Norwegian Government's concern about the situation for northern Norway was a top secret operation by which five senior German officers, all with experience of operations against the Russians on the Arctic front in 1944–45, were brought to Norway. Holed up incognito in a Norwegian hotel for a month's sojourn, they produced a series of studies that would serve as background information for the defence planning for northern Norway.

SECURITY AND COUNTER-ESPIONAGE

We have seen that from the start the Intelligence Staff had responsibilities also for security within the military. The problem, in Norway as in practically every country, was to draw the line between military security concerns and those of the civilian sector which were the province of the Security Police. Evang had himself contributed to a blurring of the border line through his JUPITER co-operation with a civilian group for the protection of industry, and by establishing a network of civilian observers to report on foreign and especially Soviet ships in Norwegian ports.

The mesh of military and civilian security activity was to become especially problematic in the sparsely populated region of Finnmark. Here the scarcity of reliable observers seemed to advise against trying to build up entirely separate networks, in spite of the Intelligence Staff's warnings against their people coming into conflict with the police. The intelligence officers in the area were also advised against using personnel from the Home Guard for surveillance or intelligence activities, as such amateurs would be impossible to keep under proper control. With such limitations both the military and the police faced serious difficulties in trying to control border crossings to and from Soviet territory. Tell-tale ski-tracks during the long northern winter showed that such traffic was going on, and suspicions were fuelled by the knowledge that the area housed a large number of active communists, some of whom had worked as intelligence agents for the Soviet Union in the wartime alliance.

In the face of these problems both the military, and particularly the Security Police, laboured under a severe shortage of resources. The Royal Commission on Defence, which reported in 1949, recognised both the importance of the tasks and the need to strengthen the secret services. But the creation of a corps of professional intelligence and security officers was bound to take time. In his budget proposals for 1950–51 the Chief of Defence Staff singled out military counter-espionage as the weakest spot:

> The situation today is that, apart from incidental and piecemeal information, the military know next to nothing about the espionage apparatus of the Soviet Union and the Satellite countries. We do not know their organisation, their extent, or their main purpose – we know so little about them that any assessment about the number of persons involved tells us little about the intensity of their efforts.[29]

On the intelligence side the most acute need was to strengthen the subsection dealing with analysis and assessment. Colonel Evang's problems in this regard reflected an anomaly which was to trouble the NIS for a long time. The Intelligence Staff, although formally a *military* intelligence service, as part and parcel of the Defence Staff, suffered from the drawback that the Norwegian armed services had no separate branch or corps of intelligence officers. Officers from the three services therefore joined the Intelligence Staff on secondment only, most of them serving only a short period before returning to their own service in order to gain promotion. The intelligence service hence had to rely on an increasing number of civilians. Evang himself was not a regular officer, having acquired a provisional officer's grade on joining the intelligence bureau of the armed forces in exile. All this contributed to giving the intelligence service an uncertain status within the military establishment. On the other hand the persons who came to form the core of the service, whether civilians with a particular expertise as radio operators, technicians, or cipher specialists, or military officers with a special interest and aptitude for intelligence work, tended to stay. In the longer term this was to give the service the advantage of a stable basis of highly qualified and experienced officers.

THE KOREAN WAR AND THE FEAR OF COMMUNISM

In April 1949 Norway together with 11 other nations signed the North Atlantic Treaty. The opponents of that new departure for European security policy – mainly the communists and communist-inspired quarters – lost no time in mobilising for action. As one historian of the period has put it:

> The aim now became one of stirring public opinion against a more intimate military co-operation with the United States. The Communist parties were not a sufficient basis for such an effort. Much more promising was the potential for mobilising the electorate in favour of disarmament and national or neutralist values. An important instrument in that regard, not least in order to put disarmament on the political agenda, was the World Peace Congresses, of which the first one was held in Poland in August 1949.[30]

In Norway the national branch of the World Federation of Democratic Women was one of the first to go into action, and among their principal targets were the trade unions. The authorities countered with a more determined effort to identify and take measures against what now came to be called fifth-column activity. An important point of departure for such measures was called the 'poster on the wall', an Order in Council dated 10 June 1949, which was issued as a poster to be displayed on the wall of every military office. The text was the result of a long drafting process led by the Defence Minister himself, in which 'we had to express basic realities of defence and the military in legal terms'.

The 'poster on the wall' had the form of a directive for all officers in the armed forces in the event of an armed attack on Norway. It was rooted in the experience of the German invasion of Norway in April 1940 and the ensuing campaign – a campaign that had had more than its share of confusion among the military and among the people at large. The essence of the directive was an order to wage battle to the bitter end and with all available means, even if communication with higher command authorities was severed. A separate section on 'fifth columnists' instructed military officers to co-operate with the police and civilian authorities in preventive measures against what was defined as 'Norwegians or foreigners who within the nation's borders work for a foreign power through illegal intelligence activities, planning and carrying out sabotage, assassinations, etc.'.

In tandem with the Order in Council a high-level group had been asked to explore the division of tasks and responsibilities between the military and civilian authorities, especially in security matters, both in peace and war. The group's report, not surprisingly, showed agreement on the principles involved, but failed to produce clear-cut conclusions about how to put them into practice. It did, however, suggest a certain extension of military authority into the areas surrounding each military camp or installation, partly for the practical reason that the military had personnel resources that the Security Police lacked. In the summer of 1950 a slightly larger committee, with both the Intelligence Chief and the Chief of the Security Police as members, was appointed to draft more detailed guidelines, based on the wording of the Order in Council.

The issue of preventive measures against communist subversion was debated at a meeting of the Defence Council on 6 July – its first meeting after the outbreak of the war in Korea. Although the Minister of Justice claimed that the Security Police were well prepared, with lists of persons who would have to be detained in an emergency, Defence Minister Hauge questioned this in relation to the requirements of the military. He wanted assurances that a mobilisation could proceed without any disturbance. The Minister of Justice then admitted that the lists were not very comprehensive: List A, containing persons who could be arrested at once, had only 100 names. A further 300 names were on List B, and could be arrested 'relatively quickly'. Defence Minister Hauge, with the support of Prime Minister Gerhardsen, concluded that not only were the lists too short, but that List A persons ought to be arrested already in the crisis alert stage, and those on List B would have to be arrested as soon as mobilisation was ordered.[31] A government proposal for quite far-reaching police powers in a national emergency was put before the Storting in the autumn and enacted, albeit in a somewhat watered-down form.

The committee set up in the summer of 1950 submitted its report in January 1951.[32] Its main findings were, first, to extend the definition of fifth-column activity to include groups and organisations which were planning infiltration and propaganda with the aim of weakening the country's defence and spirit of resistance. In addition, the Security Police and the Intelligence Staff found common ground in issuing a strong warning against the Home Guard or any elements within its units dabbling in surveillance activities. This was in fact another stage in the struggle of both the police and the Intelligence Staff to stop or at least gain control of unauthorised anti-communist vigilante activities. Some of the persons or groups thus engaged had been traced back to Home Guard circles, in many cases inspired by distrust of an intelligence service headed by a former communist in the person of Vilhelm Evang. But others had clearly been connected with British or American intelligence and counter-intelligence officers.

As for the committee's main task, it did agree to extend somewhat the jurisdiction of the military chiefs in matters of security in the vicinity of military areas. But their main proposal in the thorny question of avoiding conflicts and collisions between the police and the military was to stress the need for both to keep each other fully informed, at every level, about existing or probable security risks and about measures taken against them.

The outbreak of the Korean War created increased concern about the nation's general preparedness, and not least about internal security against communist subversion. In addition to increased budgets to strengthen the personnel of the Security Police and the Intelligence Staff, special funds were provided outside the normal budget for activities of a particularly secret nature. The 'Stay Behind' preparedness was one of those activities. Another was Humint operations outside Norway. A third, more controversial, line of action was co-operation between the Intelligence Staff and the labour movement in combating communist influence in the trade unions. Probably because of the Intelligence Staff's easier access to secret funds, it was decided that it should pay the salaries of four persons who would nominally serve as district representatives of the League for Workers' Education, an offshoot of the labour movement. In fact they would be employed in the surveillance and registration of communists.

An important internal security measure was the vetting of personnel employed or about to be employed in sensitive positions with access to classified information. Here there was no disagreement between the Intelligence Staff and the Security Police that such vetting, understood as the gathering of information, should be the province of the latter.

> Intelligence considerations advise against building up two intelligence services on the same territory. In the opinion of the military, investigation and the collection of information in civil society should be done by a civilian agency. Asking agencies under military control to carry out investigations aimed at Norwegian civilian citizens is seen as politically unacceptable and contrary to Norwegian political tradition.[33]

But Evang put his foot down when the Chief of the Security Police proposed that they should provide the military with just a simple security classification for each person vetted. 'S-0' would mean that they had nothing on the person, 'S-1' meant that the person was a definite security risk, whereas 'S-2' meant a potential security risk. Evang insisted that, as it was the responsibility of each military chief to appoint his subordinates, he would also have to make the decision on the candidate's suitability from a security point of view. The Security Police and the security section of the Intelligence Staff should therefore provide the fullest relevant information about the candidate, leaving the conclusion about that person's suitability to the responsible military chief.

This controversy between the Intelligence Staff and the Security Police turned out to be yet another instalment in the long series of conflicts between Evang, as head of the NIS, and Asbjørn Bryhn as head of the Security Police. The conflict was only in part a reflection of the seemingly inevitable clash between civilian and military security concerns. What aggravated it was the incompatible personalities of the two leaders. While a working relationship between the two agencies was kept going by their subordinates, the two chiefs were barely on speaking terms. One result of this was to disable the high-level committee set up to co-ordinate the work of the secret services. A joint intelligence committee on the British model, collating and drawing up joint assessments based on information drawn from several agencies, was an impossible dream under such circumstances.

To what extent were the heightened security concerns in the wake of the outbreak of the Korean War based on a real and present danger? One way of judging this is to look at the espionage cases that came to light in the period – bearing in mind that a number of other cases never came to court because of lack of sufficient proof. The notorious difficulty of proving the guilt of a person spying for a foreign power, unless caught *in flagrante* when handing over secret documents, was illustrated by the arrest in April 1951 of a naval lieutenant having a conspiratorial meeting with a Soviet embassy official. As the embassy official got away with the evidence the court had to declare a mistrial. Better results were obtained by the police in the border province of Finnmark, where a Soviet defector from the KGB in July 1953 gave the names or pseudonyms of several Norwegian agents. In a major court case in May 1954 seven Norwegian nationals from the border areas were convicted on charges of spying for the Soviet Union. Most of them had in fact been Soviet 'partisans' during the Second World War, when the Soviet Union and Norway had been allies, and had then been pressured or cajoled into continuing their work. Also in 1954 the police in Oslo arrested and secured the conviction for espionage of the veteran leader of a wartime communist sabotage organisation, together with a weapons specialist in the army.

The NIS throughout the 1950s did take an active part in tapping the telephone and telex lines of certain foreign embassies and agencies, from an underground bunker in the centre of Oslo. Particular targets were Soviet shipping agencies in Oslo, and the main purpose of that operation – aptly named operation MULDVARP (Mole) – was to identify Norwegian merchant ships trading to Soviet ports. The NIS could then contact a reliable officer on board with a request to observe and if possible photograph items of interest – a type of operation we shall return to in the next chapter. Other information from the tapping, if of counter-espionage interest, was then passed on to the Security Police and also to co-operating foreign agencies. It seems clear that the intelligence service gradually lost interest in operation MULDVARP, as the results from their point of view hardly measured up to the amount of work involved in reviewing and transcribing the tapes. As one senior officer observed, it was a waste of time to keep replaying tapes 'in order to find out how many bottles of milk Ivanov should buy on his way home'.[34] The work was therefore handed over to the Security Police in 1960.

A curious incident from the spring of 1956 serves to demonstrate both the general suspicion towards the secret services and the difficulty of maintaining clear lines of demarcation between the activities of the intelligence service and those of the Security Police. At a meeting of the Cabinet Defence and Security Committee on 2 March 1956 the Prime Minister accused the intelligence service of improper collection and distribution of secret information. The minutes of the meeting do not specify what kind of information, but other evidence suggests that the reports concerned more than one meeting between a KGB officer from the Soviet embassy and the Prime Minister's wife – a political figure in her own right. Those meetings were in fact kept under surveillance by the Security Police. According to a written statement by Evang, the Intelligence Staff only got involved because of information volunteered to one of its officers, information which Evang then took it upon himself to pass on to the Prime Minister's liaison officer for security and intelligence matters. 'I very much regret if this has been construed to mean that the Intelligence Staff carries on any kind of surveillance. This has never been the intention and clearly lies outside the field of activity of the intelligence service.'[35]

NOTES

1. FO/E, copy file H, Evang to Berg (personal), 5 Aug. 1947.
2. SMK, Defence Council Protocol, meeting, 14 Jan. 1948.
3. Hauge in an interview with the author on 6 May 1996 has confirmed that his approaches to the military attachés in January and February had not been cleared with the rest of the Cabinet.
4. This brief summary of international security developments is largely based on O. Riste (ed.), *Western Security: The Formative Years* (Norwegian University Press, Oslo, 1985).
5. UD 38.5/53, Hauge to Permanent Secretary R. Andvord, 6 Nov. 1947.
6. FO/E, Hauge to Chief of Defence Staff, 11 March and 14 April 1948.
7. FO/E, copy file H, Evang to Hauge, 22 May 1948.
8. FO/E, Evang Papers, Evang memorandum, 25 March 1947.
9. Ibid., unsigned memorandum dated 30 March 1950.
10. Ibid., 'Direktiv', dated Oslo, 16 Jan. 1949.
11. FO/E, E-12, Hauge to Berg 25 Oct. 1948. In conversation with the author Hauge stated that this initiative had not been cleared with his Cabinet colleagues.
12. Ibid., unsigned document 'ROC – Oversikt' dated September 1952. ROC was to be the short version of the organisation's name.
13. Ibid., 'Historie E-12', doc. no. 104.
14. This American interest may have had something to do with a visit to Oslo by General William B. ('Wild Bill') Donovan in October 1948, when he met with Defence Minister Hauge. Harold Stuart became Deputy Secretary of the Air Force in the Truman Administration later in 1949.

15. FO/E, E-12, 'ROC – Oversikt', and doc. no. 104.
16. UD, unregistered file, Gunneng to Anker, 14 July 1949.
17. FO/E, Evang papers, Evang to Hauge, 10 June 1948, with enclosures.
18. FO/E, Hallfred Skau manuscript, 'Tjeneste i Finnmark 1947–1983', p. 4.
19. Ibid., copy file H, Evang to General Berg, 2 Oct. 1947.
20. Ibid., Skau manuscript, p. 4.
21. Ibid., p. 6.
22. FO/E, copy file H, Evang to General Dahl, 16 Nov. 1948.
23. FO/E, Evang Papers, Memorandum of 29 March 1948.
24. PRO, FO 371/71499 and 71504.
25. FO/E, copy file H and Evang Papers, and UD, unregistered file 'Koordinasjons-utvalget m.m'.
26. SMK, Defence Council Protocol, 4 March 1949.
27. POT, file P-12.2 1B, Hauge to Minister of Justice, 9 March 1949.
28. FO/E, Evang Papers, Evang memorandum, 21 March 1949; copy file H, Evang to General Dahl, 6 May 1949; and General Berg to Chief of the Air Force, 7 April 1949; Skau manuscript, p. 10.
29. FO/E, copy file H, General Berg to Minister of Defence, 10 Aug. 1949.
30. Johan Kr Meyer, *NATOs kritikere: Den sikkerhetspolitisk opposisjon 1949–1961* (in the series *Forsvarsstudier*, 3, Norwegian Institute for Defence Studies, Oslo, 1989), p. 10.
31. SMK, Defence Council Protocol, 6 July 1950.
32. Ibid., unregistered file with the committee's report and a letter of transmittal dated 17 Jan. 1951.
33. FO/E, Evang papers, memorandum of 13 Feb. 1952.
34. Ibid., file 'Diverse saker', undated memo, 'Fra EJ til MM, Ad Mulvarp [*sic*]'.
35. SMK, RSU Protocol, 2 March 1956; FO/E, Evang papers, memo, 20 March 1956. For a thorough history of the Norwegian Security Police, based on unrestricted access to archives, see Trond Bergh and Knut Einar Eriksen, *Den hemmelige krigen: Overvåking i Norge 1914–1997* (I–II, Cappelen, Oslo, 1998).

3

Occupation Preparedness: 'Stay Behind'

THE ESTABLISHMENT OF 'ROCAMBOLE'

In a previous chapter we saw how the idea of an occupation preparedness was developed on the basis of Evang's SATURN radio network and the JUPITER plan for protection of industries, by way of Hauge's 'FO 4' plan and the Lien group's industrial defence, to the more diffuse ROC plan from the spring of 1949. The state of affairs at the end of 1949 appears to have been that ROC was under construction, the aim being to establish between 15 and 45 groups of five men each, and a corresponding number of secret depots containing explosives, weapons, ammunition, food supplies and personal field equipment, and communications equipment. The objective of this segment of the preparedness for occupation was partly to secure important sites and communications within free Norwegian territory under a partial occupation of the country, but mainly to prepare and carry out sabotage in occupied areas against Norwegian industrial plants which might be of use to the enemy. Central and responsible control over the activity was to be achieved through radio communications to a control centre in a free area in Norway or – if the whole country had been occupied – in Britain. For the time being only a commanding officer and a radio operator had been recruited for each of the groups. The equipment which was to be stored in the depots – called 'caches' or hiding-places – was to be acquired from the British or American side, and financing was, in principle, divided equally between Norway, Britain and the United States. Training, especially of radio operators, as well as the planning of the depots, was in full swing.

The 'philosophy' behind ROC was clearly based on the lessons learnt during the German occupation a few years earlier. In discussions about Norwegian resistance during the war it was often pointed out that the sabotage had not been particularly comprehensive and that Norwegian industry, to a great extent, had carried on much in a business-as-usual sort of way, allowing itself to be exploited to the advantage of the occupying power. An explanation for this could be that the situation during the occupation in 1940–45 was new and unfamiliar. Faced with the danger of a new occupation, there was now an opportunity to plan and prepare an alternative resistance strategy. Sabotage intended to hinder an occupying power from benefiting from Norwegian territory and Norwegian industry in a war against the Western democracies could be seen to be Norway's duty as a member of the Alliance. There might also have been an element of pure self-interest given the alternative of massive Allied bombing of enemy targets on Norwegian territory.

The basic outline of the plan was to create a top-secret network of small and well-equipped action groups which could be mobilised after the country or a region had been occupied. After an initial 'concealment period', when the groups were to find cover and carry out reconnaissance and the detailed planning of actions, selected groups would receive the signal to switch to the active phase. The depots of arms and equipment for the groups would contain sufficient supplies for a 12-month period without reprovisioning.

The central leadership of ROC, or the staff, seems to have consisted in peacetime of eight men, with Jens H. Nordlie in charge; after mobilisation the staff would be twice as large. In such a situation, the head would in all likelihood have to leave the country to attend to Norwegian interests in an Allied context. The Second-in-Command would then function as the Chief of Staff. The staff would otherwise be divided into sections for communications, operations, intelligence, training, personnel/adjutancy and supplies.[1] The plan was that, in a preparedness period, the staff, in co-operation with representatives of the CIA and SIS, was firstly to establish itself temporarily 'somewhere in Norway' – perhaps in the Setesdal hills in the interior of southern Norway – and then, after an enemy occupation, proceed to an Allied country.

During the first couple of years, while ROC was being built up, there were staff meetings at least once every week, often in the presence of Evang. From late autumn 1950, the local representatives from British and American intelligence services often took part in these meetings. Contact with the Minister of Defence was sporadic, and mostly in the form of informal conversations between Hauge and Evang or Hauge and Nordlie, in addition to written reports every now and then. After the previously mentioned meeting at the end of March 1949, there does not seem to have been any meeting between Hauge and the staff until August 1950. During a staff meeting on 8 October 1951, the issue of reporting to Hauge as well as to London and Washington, was raised. Nordlie found support for the idea that the Minister of Defence ought to be given a relatively short summary, for example concerning the work in North Norway in the summer of 1951, 'since it must be assumed that he is so overburdened with work that he cannot be expected to have the time to read the relatively lengthy summary'. The person who delivered the report to Hauge was obliged, nevertheless, to take the long version along with him, and, if required, to let him have a copy if he wanted more detailed information. It is unclear whether this was the way things were done in relation to subsequent Ministers of Defence after Hauge's resignation in January 1952. The long version of progress reports ought also to be sent to London and Washington so that they could gain some insight into 'the seriousness and the hard work involved in the distribution of more than thirty tons of equipment'.[2]

In the middle of April 1950 the ROC staff moved into a house of their own in the Smestad camp, and here the preparedness staff members met with Evang and Hauge on 8 August.[3] Of central importance at this meeting were the problems connected with the development of an occupation preparedness in North Norway. In association with existing plans for a guerrilla war in the Finnmark Army Command's combat zone, it emerged that ROC had serious recruitment problems in Finnmark county, partly because the people who might have been suitable were already involved in intelligence work. The solution which seemed the most likely was threefold: some men could be recruited from Colonel Reidar Løvlie's guerrilla unit – Colonel Løvlie was the head of FL, Finnmark Army Command. Moreover, one could attempt to find a few civilians who could move to Finnmark and establish themselves there. Finally, there was some talk – in spite of a certain amount of misgivings about this idea from Hauge – about selecting a few veterans from the renowned Linge Company who could be transferred to Finnmark in the event of a war breaking out.

With reference to the relationship with Britain and the United States and their representatives in Norway, which otherwise was considered to be satisfactory, the question of funding was also brought up. Here it emerged that in spite of the London agreement of the previous year concerning the sharing of expenses – which Hauge immediately announced had not been submitted to the Government – the analysis of the budget showed that Norway, in reality, was covering two-thirds of the costs.

According to the minutes of the meeting, Hauge then said that the operations under the ROC arrangement in his view were more in the interests of the Allies than in Norway's interest. The most reasonable approach would therefore be that when Norwegians paid the people and arranged their training, then the Allies ought to pay for all the equipment and all expenses connected with it. Nordlie was consequently instructed to submit this to the Allies. This was done by means of a memorandum immediately thereafter, which stated *inter alia* that Norway's outlay for SB – Stay Behind – now constituted over 50 per cent of the budget for the NIS. Only if the United States and Britain provided and paid for all the equipment would the original assumption of an even three-way division of the expenses be satisfied.

A cost estimate for ROC which, in the context, seems to have comprised the calendar year 1952, gives a total cost of about 1.5 million kroner. Two-thirds of this is listed as 'paid from ROC's cash funds', the rest was paid from Intelligence Staff funds and included wages, the purchasing and leasing of cars, and expenses for the headquarters at Smestad. If 'ROC's cash funds' indicates payments from the British and American side, then this could indicate that the three-way division of expenses was now in order. During a meeting in September 1952 information was forthcoming that Norway had paid its dues, the Americans more than their share, while the British still owed money, especially to the United States.

Among other proposals put forward at this meeting, there was an idea about organising frogman's training for specially selected Norwegian students in the United States. In response to this Hauge is reported as saying that in such a case the Americans would have to foot the bill, since he did not see himself going to the Minister of Finance to ask for 'dollars for frogmen'. Finally, concerning the question of a central repository for equipment for the groups, Hauge suggested utilising a bunker which was at the Government's disposition in Cort Adeler street in the centre of Oslo. The bunker was inspected three days later, and proved to be ideal for the purpose.

IN THE SHADOW OF THE KOREAN WAR

At the turn of the month October–November 1950 a new trilateral meeting was convened in London. We lack the minutes of this meeting, but from other sources it appears that it was characterised by the view that the possibility of war had crept closer since the outbreak of the Korean

War. It was decided, among other things, that as soon as circumstances permitted, depots for the groups in North Norway should be established. There is here a clear connection with the exhaustive discussions in the Defence Council on 6 July 1950, also marked by the seriousness of the situation after the outbreak of the Korean War shortly before. Halvard Lange, the Minister of Foreign Affairs, had then expressed the opinion that this event 'has increased the possibility of war considerably'. He nevertheless cautioned against immediate preparedness measures which could give rise to escalatory Soviet measures in the northern areas. 'On the contrary, we should make use of the coming weeks and months to re-appraise our longer-term dispositions so as to be able to move to a state of readiness more quickly.' In the ensuing discussion the Minister of Defence raised 'the general question of what we should do with the civilian population if we were obliged to withdraw from an area and leave it to a Russian occupation. The question is especially germane with regards to North Norway, but could also become relevant in other parts of the country.'[4]

Focusing on North Norway, one of the staff officers in ROC in December prepared a comprehensive 'status report' about the groups from the Salten Mountain region around Bodø and further north. This report mentions the groups for the districts in Nordland, Troms and western Finnmark. For several of these groups recruitment, which, to a great extent, had had to be based on the personal acquaintances of one or another person on the ROC staff, had turned out to be difficult. In three or four cases, the group leader and/or the radio operator remained outside the district for the greater part of the year and would therefore find it difficult to receive and deposit equipment in a secure place before they received the all-clear signal to recruit a third person to help.[5]

The sense of crisis in the autumn of 1950 was first and foremost marked by the Korean War. But it also received a local stimulus in the form of a serious act of sabotage at Bardufoss air station during the night of 14 November, when an airman blew up an ammunitions depot. This resulted in an immediate strengthening of security measures at military arsenals and depots. The impression of having little time to spare was also reflected in the ROC context by work on a so-called 'disaster plan' for the rapid mobilisation of the organisation and the transfer of a cadre staff to another country in a critical situation, and also in measures for 'pilot operations' in which a couple of the groups practised deploying depots in peacetime. However, a British–American proposal earlier that autumn, about carrying out a mock mobilisation, was flatly rejected as being likely to jeopardise the whole organisation.

Communist China's active engagement in the Korean War at the end of November 1950 represented a dramatic escalation of an already grave crisis. In the Defence Council, on 2 December, Lange asserted that there now was 'an acute danger of war', even if not, for the present, in Europe. His conclusion was that Norway had perhaps maintained 'security at too low levels to now, since we did not increase the immediate state of readiness at the outset of the Korean conflict. There may be reason to increase that preparedness now.' The Minister of Defence joined in saying that there 'would not be enough time to call up the forces when an acute danger of war reached Europe. By then, forces ought already to have been deployed for some time. An impending threat of attack on our country demands in response full and immediate mobilisation. If there is a danger of a rapid development in a menacing direction, the response must be to establish covering forces.' He therefore tabled a motion to step up to what he called 'Preparedness Level I', which involved, among other things, calling up a total of 5–6,000 men for extraordinary refresher courses. Those who were called up in this way would function as 'covering forces to safeguard against an enemy invading the country with very small forces, and thus destroying our chance for mobilisation'.[6]

As far as ROC is concerned, a report dating from November 1951, including a working programme for 1952, shows that course activity for participants was then well under way. After basic course no. 13, which then was nearly complete, 27 new group leaders, 27 radio operators, and 17 'third men' would have received their training. In addition to this basic course, additional courses and special industrial courses lasting two to three weeks for group leaders, as well as additional courses in two parts for radio operators, were to be held during the following six months. The deployment of depots with preparedness equipment was in full swing, and in North Norway very nearly complete. The special preparedness for Finnmark, based on a co-operative effort between ROC and four special groups partly recruited from the south, clearly had high priority. Moreover, the intelligence organisation LINDUS – to which we shall return – had five stations in Finnmark. All this went on in extreme secrecy. Personnel from the LINDUS and ROC groups knew nothing of each other, and in the eventuality of them running into – and even arresting – each other, plans were discussed to equip every single man with a special message which could be recognised by the home station. Neither had the police been informed of the SB organisation. If anybody from the Security Police should by any chance stumble across anything to do with the SB organisation in North Norway, then any reports about it would be stopped by the Commander-in-Chief North Norway.[7]

An important point in the working programme for 1952 was an intensified collection of intelligence material on what was called 'key categories of sabotage targets'. These comprised: (1) radar installations; (2) airfields; (3) lines and means of communication; (4) fuel; and (5) industry. The Intelligence Staff had to endure criticism on this point for not having provided enough of the kind of information ROC needed, and it was emphasised that 'if the groups are ever to become operational and carry out the work which we *at that time* will require of them, we will soon discover that we have neglected an extremely important area of work'. During the course of a staff meeting on 5 January 1952 it was stressed that an occupying power would probably focus on building up a network of radar stations, especially along the coast of Finnmark, and that these would have to be given top priority as a sabotage target. Other important targets in Finnmark would be Highway 50, the roads to Karasjok, Kautokeino and Skibotn; and power stations, airfields and fuel depots.

This intense concentration on plans and measures for North Norway, and especially Finnmark, does not seem to have met many objections from the leading figures of the SB organisation. The obvious explanation for this was that this area was the closest to the Soviet Union and, at the same time, furthest away from Allied support. In what must have been his last instructions as Minister of Defence to the ROC staff, Jens Chr. Hauge, in conversation with Nordlie on one of the first days of January 1952, had praised the work in general, and especially that part of it which had been carried out in Finnmark. In an appraisal of the distribution of some non-recoiling guns to the groups in the late winter of 1952, some concern was expressed that the emphasis on Finnmark ought not be to taken too far:

> It is probably mainly foreign interests, such as in connection with bombing raids across Finnmark against the Soviet Union etc., which are served by our being so strongly committed in Finnmark. Viewed in the light of a more general ROC concern, I am inclined to believe that *we would achieve greater results in the south of Norway*. In accordance with this line of argument, we should, therefore, *be careful not to mismanage our resources by allocating too much of them to Finnmark*.[8]

A distribution formula which assured 20 per cent to Finnmark was therefore considered to be a reasonable solution.

ROC's position in the autumn of 1952 was that the organisation had, at least for the time being, found its own form. By this time 32 groups had been established in all – four in Finnmark, six in Nordland and Troms, four groups for each of the regions of Trøndelag, the West and the South, seven groups in the East region and three in the Oslo area. Each of the groups had a radio station and a radio operator, and a total of 91 persons had received training. The groups in North Norway had obtained between 80 and 100 per cent of their equipment; in the rest of the country the level of provisioning varied from 0 to 80 per cent. This was not preparedness in any real sense, however, since the radio stations lacked transmission plans, crystals and codes. The plan was to have these things issued to the majority of the groups during the second half of 1952.[9]

INTELLIGENCE AND SPECIALISATION

Besides ROC it seems as if what was previously referred to as SATURN or 'the Defence Staff's secret network of intelligence officers' was, in 1950, still being formed under the leadership of Hans Ringvold, but now under a new cover name, LINDUS. In the beginning this was a network, eventually called 'Group 27', the purpose of which was to perform general military intelligence work in occupied territory. In the summer of 1950, an initiative was taken to establish two new networks. The first, 'Group 67', was an SB organisation intended to collect and pass on political and economic information, with the particular purpose of providing up-to-date information to agents who were about to be infiltrated into the country. The transmission of information to allied territory was to be done partly by radio and partly by boat or – for the eastern region – by aircraft following an ingenious procedure:

> The procedure for the pick-up of mail bags has to be left to the RAF, of course, but we know that a system has been used earlier consisting of two high masts, placed at a suitable distance from each other, and at right angles to the prevailing wind. A lengthy strap is fastened between the masts, onto which a mail bag is hung. An aircraft approaches at low altitude, towing behind it a grapnel which hooks onto the loop, carrying the mail bag away.[10]

Another project, 'Group 134', was based on a suggestion emanating from the London meeting in September 1949 about making preparations for the formation of a counter-intelligence or counter-espionage group. This group was to work against the enemy's security services in occupied territory and attempt to infiltrate them, with the aim of securing early warnings if any of their own agents were in danger. The idea had clear parallels to the German occupation during which individual Norwegian patriots enlisted in Quisling's *Nasjonal Samling* party to find out about plans for actions against the resistance movement. Characteristic of such groups, as of ROC, was that they were only supposed to be established in skeleton or cadre form during peacetime, that is, only key personnel were at that stage to be recruited and instructed as to their duties. The exception was the infiltration agents of Group 134. These had to establish themselves as trusted communists or 'fellow travellers' beforehand, so the Russians would feel they could use them in their administration of occupied Norway. The material gives no grounds to believe that anything like this was ever put into practice.

Sometime around 1950, occupation preparedness on the intelligence front was extended with a network – 'Group 33' – for reporting on enemy planes and ships, as well as a network bearing the code-name 'Group 45', which was supposed to supply meteorological data. It is doubtful whether any of these different networks had their own radio communications. In all likelihood they reported directly to the closest LINDUS station. In addition to these specialised intelligence networks, LINDUS also had a network – 'Group 74' – the aim of which was to organise the evacuation of certain categories of Norwegian and allied personnel in the initial phase of an occupation. There is reason to believe that this included the relatives of those people who would have to go underground. This network must not be confused with the more extensive 'Evasion and Escape' organisation which operated under the code-name BLUE MIX, and to which we shall return later.

NATO BEGINS TO TAKE AN INTEREST

The strategic background for NATO's interest in occupation prepared-ness in a broader European context was similar to that of the Norwegians – namely an awareness that a Soviet offensive against Western Europe, under the then prevailing balance of power in the early 1950s, could probably not be stopped until most of NATO's member countries had fallen to Soviet occupation. In August 1951 NATO's Supreme Commander for Europe (SACEUR) took the initiative to establish an *ad hoc* committee – called CPC or Clandestine Planning Committee – to plan secret operations. Represented on this committee were evidently only the three leading powers, the United States, Britain and France, which also comprised NATO's highest military body, the Standing Group. At roughly the same time, a division for special operations – the Special Projects Branch – had been set up at NATO's Allied Command Europe, SHAPE (Supreme Headquarters Allied Powers Europe).[11]

In April 1952 Evang was informed that SACEUR had given the order to CPC to summon representatives of a member country's secret service to their meetings whenever that specific country's national interests were involved. In accordance with this, Evang received an invitation to a meeting in Paris on 7 May 1952, for a briefing on the situation and a discussion on Norway's relationship to CPC. Prior to this meeting, Evang contacted his Danish counterpart to establish a common approach to the questions which were expected to be raised. Among other things, they agreed to make it clear that Stay Behind was to be used only 'in the event of a total occupation or a static partial occupation'. It was out of the question to make use of the organisation under what Evang called 'normal fighting'.

> Agreement was reached, moreover, that Stay Behind was first and foremost an instrument at the disposal of the national governments wherever they might happen to be, and that its primary task was to form the nucleus for the recapture of temporarily lost areas. The gamut of their activity had to be viewed in this light, and it is our job to see that it is the respective governments which, in the last instance, exercise control over them. It was clear that this could only be done if one controlled communications, and that the individual operator's identity was not known to anybody but a small minority of the person's own countrymen. This viewpoint must not, however, be revealed in international discussions.[12]

Six months later, the CPC presented a basic document,[13] which was circulated to the chiefs of the national secret services for comments. The plan aimed at a whole range of 'unorthodox warfare' activities. First, these concerned operations to be carried out by the secret services (Operations by Clandestine Services, OCS), which, in turn, were divided into secret intelligence activities (SI) and secret actions of an operational nature (SO or Special Operations). Furthermore they included operations by unconventional military forces or guerrilla warfare, and, finally, 'psywar' or psychological warfare operations.

As usual when NATO was concerned, this implied the delicate balancing between considerations of national sovereignty and the desire for allied co-ordination. It was emphasised that the planning and preparation of OCS operations should be the responsibility of the national services, but that the CPC in peacetime should have a co-ordinating responsibility in relation to SACEUR. Not until the active phase was SACEUR, directly or through its subordinate commands – for example AFNORTH (Allied Forces Northern Europe) – to assume control of such sections of the national secret services as were placed at the disposal of NATO.

Throughout this entire field, the Intelligence Staff was preoccupied with securing Norwegian control over the activity, for political reasons. It should therefore be regulated by agreement that the Norwegian Government retained 'the right to deal with the political situation in Norway whatever the circumstances', and the 'sovereign right to control and manage the clandestine effort which it deems necessary to exercise political control in Norway'. A special memorandum dating from January 1953 had this to say on the subject:

> During the last war, the Norwegian government was located outside the boundaries of the country, but its constitutional powers remained in legal order and it exercised its functions as government throughout the enemy's occupation of Norway ... Under the influence of these experiences, the Norwegian government views it as self-evident that it should retain responsibility for the political leadership in the country – also in occupied parts of the country. That the leadership of the resistance movement should be subordinated to an American general and his international staff would incite a political storm in the country if it became known before an occupation – and after an occupation it would provide an excellent basis for enemy propaganda.[14]

Another element which NATO, for good reasons, was interested in developing and co-ordinating was an 'Evasion and Escape' organisation.

The objective was to create a network which could rescue, receive and repatriate Allied military personnel – especially air crews – who had to eject by parachute or make a forced landing in enemy-controlled areas. Fragmentary written material indicates that such a network was organised as an element of SB early in the 1950s under the code-name BLUE MIX. The initiative was American and, even though this organisation was also under Norwegian command and control, a report from 1956 admits that 'the American influence made itself more directly felt in this area of work'. The development of this organisation seems otherwise to conform relatively closely to ROC and LINDUS, but on a smaller scale, being subdivided into districts – apparently ten in number – with district chiefs, group leaders, radio operators and secret depots.

The relationship between national control and NATO supervision was to become a recurring subject in discussions on co-ordination of the secret services in the Alliance in operational contexts – whether they were special intelligence operations, Stay Behind, 'retardation' which we shall consider later, or 'Evasion and Escape' for Allied military personnel. Towards the end of 1954 a *modus vivendi* seemed to have taken shape in the form of a design for Allied coordinating bodies – 'Allied Clandestine Co-ordination Groups' or ACCG – both at SHAPE and in subordinate commands such as, for example, AFNORTH with headquarters in the Oslo area. The intention was that ACCG AFNORTH would be an integrated staff under a directorate in which all participating nations would be represented. At the SHAPE level, ACCG's directorate would have only three members from the three leading NATO powers, the United States, Britain and France. But every member country would have a national delegation linked to the group, and in the documents it was stated 'positively half a dozen times: "Command and control will at all times be retained by the respective National Clandestine Services"'.[15] Nevertheless, in another memorandum from the same time, misgivings are expressed concerning the superior role assumed for ACCG SHAPE where Norway was not represented in the directorate.

1957–58: NEW PROBLEMS WITH NATO

In light of these NATO plans and the 'retardation' plans, to which we shall return later, there appears from 1955 onwards to have been a feeling in the Intelligence Staff that NATO and CPC were mainly interested in operations in the opening stages of a war, and mostly outside the territory of the member countries in NATO at that. The leadership of the Norwegian SB organisation, however, considered it a clear premise that the activation of their networks would not take place until 'after a fully completed occupation'. That was the basis of the trilateral agreement between Norway, Britain and the United States. In line with this, the Norwegian side proposed in 1957 that the 'Country Section', or the national headquarters, should be established in Norway instead of Britain, also because Norway, in the first phase of an unlimited nuclear war, would be just as safe a location as Britain.[16]

This proposal may have been inspired by the fact that the Dutch, during a Norwegian–Danish–Dutch consultative meeting in May 1957, had signalled a strict 'national' line under forthcoming meetings with Britain and the United States. Among other things, they would argue for a purely Dutch 'country section', even if this might be localised in Britain – a concession probably explained by the difficulty of finding secure hiding places on Dutch territory. But the proposal may also have been connected with a certain uneasiness over a growing NATO-inspired 'mix-up' between 'retardation' and occupation preparedness which could lead to reduced national control and, perhaps, to the 'proper' SB being moved further down the list of priorities. Evang's dilemma was, nevertheless, that he neither would nor could relinquish the intelligence service's responsibility for planning and overseeing even the sort of operations by the clandestine services that he was sceptical about, although the organising and execution of armed action behind enemy lines had now been transferred to the army.

The 1957 memorandum thus emphasised that also the OCS (Operations by Clandestine Services) in the first phase of a war would have to be a purely Norwegian affair. The desire for national control had come up in yet another connection in 1955. In a memorandum to Evang, Harbitz Rasmussen of the SB staff said that copies of the records of personnel in ROC and BLUE MIX had been deposited in a sealed form in Washington and partly in London, and that the information needed to establish and run the radio communications for the various networks could also be found there. But the plan, as he reassured Evang, was to have this material deposited under 'exclusive Norwegian control' – meaning, reasonably enough, at the Norwegian embassies in the two capitals.

In 1957 an acute crisis developed in the relationship between the Intelligence Staff and NATO in connection with the secret services. In September Evang received information that an American officer, who was a member of the staff at HQ AFNORTH (Headquarters Allied Forces Northern Europe) at Kolsås, 'was showing a distinct interest in general military intelligence material and had also had translated at AFNORTH data on Norwegian citizens, especially people who had strongly pacifist and negative attitudes to NATO'. A superior officer in the operations section had summoned the officer in question and asked him about his work, and had been told that he worked on psychological warfare and 'Evasion and Escape', and that he reported to a named officer at SHAPE.[17] At Evang's demand this matter became the first item on the agenda at his meeting with CPC in Paris on 19 November. A British officer, Colonel Blaer, was the chairman of CPC, and he began by indicating that the NIS 'was extremely worried about activities carried out by officers at Kolsås. This concerned SB, Psywar and Counter Intelligence'. Evang then took the floor and, according to his own report of the meeting, delivered a stern warning to AFNORTH to keep its hands off SB and other clandestine activities. It now seemed that his previous warnings had gone unheeded:

> Things were quiet until the past year when one became aware that there were still officers at AFNORTH who worked on Psywar, E&E and, in this connection, also with the blacklisting of people at high levels. When high ranking persons in Norway are being included on such a blacklist, then something must be wrong. My government also views this in a very serious light, and I have standing orders not to take part in international planning if such activities are going on.
>
> As far as Norway is concerned, our interest in CPC planning as such has, since 1954, declined steadily because there is no future in it for us. We are of the opinion that we are developing a Stay Behind which is to be used at home for the purpose of liberation from an occupation. No organisation for retardation can be prepared for Norway or Scandinavia, just possibly for the rest of Europe. He [Evang] understood well SACEUR's interest as far as retardation was concerned, but our defence would make use of these people. It is the excessive infiltration of both phases, as well as the extremely vague directives, which in his opinion have made the work so difficult.[18]

During the extended discussion which followed, the chief of the Special Projects Branch at SHAPE, Brigadier Simon, finally took upon himself the job of cleaning up the affair. The two officers, the names of whom Evang gave him, were evidently working in a section for 'Special Projects' at Kolsås, but Brigadier Simon denied that they had instructions to act in the way Evang had recently uncovered. Evang maintained that it was the blacklisting and contact with Norwegian civilians which was of such a serious nature that he could not participate in CPC until things had been put in order.

After a certain amount of prevarication, a letter was finally despatched in May 1958 from one of the senior officers at SHAPE, General Schuyler, to General Øen, the Chief of the Defence Staff. Here General Schuyler apologised for any planning activity of a clandestine nature which had exceeded purely wartime needs. Then, on 14 October 1958, Evang had a meeting with an American general who clearly had as his task to get Norway to return to the CPC. Evang then stated that an official letter to Norway on the matter would have to contain the following main points: '(a) The affair had been resolved, (b) SHAPE would promise not to continue activity of the sort that has been criticised, (c) An appeal to Norway to rejoin.'[19]

The available material shows clearly that Evang and the Intelligence Staff relatively early on won through at NATO with their principal viewpoints about Stay Behind. The plans were only to be put into effect after an enemy occupation of the country was an established fact, and the arrangement and control of the organisation was solely Norway's business.

'RETARDATION' – GUERRILLA WARFARE AGAINST A SOVIET ASSAULT

A comprehensive document of July 1961[20] provides interesting and detailed insight into how NATO then viewed a probable development if war were to break out. The planning assumption was that a general war in Europe would begin with the use of nuclear weapons, and would have two phases: a first phase of large-scale organised warfare, which would probably not last more than 30 days, and a second, more long-lasting phase, characterised by regrouping and resupply with a conclusion of the war in view. NATO now planned for a forward strategy, and did not expect the enemy to be able to occupy extensive parts of the European area. SB preparations in the member countries would nevertheless still be desirable in the event of NATO forces having to retreat temporarily, especially from border areas.

Both SHAPE and CPC now accepted that such SB activity was a purely national responsibility, limited to the territories of the member countries, and neither SHAPE nor CPC was involved in its planning. SACEUR's need for operations carried out by the secret services were primarily secret intelligence operations, especially in relation to the satellite states and in the first phase of the war, and subsequently, 'Evasion and Escape' operations during the nuclear-war phase. It was with an eye to such needs that SACEUR desired the co-ordination of plans in peacetime as well, to avoid any duplication of effort. In wartime, the co-ordination effort would go through ACCG, which had now been renamed 'Allied Consultative and Co-ordinating Groups', at the NATO commands. In a Kolsås context this ultimately resulted in a special arrangement which further strengthened national control, in that ACCG AFNORTH became physically located at Intelligence Staff Headquarters and comprised a representative from Norway, Denmark, Britain and the United States, respectively.[21]

But if SB thus became, to an increasing degree, a purely national concern, albeit with support from the United States and Britain, what still remained was to define what the Norwegian secret services could contribute to the alliance in the war-fighting or campaign phase while regular troops were still fighting in the area. Intelligence operations would continue as a natural part of the activity of the Intelligence Staff. 'Evasion and Escape' already existed in Norway in the form of the BLUE MIX network. We gather, however, that for both of these fields of activity, a special Norwegian counterpart was established from the mid-1950s, spoken of as Phase I in the language of occupation preparedness. Phase I was designed for a situation in which war-fighting was still going on in the country, but only parts of the country had been occupied. This was in contrast to Phase II, in which the whole country had been occupied and Stay Behind was led from abroad. Phase I comprised a special communications network under Norwegian control alone, under the leadership of a 'base element' or a master station on Norwegian territory, and with a limited number – up to half the total number of field stations under Phase II – of specially selected stations which 'were to be activated immediately a state of war had been proclaimed'.[22]

This informal arrangement was replaced in 1970 by an organised variant under the code-name ARGUS. The ARGUS people, as far as we have understood, would communicate with the Chief of Defence via a headquarters in the region – somewhere in the county of Nordland or, alternatively, in Telemark – to keep him informed about developments in the combat phase of an invasion. The idea behind an alternative base in Nordland was, of course, that an attack on the country could also start in southern Norway. In addition, special evacuation routes were organised for Norwegian key personnel with, among other things, the use of submarines.

Nonetheless, one issue remained: 'retardation', now also with regard to Finland. The main objective of operations carried out by the secret services was, in the campaign phase, to provide support for NATO's short-term 'Emergency Defence Plan' in the form of what was called 'retardation' – the delaying of an attacking enemy's advance. In Norway, planning for such operations had started in 1953, and it became immediately apparent that this would have to be a special arrangement which would without doubt become the responsibility of the Intelligence Staff, but which should not get mixed up with SB. A special 'retardation' organisation would have to be built up, derived from the army and combined with the local defence, based on combat units of about 20 men each.

In a planning document from the summer of 1953 it is recommended that 'retardation' should become a separate organisation under the Defence Staff, and that the leaders would mainly have to be veterans of the wartime special service 'Linge company', who would then recruit men from their respective districts. Later, one returned to the idea of building the whole affair on the Home Guard. In the summer of 1953 the blueprint reckoned with 20 groups comprising a total of 375 men, distributed over the whole of the country as far north as Tromsø. In Finnmark it was envisioned that Finnmark Army Command's guerrilla scheme would be able to cover any contingencies.[23]

In accordance with the 'Emergency Defence Plan', the most important tasks would be to assist during an early phase of the war by obstructing the most strategic railway lines, oil pipelines and ports and, in addition, supporting Allied air activity with the aim of achieving air control, and hindering the enemy's advance movement of bases for tactical air forces. Interest was also expressed by the American side for this type of guerrilla activity. Hence, in a meeting of the Co-ordinating Committee, an initiative from a representative of the CIA was referred to in which the representative had wanted to know what type of material support was needed for such action groups for a period of up to two years after an enemy occupation was a *fait accompli*.

Military logic and basic principles of tactics suggested that 'retardation' operations directed against a Soviet offensive with Norway as the target should be launched at the earliest possible stage. This could involve operations also on Swedish territory. This first planning document[24] hence envisioned five groups established within the triangle southern Sweden–Stockholm–Oslo. Five other groups would take care of 'retardation' within the triangle Oslo–Rogaland–Sørlandet. Equally important as a deployment area for operations against Norway was northern Finland. In a relatively extensive dossier from November 1953 in the archives of the Intelligence Staff, an assessment is made concerning whether and, if necessary, how potential 'retardation' operations – but also intelligence and SB activities – could be carried out on northern Finnish territory, preferably in the form of a Finnish–Norwegian co-operative effort.[25]

Regarding 'retardation', the premise seems to have been that larger-scale operations in Finland, such as, for example, the destruction of road-bridges at Ivalo and Inari, would have to be carried out by Finnish soldiers organised into two groups with a total of 56 men, and with cover detachments of about 100 men for each group. Norway could make a contribution here with plans and support in the preparation phase, performed by Finnmark Army Command. However, as far as Stay Behind was concerned, the NIS could play a more active role. The proposal aimed at establishing three observation posts for intelligence-collection purposes after the model of the LINDUS 'Group 27' in the areas of Salla–Rovaniemi and Ivalo–Rajajoseppi. The agents would be recruited locally, and the posts established immediately before or after the outbreak of war. SB groups on the ROC model, for sabotage operations, would be needed only 'when the country is firmly in enemy hands, and after the enemy is well on his way in repairing the damage done by the Army and the Retardation units'. The idea here was to insert Norwegian or Finnish units from the outside in the manner of 'hit-and-run-raids'. But a certain amount of explosives, weapons and food had previously to be deployed in depots in peacetime.

As early as 1953 plans were thus being laid for a special organisation for 'retardation' operations in Finland, based on a Norwegian–Finnish co-operative effort in which the Norwegian SB organisation was to provide support in the planning and preparation, while the 'foot soldiers' were to consist of Finnish troops. The available material, however, provides no precise indications of the degree to which these plans were realised.

Several years later, in 1961, a similar project was presented by the CPC committee in NATO, this time again as an element in SACEUR's defence plan for emergency situations – the Emergency Defence Plan. The aim was to identify targets for secret intelligence and sabotage operations in the eventuality of Soviet forces invading Finland or Finland becoming a base area for war operations against NATO in Europe. The intelligence measures were to be carried out as soon as the defence plan had been put into effect, while the action plans were to be put on hold until special orders were received. In the event of a communications failure, the actions could still be carried out immediately after Soviet forces had invaded Finland. As far as possible, all preparations were to be made in peacetime. The principal objective for all the operations would be to localise and destroy Soviet nuclear-weapon and air-defence installations. Moreover, Finnish resistance groups were to be organised for actions against enemy forces and their supply lines.[26]

These plans were based on a scenario in which the war would break out without or with only a brief warning, and in which nuclear weapons would be used in the initial stage. The objective of the Soviet Union was assumed to be to establish a forward set-up for early warning, fan out its air force and rocket units, construct mobile short-range missile launch pads directed at targets in northern Europe, and secure transit areas for ground forces for the invasion of North Norway. The planners anticipated that Finland, with its small military resources, would be unable to maintain organised resistance over a protracted period. Finland would, therefore, declare neutrality and attempt to avoid war by acceding to a number of Soviet demands. But the Finns possessed a strong will to resist, and would be able to carry out an extended guerrilla war against the interloper, with Western support.

The planning document was careful to give an assurance that the choice of objectives and means for such a scheme would be the prerogative of the national secret services. The Intelligence Staff drew up a short outline to show how Norway could contribute to such a scheme, especially with a view to the organisation and build-up of a reporting and sabotage network on Finnish territory. The first thing that had to be done was to get hold of contact persons within the Finnish armed forces and political institutions, and thereafter to find five to ten Finnish or Norwegian radio operators, and provide the necessary equipment. A separate staff would have to be set up for the project, with a permanent nucleus consisting of two men, and otherwise with the participation of SB instructors.[27] We have no material showing whether this project got any further beyond the drawing-board stage than the previously mentioned plan. But it is possible that elements of these, as well as earlier plans regarding Finland, were realised.

At the beginning of the 1960s, the Norwegian SB organisation seemed more or less to have settled into the pattern it was to maintain during the rest of the period covered by this study. The most important change was that the intelligence organisation LINDUS abolished the meteorological network, the 'Group 45', as well as the part of the shipping-control network – 'Group 33' – that had been based in south Norway. Annual reports throughout the 1960s tell mostly of courses and training for the three branches which constituted the actual occupation preparedness plan – ROC, LINDUS and BLUE MIX. With the exception of funds for the renewal of the technical equipment, especially radio equipment such as high-speed transmitters, the costs were minimal. The majority of personnel were volunteers and unpaid, whose motivation in offering their services was idealistic and who gained no other form of recompense than the gift of a book or the like at Christmas, and a sum of money as compensation for lost earnings. A certain amount of recruiting had been necessary to replace the older people who had been involved since the start, but in the main the personnel situation remained stable. The last annual budget under the trilateral British–American–Norwegian financing agreement – for 1965 – was in the order of 600,000 kroner. The British side had for some time shown diminishing interest in the work, and, from 1966, the financial contribution from that source dried up. The grant from the United States disappeared after 1968.

In spite of the loss of the economic grants, both the United States and Britain claimed during the annual co-ordination meeting in 1968 that it was still worthwhile to sustain the organisation. The new NATO strategy, based on 'flexible response', implied a certain increase of interest in a possible limited Soviet aggression against the flanks. The events in Czechoslovakia in the summer of 1968 had also accentuated the value of an occupation preparedness, and, concurrently, underlined the time factor. In a conventional war scenario, a thrust could happen so quickly and unexpectedly that the main SB operating base in Britain would have to be prepared to take over the operative leadership at very short notice indeed. The general idea was, nonetheless, that the activity would be led from a base on Norwegian territory. The new head of the Intelligence Staff, Colonel Johan Berg, concluded in a memorandum to the Chief of Defence in November 1968, that the work should continue, based on

Norwegian needs and economic resources, but with the practical support which the co-operating parties were still willing to give. Nevertheless, the Intelligence Staff was still wary of any suggestion which could lead to British or American interference in the work on Norwegian soil. This concerned, among other things, a proposal of support from the American 'Special Forces' which were stationed in Germany, or the British 'Special Air Service' units, whose tasks included the support of resistance groups in the NATO countries.

NOTES

1. FO/E, E-12 II, 'Mobiliseringsoppgjør for ROC', undated, but c. Sept.1952.
2. Ibid., agenda for meeting, 8 Oct. 1951.
3. Ibid., minutes of meeting, 8 Aug. 1950.
4. SMK, Defence Council Protocol, 6 July 1950.
5. FO/E, E-12 II, five-page report dated 9 Dec. 1950.
6. SMK, Defence Council Protocol, 2 Dec. 1950.
7. FO/E, E-12 II, undated, probably Nov. 1951, preliminary survey of the work programme.
8. Ibid., Note on the distribution of ten 57-mm guns, 5 March 1952.
9. Ibid., E-12 I, 'ROC' survey of September 1952.
10. Ibid., Notes 67 and 134, 28 July 1950.
11. FO/E, file 37.00 CPC, Reputation doc., 8 Oct. 1952.
12. FO/E, E-12 I, Evang note, 30 April 1952.
13. FO/E, file 37.00 CPC, doc. no. CPC/4/52.
14. FO/E, file 'CPC', two-page memo, 'Reputation', 28 Jan. 1953.
15. Ibid., unsigned memo, ref. 'S/19/54, S/20/54, Oct. 1954'.
16. Ibid., unsigned memo of 16 Nov. 1957 'Ad RV/6/57 og CPC/2/57 from 19/6/1957'.
17. Ibid., unsigned memo, probably by Evang, 2 Sept. 1957.
18. Ibid., memo, 16 Nov. 1957, 'Møte CPC tirsdag 19. November, avenue Deloison, Neuilly, Paris 14.30'.
19. Ibid., Evang's memos of 14 May and 14 Oct. 1958.
20. Ibid., file 'CPC', doc. CPC/1/61, 18 July 1961.
21. Ibid., doc. RV/1/62, 3 April 1962.
22. Ibid., unsigned memo entitled 'Historikk – ALF (1987)', and interviews.
23. Ibid., file 'CPC', two planning documents dated 4 Feb. and 22 June 1953.
24. See also FO/E, E-12 I, doc. CNCS/I/53.
25. FO/E, E-12 I, file 'Retardation in Finland', dated 13–16 Nov. 1953.
26. FO/E, file 'Vagrant', 16 June 1961.
27. Ibid., unsigned memo from June 1961 'Utkast til OCS Plan Finland'.

4

Through the Iron Curtain: Humint and Photint

We mentioned earlier a plan from the summer of 1949 for sending agents across the border from Finnmark into Soviet territory. Lieutenant Skau, who as acting intelligence officer for the border garrison would have been in charge of such operations, had then turned down the plan as too risky. In the autumn of 1950 Skau, in co-operation with Captain Arne Ekeland as intelligence officer for Finnmark Army Command and with the approval of the Intelligence Staff, organised two brief border crossings to test the vigilance of the Soviet border troops. Both operations – GJEDDE in the middle of September, and DUE in the following month – went well, and seemed to show that it was possible to cross the border in spite of watch-towers, patrols, and wire fences. In operation DUE the agent reached a point where he could see and report on the Luostari airfield and the traffic on the Arctic highway.[1]

In spite of these relatively promising attempts it was not before 1952 that Norwegian-led intelligence operations across the border from Finland and Finnmark got under way. The planning and organisation of the operations was all the time in the hands of the Intelligence Staff. They determined the targets – presumably often together with the British and American secret services – and recruited the agents, most of whom were Finnish nationals picked by the Intelligence Staff's representative in Finland. Training, equipment, briefing and debriefing was also in the hands of the Intelligence Staff, and carried out either in Oslo or in Finland. Local arrangements for operations from Norwegian territory were in the hands of Skau and Ekeland.

In order to be able to operate from Finnish territory, Evang during the winter 1951–52 had secured tacit approval from the Finnish intelligence service and their military. In a personal letter to Norway's new Defence Minister, Nils Langhelle, dated 29 February 1952, he wrote that the 'Finns will permit and secretly assist so that the planned operations from central Finland may begin this summer'.[2] The first such operation registered in Norwegian source material, operation UPPSALA, took place at the end of June. Then two agents crossed the border south of Inari Lake on their way to Murmashi southeast of Murmansk, and returned after three weeks on Soviet territory. One month later two other agents – operation OCEAN – crossed the border east of Rovaniemi on their way to Kandalaksha. But they returned after only seven days. In September a third operation – operation HAVANA, also with two agents – crossed from southern Finland in the direction of Sortavala. Here the agents came back after only five days. The information available from these operations is sparse, but the geographic spread – one each from northern, central and southern Finland, suggests that they were meant to test the Soviet frontier watch in the different sectors.

Operation RENA, commencing 31 August, was the first real intelligence operation across the border from Norwegian territory. Like UPPSALA, RENA had Murmashi as its target. The two agents – referred to only under their cover names of 'Pelle' and 'Kalle' – travelled by civilian aircraft from Oslo to a lake in Finnmark, and from there by car and jeep to a hut near the border. The plan involved an 18-day stay on Soviet territory. But it turned out to be an operation in which most things went wrong. After crossing several rivers by rubber dinghy they reached the Tuloma area on 9 September. Here they split up to observe and photograph different targets. But when 'Kalle' returned to their depot and saw it had been found by a Russian soldier, he concluded that his companion had been taken prisoner and decided to go back. As 'Pelle' came back to the depot he was seen by the Russian soldier, and decided to shoot him. Carrying some supplies and the rubber dinghy he started to go back. A Russian frontier guard fired a shot at him by the Pechenga River, but missed. Thus, after 16 and 18 days respectively, both agents returned – shaken and somewhat dishevelled – to safety on Norwegian territory, and were hastily whisked away to Oslo.

At least two of the three operations from Finnish territory this autumn had repercussions. A handwritten note from the chairman of the Co-ordination Committee for the secret services states that on 18 November he informed Prime Minister Oscar Torp that two 'offensive intelligence missions' had run into problems, and that Finnish reactions had to be expected. And at a meeting of the Co-ordination Committee in March 1953 Evang reported that Finnish police had carried out investigations and arrests. Evang assumed that Finnish Prime Minister Urho Kekkonen was behind the police actions. The consensus at the meeting seems to have been that it was the sum total of espionage activities by US, British and Norwegian intelligence services that had passed a threshold, making it necessary for the Finnish Government to act. It was known that the Soviet ambassador in Helsinki had complained directly to Kekkonen about two border crossings.[3] Evang later informed the Co-ordination Committee that 'a couple of accidents' in the autumn of 1952 had led to a few Finnish citizens being convicted for illegal border crossings. In the autumn of 1953 a Soviet defector also informed the Norwegian Intelligence Service that Soviet intelligence was in contact with Finnish circles who knew about such operations – in one case they knew beforehand that an operation was to take place.

In spite of the problems thus encountered the operations were resumed in 1953. In order to have more secure means of transport for the agents in Norway, the Intelligence Staff had borrowed a single-engined De Havilland 'Beaver' aircraft from the Americans. The plane was registered and operated by the civilian Widerøe air transport company. In the aircraft's log-book the agents were registered as geologists on scientific survey missions.[4]

The first two operations in 1953 started out from Finnish territory. Operation ANNY had as its task to place supply depots for the next operation, BARBARA. The target for the two agents of operation BARBARA was the so-called Stalin Canal, a waterway connecting the White Sea with the Baltic by way of Ladoga Lake. This was strategically important as a means of allowing small and medium Soviet warships to move between the Baltic and Northern Fleets. BARBARA crossed the border on 17 August, and came back three weeks later. The agents seem to have had very little to report, and the Norwegians suspected that they had stuck to the depot tents most of the time.

On 14 July everything was ready for the first 1953 operation across the Norwegian–Soviet border: operation FILTER. This time the two agents were Soviet defectors, and the plan was for them to make their way across to the Luostari air base, and then take the train from Murmansk to Leningrad and back before returning across the border to report on anything they had observed. They did not come back, and in the autumn the defector Pavlov could report that the two agents had been caught 100 kilometres into Soviet territory. They had apparently fired shots at each other, and one had been wounded. The next year *Pravda* reported that two agents had been sentenced to 25 years hard labour for having entered Soviet territory in the service of a foreign power for the purpose of espionage. Whether this was what happened, or whether the two men were really KGB or GRU agents, has never been established.

In two other operations that summer a different pattern was tried, in which the agents would enter Soviet territory from Finland but return across the border to Norway. Both operations – NILSEN and DOROTHY – appear to have gone without any particular difficulty. Then came operation BAMSE, which ran into trouble. This was an operation in which a single agent crossed from Norwegian territory towards Liinahamari and Pechenga at the end of July. When the agent returned after three days he said that he had been discovered soon after crossing the border by two frontier guards. They had exchanged shots, but the agent had gone on to complete his mission, and returned afterwards with only a bullet hole in his rucksack. Very soon after, the Soviet Frontier Commissioner requested a meeting with his Norwegian opposite number, and formally complained against illegal espionage activity by Norway. The result of this was that the Norwegian police became involved, and the Intelligence Staff had to busy themselves with removing all traces of the operation, including sending the agent post-haste to Oslo. The two Norwegian intelligence officers involved also left the area, officially for 'holidays'.

Skau was then called back to Finnmark after three weeks to arrange reception of two Soviet agents who were supposed to come across. One of them did in fact turn up on 17 October. His story was that he was an Estonian agent for Swedish intelligence, and had met the other agent, a somewhat elderly Estonian, in Pechenga. On the way to the border the older man became ill, and had to abandon the trip. Skau's account makes clear that he found the whole story highly dubious.[5]

In the autumn of 1953 Evang gave his first report to the Co-ordination Committee about the Finland operations. He explained about his political contacts in Finland, and about the stationing of intelligence officers at the Norwegian Legation in Helsinki. He then told the committee about certain 'patrol forays' into Soviet territory during the summers 1951,[6] 1952 and 1953, carried out by veterans from Finnish long-distance patrols who had penetrated deep into Soviet territory during the Soviet–Finnish war. Evang claimed that the operations had been of great value. 'Valuable intelligence material has been obtained, especially detailed information about Soviet communications and transport and supply facilities in areas of great importance for Norway. The material we have got and have been able to process has also given us a good standing within NATO.' He admitted there were certain risks involved, as it required contact with many persons in Finland, but liaison with Finnish authorities was good:

> There is reason to believe that the Finnish authorities (Kekkonen's government) will keep a benign attitude as long as the Norwegian activity does not complicate Finland's relations with the Soviet Union. Prime Minister Kekkonen was informed at a fairly early stage that a certain activity went on in Finland on Norwegian initiative. We have reason to believe that Prime Minister Kekkonen directly or indirectly will warn Norwegian quarters whenever the Finns no longer feel able to tolerate such Norwegian activity.[7]

Evang further claimed good relations with the Finnish border police and military security authorities, to which Asbjørn Bryhn, the Chief of Security Police, added that he had good contacts with his Finnish colleagues. Evang finished by stating that similar operations might be carried out the following year, but that no operations of any size would be undertaken without previous approval in principle by higher authority. The committee members appear not to have had any objections to Evang's report, beyond stressing the importance of close co-operation between the intelligence service and the Security Police.

On 20 April 1954 Evang outlined for the Co-ordination Committee the operations planned for that summer. One was a border-crossing operation with the cover name LOG CABIN. Two agents – one British national called 'Philip' and one Norwegian named 'Svein' – duly crossed the Soviet–Norwegian border on 17 August. Their task was to tap a communication line which had been identified by operation BAMSE the year before. But after their return three days later it turned out that they had tapped the wrong line. The next operation, LINDA, was very special, and rather more successful. The agents 'Jussi' and 'Willy' came by boat to Finnmark at the end of August, and on 8 September a balloon rose from the boat deck with the two men on board. Returning on foot one week later, they reported that they had flown for three hours until daylight forced them to land nine kilometres into Soviet territory. They then continued on foot to Luostari airfield, and kept the area under close observation for three days before making their way back to Norwegian territory. Although the original plan had been for them to go further east and report on traffic in the Kola inlet and Vaenga airfield, the operation was considered to be successful. That was not the case with the three operations planned with Finland as the starting point that year. One, operation RITA, with the Alakurtti airfield in Soviet Carelia as the target, had to be abandoned after two unsuccessful attempts. The other two – ALICE and BETTY, intended to start from Finland and return to Norwegian territory – were for various reasons cancelled.

As far as can be ascertained from the available sources, 1954 saw the end of Humint missions across the border from Finland and Norway as organised by the NIS. In 1956, and again in 1958, plans were studied for landing agents by boat on the Murmansk coast. The last one, operation PEGGY, got to the stage where a landing craft was being tested, but nothing came of it.[8] In a kind of epilogue the Americans in 1959 hatched a plan to fly agents into Soviet territory in order to plant remote-controlled radio equipment at selected sites. The aim may have been to obtain early warning of operations by Soviet strategic bombers, since it was suspected that the Soviet air force planned to use the Kola Peninsula as a base for bombing missions against the United States. Some testing of the radio equipment was carried out in late 1959, but the project was then postponed, and probably abandoned.

Notwithstanding Evang's optimistic reports to the Co-ordination Committee, and with the necessary reservations due to the scarcity of documentary evidence, our conclusion is that the intelligence outcome of these border crossings was very limited. Of the 17–18 operations registered in our material, less than half were carried out more or less according to plans. Three or four were cancelled or abandoned, and three others – RENA, FILTER and BAMSE – ran into serious problems. From the purely operational point of view, the fact that no agent's life was lost could be said to make the operations a success, especially if compared to the series of catastrophes that befell comparable ventures by SIS, CIA and Swedish intelligence in Eastern Europe and the Baltic. Whether the Norwegian operations were worth the risks involved – to the agents as well as to the political relations between Finland and the Soviet Union, or Finland and Norway – is a different question. Perhaps the main significance of the operations is the way they bear witness to the desperate lack of and need for reliable information about 'the other side of the hill'. That need was no less urgent after the abandonment of those missions.

Other means of intelligence collection therefore had to be tried, one of them being the now well known – and from an intelligence viewpoint equally unsuccessful – experiment of sending huge unmanned balloons drifting with the wind from Norway into and over Soviet territory with a payload of cameras and other instruments.[9] In the context of the NIS, the collection of intelligence in the later half of the 1950s came to be centred on three sectors: Sigint, which will be the topic of a later chapter; 'shipping', or the collection of intelligence by means of the Norwegian merchant navy, which we shall return to later in this chapter; and aerial photography which is our next subject.

AERIAL PHOTOGRAPHY

Aerial photography from along the Norwegian–Soviet border was in a way a parallel to the Humint missions across the border. Neither could reach very far into Soviet territory, but both had high priority since they covered the most forward positions for any Soviet activity directed against Norway. Hence both activities began on an experimental basis already in 1949. Air photography from planes flying along the Norwegian side of the border had to be done with cameras positioned at an oblique angle. The pilots had strict orders not to get so close to the border that the Russians might suspect a violation of their airspace. Such activity did have its dangers. While no Norwegian aircraft was shot down or even fired at, there are many examples of other countries' reconnaissance planes being shot down although their own observations put them well outside Soviet territory.[10]

The first such reconnaissance mission along the border, by an aircraft from the Royal Norwegian Air Force (RNoAF), took place in August 1952 with a C-47 Dakota – operation PEDER. An after-action report shows that besides photography such missions had the important side effect of allowing the intelligence service to identify Soviet radar and other signals installations which had been alerted by the flight. Thus PEDER had enabled the intelligence service's monitoring stations to identify two Soviet air control stations in the Salmijärvi area: one main station by Murmansk and one in the Belomorsk area which appeared to be the headquarters of the Soviet air control and warning service for northwest Russia.

Some time was to elapse before the next such operation by the RNoAF.

In the meantime British intelligence had begun to show great interest in northern Norway as a platform for operations to collect information about northern areas east of the iron curtain. On 3 November 1952 Evang informed the Co-ordination Committee about a visit from Rear-Admiral Anthony Wass Buzzard, head of British Naval Intelligence. The subject was deemed so sensitive that only handwritten notes were produced. Among the operations that the British wanted permission for were two types of aerial reconnaissance missions. One concerned reconnaissance flights by twin-engined British jet aircraft of a new type – presumably English Electric Canberra planes – towards northwestern Russia, staging through the Norwegian air station at Bodö. The other operations were by specially equipped radar aircraft 'which will keep to Norwegian air space throughout'.[11]

The sensitive nature of the British plans led the chairman of the Co-ordination Committee to put them before the Prime Minister two weeks later. He had also proposed to Defence Minister Langhelle that the Cabinet Defence and Security Committee ought to look into the matter. There is no record of what further happened, but it seems safe to assume that at least the Canberra plan was turned down by the government. As we now know, British Canberra aircraft did carry out high-risk overflights over Soviet territory from bases in Germany and the United Kingdom.[12]

Before new Norwegian flights could be organised, an observation post for stationary surveillance of the important Soviet airfield of Luostari was established at Korpfjell, less than a kilometre from the Soviet–Norwegian border. At times pilots from the RNoAF – nicknamed 'peeping pilots' – were stationed there, and the post remained active until 1962. In the later 1950s even army and naval officers were posted to the border to obtain more qualified assessments of observable Soviet military activity.

In the autumn of 1954 the Intelligence Staff together with the RNoAF again tried air reconnaissance near the border, this time with the same 'Beaver' single-engined aircraft which was used to ferry agents to Finnmark. The order for the operation, which was codenamed MINERAL, gave priority to photography of airfields, control and warning installations, naval installations, industrial sites and communications within 8–10 kilometres from the Norwegian border. In addition the operators were to 'register and plot Soviet Russian stations and record their signals characteristics', in other words a Sigint operation. The aircraft was to fly at a height of 10,000 feet, and about four kilometres inside Norwegian territory. It was expected that the flight would be registered by Soviet radar, and the MIG-15 planes stationed at Luostari were known to have a high state of readiness. The operation was nevertheless seen as involving little risk: 'On the firm condition that the border regulations are observed to the letter, so that no territorial violation can be suspected, it is considered highly unlikely that Russian aircraft or anti-aircraft artillery will try to prevent the operation from being carried out.' But the instructions emphasised that the flight '*must be halted immediately* if the crew observe aircraft in the vicinity or the Beaver is attacked'.[13]

This first MINERAL operation was unsuccessful for several reasons. The weather was bad, the type of aircraft was unsuitable, and the planning and co-ordination was faulty. In the following year it was decided to mount operation MINERAL 2, this time with a C-47 Dakota aircraft. Although the chief of staff of the RNoAF was worried about the danger of such missions, a study of the photographic material convinced the air force that the intelligence value made it worth while to continue. C-47 flights were thus repeated twice in 1956 and again in 1957 and 1959. In the meantime a new series of reconnaissance operations had begun, using RF-84F 'Thunderflash' which was a version of the Thunderjet that had been specially adapted for photo reconnaissance. Under the code names RETINA, FOKUS and VEGA, this series of operations all had photography of the Soviet border areas as the main purpose. In tandem with this the air force worked with the intelligence service on a new type of operation, called KORNELIUS. Here the purpose was to map out Soviet radar coverage of Norwegian territory, and to monitor Soviet reactions to Western aircraft approaching the border. This meant sending a formation of F-84G 'Thunderjet' planes heading straight towards the border, before breaking off and returning to base. During the operation all stationary and some mobile monitoring posts of the intelligence service and the air force were on high alert to register Soviet radar activity and signals traffic.

This multifaceted reconnaissance activity was actively pursued during the following years, in spite of recurring problems of co-operation between the Intelligence Staff and the air force. The air force complained about the lack of feedback from the Intelligence Staff concerning Russian reactions to the flights. On one occasion they claimed that the Staff had failed to inform them of an exchange where Russian fighter pilots had requested permission from ground control to shoot down a Norwegian reconnaissance aircraft. This allegation was dismissed by Evang, and the consensus that gradually emerged was that these flights were comparatively risk-free. A quite different complaint concerned the delay in providing tactical intelligence to the air force about day-to-day activity in Soviet air space. To this Evang responded with a detailed explanation of the time-consuming effort involved in assembling, collating, analysing and retransmitting the gist of the voluminous Comint material that was pouring in from the monitoring stations. The Soviet air command centres did routinely communicate flight plans to outlying radar and control stations the night before an operation was to take place. But the effort required to analyse the signals meant that only in exceptional cases could the Intelligence Staff provide advance warning to the air force.

The intelligence provided as the result of the RNoAF's air reconnaissance activity in the northern areas bordering on the Soviet Union was shared with Allied air forces. The available material suggests that such bilateral exchanges tended to be with the British during the 1950s, but mainly with the Americans during the 1960s. One reason for the switch to the Americans may have been disappointment with the lack of a quid pro quo from the British. The head of the intelligence section of RNoAF, who visited the UK in 1956, wrote in his report that 'our experience shows that the British authorities are far more interested in receiving information and intelligence material than in giving something in return, and they usually try to get material with a minimum of reciprocity'.[14] The Norwegian air force at that time had a particular need for intelligence assistance concerning airfields and radar stations in Finland and Estonia. The reason was that the Air Commander at AFNORTH – Allied Forces Northern Europe – had ordered the RNoAF to take part in operations against targets in Finland and Estonia on the outbreak of war.[15]

The Norwegians were by no means alone in their air reconnaissance activities in the north. British and American aircraft took an active part from the beginning. Much of this Allied activity required use of Norwegian air bases and facilities in order to get the most economical use of the available resources, although aircraft with extended range flew missions from Thule air base in Greenland or bases in Iceland and the United Kingdom. In line with the established Norwegian policy of trying to keep tensions low by avoiding unnecessary provocations in the northern areas near the Soviet Union, the Norwegian authorities kept a wary eye on such Allied air activity. The mainstay of Norway's policy of 'reassurance' towards the Soviets was the ban on the peacetime stationing of foreign forces on Norwegian soil. This did not preclude visits or short stays by Allied military aircraft, but any operations by Allied planes from Norwegian air bases had to keep west of 24 degrees east – roughly 300 kilometres from Soviet territory – and were prohibited from overflying Soviet territory.[16] Reconnaissance flights covering the northern areas from foreign bases could in many cases be tracked by Norwegian radar stations, but were of course beyond the control of Norwegian authorities. They could nevertheless create problems in Norwegian–Soviet relations if they penetrated Soviet air space and then took evasive action that brought them into Norwegian air space.

Allied reconnaissance aircraft on short-term operational or training visits to Norwegian air stations had of course to obtain permission from Norwegian authorities, and so had to conform with the regulations. This was the case with a series of operations by the British RAF from 1956 to 1959, using Washington, Canberra and Comet aircraft. Their flight patterns normally took them out to sea, reconnoitring over international waters in the Barents Sea as far as Novaya Zemlya. But in 1958 Evang confessed to misgivings about British 'ferret' operations, by which their aircraft flew in from the sea towards the Russian coast to test Soviet radar reactions. The pattern was similar to that of the RNoAF's overland KORNELIUS operations, but Norwegian radar had noticed that the British pilots took greater risks, and did on occasion come close to collision course against scrambled Soviet fighter planes. Long-range American planes, flying from Thule air base on the so-called 'Murmansk Run', also went close to and perhaps occasionally into Soviet air space in the Kola area.[17] But reconnaissance aircraft from the US navy also carried out a series of operations from Norwegian airfields in 1958.

By the end of 1958 the sum of all these activities had reached proportions which made it necessary for the Soviet Union to protest. On 19 January 1959 the Norwegian Ambassador in Moscow, the former Justice Minister O.C. Gundersen, was summoned to Deputy Foreign Minister Valerij Zorin and handed a protest note. In relatively mild terms it referred to reports in Norwegian and Finnish newspapers about British and American reconnaissance aircraft operating from Bodø air station in northern Norway 'towards the border of the Soviet Union'. The note referred to Norway's ban on the peacetime stationing of foreign forces, and urged the Norwegian Government to take the necessary measures to prevent such use of Norwegian airfields. 'This would contribute to the maintenance of calm in Northern Europe, as well as to the continued development of good neighbourly relations between the Soviet Union and Norway, which is founded on mutual trust.' Norway's reaction was to make public its decree against Allied air activity in northern Norway east of 24 degrees. The official reply to the Soviet note stated that short visits by Allied aircraft to Norwegian bases was in full accordance with the Norwegian policy on bases. This was the first Soviet protest against Allied reconnaissance activity from Norwegian territory. It was not to be the last.

U–2 IN NORTHERN LATITUDES

The first Allied overflight over Soviet territory in the north, as registered by the NIS, occurred on 8 May 1954, when what proved to be an RB-47E plane crossed over the Kola Peninsula before exiting over Finnish territory. At the same time one or several Allied aircraft violated Norwegian air space, probably as a diversionary manœuvre. It seems likely that Evang discussed this incident during meetings with Allen Dulles in Washington the following month. At any rate he informed the Co-ordination Committee about the overflights in July, and added that they must have occurred with 'approval from very high authority'.[18]

In October 1957 there occurred two potentially alarming incidents, closely monitored by Norwegian radar and Sigint stations. On 11 October an American reconnaissance aircraft was detected by Soviet radar about 60 nautical miles off the Murmansk coast. Several MIG-17 fighters were scrambled to intercept the flight, but were unable to reach the altitude of the intruder. The US plane had then turned back and into Norwegian air space.[19] Two days later a similar incident occurred, and this time the intruder was able to overfly a large part of Kola before continuing into Norwegian air space, in spite of several attempts at interception by MIG-17 and MIG-19 fighter planes.

The Norwegian Government protested against these violations of Norwegian territory, and Allen Dulles sent a personal telegram to Evang with apologies. Evang in his turn briefed both the political and military authorities about the flights, which he assumed were aimed at photographing alleged missile bases as well as known air stations in the area. As for possible political complications Evang was not unduly worried:

> Taking into account that foreign aircraft remained over Soviet territory for about one hour without Soviet aircraft succeeding in intercepting the intruder, the loss of prestige involved makes it unlikely that the Soviet Union will publicly admit to the overflights

through a formal protest. Especially not at a time when Soviet political propaganda relies so heavily on the efficiency of their air and missile forces.[20]

We do not know if alarm bells were heard in the Intelligence Staff or the RNoAF staff as it became clear that the American planes in action that October had operated at altitudes of 62,000 and 65,000 feet, far beyond the known ceiling for RB-47 aircraft. The solution to that riddle came in the following year: the plane in question was a new type, designated U-2. In August 1958 this new aircraft made its first appearance in Norway, at Bodø air base.

The first U-2 operation from a Norwegian air base had the code name BABYFACE, and the stated purpose was meteorological observations over international waters in the northern area. It had advance approval from the Cabinet Defence and Security Committee. It involved two U-2 planes – or articles as they tended to be called by the CIA – and several transport planes carrying supplies for the mission. All was in place at Bodø at the beginning of September, and one U-2 flew on a night mission in the middle of the month. The other one developed technical problems and was replaced by another one later in September. The two 'articles' then remained at Bodø through October, but no further operations were flown before they returned to their bases. So far it seemed to be 'much ado about nothing'.[21]

Since BABYFACE was a CIA operation the latter had provided Evang with advance information. But in after-action reports to his Norwegian masters he made clear his dissatisfaction. 'It is evident that the Americans in this case have only provided the minimum information necessary in order to obtain clearance. Their initial information was not complete. In any future request for similar operations we must demand more adequate information.' He added, somewhat enigmatically, that the real purpose of the operation had not been achieved, partly due to the weather, but also on account of American political misgivings. Two years later a Defence Staff memorandum for the Defence Minister stated that the original plan had been for one or two flights from Bodø along the northern Soviet rim to Alaska and back, for various intelligence purposes.[22]

The political repercussions of operation BABYFACE came several months later. One of the U-2 planes, on the way back to its base in Adana in Turkey, allegedly violated Soviet air space in the Baltic. At least that was Khrushchev's point of departure when – on 9 February, less than three weeks after Zorin's protest about 'flights towards the borders of the Soviet Union' – he berated the Norwegian ambassador in Moscow about Norway having allowed US aircraft to use Norwegian air space for flights that violated Soviet territory. In the course of the conversation it became clear that the Russians in fact had no evidence that the plane had come from a Norwegian airfield. It could, Khrushchev admitted, be a case of 'one of those big planes which Norway did not possess, and which flew at very high altitudes where they could not be detected by the Norwegians'.[23]

In 1959 both the British and the Americans showed a markedly increased interest in reconnaissance flights in the north with the use of Norwegian bases. The probable reason was a combination of concern about Soviet atomic bomb tests on Novaya Zemlya, and worries about Soviet development of long-range missiles following the 'Sputnik' shock in 1957 – the famous 'Missile Gap'. For this latter concern the northern areas had come into focus because of indications that the Russians were here – subsequently pinpointed at Plesetsk, about 200 kilometres south of Archangel – building their first firing range for ICBMs that could reach targets in the United States.

The first request for clearance to use Norwegian air bases came in January 1959 from the US air force. The operation was codenamed DREAMBOAT, and concerned Elint–Comint flights with C-130 aircraft flying a triangular pattern over the Barents Sea, keeping at least 120 kilometres from the Russian coast. The main base for the planes was in Germany, but with the use of Bodø air base in northern Norway they could have four full hours over the operations area.[24] The use of Bodø was also a requirement for a simultaneous British proposal for a series of three to five flights with Comets and Canberras over the same area in January–February and in the late autumn. Other requests, which did not involve Norwegian bases but would entail flights across or near Norwegian air space, concerned a B-47 operation which would cross over Norway, skirt the Finnish–Soviet border, and return to Germany via the Baltic, and a U-2 with British markings and crew which would fly along the Kola coast but outside Soviet territory.

In presenting those 'applications' to his superiors, Evang drew attention to the political risks involved. The Russians might interpret them as preliminaries to an attack, and shots could be fired in anger. Norway would be involved since the Russians would detect the use of Bodø, which would engender new protests about breaches of Norway's 'no foreign bases' declaration. Evang therefore advised granting only a limited number of operations. He also took this opportunity to promote his programme of increased Norwegian Elint efforts, in order to reduce the need for the more dangerous Allied 'ferret' flights. He admitted, however, that much of the necessary intelligence could only be obtained through high altitude flights, and so long as the British and the Americans feared that this area contained long-range missiles targeted on their territory they would go to great lengths to ascertain their whereabouts.[25]

All those requests were considered at a meeting with the Defence Minister and the Chief of Air Staff on 21 January, by which time the Soviet protest note from two days earlier was known. The Defence Minister declared that it was unacceptable that the Russians, through their protests, could put a stop to a perfectly legal activity such as flights from Bodø over international waters by British or American aircraft. That the purpose was intelligence collection was in this context irrelevant. Norway could not on the other hand condone violations of Norwegian air space, or flights from Norwegian bases over the territories of neighbouring states without clearance from those states. The meeting then approved one British operation for February, but decided to postpone consideration of the American requests.[26]

BODØ, 1 MAY 1960: THE U–2 THAT NEVER CAME

It is uncertain how many of the operations planned for 1959 actually were carried out. But towards the end of that year a series of new US and British requests for flights from Norwegian bases poured in. At a meeting on 1 December Evang put them before State Secretary Erik Himle and senior civil servants from the Defence and Foreign Ministries. To a question about the intelligence value of such flights Evang replied that it was a vital interest for the Allies to find out about the control systems of Soviet ICBMs, and that sort of information had to be collected by aircraft at high altitudes: 'one hopes in other words to come across signals that make it possible to locate bases for ICBMs.' These were missiles that were not targeted on Norway. But in matters of such weapons one could not separate Allied from Norwegian interests. When pressed on this point by State Secretary Himle he repeated that knowledge about such missile bases was of decisive importance to the Allies, but ultimately also for Norway. He personally had some doubts as to whether the flights in question would obtain the desired results, but added that he did not have the expertise that the planners of those flights possessed.[27]

The matter, and the wider context of Norway's collaboration in Allied intelligence collection, was now put before the Cabinet Defence and Security Committee, where the following conclusion was recorded:

> The Prime Minister agreed that Norway could make a valuable contribution through the control and warning system being built up in northern Norway, and that this was an activity which the Soviet Union could not object to. He further stated that no great consequence could be attached to Allied overflights of Norway without landing. Flights that departed from Norwegian airfields, on the other hand, could be permitted from time to time but only within strict limits.[28]

The Defence Staff was instructed to co-ordinate all such activities, but the Allied ambassadors concerned should be informed about the policy. The British ambassador, Sir Peter Scarlett, and the US *chargé d'affaires*, Fisher Howe, were instructed accordingly. They were told that the number of flights from Norwegian bases would have to be reduced, the operations ought to take place at variable intervals, and the length of stay on Norwegian territory should be as brief as possible. Finally there was an absolute condition that the flights did not operate 'in the vicinity of Soviet territory'.[29]

In February 1960 Evang went to London to discuss the flights with representatives of British and American intelligence agencies and air forces. There he emphasised the need to show a clear military requirement for the planned flights. He was then given a list of all of 19 flight requests, averaging two per month beginning in April. The predictable reaction from the Defence Minister was that this was excessive, and contrary to the Government's guidelines. For the time being only one flight in April and one in May could be approved.

A plan for an April flight was presented for Evang on 1 April, and concerned electronic searches over international waters in the area Svalbard–Franz Joseph Land–Novaya Zemlya. The Norwegians objected to the size of the operation, involving three C-130 transport aircraft and two U-2 planes, and also to the proposed use of Andøya air base. There followed a series of changes of plan, mostly discussed between Evang and CIA representatives with occasional involvement of air force officers. On 27

April Evang was finally informed that the operation would involve two C-130 aircraft. Two days later he reported to the Air Commander North Norway that the flight would be reversed, so that the two U-2 planes instead of starting from Bodø would land there after completion of the mission. On 30 April Evang was told that the operation would go ahead, and at dawn on 1 May the two C-130 planes left their base in Germany with course for Bodø, where they arrived before nine in the morning. Shortly after landing, the senior USAF officer stated that only one U-2 aircraft was expected, with noon as the estimated time of arrival. In the early afternoon the Air Commander North Norway was told that the flight must have been cancelled, and that the two C-130 planes would immediately return to Germany.[30]

As we know, the U-2 aircraft expected at Bodø on 1 May 1960 was shot down over Soviet territory. It had left its base at Peshawar in Pakistan, and after entering Soviet air space had overflown the missile-testing base at Tyuratam in Kazakhstan before setting course for its next main target, the missile base at Plesetsk south of Archangel. The flight ended near Sverdlovsk, possibly because the aircraft was disabled or destabilised by the shock-wave from a ground-to-air missile exploding near the tail. The pilot, Gary Powers, bailed out, was taken prisoner, and it was revealed that he had been on his way to Bodø.

The downing of Gary Powers and his U-2 had a series of grave political repercussions, of which the most spectacular was of course Khrushchev's break-up of his summit meeting with President Eisenhower in Paris shortly afterwards. That story is well known. Here we shall review briefly the consequences of the affair for Norway's relations with the two superpowers, before considering its impact on Vilhelm Evang's position as intelligence chief, and on the US–Norwegian intelligence relationship.

The Soviet reaction to Norway's involvement in the U-2 mission was sharp, and took the form of oral statements from Khrushchev himself as well as from Defence Minister Malinovski, topped up by an official protest note on 13 May. There were threats of retaliatory strikes against Norway, reserving the 'right to initiate any measure we like against these bases and airfields, and we can hit these bases so that nothing is left of them'.[31] The alarm that these threats produced in Norway exacerbated the Government's anger about the inadequacy of the information initially provided by Evang and the air force chiefs about their involvement in the operation, which had led Foreign Minister Halvard Lange to give misleading statements to the Storting. Under subsequent cross-questioning in the

Ministry of Defence, Evang and the military chiefs maintained their denial of any foreknowledge of the U-2's overflight of Soviet territory, which was of course the crux of the matter. But suspicion remained that at least Evang knew more than he was willing to admit. The Government nevertheless made a sharp protest to the United States against the unwarranted and unacceptable use of a Norwegian air base as destination point for an operation violating Soviet air space.

The important question from our perspective is whether Evang knew or should have understood more than he was willing to admit to his masters about the plan and purpose of the U-2 mission. It seems clear to us that the Americans could not have informed Evang that the U-2 flight expected at Bodø on 1 May was on a mission which involved deep penetration and overflight over Soviet territory. The Americans knew full well that the use of a Norwegian base for such an operation was in flagrant contravention of specific Norwegian conditions for such use. And both they and Evang would have known that making Evang an accomplice would put him in an impossible situation if, as was not unlikely, the secret of the U-2 mission was revealed. Evang would therefore have had every reason to pass on such information to his political superiors, with the inevitable result that the operation would have had to be cancelled.

A different question is whether Evang should have surmised or suspected that an overflight of the Soviet Union was intended. Alarm bells should perhaps have rung when the operation was 'reversed' to involve landing and not starting from Bodø. Evang and one or two senior air force officers probably knew that the U-2 operated from bases in Pakistan, Turkey and Western Germany. Flights from the two first countries destined for Bodø would seem rather pointless unless the purpose was to penetrate or at least skirt Soviet air space. Flights from Germany, on the other hand, might well have the Barents Sea as their target area, in line with the flight plan given to Evang on 1 April, with staging through Bodø on the return journey.

A final question concerns whether Norwegian intelligence and radar could have tracked the flight so as to establish *at the time* whether an overflight was in progress. This is most unlikely, seeing that Norwegian radar had an operational ceiling of about 50,000 feet, while the U-2 flew at over 60,000 feet. Sigint monitoring of the Soviet control and warning network may have alerted the Norwegian intelligence service that something unusual was happening. But analysing and interpreting the signals was bound to take some time before any conclusions could be drawn.

We therefore conclude that the planned use of Bodø for Gary Powers' ill-fated mission on 1 May 1960 was a deliberate American contravention of agreed conditions for flights involving the use of Norwegian air bases, in breach of the mutual trust on which the intelligence co-operation was based. As Evang stated to his political masters at a meeting on 13 May: 'I have been thoroughly led astray, and must see this against the background of the vital US interests that are involved. I believe the President knew. I did not expect that the United States would do something like this.'[32] It must be assumed that the CIA in planning the operation had calculated the risk of Soviet and Norwegian protests against the need to obtain more information about Soviet ICBM developments, and that the latter consideration had prevailed.

As far as Soviet–Norwegian relations were concerned, the menacing Soviet utterances in the initial aftermath should be contrasted with the mild language employed by Deputy Prime Minister Mikoyan in a conversation with Halvard Lange a few weeks later: 'Mikoyan stated that in relation to the U-2 affair the Soviet government believes the statements made by the Norwegian government. The Soviet government was pleased that Norway had taken such an unequivocal stand against such a violation of the Soviet Union.'[33] Shortly after that, however, an American RB-47 E aircraft was shot down by Soviet fighter planes north of Kola. Although Norwegian radar observations confirmed American assertions that the plane was over international waters when shot down, the Soviets claimed that it had penetrated Soviet air space, and that Norway in various ways was involved in the operation. New verbal attacks on Norway followed, which strengthened the Norwegian Government's resolve to tighten even further its policy on Allied use of Norwegian air bases – the most significant new restriction being a ban on flights east of 24 degrees even over international waters without prior approval. This new policy was acknowledged by the Americans through the following official statement:

> If and when a decision is taken to resume RB-47 type peripheral reconnaissance flights – and it should be understood that these do not involve penetration of Soviet air space – which might be construed in the event of publicity regarding them as having involved Norwegian co-operation or participation, the United States will be prepared to give advance notification of the flights to Norwegian authorities.[34]

The epilogue to the U–2 affair came in February 1961, at a lunch which Allen Dulles and other senior CIA people gave for Evang in Washington. To the consternation of his hosts Evang then lashed out at CIA's behaviour in the matter:

> Evang mentioned that the U–2 affair had set the Norwegian Intelligence Service back 3–4 years. Our excellent relationship with the authorities was destroyed. The few persons in the higher levels of the Norwegian administration who understood something about modern intelligence had never accepted the cover story that had been produced. None of them seriously believed that this airplane would approach Bodø without certain advance agreements. The CIA had given the NIS an explanation, which was incorrect. On that basis the NIS had produced a cover story for Norwegian military authorities, especially Air Command North Norway. A cover story based on wrong information always becomes nonsense. The Oslo prelude to the operation was the stupidest possible from a security point of view. After the accident had happened the NIS did not within reasonable time get any kind of answer from the CIA to even the simplest of questions, such as whether Powers had previously been to Bodø. Hence the cover story that NIS had to present to the Norwegian authorities was unusable. NIS had on this occasion, as also later during the RB–47 episode, felt completely let down by the CIA.[35]

DELFINUS: MERCHANT SHIPS AS OBSERVATION PLATFORMS

Although enclosed by what was in many ways an impenetrable iron curtain against unwanted entry and sojourn, the Soviet Union and other communist countries were not hermetically sealed. Through organised visits by official delegations, and visits by representatives of Western firms that specialised in trade with the Eastern bloc, a certain amount of approved travel activity took place even in the height of the Cold War. The NIS made sporadic attempts to utilise such 'legal travellers' – referred to in the trade as LT – to obtain information of interest to intelligence services, but apparently without much success. One reason for that was the obvious one that such visitors were always under tight surveillance and kept away from military and other forbidden areas. In 1956 Section VI of NIS tried 11 such LT operations, in order to 'gain insight into the operational possibilities in a field of activity that is new to us'. The section concluded that this was a promising field, and proposed to extend the activity. In addition the section suggested placing NIS agents in important Soviet and East European cities, and pointed to the useful intelligence obtained by one of their officers while attached to the Norwegian legation in Prague in 1956. 'We must operate where the intelligence is to be found, primarily in places like Warsaw, Prague, Budapest, Moscow.' Evang, however, remained sceptical.[36]

The transport of goods by Western merchant vessels to and from the communist bloc was a different matter altogether. Since the merchant navies of those countries lacked transport capacity for their import and export needs, a major share of their maritime trade had to be carried on Western ships. Norway, with the world's fourth largest merchant navy, was very active in this trade. The ships called at important ports, and while sailing in coastal waters, in the approaches to major ports, and while in harbour, the ships' officers and crew could observe and photograph objects of intelligence interest – naval vessels, port installations, radar and radio aerials, etc. While on shore leave they could relatively freely walk about and identify military buildings, police stations and other more or less strategic targets. In addition to observing and photographing, the crew might on occasion have other tasks like collecting sea water samples for analysis for radioactive fallout from nuclear tests, or Elint missions targeted towards investigating radar stations on the Soviet Arctic coast. On shore leave they might also be charged with posting letters – presumably to agents of US or British intelligence.[37]

The NIS was early on – already in 1948 – aware of the potential value of such observations behind the iron curtain. Organising such activity so as to obtain the best possible results was however no easy task. Firstly, extreme secrecy was required. For instance, a Norwegian sailor in the town of Murmansk who showed a strong interest in particular buildings or installations, especially if he also tried to take pictures, would risk being arrested and sentenced for espionage activity. The observers, or agents, and their ships, were therefore never named in the reports. There was also a risk that Norwegian vessels might be excluded from such trade if there were grounds for suspicion that they were used for intelligence purposes. All this helps to explain why such operations were kept at a fairly low level during the 1950s. One section chief of NIS nevertheless in 1958 found reason to call these shipping operations 'our most reliable source of offensive intelligence'.[38]

Intelligence from the shipping operations was acquired in different ways. The most common method was to assign such tasks to specially recruited contact persons on Norwegian ships trading to eastern ports. A vital source for information as to which vessels were chartered for such traffic was the monitoring, through the underground bunker in the centre of Oslo, of telex and other messages to and from the Soviet shipping agency 'Sovfracht'. The persons recruited were briefed about what to look for, and provided with special cameras if photography was required. They were then debriefed when the mission was completed. As many Norwegian merchant vessels traded between foreign ports, the NIS had from the early 1950s briefing officers stationed also in certain important foreign ports, such as in London, in Kiel, and in Singapore with a view to shipping traffic to China. In Norwegian ports the briefing officers were often the intelligence officers of the local naval commands. Crews on Norwegian fishing vessels operating on the Barents Sea would also be asked to observe and report on Soviet naval vessels and their exercises, for which purpose they were given brief training courses.

On particular occasions the NIS also placed specially trained officers on board vessels bound for eastern ports. One such occasion came when in 1956 exchange visits of Soviet and Norwegian naval vessels were arranged. A Norwegian flotilla visited Leningrad in the summer of 1956, and on that occasion three or four NIS officers dressed in naval uniform were put on board. Besides photographing items of interest they were also provided with special electronic equipment supplied by the United States and Britain for various monitoring activities. Similar arrangements were made for the return visit by the Soviet navy. Plans to employ frogmen to examine the bottoms of the ships while in Oslo harbour were discussed, but abandoned in the light of the disappearance a few months earlier of the British frogman 'Buster' Crabb while examining the Soviet cruiser which had carried Bulganin and Khrushchev on an official visit to Britain.[39]

As late as in 1955 the sailors of the merchant navy entrusted with such missions received no remuneration for their work. This created problems as it appeared that intelligence officers of other countries were interested in the same kind of information and willing to pay for it. From 1956 or 1957 the observers hence seem to have been paid a monthly retainer fee of 300 kroner, plus a bonus of 200 kroner for each mission.

The existing source material for this shipping activity is somewhat fragmentary. But the evidence shows clearly that the Kola Peninsula and the White Sea were the focus of NIS attention, for obvious reasons. A survey of the activity in 1957 shows that of a total of 167 mission reports – 40 fewer than the previous year – about half were from that area, with an emphasis on Murmansk and Archangel. Strongly represented also was the Baltic area, and particularly Leningrad. Here there was close co-operation between the NIS and the Swedish secret intelligence agency 'T-byrån'. Led by Thede Palm, who early on had formed a close personal friendship with Evang, that agency carried on a multifarious activity in the Baltic based on Swedish sailors and fishermen as well as some Baltic refugees. A third area, the Black Sea, was represented with a smaller number of reports. From 1955 to 1960 the NIS received an average annual total of about 250 reports, up to 150 film strips, and a number of cine films. An annual report from 1959 shows that the NIS also had reports from German and British merchant vessels and trawlers operating in the Barents Sea and adjoining sea areas. German shipping was increasingly active there, but this had so far resulted in few reports. Contacts on British ships were more active. In 1959 the NIS registered almost as many British as Norwegian reports.[40]

During the years 1956 to 1958 the NIS also carried on some activity in the Far East based on Norwegian ships. This was due in part to reports from the Norwegian consulates in Manila and Hong Kong in 1956 about British and American intelligence officers eager to come on board and question officers on Norwegian ships coming from mainland China. The Norwegian consul in Manila had misgivings about this, and when he told the American naval attaché about his concern, the reply was that he would only cease this activity if a better alternative for obtaining such information could be found. The consul then offered to arrange meetings between the naval attaché and Norwegian ships' captains at his home. The Foreign Ministry in Oslo was informed, and seems to have found the arrangement acceptable. However, when the consul in Hong Kong later that year reported similar problems and asked for instructions, the matter was brought before the Co-ordination Committee. There the Foreign Ministry representative cited numerous reports suggesting an increasing pressure from British and American intelligence for access to Norwegian ships and their officers. The Foreign Ministry was apprehensive about the involvement of Norwegian consular officers in such activities. Evang's reaction was to inform the committee that the NIS planned to post its own officers in those ports, because if the NIS did not do this work the pressure from US and UK agencies was bound to increase. The committee was clearly unhappy about the situation, and the chairman, Andreas Andersen, put his warnings on paper. He saw no reason for Norwegian intelligence activities in such far-away areas with only the remotest relevance to Norwegian national security. It was more important for Norway to have good relations with the countries of that area, due to its shipping and economic interests.[41]

The outcome of the committee's discussions was an instruction to the Norwegian consulate in Hong Kong which advised against participation by consular officials in arranging interviews for other countries' intelligence officers with Norwegian citizens, except in special circumstances. Reports during 1957 nevertheless suggested that the problems persisted. The Legation in Tokyo reported that American intelligence officers operated in the same manner in Japanese ports. And when a temporary consul official in Manila refused to co-operate with the Americans, the US naval attaché began to send his own people on board Norwegian ships. This led to a meeting of senior ministry officials with Evang in May 1958, at which Evang proposed a solution. The Norwegians would have to do this work themselves, since the information obtained was of considerable intelligence value to Norway as well as to its Allies. Evang would therefore arrange a suitable cover for one of his officers to be stationed in the Far East.[42] This was then accepted, and soon afterwards one of Evang's most trusted officers, Commander Martens Meyer, was sent to Hong Kong as 'Maritime Inspector'.

Martens Meyer had not been long in his new post before Norwegian shipping circles understood the real purpose of his presence – the consul reported that he had quickly acquired the nickname 'Mata Hari'. Some ship-owners' representatives became increasingly concerned lest the activity of Martens Meyer and his successor might damage Norway's position in China's maritime trade. One Norwegian ship-owner also threatened to go to the newspapers with the story. At a meeting in Oslo with the President of the Norwegian Ship-Owners' Association, in December 1959, it was finally decided to abandon NIS operations in the Far East.

This, however, was not a satisfactory solution from the viewpoint of the NIS's American partner, which soon began to urge a resumption of the operation. During a visit to Washington in February, 1961, Evang and Martens Meyer discussed the matter with Bill Welsh, who was the CIA's main expert for the area.[43] Welsh stressed the great importance attached to the Norwegian effort based on Hong Kong, and Evang agreed to reconsider the matter, since he also saw some long-term value in building up Norwegian knowledge about China. But it would be impossible to establish a Norwegian shipping office in Hong Kong without the Ship-Owners' Association and the Foreign Ministry knowing about it.

There is only scanty evidence about further developments on that particular score. Some sort of co-operative arrangement between the NIS and the CIA seems to have been established in Hong Kong, and at a meeting in the United States in March 1964 it was agreed 'to continue the present arrangement'. There was also some mention of Norwegian operations in China in the scientific and technical intelligence fields, and a concrete plan for an operation 'in the forestry field'.[44] However, the statistics from the shipping section of NIS has only two operations in the Far East in 1962, and none in the period 1963–66, which suggests that any operations by Norwegian agents in that area have been run by the Americans. From 1967 about 20 operations were recorded each year, with a yield of from 376 to 2,421 film strips. In the autumn of 1969 the Americans again signalled strong interest in operations in China, with special regard to 'the Chinese navy which is now on the move'.[45]

In the European area the 1960s showed a marked increase in the reporting and photographing activity of the merchant ship agents, especially in the northern areas, where each year there occurred between 200 and 500 operations. The annual yield of film strips was 3,000–8,000, with the addition of several cine films. Highest priority in this area was towards the end of the 1960s accorded to the shipyards building nuclear submarines, but intelligence about nuclear installations was also well up on the list. Towards the end of the decade there was a certain increase of activity in the Baltic, but something of a standstill in the Black Sea.

This chapter has dealt with three different ways of obtaining intelligence from behind the iron curtain – by agents crossing the border, by aerial photography and monitoring in the border areas, and by agents on board merchant vessels. In the period up to 1960 those were in the main the only ways for Western intelligence to obtain visual information about the military capacity of the Soviet Union. By the early 1960s the two first methods had largely been made obsolete by the advent of an epoch-making technological innovation: reconnaissance satellites. But the third method, observations based on agents on board merchant vessels in eastern trades, saw a sharp increase from 1962. It may at first sight seem surprising that this source did not also lose its value in the satellite age. But photography from above, the bird's eye view, had its limits. It required mostly clear weather, and for many years the 'solution' of satellite photographs – the ability to distinguish smaller objects – was insufficient for a detailed picture. Also it gave a one-dimensional vertical picture that could be misleading. A well-known example of how 'horizontal' photography could provide a necessary corrective to aerial photography is the first batch of aerial photography over Tibet. They showed a series of constructions on mountain tops which from above looked like little forts surrounded by ramparts. Only after obtaining close-range photographs at ground level did it become possible to establish that the objects were small temples containing statues of a god who is the protector of wayfarers.

Another strong indicator of the value of Humint observations based on merchant vessels even in the satellite age is the fact that the US Navy in 1966 began its own 'shipping' operation under the cover name 'Task Force 157'. The purpose was 'collecting intelligence on the naval movements and capabilities of the Soviet Union, China, and other target nations (North Korea, Vietnam, and the Eastern European countries) ... via the recruitment and running of agents employed by merchant marine fleets, particularly those that entered denied areas'.[46] Since that operation was particularly aimed towards navies it was hardly meant to replace the Norwegian shipping operations. Nor is there any indication that the operations were co-ordinated, even though the US operation also covered the Kola and Leningrad areas. In fact, according to Richelson's account, the very existence of 'Task Force 157' was kept secret from all countries except Britain. Even in the United States it appears that only a few people at the top of the intelligence community were aware of it until its existence was revealed by the *Washington Post* in 1977 – shortly before the operation was closed down.

New indications of the intelligence value of the Norwegian shipping operation came towards the end of the period covered by this book. The new – since 1966 – chief of the NIS, Colonel Johan Berg, visited Washington for top-level consultations with the CIA and the Defense Intelligence Agency in February 1969. At those meetings the Americans strongly praised the value of the intelligence collected by the Norwegian sailors, and urged the NIS to extend the operation:

> We were asked whether we could extend our activity in the Mediterranean regarding Soviet maritime movements there. Due to political restrictions the Americans were unable to reconnoitre closer than 80 nautical miles from the coasts of Arabic states or east of Cyprus. This hampered the efforts to maintain an up-to-date surveillance of

the deployment and activities of Soviet ships, especially the possible development of bases.[47]

Finally, during a working conference in Washington in November 1969, attended by three leaders of the Norwegian shipping operations, the value of the intelligence thus collected was again stressed: 'In spite of the steady improvements in satellite and aerial photography, it was pointed out that our clandestine collection programme could not be replaced by those systems, and hence was very valuable to the United States.' As a token of US appreciation the Norwegians were given an up-to-date map of all installations in the northern part of the Kola Peninsula, based on the whole gamut of collection means. 'They mentioned that the map represented a tribute to the Norwegian collection work, and that similar data had not been made available to other nations. It was repeatedly stated that Norway occupied a unique position in regard to feedback from the CIA and NSA.'[48]

NOTES

1. The main source for these border crossing operations is H. Skau's manuscript memoirs 'Tjeneste i Finnmark 1947–1983'. While there seems no reason to doubt the veracity of his account, it is lacking in detail, and his information about operations from Finnish territory was, as he states, mainly second-hand.
2. FD, file 'Koordineringsutvalget for 1952–53', Evang to Langhelle, 29 Feb. 1952. In the same letter he writes that the Finns will also facilitate Norwegian technicians' monitoring of Soviet military signals traffic in the Salla and Porkkala border areas.
3. SMK, file KK, 'mappe nr. 3', handwritten note by 'AA' (Andreas Andersen), 11 March 1953.
4. FO/E, file 'Beaver'.
5. Recent reports in Swedish media about massive KGB penetration of Sweden's network of agents in Estonia suggest that Skau's suspicions were well founded.
6. Skau's manuscript has nothing on any such operations in 1951.
7. SMK, file KK, 'mappe nr. 4'. Two-page memorandum 'Visse etterretnings-operasjoner i Finland', 15 Oct. 1953.
8. FO/E, Skau manuscript, pp. 40 and 45.
9. On this see R. Tamnes, *The United States and the Cold War in the High North* (Ad Notam, Oslo, 1991), pp. 125–6, and R.W. Sørdahl, *U-1* (Cappelen, Oslo, 1985).
10. The best-known case from Northern Europe in this early period is the DC-3 aircraft from the Swedish Air Force which was shot down while on a Sigint mission over the Baltic Sea. See R. Älmeberg, *Flygaren som försvann* (Askelin & Hägglund, Gothenburg, 1983). In a commentary to that incident FST/E stated that it was 'a clear warning from the Soviets that they will tolerate no form of technical surveillance

over the territories they control, however legitimate' (SMK, file KU, memo, 20 Aug. 1952).

11. SMK, file KU, memo by 'A.A.' (Andreas Andersen, the chairman of the Co-ordination Committee), 3 Nov. and 18 Nov. 1952.
12. For those operations see Paul Lashmar's articles in *Aeroplane Monthly*, Oct. 1994 and Feb. 1995.
13. FO/E, file 'Div. materiale. Mappe: Major Stray'. This file contains the operations order as well as other papers relating to the operation.
14. FO/E, file 'Diverse saker', report by Captain Bibow, dated 11 Nov. 1956.
15. FO/E, SH archive, RNAF to Chief of Intelligence Staff, 20 Nov. 1998.
16. The most complete and authoritative study of Norwegian postwar security policy, with particular regard to relations with the major Allies, is Rolf Tamnes, *The United States and the Cold War in the High North*.
17. FO, SH archive, folder 'U-2', six-page memorandum reviewing the history of such flights, dated 15 Oct. 1960, and SMK, KU protocol, 17 Nov. 1958.
18. SMK, KU protocols, 6 and 7 May 1954, with annexed memoranda, and protocol, 19 July 1954.
19. Information recently released by the CIA suggests that the purpose of this first mission was to observe the Soviet Northern Fleet's manœuvres in the Barents Sea, and that no overflight of Soviet territory took place. See D. Welzenbach and N. Galyan, 'Those Daring Young Men and Their Ultra-High Flying Machines', in *Studies in Intelligence*, Vol. 31, No. 3.
20. FO/E, file 60.80, 'Diverse flytokt', memos by J.L. Sveinsson, 1 Nov., and Evang, 31 Oct. 1957.
21. UD, file 33.6/14b, various memoranda.
22. FO/E, Evang Papers, memo 'Operation "Babyface"' of 17 Nov. 1958, and FO, SH archive, file 'U-2', note for General Øen for delivery to Minister Handal, 4 Oct. 1958.
23. SMK, file KU, Ambassador Gundersen's memo, 9 Feb. 1959.
24. FO/E, file 60.80, 'Diverse flytokt'; memo, 'Operasjon "Dreamboat"' of Jan. 1959.
25. FO/E, Evang Papers, memo of 8 Jan. 1959, 'Amerikansk/britiske forslag om flyginger fra Norge'.
26. Ibid., memo of 21 Jan. 1959.
27. UD file 38.17/13b, memo by G. Kristiansen, 1 Dec. 1959.
28. Ibid., memo, 4 Dec. 1959, 'Amerikansk/britiske rekognoseringsflyginger i arktisk område'.
29. Ibid., G. Kristiansen, memo of 9 Dec. 1959.
30. FO, SH file, folder 'U-2', various memoranda. See also Tamnes, *The United States and the Cold War in the High North*, for a more detailed account of the event.
31. More details ibid., p. 180.
32. UD file 33.6/14b, Rolf Busch memo, 13 May 1960, 'Allierte oppklaringsfly i Norge'.
33. Ibid., Vol. II, Lange memo, 24 June 1960.
34. SMK, file KU, Foreign Ministry to Prime Minister, 15 Oct. 1960, enclosing a report from ambassador Paul Koht in Washington.
35. FO/E, file 'X-Z Elint–Comint drøftelser'. Memo dated 24 Feb. 1961: '15 februar 1961. Lunsj'. The cover story mentioned is presumably the first, incomplete, version that Evang gave to his political masters, on which the Foreign Minister had based

his first, inaccurate, statement to the Storting.

36. FO/E, MM/Ollestad Papers, file 'Diverse saker'. Various memos from March 1957.
37. FO/E, file '136. VI avdeling', E. Jensen to Martens Meyer, 11 Jan. 1956, reporting on activity by FST/E/VI/B in 1955.
38. Ibid., unsigned proposal for a programme of operations for VI section, minuted as handed to the chief on 15 Feb. 1958.
39. See Tom Bower, *The Perfect English Spy* (Heinemann, London, 1995), pp. 159 ff.
40. File '136. VI avdeling'. Various reports from the period 1955–1960. Discrepancies between the figures in the reports and those in the Appendix are because the latter contain figures only from missions by Norwegian agents.
41. SMK file '013.0 Diverse', Andersen's note of 24 Nov. 1957.
42. UD 38.5/53, Note signed F. Jacobsen, 31 May 1958.
43. FO/E, file 'X-2 Elint–Comint drøftelser', note about meeting, 14 Feb. 1961.
44. FO/E, file 40.04, memo for Evang, 10 April 1964.
45. FO/E, file 'Sjef E Notater 1970', with report of a meeting in Washington, 24–28 Nov. 1969.
46. Quoted from Jeffrey T. Richelson, 'Task Force 157: The US Navy's Secret Intelligence Service, 1966–77', in *Intelligence and National Security*, Vol. 11, No. 1 (Jan. 1996), p. 114.
47. FO/E, file '1 | 969: SJ E/A Notater Inn/Ut', memo from the Chief of NIS to the Defence Chief, 12 March 1969.
48. Ibid., file 'Sjef E Notater 1970', memo from the Chief of NIS to Chief of Staff Defence Command No. 1, 5 Jan. 1970, annex 'Internt notat: Møte i Washington 24–28 November 1969'.

5

Comint: Communications Intelligence

In a previous chapter we have seen that monitoring of Soviet military communications in the northern areas – operation TORKEL – was the first 'offensive' intelligence operation undertaken by the NIS. After a period of testing in the area around Kirkenes, TORKEL moved to a new building at Vadsø in the autumn of 1951. Here the station established itself by the official cover name of FFSV – Forsvarets Forsøksstasjon Vadsø (Defence Experimental Station Vadsø). With an initial personnel of 20, FFSV was destined to become the main station for NIS activities in the North in the field of communications intelligence. The other elements in the Comint network were the listening and radio direction-finding stations near Trondheim and Stavanger, and the headquarters in Oslo. The headquarters had in 1947 been moved to its more permanent location at Sæter on the eastern outskirts of Oslo, and included an element engaged in final analysis of the collected material.

Comint would for a long time be the dominant activity of the NIS. They defined it as being 'electronic intelligence directed towards monitoring and analysis of foreign military communications for the primary purpose of obtaining early warning of extra-ordinary military activity, and to provide information about organisational structures, order of battle, exercises, and other activity'. As the NIS in the 1950s began to move into the field of what was sometimes called Non-Comint electronic intelligence, but more often Elint, the designation Sigint, Signals Intelligence, came into use as covering both Comint and Elint. Elint was then defined as electronic intelligence directed towards electro-magnetic radiation from foreign military radar, guidance and navigation systems for the primary purpose of obtaining information about equipment capacity and weapons development, and to monitor tactical activity. A first aim was here to locate and monitor the Soviet radar stations on the Kola Peninsula.

Ideally the collected coded Comint material should be decrypted – translated into plain language. But with the ever increasing amount of material collected, this would have required a much larger investment in personnel and machinery than was possible within the limits of the combined resources of the radio and cipher sections of the NIS. The mainstay of NIS achievements in the Comint sector would therefore be on a different level: even if you could not read the contents of the messages, it was still of major importance to identify and locate the sender and receiver by direction finding and analysis of call signs. This made it possible to establish and maintain a 'map' of Soviet military air and naval movements, in northern Russia, and to monitor the development of stations and bases in the area. Over time one could thus establish a pattern of normal activity, and be alert to any alterations or deviations from that pattern: could they be preparing a major military exercise in the area? Were new types of submarine or surface naval vessels being tested? Were new atomic bomb tests being organised? Were they about to test-fire ship-based missiles? With any such extraordinary activity the relevant parts of the intelligence apparatus would then be alerted, and counter-measures instituted.

With its modest personnel strength, and with equipment that was hardly 'state of the art', FFSV, working together with the main station in Oslo, seems relatively quickly to have established itself as an important source of knowledge about the Soviet Northern Fleet and Soviet air and army strength in the northern areas. In particular, the radio operators developed a high degree of expertise in identifying ships, aircraft and ground stations from the patterns of changing call signs used. Soon the Americans began to take an active interest in the results. In June 1952 two US experts came to Norway. The most prominent of the two was the cryptologist Dr Louis Tordella, who had already established himself as a central figure in AFSA, the Armed Forces Security Agency, which was the US military Comint and cipher agency. AFSA was at this time on the way to being transformed into NSA – the National Security Agency, sometimes referred to as the 'No Such Agency' in view of the extreme secrecy surrounding the organisation: it did not exist in any public document, and the Presidential Directive that established it was in addition to its Top Secret classification protected by a codeword which only a few highly placed persons had been entrusted with. Accompanying Dr Tordella to Norway was Commander Griffin Chiles from the US navy.

1952: THE NORUSA CO–OPERATION GETS UNDER WAY

In Oslo the two Americans had several meetings with Evang, and with two of the leading men in the Norwegian Comint section, Dag Falchenberg and Erling Hellerslien. Falchenberg then took them – camouflaged as Mr Jones and Mr Williams – on a visit to FFSV at Vadsø to study the set-up there. They showed a particular interest in information from Soviet short-range communication stations in the Barents–Murmansk area, and they had beforehand been provided with samples of what the Vadsø station had picked up from Russian radio transmitters. Back in Oslo Tordella and Chiles had further meetings with Evang and his people, attended also by the CIA representative Robert E. Andersen. The Americans considered the set-up in Finnmark as very promising, particularly with regard to EW or early warning: firstly as warning of a build-up or redeployment of Soviet sea, land and air forces in the area, 'which were of direct concern to Norway and a real concern to us and to NATO', secondly in the context of mapping out the Soviet control and warning organisation with a view to finding the safest flight paths for US bombers. Tordella therefore advised a strong expansion of the Norwegian Comint activity.[1]

As a naval person and radio specialist, Dag Falchenberg occupied a central position in this work. He has in later years emphasised identification and localisation of Soviet naval vessels as a field where the Norwegian service was particularly advanced and hence could offer the Americans valuable information. At first the Norwegian radio specialists had profited from assistance from Sweden, where FRA – Försvarets Radioanstalt (the Defence Radio Agency) – had during the Second World War developed its own particular skill towards Soviet signals systems. But the Russians had in the meantime – apparently in 1948 – refined their systems, 'so that what we had learnt from them [the Swedes] was out of date and we had to start finding our own ways'. This was specially so regarding the Soviet navy's system of call signs, which of course was hedged about with particular secrecy to prevent adversaries from identifying and determining the position of the different ships:

> Each vessel could have towards one hundred different call signs one day and an equal number next day which had not been used before, so it never had to use the same one. This was a very complex system which both the Americans and the Swedes had employed many mathematicians and university people to try to solve, but our radio

operators had succeeded. This somehow served to advertise us, so that the Americans became interested in working with us. That is how NORUSA came into being.[2]

The June 1952 meetings resulted in a preliminary, bilateral Norwegian–American agreement for Comint co-operation. The United States would provide equipment and financial support, in return for copies of material collected as intercepts or as recordings of Soviet signals traffic. The American desires were specified to the following types of information: primarily 'early warning' signals in 'perforated tape' version, with the ultimate aim of providing sufficient data for a relatively complete reconstruction of daily Soviet signals activity in the north. Until such time as a direct teleprinter communication could be established, this material was to be delivered to the CIA station at the US embassy the day after being recorded. In addition the Americans desired copies of signals traffic, logs and direction-finding results from other stations that could supplement the Vadsø material. The Americans also requested a gradual expansion of the NIS intercept activity towards a nearly complete coverage of all Russian radio traffic in the north, including navy, army, air, police, anti-air, shipping, etc. Suggested targets for the increase of personnel were 30 by January 1953, 40 by July 1953, with a further expansion to about 175–200 over and above the personnel strength as of June 1952. Finally the Americans requested the loan of copies of intercepts from earlier years. The equipment to be provided by the Americans included teleprinter machines for production and transmission of EW material, radio receivers, aerials, direction-finding instruments, etc.[3]

Co-operation on the basis of this first NORUSA agreement seems to have been quickly established. On 16 September the Intelligence Staff notified the CIA station at the US embassy that delivery of EW reports would begin that day. The service would then expand as soon as more personnel could be hired. During the autumn the network of collection stations was expanded with the establishment of a new station at Fauske near Bodø – called FSTF I, Forsvarets stasjon Fauske (Defence Station Fauske). Its geographical location was determined after tests in the Bodø–Salten area conducted by the radio operator Erling Jensen. Jensen had been station chief on TORKEL from the spring of 1948, first at Kirkenes and then at Vadsø, until appointed chief of Fauske I. The 'headquarters' was established in two rented rooms on the top floor of a house in the centre of Fauske, and the radio station with its aerial masts was set up in a marshy area nearby. The 'station' was an uninsulated 2 x 2-metre cabin, equipped with a 1,000 watt electric heater which could not be used on full power since the consequent voltage loss in the power supply to the cabin would disable the radio equipment. An urgent request to Oslo for more comfort resulted in the provision of sheepskin motorbike dresses which was in fact war booty from the German army's motor cycle troops.

In the summer of 1953 FSTF I 'headquarters' was moved to some barracks in a German-built army camp nearby, and there new purpose-built housing was put up in 1956. The operational personnel then counted 11 persons. Equipment was still very primitive: 'Standard equipment for an operator in those days was a couple of radio receivers, a pencil, two crayons (red and blue), some writing paper, and a post log in quadruplicate.' Whenever the station being monitored changed frequency the operator had to fetch a portable frequency meter and put another notch on the receiver scale. Adding to the difficulties were the mediocre receiving conditions in the camp area.

From 1952 the Comint activity in the county of Finnmark was also expanded somewhat. At Vadsø there was the main station at Tomaselv, on the outskirts of the town, and two direction-finding stations, one at Vadsøy islet, the other on the Melkevarden hilltop to the north. In addition the NIS from 1952 to 1957 operated a mobile summer station in the south Varanger area, the district adjoining the Soviet border. At first this was located at Vaggetem, with four men living in a tent. 'The area was mostly bog, and the mosquitoes were a great nuisance. It was therefore natural to name the station "Mygg"', says Hallfred Skau in his memoirs. During the two last years of its operation the station was on a hilltop – 'Hill 96' – further north. Some test monitoring in the VHF band was also conducted at Korpfjell a few kilometres from the border. From that hilltop there was a good view towards both the important Soviet military air base at Luostari and the main highway towards Pechenga and the coast.[4]

In the spring of 1954 preparations for a more formal NORUSA agreement got under way. In May–June Evang visited Washington for talks with CIA Director Allen Dulles, and on 8 June he gave an account of the meetings to the Co-ordination Committee. The talks had shown that the CIA was becoming particularly concerned about what appeared to be the construction of large air bases in northwestern Russia, presumably intended for bombers that could reach targets in the United States. They were therefore specially interested in intelligence from this area, and 'valued very highly the reports provided by the radio monitoring service of the defence staff'. This is an early indication of the so-called 'Bomber Gap' fear which hit the United States a year later, based on suspicions that the Soviet Union was developing a long-range bomber force capable of reaching the American continent. One such strategic bomber aircraft, the M-4 Bison, had been displayed during the May Day parade in Moscow. With such a force the United States would for the first time become exposed to a direct threat of attack with atom bombs.[5]

Evang's comment to the Co-ordination Committee about the value of the Norwegian Comint efforts may well have been intended to stimulate the committee's appetite in the advent of discussions about an expansion of the activity. A parallel proposal for expansion of Elint activity came before the Co-ordination Committee on 23 August, when State Secretary Sivert A. Nielsen from the Defence Ministry reported a conversation with H.F. Matthews from the US Embassy. Matthews had outlined a proposal for a considerable build-up of what was termed 'the electronic intelligence activity in Finnmark'. Beside the radio monitoring service and the work of the radar stations in the area, it was now also a question of 'installations which can intercept electronic emissions of a non-communications character', for example from launching sites for guided missiles. A personnel requirement of nearly 300 was indicated. Andreas Andersen, chairman of the committee and representing the Prime Minister, reacted very negatively to this proposal, which may explain why Evang offered very little information when the issue next came before the committee, on 18 September and again on 8 October. Still Evang did not hide his concern about the global dominance of the United States in the field of intelligence, and he stressed the need to ensure an adequate quid pro quo from the Americans with both intelligence material and equipment.[6]

Co-operation in the Comint field had in the meantime grown apace, although the increase of personnel lagged behind the tentative targets set in 1952. A survey from the autumn of 1954 showed that there were then 80 radio operators employed on the monitoring stations. The Americans at that stage wished to see this increased to 180 in the next three years, with 70 at Vadsø, 35 at Fauske, 15 at Trondheim, eight at Stavanger, plus 30 at the Oslo Comint centre. A personnel of ten was foreseen for the analysis section, and seven radio operators were needed for rotation at the mobile stations. It was becoming increasingly clear that the supply of trained radio operators was the bottleneck, and recruitment to the remote Finnmark stations seemed to depend on satisfactory salary compensation for the hardship involved. More up-to-date equipment would have to be provided from the United States, but there was also an urgent need for new building construction, for the stations themselves as well as housing for the personnel. A particular requirement which it was hoped the Americans could fill was Russian language training for about ten operators to monitor Russian voice communications.[7]

THE NORUSA AGREEMENT OF 10 DECEMBER 1954

Formal negotiations for an official NORUSA agreement began in Oslo on 8 December 1954, and the composition of the US delegation attested to the importance which the Americans placed on the co-operation. It was led by Frank B. Rowlett, who was then attached to the CIA, but was one of the true veterans of US signals intelligence, having served since 1930. He was later in the 1950s to return to NSA as special adviser to the director. Accompanying him was Louis Tordella, who was shortly to become deputy director of NSA – and regarded by many as its real boss. Both Rowlett and Tordella were later to be awarded the exceedingly exclusive and prestigious 'National Security Medal'. The US delegation was completed with three men from the CIA's Oslo station and two Comint experts.

In preparation for the meeting the two parties had put on paper their requirements. From the American side the need for intelligence was divided into a number of different categories. The daily reporting should contain two elements: a 'tecsum' to sum up the activity on Soviet signals networks as regards technical details such as call signs, frequencies used, timings, etc., and eventually also an 'intsum' which would sum up the activity in meaningful plain language, such as number and types of ships from the Soviet Northern Fleet cruising in the area. In addition the NIS should provide 'spotsum' – instant reports on unusual or specially important detections which should not await the daily routine reporting. This might be such things as new submarines appearing in the area, increased air traffic, or a marked increase in signals traffic. These reports should also be provided in plain, non-technical language, and should contain any supplementary comments or interpretations which the NIS experts could supply. All of this should hereafter be transmitted electronically by teleprinter. Topping the list of target priorities was the Soviet Northern Fleet and their fleet air arm; next came Soviet air defences, tactical air, ground forces, the Soviet merchant navy, the police and the strategic air force.

On the Norwegian side there was a growing awareness of the value of such Comint material for the Americans. A summing-up, which was probably written by Jon K. Brynildsen, the radio section chief, put it this way:

> Our 'Early Warning' reporting contains a rich concentrate of the radio traffic in the following categories: the Arctic fleet, the Arctic fleet's air force, their air control and warning system, the coastal, maritime, and border police, tactical air, etc. It embraces the number of stations of different types monitored within each network, radio direction findings, extracts of important messages, etc.
>
> Through this EW the Americans can with 2–4 days' delay have a fairly complete picture of what has been going on in the area from the Arctic Ocean to Petrosavodsk and eastwards to the Dickson area. When they then one month later get sent the total amount of traffic monitored and recorded by us, they have full coverage to the extent made possible by the current personnel strength at Vadsø and Fauske.[8]

In the light of this, and seeing the Americans' requirements of 'intsum' and 'spotsum' with NIS comments and interpretations, the writer's view was that the NIS could reasonably expect to be provided with various codes and ciphers and other kinds of information to enable them to expand the coverage and give fuller analyses and commentaries. The NIS was also interested in expanding coverage of Soviet military voice-communication channels. This would be specially valuable for the monitoring of Soviet aircraft operations, for example in order to map out the tactics used when intercepting Western planes that approached Soviet territory. Through its monitoring of Soviet air control's telegraph traffic the NIS was already able to follow the pre-notification of flights sent by the Russians to their own radar stations in order to avoid confusion with any Western intruder. 'They provided point-to-point positions for next day's flights, which enabled us to notify our side about impending operations.'

During these December 1954 meetings it was also agreed that the geographic area of coverage for the Norwegian stations would be extended. Up until then coverage had been largely limited to the Barents and White Seas and the Kola Peninsula. The expansion of the area was aimed at covering the Soviet air forces and armies, especially in the Moscow area

– air defence being a particular concern – and also the White Russia military district.[9]

The final agreement – the first official, formal NORUSA agreement – bore the title 'Communications Intelligence Agreement', and was dated 10 December 1954. It was to mark the start of a long-lasting close bilateral co-operation. One of the clauses stated that neither of the two parties would disclose information from this co-operation to third countries without the consent of its partner. Exception was made for the UK, which might receive material through the United States, with British material being similarly supplied to Norway through US channels. In addition to material being transmitted electronically on a day-to-day basis, NIS officers and the CIA and NSA representatives stationed in Oslo maintained regular personal contact. Then there were annual review meetings, alternating between Washington and Oslo, in which leading men from the different services took part. For the NIS the agreement became the vehicle for a strong expansion of its Comint work, regarding collection as well as analysis and assessment of the intelligence material. The tempo of the expansion was however limited by the availability of qualified operators. Thus it seems that delivery of daily 'intsum' reports only got under way in the summer of 1957, and then only after thorough scrutiny 'to check that there is nothing there that NSA ought not to be given (e.g. matter obtained through external sources)'.[10]

MAKING SENSE OF THE MATERIAL: THE CIPHER SECTION

'Ciphering', 'coding', 'encrypting', and, inversely, 'forcing', 'deciphering', 'decoding', 'code-breaking', 'decrypting' – the terminology varies. NIS tended to use 'chiffrering' and 'dechiffrering' (ciphering and deciphering), but for our purposes we shall use the terms 'encrypting' and 'decrypting'. Whatever term one uses, however, it denotes a very ancient art which has always fascinated mathematicians and diplomats, not to mention authors and readers of spy stories. Few can have avoided a sense of exhilaration and admiration when reading about the code-breakers at Bletchley Park during the Second World War, and their race against time to decrypt the signals going to the German submarines.

A more down-to-earth approach is needed as regards the cipher section of the NIS after the war. To begin with, there have always been codes which are impossible to break without possession of the key. A good example is the KGB signal traffic to and from its agents in the United States, which the American services – mainly AFSA and FBI – with all their resources spent years to decrypt with only partial success. The snag with such unbreakable codes is that they are clumsy and time-consuming to use. Machine encrypting and decrypting were important steps toward the secure and fast communication of secret signals. With possession of the machinery, and the code determining the setting of the movable parts, the code-breakers could set to work. But a fair amount of telegram traffic would still be needed before patterns could be discerned.

Machine cryptography saw rapid advances after the war, and before long only the simplest of systems could be decrypted without a massive effort from highly specialised personnel and access to state-of-the art punch-card machines and eventually computers. Most of the highest grade Comint traffic could therefore not be read by the NIS, and could only be decrypted with the help of the huge resources of the NSA in its new headquarters outside Washington DC.

Next in importance to reading the actual contents of Comint traffic was the capability to monitor and analyse the radio traffic in order to identify and locate sender and receiver. That made it possible to map out Soviet military air and naval activity, and to track the build-up of stations and bases in their Northern Military District. The evidence suggests that the operators in the Norwegian listening posts, together with the analysts there and at the central station, early on developed a particular expertise in deciphering or identifying the call signs of Soviet aircraft, warships and army units, as well as their home stations. Such 'traffic analysis' made it possible to determine the pattern of operations for the different categories of Soviet military activity in the north. But the deciphering and analysis that this involved was part of the Comint effort, albeit with the assistance of the cipher section.

We have earlier touched on the cipher section as a small unit with two main tasks: developing and securing national cipher systems, and decrypting of other countries' codes and ciphers. In the first, more technical–scientific field, the section with its chief, Nils Stordahl, succeeded in developing considerable expertise in analysing cipher machines and systems, and in the construction of cipher machines. With such specialists as the mathematician Ernst S. Selmer and the engineers Bjørn Rørholt and Odd Nilsen, the cipher section of NIS became an important constructor and supplier of machines and equipment to several NATO member countries. However, since such activities were not a part of intelligence work as such they will not be further considered in this book.

As regards decrypting of other countries' code traffic the cipher section started out with quite an ambitious programme, particularly for breaking diplomatic telegram traffic. But the results turned out to be quite modest. A survey in the 1955 annual report leaves an impression that only a few relatively unsophisticated ciphers, used for low-grade traffic in, for example, French and Italian diplomatic correspondence, had been decrypted. Attempts at deciphering telegrams to and from other countries such as Egypt, Albania, Belgium, Switzerland, Czechoslovakia, Western Germany, China, Turkey and Israel had been largely fruitless. In some cases the systems were too complex to solve, given the limited resources in personnel and machines available to the cipher section. In other cases the volume of traffic was too small. The material was collected in part through the NIS's own eavesdropping service. Some of it was provided as copies of telegrams transmitted through the Norwegian Telephone and Telegraph Office, or obtained through an exchange agreement with the Swedish FRA.[11]

An important target area for the decryption effort was Soviet military traffic. A five-year plan for expansion drafted by the cipher section in February 1956 gave top priority to the establishment of a special section for that purpose. Included in the plan was an expansion of the personnel from 12 permanent and 18 short-term posts to a total of 45 persons. But there is no indication that this was achieved. The conclusion therefore has to be that the cipher section as regards code-breaking did not get very far. A memorandum written in connection with an inspection which the Control Committee for the intelligence service carried out in October 1960, put it this way:

> In connection with the material collected it was stated that between one and ten per cent is immediately intelligible. The rest consists of telegrams and messages which it has so far been impossible to decipher. The material is however systematically filed in the hope that some time in the future it will be possible to break the codes for such telegrams.[12]

That stage was never reached by the NIS, since it never obtained the necessary resources. In this particular field it has to be said that the NIS was nothing more than a supplier of raw material for co-operating services.

The final blow for Norwegian cryptography came in 1965, when the cipher section was transferred to the newly established separate Security Staff. There its tasks were largely limited to developing and securing indigenous cipher systems. One of the veterans of the NIS, Knut Willy Kval, who rose to become its deputy director before retiring in 1996, has offered this merciless comment:

> Once Evang had been winged, cipher was taken away from the Intelligence Staff. We then became perhaps the only service in the world which did not do cryptography, and as a result the NSA had two organisations in Norway to play on instead of just one. When such matters came up, where it was not in the interest of NSA that we should possess cryptographic insight, they did not have to share such matters with us.[13]

THE GROWTH OF COMINT 1955–57

The NORUSA agreement was the foundation for a strong expansion of the NIS's Comint activity. A five-years expansion plan from 1955, drafted in consultation with the Americans, looked to an annual increase of 27 radio operators. This would bring the total personnel of the radio section to 290 by 1960, which was roughly double the number in 1952. There would of course be a corresponding increase in the amount of new equipment provided, particularly with regard to radio receivers. As a sign of the times the NSA now got its own representative in Oslo, working with the CIA's Chief of Station. Technical consultation meetings would now be held about once a week with one or more of the Norwegian Comint specialists Brynildsen, Falchenberg and Hellerslien. Some of the Norwegian radio operators were sent to the United States for language training.[14]

In 1955 the NIS also noted a growing interest in Norway's Comint activity from the British. As a later chapter will show, the Royal Air Force (RAF) early on had become a natural partner in the work of the Royal Norwegian Air Force concerned with tactical electronic intelligence. That co-operation was the main reason for the visit to Oslo of Mr Poulden from GCHQ in February 1955. But as in Britain GCHQ – Government Communications Headquarters, since 1952 located near Cheltenham – handled both Comint and Elint, it was natural that Mr Poulden should also contact the NIS. On 24 February 1955 he met with Lieutenant-Commander Falchenberg from the NIS and Major Knut Haugland from the Royal Norwegian Air Force. Mr Poulden introduced himself as a senior figure on the British side as regards both Comint and what he called Non-Comint, and appeared to be well informed about the NORUSA agreement. Britain of course had its own intelligence agreement with the United States from 1947: the UKUSA agreement.

Mr Poulden expressed strong interest in the monitoring activities of the NIS, and stressed Norway's favourable position as an important contributor on account of its geographical situation. He also stressed the general trend towards seeing Comint and Non-Comint as two sides of the same coin – as was the case in Britain, but unfortunately not in the US, 'due to turf battles between the armed services'. He praised the Norwegian division of labour whereby the air force dealt with the tactical intelligence picture, while the NIS processed the same intelligence and the Comint material for strategic purposes. 'It all gave me the impression that it had been pre-arranged with the CIA to persuade the air force to see things the way the NIS wanted.'[15]

We mentioned earlier that during the talks leading up to the NORUSA agreement of 1954, the NIS had been encouraged to expand the geographic scope of its Comint activity in a southerly direction, towards the Moscow area and White Russia. A memorandum from April 1957 shows that up to the end of 1955 the coverage was still mainly limited to the areas north of 60 degrees north. But in the spring of 1956 the Swedish FRA had handed over a lot of material from Leningrad Military District. By that time the NIS stations had also begun to extend their coverage southwards. The United States still had Soviet air force and navy at the top of their target priority list, but the expansion plan now took special note of Norway's interest in monitoring the military developments on the ground in the Kola Peninsula.

In line with general NIS policy the radio section was still determined not to become a mere supplier of raw data to co-operating services. A memorandum from Hellerslien, and a directive from section chief Brynildsen, both from 1957, described in some detail how the collected material was processed and analysed. The raw material – defined as 'telegrams intercepted from transmissions by hand or speed morse, by teleprinter or other pulse systems, tape recordings of voice transmissions, plus intercept journals and radio direction findings' – was analysed in three stages. First came what was termed 'system analytic processing', which consisted of analysis of signals procedures, reconstruction of call signs, frequency tables, traffic codes, etc. The next stage was called 'draft processing', defined as 'plotting in sketch form of raw traffic, and setting up monthly surveys', and 'establishing 'a day-to-day identification of the stations by frequency, station number, etc.' Last came the intelligence-processing stage, which meant 'setting out, as required, in readable and intelligible form, the intelligence which can be inferred' on the basis of all the available material. In terms of geography the highest priority was accorded areas north of 60 degrees as far as 100 degrees east, including the whole of the Soviet Arctic coast. Material from the second priority areas – the Baltic Sea, Leningrad, the Baltic republics, White Russia and Moscow military district, and the third priority, which covered the rest of the Soviet Union and the satellite countries, was less thoroughly analysed.[16]

At Evang's request Brynildsen and Falchenberg in the spring of 1957 put on paper a preliminary assessment of the status of NORUSA co-operation. This showed that the material provided by Norway was both varied and extensive. For the purpose of more long-term analysis, the NIS on a daily basis, by courier to the American embassy, delivered copies of monitoring logs, intercepted telegrams and lists of direction-findings. The sheer amount of this material – averaging 1,000 telegrams, 350 log sheets, 500 direction-finding data, and four or five reels of tape recordings – meant that only the NSA with its thousands of analysts and massive array of processing equipment had the capacity to subject all this to thorough analysis. Other written material included periodic reports and various special reports on Soviet signals traffic and the conclusions drawn in terms of the number of commissioned naval vessels, their basing and exercises; surveys of air units with numbers and types of aircraft stationed at each air base; organisation and capacity of the Soviet air control and warning network, particularly in regard to location and range of the radar stations.

In a different category came intelligence of EW or early warning character, which on account of its urgency had to be transmitted electronically and in crypted form. Such material went either by line teleprinter to an American communications centre at Gardermoen, north of Oslo, or by wireless teleprinter via the large Chicksands communications centre in Britain to the huge newly built NSA headquarters at Fort Meade, between Washington and Baltimore. As explained above, this special material was divided into 'tecsum' – a highly concentrated compilation

of the signals traffic comprising 'all information necessary for a reconstruction of the activity within the different networks in all the armed
services during the last 24 hours'; 'spotsum', on a more irregular basis;
and from the summer of 1957 daily 'intsum'. The two latter categories
were in plain language but transmitted in cipher.

So what did the Americans provide in return? Their contribution was
of two kinds. First they provided first-class technical radio equipment,
specially radio receivers and direction-finding apparatus. In addition the
NIS received the results of the more long-term and partly machine-
processed analysis of collected intelligence, both that delivered by the
NIS and that intercepted by the NSA's own monitoring effort, if relevant
to Norway. Brynildsen and Falchenberg summed up the 'trade balance'
in this way:

> It is difficult to weigh the value of the contributions from each side,
> as they are different in kind. If judged qualitatively in terms of the
> effort involved we feel that what we deliver is more than what we
> receive. On the other hand it would be difficult on a day-to-day basis
> to do without the sheer size of the effort taken care of by the
> American punch-card processing of the material. Also the material
> assistance represents a very considerable saving for us in economic
> terms.[17]

NIS AND THE DEFENCE FIVE-YEAR PROGRAMME, 1957–63

The Ministry of Defence in January 1957 presented to the Storting a five-
year programme for the continued defence build-up. This was based on
a secret report from 1955 produced by a committee known as the Boyesen
Committee. The report had been examined by the Chiefs of Staffs'
Committee in the spring of 1956. The debate about that report, and the
discussion of the five-year programme, has been focused on the issue of
the role of nuclear weapons in the defence of Norway. But the programme
also signalled a new deal for the intelligence service, although the
unclassified version of the programme, as presented to the Storting, was
suitably vague on the matter. It said that the ministry fully agreed with
what the Chiefs of Staffs had emphasised in their assessment of the
programme:

> The intelligence and warning service is important for the evaluation
> of the situation at any given time. The earliest possible warning is a

precondition for an effective defence. In the years to come there must be an increased emphasis on making the intelligence service more efficient, on expanding and ensuring the effectiveness of our warning and communications system, and on the surveillance of possible routes for surprise attacks.[18]

In October 1956 the Intelligence Staff prepared a draft for a detailed statement which they wanted the Defence Chief to submit to Defence Minister Nils Handal. Here the NIS put forward its own reasons for a greater emphasis on what they called 'the electronic intelligence service'. In the light of what actually happened later, the concrete proposals – 58 new positions for operators in the period up to 1962–63 – seem modest. But at the base of the proposals lay a detailed assessment of the value to Norway and to the allies of the Comint–Elint effort which deserves to be quoted in full, both as a status report and as a relatively balanced evaluation of Norway's role:

Electronic intelligence was started by the great powers some time before the Second World War, and saw a strong increase during the final years of the war. After the war, and in our case since 1948, it has in steadily growing measure constituted the basis for, and provided a major share of, our military information about the Soviet bloc. It provides the raw material which is then subjected to technical analysis. The field covers
(a) the military–strategic picture,
(b) the immediate tactical picture, and
(c) warning.

In the east/west conflict it has increasingly become clear that Norway, and especially North Norway, has an exceptionally favourable geographic position for the coverage of very considerable parts of the northern and central regions of the Soviet Union. Experience has shown that Norwegian personnel have the special abilities required to reach a high standard of achievement in this field, and that Norwegian mathematicians are well placed to analyse the results.

Since NATO was established, defence planning has proceeded on the basis of an estimate of Soviet capabilities known as the 161 series of documents, entitled 'Soviet Strength and Capabilities'. That estimate is updated once a year. Through the years that the Defence

Staff has been involved in this process, it has become evident that NATO's northern flank will not get sufficient attention unless Norway herself can provide adequate information about potential threats from those parts of the Soviet and Eastern bloc. It is the electronic intelligence effort which has constituted the main basis for Norwegian threat assessments, and since the information has been reliable we have in the main got acceptance for Norway's evaluations.

During the last couple of years electronic intelligence has expanded to embrace, in addition to the field of communications, also all electronic emissions of a technical nature from sources such as radar, bases for rockets and guided missiles, artillery positions, naval on-board systems, electronic installations at air bases, etc. Through extended communications analyses it is also possible to assess Soviet capabilities for jamming or in other ways disturbing or interfering with our own communications and electronic installations. The electronic intelligence service thus also provides the necessary foundation for building up the Norwegian ECM (Electronic Countermeasures) apparatus, which is needed for the operations of our navy and air force.

Norway's position as a warning area for the Western great powers – North Norway especially for the US and Canada, South Norway for the United Kingdom – ensures that the Western interest in expanding the electronic intelligence effort in Norway is very strong. The effort is still and will probably remain during the next five years officially kept away from NATO, and the co-operation will rest on bilateral agreements.

The Americans are particularly interested in seeing a strong expansion of this service, and the Defence Staff thinks that it would not be difficult to get them to establish American stations manned with American personnel. From a national standpoint this cannot be recommended. We have however obtained commitments for technical support on conditions that are not seen as nationally damaging. The existing budgetary proposals do not therefore include expenditure on such kinds of equipment.

Our investment in the field of electronic intelligence is minor in relation to the results we know can be obtained. There is today also the very real situation that Norway is needed as a warning platform for the United States not only in the opening stages of an eventual war, but also for the duration of belligerent activities. This engenders a strongly increased American interest in Norwegian territory remaining unoccupied, on condition that Norwegian warning efforts are maintained at an acceptable level.[19]

1958 – AMERICA URGES FURTHER EXPANSION

In a memorandum dated 13 January 1958 the CIA Chief of Station in Oslo expressed a very serious concern about the increased pace of Soviet build-up of the Northern Fleet and of the air forces in northwestern Russia. It alleged a tripling of the Northern Fleet during the last few years, and characterised the roughly 100 submarines there, many of them new and very long-range, as the greatest potential single threat to Atlantic shipping in wartime. The Soviet air forces had at the same time developed a network of bases in northern Russia, and their heavy and medium-heavy jet bombers were conducting flight exercises as far as the North Pole. All this made it desirable to expand the Norwegian Comint effort considerably beyond that planned in the five-year programme from 1955. Instead of the programmed target of 50 'tables' or positions served by about 225 operators, a complement of 80 tables and 360 operators should now be set as the target. This would mean an increase to about 450 men for Section V. The particular requirement was for a greater concentration on Soviet naval and air activity in the north, with round-the-clock manning at all tables to ensure early warning of enemy action.[20]

At the root of those urgent requests lay the American fear of a 'bomber gap' – the concern that the Soviet Union was about to get an upper hand through the development of long-range strategic bombers which could reach targets in the United States. In a National Intelligence Estimate from March 1956, regarding the probable strategic attack capabilities of the Soviet Union through mid-1959, the CIA had concluded that the Soviets' principal weapon against the United States would be bombers carrying atomic weapons. As for possible base areas for the opening phase of a bomber offensive, the CIA put the Kola Peninsula at the top, since the bombers could proceed from there directly towards the United States without alerting the warning and control networks of Western Europe. The CIA estimated that by mid-1956 the Russians had at least six airfields suitable for mid-range bombers with a full load, and that at least one of those could also handle the heaviest bombers. A crash programme to expand the bases on Kola and other northern areas could be expected, which would allow the Soviet Union to base the whole of its strategic bomber force there.[21]

An initial comment on the US expansion requests, from Jon K. Brynildsen as head of the Comint section, showed clear reservations against such a sharp increase, for several reasons. His primary concern was the shortage of qualified radio operators or telegraphists. But it was also a question of money, for salaries for such a number of personnel as well as for investment in buildings both to expand the stations and house the personnel. Radio receivers and other equipment he assumed the Americans would provide. Presumably, however, Evang had already received assurances that the matter was of such importance to the Americans that money would not be a problem.[22]

At a three-day Comint conference in Oslo in March 1958 the participants worked out a preliminary agreement on expansion of the Norwegian effort. In addition to other priority items there was full agreement that the Northern Fleet's submarine activity was of great interest, and that the Soviet fishing fleet also was an important target. This interest in the fishing fleet was evidently connected with frequent sightings of Soviet intelligence ships camouflaged as fishing vessels. Monitoring the activity of the Soviet air forces nevertheless remained Comint priority number one.

In tandem with the talks on expanding the Comint effort, Evang and Martens Meyer discussed with the Americans the question of co-ordination of Comint and Elint activities. As will be seen in a later chapter it was the Norwegian air force which ran most of the Elint effort in Norway, in close co-operation with the US air force and – to a lesser extent – the RAF. It was becoming increasingly clear that the two fields were two sides of the same coin, jointly termed Sigint – signals intelligence. The UK had, as we have seen, put this principle into practice by joining the activities together under the aegis of GCHQ – Government Communications Headquarters. But on the American side, with their strong tradition of services' separation, rivalry and even duplication of effort, control of the two fields of activity remained a bone of contention. The US navy and the US air force in particular hung on to their own intelligence services. A joint organisation – the Defense Intelligence Agency, DIA – only came about in the 1960s. As the United States in addition built up a steadily bigger and stronger Comint organisation in the NSA, it was inevitable that the CIA should experience great difficulties in establishing itself as the superior co-ordinating agency for all American intelligence activities towards, and in, foreign countries. On the Norwegian side the Intelligence Staff was the channel for co-operation with both NSA and CIA. It was therefore natural that it should also wish to control or at least co-ordinate both Comint and Elint work in relation to the Americans, with the link between the NIS and the CIA Oslo station as the main conduit.

It is against this background that we must see Evang's desires as to the pattern of co-operation, considered at a meeting on 12 March 1958 in preparation for a visit to Washington to discuss the matter. Evang's point of departure was that the stations collecting intelligence material, and the personnel there, often handled both Comint and Elint data, and the final product was based on information from both those two as well as other sources. Therefore the NIS should also co-ordinate both collection and analysis of Elint material. In regard to transmission of material and analyses to the Americans Evang wanted all of it to go to CIA Oslo, which would in turn be responsible for passing on to the US navy and the US air force what they should have.[23]

The question of a supplementary agreement about extending Comint activity in Norway came before the Cabinet Defence and Security Committee on 20 May 1958, under the heading of 'The question of extending the electronic intelligence effort in Norway'. Defence Minister Handal introduced the matter with the following statement:

> The Defence Minister stated that the electronic installations already active in North Norway have produced much information that is of interest. The American government is strongly interested in a further expansion of the system, due to the significance of the military activity in the Kola–Murmansk region. The question now is whether Norway is willing to carry out an expansion financed by the Americans. It concerns an investment of 10 million kroner in the course of 2–3 years and running costs of 9 million kroner annually. We are talking about one station in Eastern Finnmark, one at Fauske, and one in the Oslo area. The stations will be manned by Norwegian personnel. The Americans will cover also the running costs.[24]

Handal continued that the Defence Staff strongly favoured such an extension, among other things because it would be of value in verifying a nuclear test ban.[25] He emphasised the need for strict secrecy, and averred that the matter would have to be kept out of the public account procedures. The Auditor General's office had agreed to this, on condition that the plans should be approved by the chairman of the Storting's military affairs committee. Prime Minister Gerhardsen remarked that 'one should in principle take a positive attitude whenever Norway on account of its geographical situation could be of particular service to the common defence through such clearly defensive measures.' The committee then agreed that the Defence Ministry should pursue the matter.

On 3 July 1958 the Defence Minister put to the Committee a draft agreement, and gave some details about the size of the effort, which he said would involve a personnel increase from the current 158 to a total of 478 persons. He stressed that the activity would not be a one-way arrangement: 'The condition is that the collected intelligence will as quickly as possible be put at the disposal of the Americans. But the intelligence will also be for use by Norwegian military authorities, and the Americans have declared their willingness to share with the Norwegian military authorities the results of their analyses of the collected material.' Eight days later State Secretary Erik Himle informed Evang that the ministry had settled the matter with the then chairman of the Storting's Military Affairs Committee, Henrik Svensen.[26]

The final agreement, in the form of a supplement to the NORUSA agreement of 10 December 1954, was dated 26 August 1958 and signed by Vilhelm Evang on the Norwegian side and CIA Station Chief Louis Beck on behalf of the Americans. The agreement was on all major points in accordance with the results of the March discussions, with the added specifications outlined by the Defence Minister to the Cabinet Committee. Thus it was stated that 'The activity in the expanded electronic intelligence effort will in its entirety be carried out by Norwegian personnel and under complete Norwegian leadership and administration.' Priority of coverage was specified as follows: 'There is agreement that coverage of the submarine activity of the Soviet Northern Fleet is of major interest to the defence of the West and should be given high priority. There is also agreement that coverage of the Soviet fishing fleet is a high priority target.' The fact that the Soviet strategic air force no longer topped the priority list suggests that the fear of a 'bomber gap' had diminished. This is also borne out by estimates from the CIA which have subsequently become available.[27]

One concrete result of the expansion of the Comint activity was the establishment of FSTM – Forsvarets stasjon Moen (Defence Station

Moen) – at Høybuktmoen by Kirkenes. Planning for this station got under way immediately, and the initial construction in 1959 embraced housing with 22 apartments for the personnel, at Hesseng between Høybuktmoen and Kirkenes, and a station building at Høybuktmoen itself. The station, however, only began operations in the summer of 1960. Its main mission was to monitor the telegraphic communications of the Soviet army and border guard units on Kola. Moen belonged to Section V of the Intelligence Staff, but came under the administration of FFSK – Forsvarets Forsøksstasjon Kirkenes (Defence Experimental Station Kirkenes). This was an establishment created in 1960 which also ran the METRO station at Korpfjell near the Soviet–Norwegian border. METRO was an Elint station established by the Intelligence Staff in 1957 and subsequently expanded. In 1958 and 1959 there was also a mobile station at Høybuktmoen for the detection of Soviet nuclear tests – station CROCK POT – whose establishment had been approved by the Cabinet Defence and Security Committee in the spring of 1958. FFSK served as an administrative superstructure for those stations. The air force Elint station at NABBEN near Høybuktmoen was, however, not included in that arrangement.[28]

FURTHER DEVELOPMENTS THROUGH THE 1960s

The supplementary agreement from August 1958 became the point of departure for a very strong expansion of NIS activity in the field of Comint. For the period until the late 1960s Comint was to constitute the dominant feature of the work of Norwegian Intelligence Service. The expansion programme soon acquired the designation 'the HP project', where HP stood for High Priority. Finance was no longer a limit for the development. Somehow the NIS managed to arrange for a sufficient recruitment of radio operators and technicians to fill the projected need for about 60 new officers each half year up to mid-1962.

We do not know if this development was in complete accordance with Evang's desires for the development of the service. A tinge of some regret may be deduced from a statement from him in the spring of 1958:

> Colonel Evang stated that it must be borne in mind by the Americans that a tremendous buildup such as was planned for the Comint program would mean that the amount of his time spent on this

programme would be raised from one fourth to one half and that consequently it could be expected that some other portion of the over-all intelligence program would suffer because of this change of emphasis.[29]

The Control Committee also had some reservation against a too accelerated expansion. When the Americans in the spring of 1961 again urged an expansion to 80 'tables', the committee pleaded that 'we must first concentrate on reaching the current target and see how far we get. We can then later come back to the question of still further expansion.' But American urgings for a more extensive effort continued. At a US–Norwegian Sigint review conference in Oslo, 5–7 February 1962, the Americans proposed a target of a minimum of 75 but preferably 120 'tables'.

At that meeting Louis Tordella, Deputy Director of the NSA, outlined a partly new list of priorities for the Sigint activity. At the top of the list now figured Soviet development of SSBN – nuclear submarines equipped with missiles. In part through intelligence collected by the NIS, the Americans had now identified the Barents Sea as one of two testing areas, the other being near Sochi in the Black Sea. It was deemed important to penetrate the signals activity while it was still in the experimental stages when the Soviet operators had not yet finetuned their routines against interception. The search for unidentified Comint or Non-Comint signals therefore should be given top priority. Next in the order of priority came the task of determining the location of and gaining knowledge about the operational readiness of land-based Soviet intercontinental and medium-range missile bases, particularly about possible development of ABM defence systems against missiles. Tracking the Soviet nuclear tests in the north was part of that effort. As a third priority Tordella mentioned information about the movements of both nuclear- and diesel-powered submarines patrolling in northern waters. Only in fourth place – down-graded from occupying top priority in 1957 – came the Soviet strategic air force.

Even further down the long list came the Soviet naval air force; new communication systems codenamed MERCURY GRASS which made possible simultaneous transmissions on multiple channels from the same transmitter; information about Soviet capability for registering, locating, deterring or in general defending against incoming bombers; Soviet activity in northwestern Russia both generally and in regard to ground forces; intelligence about the surface ships of the Northern Fleet; information about the Soviet merchant and trawler fleets; and finally civilian air traffic. Throughout this lengthy menu the Americans put great store on the collection of Comint material, and in some areas also Elint material. The list of priorities presented had been confirmed by the United States Intelligence Board (USIB), which was then the central co-ordinating authority for the CIA, the NSA, the armed services, the FBI, the Atomic Energy Commission and the State Department.[30]

It was Vilhelm Evang who mostly spoke from the Norwegian side during these discussions. Concerning the list of priorities he stressed that there were particular Norwegian requirements for intelligence which had to be met. The Norwegians would thus emphasise in particular the items regarding Soviet ground forces in the Northern and Leningrad Military Districts, and also the Soviet merchant and fishing fleets – the latter because its ships could easily be converted for military purposes:

> These national requirements and desires were dictated by a fear, not only in Norway but also in SHAPE and NATO's Northern Command, of the military as well as naval threat against Northern Norway. This was also the view of C-in-C Northern Norway. We feel a strong requirement to keep an eye on what happens on the Russian side up there, from the point of view of warning.[31]

A recurring theme in Evang's comments during these meetings was a desire for additional information from the American side about Soviet development of new weapon systems, in order that the Norwegian stations could possess an up-to-date frame of reference for the type of signals activity they should search for. In particular he mentioned that they had only now been informed that a certain signal traffic, which the Norwegian stations had not been able to analyse, in fact stemmed from missile-firing tests by Soviet submarines in the Barents Sea. There was here a concern that the Norwegian Sigint service might be reduced to a supplier of raw data. In part this raised the question of obtaining the right equipment for analysing and processing the collected data, but there was also the matter of insufficient feedback from the Americans. Tordella quickly responded by handing over a list of dates for 20 missile-firing tests, and explained the delay by the long time taken before the NSA had been able to discern a pattern which pointed towards that kind of missile-testing.

There is no need here to enter into details about the planning and

build-up of the different stations under the High Priority (HP) programme. Instead it is worth taking a look at an important special feature
of the evolution of electronic intelligence activities in North Norway:
namely the increasing integration of the different specialities – first
Comint and Elint, further Radint or radar intelligence, Seismint or seismic
intelligence, and eventually Acoustint, acoustic intelligence, which
together with Seismint had Soviet nuclear tests as a primary target. One
consequence of this integration was that several of the stations acquired
equipment and specialist personnel which turned them into combined
installations. A map – undated, but probably from 1963 – shows that
BARHAUG (Viksjøfjell), METRO (Korpfjell) and a station on Hill 96
in the Pasvik valley were all designated as combined Comint and Elint
stations, whereas NABBEN by Kirkenes was a 'pure' Elint station. On
the Varanger Peninsula we find FSTV Vadsø dealing only with Comint,
whereas the air force station HEKLA at Vardø, with its FPS-8 radar,
combined Elint with Radint.[32]

Comint, in the shape of the HP programme, still remained the dominant field of activity. The agenda for a meeting of the Control Committee
on 2 January 1964 contained the information that the existing upper limit
for personnel employed in HP, 343 persons, was about to be reached. The
question for the meeting was whether to raise the ceiling to 506 persons,
which would be needed to meet the target of 80 'tables' desired by the
Americans. No decision was taken, but on 6 January Evang raised the
matter with Defence Minister Gudmund Harlem. Evang had before that
discussed it with his superiors in the Defence Staff, Vice-Admiral Folke
Hauger Johannessen, the Defence Chief, and his Chief of Staff, Major-
General Harald Løken, and found there 'a markedly negative attitude.
Johannessen had said that one must of course try to obtain all sorts of
information, but one must not do things that might irritate the Russians.'
Evang's own view, as stated to Harlem, was this:

a. An increase in numbers was necessary.
b. It was conceivable that such an increase in numbers might irritate
   the Russians.
c. If there was no increase, the consequence would be that the
   Western powers would seek to obtain the information in other
   ways, which in Evang's opinion would certainly become a greater
   danger to Soviet–Norwegian relations that an increase in personnel for Section V.[33]

Harlem's intention had been to bring this matter before the Defence Council, which had a meeting scheduled two days later, but now decided that it was too sensitive an issue for such a large body. Instead he took the issue to the Cabinet Defence and Security Committee, which approved the personnel increase four weeks later. The Control Committee concluded after this that the total manpower for the HP programme, including analysts, technicians, signals specialists, etc. would now reach the figure of 624. They also drew the conclusion from the Cabinet Committee's decision that 'there is no longer any definite ceiling for the number of personnel'.[34]

In fact the Cabinet Committee had evinced clear political reservations against the existing and projected concentration of intelligence activity in Eastern Finnmark, so close to the Soviet border. Evang thought that increased automation of some of the activities might produce a reduction. But Transport Minister Himle suggested exploring the possibility of transferring part of the activity further west, to western Finnmark or to the counties of Troms and Nordland. At the next review conference with the Americans, in Washington in March 1964, Evang made this his main topic. He himself thought that the Cabinet's worries were exaggerated, and may have intended the talks to provide him with arguments against such moves. But he loyally argued the views of his political masters, with the result that the US air force expressed a willingness to set a ceiling for the number of personnel employed at POLAR REIN, a nuclear test monitoring station established in 1962. It was also decided that a planned new AFTAC (Air Force Technical Applications Centre) station would now be located further west in Finnmark. That was the origin of the PINE FOREST Acoustint station at Karasjok, established to monitor Soviet nuclear tests.[35] For its part the NSA expressed a willingness to study which categories of signals could successfully be monitored at locations further west.

In accordance with Evang's determination that the NIS should not only collect but also process the intelligence material, the expansion of Comint carried with it an enlargement of the sections for analysis and processing at headquarters in the Oslo area. A proposed reorganisation plan from 1963 for those parts of the Intelligence Staff showed a personnel strength of 96, engaged in traffic analysis, solving tactical codes for identification and plotting of stations, transcription and translation of voice communications, and direction-finding of transmitters.

We have a survey of the out-stations in the Comint sector from the spring of 1965 which also states the missions of each station. By far the largest of them was still Vadsø, FFSV, with its headquarters at Tomaselv, the radio direction finding station on Vadsø island, and a VHF station at Melkevarden. Its monitoring and listening coverage stretched far into the Soviet Union, and included also the whole of the Arctic Ocean area including Svalbard and Frans Josef Land. Vadsø further co-operated with Fauske to cover air and ship traffic north and west of Finnmark. The second largest station was now Kirkenes/Moen, FFSK/M, with its sub-station BARHAUG (Viksjøfjell); the tasks here were similar to those of Vadsø, but with northwestern Russia as a particular target area. Fauske, as the third largest station, worked as mentioned in tandem with Vadsø. The old stations near Trondheim (Heimdal) and Stavanger (Randaberg) were primarily engaged in radio direction-finding. Finally there was the radio station at Nordstrand outside Oslo, which covered Soviet ship movements in addition to being responsible for the southern regions of the Soviet Union and the satellite countries.[36]

This survey was annexed to a proposal from the Comint section for yet another personnel increase, from the existing total of 451 to a projected 669 persons. However, the Control Committee now decided to set a ceiling of 527 employees for the HP project, and that limit was finally confirmed in 1967. That ceiling was then, as far as we can see, maintained for the rest of the period until 1970 which we are concerned with here. The total for the whole of the NIS was then just over 1,000 persons, which means that Comint, with over half that number, remained by far the largest section. In addition to the HP programme, and not managed by Section V, came the intelligence ships which from time to time operated in the Barents Sea. Those ships also had Comint tasks in addition to their Elint and Radint missions, and will be dealt with in Chapters 6 and 7.

SPECIAL COMINT OPERATIONS

The Comint section of NIS had two special tasks outside the very extensive monitoring and listening effort directed towards Soviet military signals traffic. One of them was to locate, identify and monitor communication to and from KGB and MVD stations in the Soviet coast guard and frontier guard services, and KGB traffic on the diplomatic networks. It seems that the Comint specialists of the NIS early on developed a certain expertise in locating and identifying such stations. An example of this is a special operation – operation EFRAIM – which in 1953 succeeded in identifying and listening in to a KGB station at Svalbard. Bjarne Thorsen was the intelligence officer in charge of that operation. Armed with fairly primitive direction finding equipment – one set being a reconditioned commercial radio receiver – and a list of frequencies and call signs, Thorsen and a telegraphist soon pinpointed a fjord on the western coast of Svalbard, and there found a Russian combined trawler and tugboat with tell-tale special aerials.

With particular regard to the KGB communication between Moscow and Oslo, the NIS monitored and intercepted an average of 2,000 and 2,500 telegrams annually during the 1960s.[37] We have been unable to determine whether or to what extent this yielded information of any intelligence value. But seeing the serious problems which the NSA and its predecessor agency experienced in trying to break KGB traffic from the war years – project VENONA – it is extremely doubtful whether the NIS had much success in their venture.

One of the early aims of the NIS radio section was to uncover illegal radio transmitters used by Soviet agents in Norway. We have in an earlier chapter touched on the unsuccessful attempts to locate and identify such a clandestine radio transmitter in the Bakfjord area in 1949. (The agent was finally uncovered by other means and arrested in 1961.) It appears that such operations were only sporadically attempted after that. In 1968, however, a working group was set up, apparently at the behest of the Security Police, to advise on whether to instigate such radio surveillance on a more regular basis. Their conclusion was affirmative:

> The unmasking of East bloc agents in several countries has shown that radio is to a considerable extent used as their means of communication with their task masters. Although only one agent has been caught with such equipment in this country (the Bakfjord case), there is every reason to think that there are other agents using the same means to communicate.
>
> The police have during the years received numerous reports of suspicious radio transmissions which have been investigated, but without results worth mentioning. The police in 1949–50 called on the assistance of the Defence Staff in connection with the reports about illegal radio transmissions from Bakfjord. But the presence of persons from the Defence Staff in this remote area must have alerted the agent, and the listening and direction finding efforts were

fruitless. About twenty years later the case was solved by other means, and it was found that the transmitter had in fact been working at more or less regular intervals throughout that time. With an organised listening and direction finding service there is reason to believe that the transmitter could have been uncovered much earlier.

Another and very strong argument in favour of organising such a service in peacetime is the difficulty of building up an organised service in times of crisis or war, without the benefit of experienced personnel and well-tried equipment. The group's conclusion is therefore that there is a need for an organised radio surveillance.[38]

Still the working group had to conclude that none of the interested institutions – the police, the Telecommunications Office, or the Defence Staff – possessed the personnel resources or the equipment necessary to establish such a surveillance service. Whether this was established at a later stage is a question which lies outside the time-frame of our study.

NOTES

1. Tordella in conversation with the author, 17 Oct. 1994.
2. Author's conversations with Dag Falchenberg, 13 March 1996, and Erling Hellerslien, 7 March 1996.
3. FO/E, file 'X-2 Elint–Comint talks': 'Preliminary NOR–US Agreement on Certain Communications Intelligence Matters, June 1952'. The available material is inconclusive as to whether this first NORUSA agreement was officially approved by the two governments, as intended. But there is every reason to believe that at least the Chief of Defence Staff and the Defence Minister were fully in the picture.
4. FO/E, H. Skau manuscript, and the mimeographed booklet 'Erindringer fra E-tjenesten i Sør-Varanger ...' (Reminiscences of intelligence service in the south Varanger area).
5. SMK, KU protocol, 8 June 1954. See also CIA, History Staff, *Intentions and Capabilities: Estimates on Soviet Strategic Forces, 1950–1983* (CIA, Washington, DC, 1966), pp. 5–54.
6. SMK, KU protocol 18 Sept. and 6 Oct. 1954. It is unclear whether the manpower figure was for the Elint stations alone or if the radio stations were included. There is in this period no specific mention of the Comint co-operation with the United States in the committee's minutes. This may be because the matter was so sensitive that it was not included in the official protocol, and was only discussed verbally. It is also possible that Evang communicated directly with the Defence Minister, and left it to him to handle the matter with the Cabinet Defence and Security Committee and the Prime Minister. New – from 1954 – guidelines imposed a general duty on the members to inform the Co-ordination Committee, but left a loophole for exceptions.

7. FO/E (Sæter), Radio section chief Brynildsen to Evang 18 Nov. 1954: 'Summary of major US Comint requirements', with Brynildsen's comments annexed.

8. FO/E (Sæter), P.M., 14 May 1954, 'Samarbeidet med amerikanerne på radioom- rådet' (Co-operation with the Americans in the field of radio).

9. FO/E (Sæter), 'Rapport vedrørende drøftelser USA–Norge' (Report on US– Norwegian talks), 8 Dec. 1954.

10. FO/E, file 'Sammenheftet korrespondanse til X 1952–1959', 'HSN [Hellerslien] kommentar i forbindelse med saker på møtene 13. og 21. juni', dated 24 June 1957.

11. FO/E, file 'Skuff 16. X-43. IV avdeling'. Various memoranda.

12. Ibid., FST/E/IV to Chief FST/E, 16 Feb. 1956: 'FST/E/IV. 5-års plan (1956– 1960)'.

13. Knut Willy Kval in conversation with the author, 15 Jan. 1997.

14. FO/E (Sæter), Evang to 'X' [the US liaison], 11 Nov. 1955.

15. FO/E, file 'X-2 Elint–Comint drøftelser', memo. from Falchenberg to Evang 25 Feb. 1955, with report of meeting with Mr Poulden, 24 Feb.

16. FO/E (Sæter), Hellerslien memo, 15 April 1957, 'Forslag til den videre organisering av bearbeidingstjenesten', and J.K. Brynildsen's standing order No. 1/57: 'Instruks for bearbeidingstjenesten ved Avd. V', 13 Nov. 1957.

17. FO/E (Sæter), Brynildsen to Chief of Intelligence Staff, 25 April 1957: 'Oversikt over samarbeidet Norge–USA på radio-etterretningsområdet (Comint)'. For the NSA headquarters see J. Bamford, *The Puzzle Palace* (Houghton Mifflin, Boston, MA, 1982). According to Bamford, punch-card processing was at that time still the most important tool, due to the limited capacity of the computers which IBM and NSA had developed for the purpose.

18. *Stortingsforhandlinger* (parliamentary proceedings), 1957, Section 2a, St.prp. No. 23 (1957), pp. 7 and 15.

19. FO/E, copy file H, draft letter from Lambrechts to Handal, 12 Oct. 1956.

20. FO/E (Sæter), Memorandum for Evang, 13 Jan. 1958. Each 'table' or position comprised a set of radio receivers and other necessary equipment for one operator.

21. CIA, History Staff, *Intentions and Capabilities: Estimates on Soviet Strategic Forces, 1950–1983* (CIA, Washington, DC, 1996), pp. 28 and 35.

22. FO/E (Sæter), Brynildsen to Evang, 31 Jan. 1958, 'Review of Comint requirements'.

23. FO/E, file 33.01.5 'MOU', doc. no. 10: 'MOU 14.3.1958 – discussions 12.3.1958'. It is quite possible that Evang's desire for overall control was prompted by an expressed wish from the US Air Attaché shortly beforehand, for the establishment of a mobile Elint station near Kirkenes for monitoring Soviet nuclear tests. See SMK, RSU protocol, 26 Feb. 1958.

24. SMK, RSU protocol, 20 May 1958.

25. In March 1958 the Soviet Union had declared its willingness to suspend all testing provided the United States did the same. A one-year test ban went into force in Nov. 1958.

26. SMK, RSU protocol, 3 July 1958; FO/E, file 'MOU', doc. no. 7, Evang note, 14 July 1958.

27. FO/E, file 'MOU', doc. no. 6, 26 Aug. 1958. Oddly enough the supplementary agreement gives 9 and not 10 Dec. 1954 as the date of the first NORUSA agreement. An explanation may be that the English and Norwegian texts were not signed on the same day. For the 'bomber gap' estimates see also John Prados, *The Soviet Estimate*

(Dial Press, New York, 1982), pp. 41–50.

28. FO/E, Hallfred Skau manuscript, and mimeographed booklet 'Erindringer fra E-tjenesten i Sør-Varanger, og tilbakeblikk på Moens 30-årige historie'. See also the subsequent chapter on the Air Force and Elint.
29. FO/U, file 'MOU', doc. no. 10.
30. FO/E, 'Skuff 12: X2. Elint–Comint drøftelser 1958–1962'. Minutes of Sigint meeting in Oslo, 5 Feb. 1962.
31. Ibid., Minutes of meeting, Wednesday, 7 Feb. 1962.
32. FO/E, green binder, 'Historisk materiale: Organisering m.v. av E-tjenesten'. Appendices B and C.
33. FO/E, 'Skuff 5: 10.01 FD–Forsvarsministeren–Statssekretær'. Evang memo of conversation with Harlem, Monday, 6 Jan. 1964 at 1300–1430 hours.
34. FO/E, Control Committee file, agenda for 2 Jan. and minutes of meeting, 2 March 1964.
35. The story of POLAR REIN and PINE FOREST will be taken up in Chapter 9.
36. FO/E (Sæter), annex 5 to a memo of 25 May 1965 from FST/E-V: 'FST/E organisasjon: Electronisk etterretningstjeneste'.
37. FO/E (Sæter), Box A. Annual reports from 1963 and 1965.
38. FO/E (Sæter), Box 1, file 'Samarbeide m/politiet. Agentvirksomheten 1969–72'. Working group's report dated 18 Nov. 1969.

6

Electronic Intelligence (1):
The Air Force as Elint Pioneer

Behind the development of Elint installations in North Norway in the 1950s lay a whole set of Western strategic considerations. From British and American viewpoints, there was a particularly strong interest in getting up-to-date information about radar systems in northwest Russia, and for two reasons. Firstly it was important to register all unusual or irregular activity as quickly as possible, in order to obtain early warning of military movements of a potentially offensive nature. Such early warnings were, of course, viewed with equal interest by the Norwegian armed forces. But in addition, a Soviet bombing raid against Britain or the United States would in all likelihood use its northern bases as one of its main points of departure. From there, the bombers would be able to fly over the Arctic or over the open sea, with far less risk of detection than if they took off in central Soviet Russia and had to fly over land across Western Europe, where they would soon be picked up by the continental radar chains. As early as in 1954 the CIA were expecting an accelerated expansion of Soviet aircraft bases in the north, and two years later the CIA committed to paper a prophecy that the aircraft bases on the Kola Peninsula, in addition to the bases on Chukotskiy and Kamtschatka Peninsulas at Russia's eastern extremity, would lead off in the opening phase of any bombing raid against the United States.[1]

The second main area of interest concerned what was often called 'route planning' in US air force terminology. Here the task was to pinpoint radar installations and other elements of the Soviet air defence system, *PVO-Strany*, to find the safest approach routes for American bombers on the way to attack strategically important targets in the Soviet Union. In 1954 the CIA expressed certainty that the Russians in the years up to 1960 would use considerable resources in developing effective surface-to-air missiles with accessory radar systems as a defence against American bombers. The Russians could here build on the work of the German experts who had been brought to the Soviet Union immediately after the war. Before the end of the 1950s Norwegian intelligence was in a position to identify the Soviet P-14 radar systems on the Kola Peninsula, known by the NATO code name of 'Tall King', which constituted the core of an advanced early warning radar chain along the Soviet border. They had also located and identified the characteristics of the P-8 'Knife Rest' and the P-12 'Spoon Rest', which were combined 'acquisition and target tracking' radar systems attached to the Soviet air defence system SA-2 'Guideline'. SA-2 was one of the first really efficient surface-to-air missiles and was, at the beginning of the 1960s, deployed at more than 2,000 launch sites. It has also been claimed that it was a volley of 14 such missiles that obliged Gary Powers to eject from his U-2 after a missile had exploded close enough to cause him to lose control of his aircraft.[2]

THE DEVELOPMENT OF ELECTRONICS

Not unexpectedly, the rapid technological evolution during the first postwar years presented major challenges to the various methods of intelligence collection. This applied in particular to weapon systems, in which electronics achieved a more and more dominating position. Since electronic equipment radiates electronic energy in one form or another, it leaves 'traces' or, for that matter, 'finger prints'. For the military tactical and strategic planners, it was therefore of great importance to access information about the opponent's electronic equipment and its function in a weapon system. Together with other information, this could provide a better basis from which to assess the opponent's war-fighting capabilities. Consequently, everything in this area was surrounded by strict security measures, which meant that intensive efforts were required to procure the necessary intelligence.

During the war both sides had developed methods by which to exploit as well as guard against electronic intelligence. Centrally placed persons in the Norwegian armed forces knew from wartime service with the forces of the Norwegian Government-in-exile that the British had made great advances in the field which they called 'Y & RCM service'. With this in mind, the Norwegian Air Force High Command in 1949 asked the Intelligence Staff what they were doing in this field.[3] A corresponding initiative came from the navy, which in addition had concrete suggestions to make as to how electronics and electronic warfare might be developed for its own benefit.[4] The reply to both was that the Intelligence Staff was carrying out a limited Y service, but no RCM service (Radio Counter Measures), and that the whole field ought now to be looked into. In a letter to Evang at the end of the year, the head of the Radio Section, John K. Brynildsen, made an effort to clarify the terms used. The Y service, he explained, covered a large area of which RCM was the offensive component, while the rest constituted the passive element. The offensive activity was directed at disrupting the enemy's radio communications and developing countermeasures to deflect similar efforts from the other side. The passive component involved intercepting the enemy's radio communications for intelligence purposes.[5] This passive Y service corresponded, in other words, to what came to be known as an electronic intelligence service.

However, labels and contents were not always consistent at this early juncture. Very often the term electronic intelligence was used in a kind of short-hand to include both Comint and Elint, when in fact Sigint or signals intelligence would have been the correct term. At the same time, in more precise contexts, the term electronic intelligence would be defined as limited to the Elint part on its own. In the Norwegian service, the Elint part would in this context be defined by being specified as 'all other forms of electronic activity that are not based on the transmission of communications'. In a memorandum from the Intelligence Staff from the beginning of the 1960s, we found this definition:

> Elint (Electronic Intelligence) covers everything that has to do with
> a. the collection of technical data about all kinds of electronic equipment and systems such as all types of radar, weapon systems, remote guidance, radio lines, navigational systems, data transmissions from satellites, electronic radiation from e.g. industrial plants, etc.
> b. the processing and analysing of this material.[6]

The memorandum states additionally that by analysing the emissions in the form of electromagnetic energy which is radiated from electronic equipment and processes (missile launches, etc.), it becomes possible to ascertain the type of equipment producing the signal, how it works, its location, its connection with other types of equipment or processes, etc.

A significant portion of such electronic emissions are in the higher end of the frequency spectrum, which means that the signals follow a near 'line of sight' path. In practical terms, therefore, the closer and higher an intercept station is located in relation to the emitting target or target area, the better the conditions for a successful intercept. From the point of view of finding the best locations for Norwegian Elint intercept stations, the requirement hence was to place them as high as possible and as close as feasible to the border, so as to attain a maximum 'line of sight coverage' relative to the target area. Also, in order to enable two stations to obtain reasonably accurate cross-bearings for locating the target's position, they had to be placed at a sufficient lateral distance from each other, and – in this particular case – roughly on a north–south line, since the general target area was to the east.

An Elint facility could be either stationary, in a permanent land-based station, or mobile on board ships or aircraft. Each of those positions had its particular advantages and drawbacks. In the permanent ground stations there was ample space for search equipment irrespective of size (unless political considerations advised against too conspicuous aerials); the target area could be covered continuously; it would be possible to achieve quite accurate bearings when working in tandem with another ground station; and one could also study selected types of signals or the use of certain types of equipment over extended periods of time. The drawbacks were a limited coverage area, since directional transmissions which beamed away from the station were missed. Ship-based Elint could accommodate fairly large installations, and allowed greater operative freedom, with the possibility of staying close to the target for extended periods of time. The drawbacks were related to considerations of aerial size, which limited coverage radius unless compensated by more sensitive pre-amplifiers; less accurate bearing data than that provided by the permanent stations; and limitations on the range of each tour of operations due to bunker capacity and, partly, weather conditions. (Most of those drawbacks were reduced when the NIS acquired its own ship.) The Elint equipment used under air reconnaissance was able to cover all the relevant frequency bands; the operating altitude provided a considerably wider radio horizon and could therefore result in the coverage of areas which otherwise were unreachable; and by being more mobile it was possible to find the most advantageous intercept position for a given signal source. Obvious limitations were the restricted size and weight of the equipment that could be accommodated; relatively brief search periods; less accurate bearing data compared with the permanent stations and boat operations; and cost considerations.[7]

The rapid pace of developments in the field of electronics was to some extent reflected in changes of terminology. Quite soon the designation 'Y service' was replaced with 'Electronic Warfare', and RCM became ECM – 'Electronic Counter Measures'. 'Elektronisk krigføring', abbreviated EK, was a natural choice for the Norwegian version. But difficulties with definitions and demarcations remained. In the sources we have from the 1950s it is sometimes difficult to distinguish what is *intelligence* and what is *warfare* when EK is aired in various contexts. Precisely because electronic warfare embraced both offensive and defensive measures, as did the Y service, this mix-up was exacerbated.

In 1953 the Intelligence Staff defined the EK field as, 'in the widest sense, any form of military activity in which electronic aids are utilised (offensively or defensively) to advance the objectives of the war'. The Intelligence Staff tended to distinguish four components of EK: (1) ECM Monitoring – 'Listening in on the enemy's radio and radar signals with a view to directing jamming transmitters'; (2) Jamming – 'Disturbances whose aim is to complicate the use of radio and radar by the enemy'; (3) Beaconing – 'Reception and re-transmission of signals from the enemy's navigational aids to make direction-finding unreliable or impossible'; and (4) Anti-Jamming – 'Technical devices in radios and radar equipment to make them less susceptible to the effect of enemy jamming'.[8] The more updated designations are Electronic Support Measures (ESM), which is interception in support of ECM; ECM, which generally stands for jamming; and Electronic Counter Counter Measures (ECCM) which stands for counter-measures against an adversary's ECM. A current and more practical definition of the whole field is that given by a British expert: 'Electronic Warfare – typically involving receivers aboard aircraft which give immediate warning when a hostile missile radar is locked on, and the on-board jammers which then counter the radar.'[9] Here the intelligence element is completely absent.

Not unexpectedly, NATO needed to get involved with such a wide-ranging and pioneering military effort: SHAPE wanted to establish Electronic Warfare Units, and this had to be co-ordinated with what was already going on at the national level. Evang asked Falchenberg of the Radio Section at the Intelligence Staff to look into this from an NIS point of view, and early in 1952 he reported back that the NATO initiative risked interfering with some of their ongoing activities, primarily interception of radio signals. He thought that jamming, too, ought to be conducted, or at least led, by the Radio Section: the personnel needed to be 'first-class', closely associated with the interception service, and only those with the 'best possible' knowledge of the enemy's procedures ought to work in this field. Protection against corresponding activity on the part of the enemy was, on the other hand, a matter for the armed forces and NATO. As far as radar was concerned, this was characterised as an enormous area of work. Radar jamming and radio jamming would have to be co-ordinated, in conjunction also with the intercept service.

The Intelligence Staff were clearly sceptical towards NATO getting too involved in the matter, and Falchenberg calculated that the Defence Staff was generally not much in favour of any form of earmarking of Norwegian intelligence results for SACEUR. But the results of Norway's ECM activities ought, he thought, to be passed on to its allies, and Norway might take on assignments to a certain degree, even though its units would not be subject to any international body. The latter was probably an utterly crucial precondition for entering into any form of collaboration with NATO in this area. Falchenberg therefore recommended a response to SHAPE in which it would be informed that there was some activity in this field in Norway, in terms of a monitoring service, but that it was under such difficult circumstances that the work could hardly be led by anyone else but the national authorities. The results, however, would be placed at SACEUR's disposal.[10]

In a memorandum from SHAPE in 1952, the Headquarters Allied Forces Northern Europe (HQ AFNORTH) was entrusted with the task of formulating a proposal concerning the establishment of an organisation for 'Intercept, D.F. and Jamming', in other words, electronic warfare. The organisation was to be attached to the tactical headquarters for air and ground forces that was being planned near Bodø. Wing Commander Abrook, who was in charge of the issue in HQ AFNORTH, was briefed on the Norwegian air force's plans in the area, and explained his own ideas in a meeting with Evang in June 1952. Abrook was of the opinion that there ought to be Electronic Warfare stations in the Oslo area, at Sola, in Trondheim, and in Bodø; that Norway ought to be able to manufacture the equipment; that one was talking in the range of a total of 100 men;

and, since listening in on the enemy's radio communications constituted a part of these EK plans, knowledge of Russian was required for the operators.

Evang probably attempted to be as accommodating as possible, though without binding himself to any concrete plans. He intimated that the four stations could be attached to institutions that had already been established or were in the process of being established, but that the questions of equipment and manning would have to be dealt with at a later date.[11] This evasiveness suggests that the Intelligence Staff needed to gain time in order to consider the whole field of electronic warfare, and to determine their own role in it. As it happened, an initiative from the air force was already on the table, by way of a proposal for a 'Section for Tactical Radio Warfare in the Air Force', in which electronic warfare and electronic intelligence seemed inextricably intermingled.

AIR FORCE INITIATIVES AND SETBACKS

The air force leadership had as early as 1951 taken up the question of obtaining from the United States equipment for a tactical electronic intelligence section, as well as assistance with training of personnel. This had been done through the Military Assistance Advisory Group (MAAG) in Oslo, an American body which had been founded to administer American weapons aid. One of the purposes of such a unit would be to study the Soviet Union's air order of battle in northwestern Russia. The Air Force High Command and MAAG had then agreed that the best way would be to start building up such a section with a mobile radio squadron 'after the American model'. MAAG promised to get hold of all the equipment needed for such a radio squadron, and to get the requisite number of specialists on to training courses in the United States.[12]

Knut M. Haugland, whose background included work as a radio operator during the German occupation of Norway, as radio operator on Thor Heyerdahl's 'Kon Tiki' adventure, and experience with Stay Behind, was now called home from service in the Norwegian Brigade in Germany and ordered to report to the Intelligence Staff. He was informed here by Evang and the chief of the intelligence section (O IV) in the air force, Lieutenant-Colonel L. Wilmer Robertsen, about existing plans. In January 1952 he was then charged with formulating a detailed inventory of material and personnel and, in addition, proposing station locations. The plan itself no longer exists, but we do know that it was despatched to Evang in May, and that he stated his agreement with 'the main thrust' of the plan.[13]

After approval of the personnel inventory by the Ministry of Defence and the Air Force High Command, Haugland was given an office and started the work. The first step consisted of a comprehensive search for possible station locations in Finnmark. For two weeks in the summer of 1952, he and Lieutenant Asbjørn Thon criss-crossed the area, and with good results. Haugland concluded that the listening station for shortwave ought to be located either at or around Banak air base, or in Alta. One of the two shortwave direction-finding stations ought to be placed in Kautokeino, the other one near the Banak listening station, whereas the Vardø area was the best place for a UHF listening station.

Even while Haugland was still doing service in the Intelligence Staff, recruitment to what was now called 'the Air Force's electronic intelligence service' had already started. The High Command had been offered three places at an American radio school, and three soldiers were sent over for six months' training. In July 1952 the air force, in close collaboration with the Intelligence Staff, advertised in the newspapers for radio operators. The required personnel thus recruited, the Intelligence Staff took upon itself the basic training of radio operators. Eight sergeants received a period of 18 months' training, after which they were ready for the American courses. But unexpected obstacles intervened, in the shape of problems with the delivery of the equipment. MAAG had placed the order in 1951, 1952, and again in 1953. From Washington word came that someone somewhere in the system had stopped the order. It was now entered into the 1953/54 delivery programme. The training in the United States, which was an essential prerequisite for the handling of equipment valued at more than three million kroner, also encountered problems. For three years in a row, from 1952, the course was cancelled just before the departure of the students, again on orders 'from the highest sources' in Washington.

Undaunted, the air force carried on with its own courses for the personnel. Participants followed courses in administration, air intelligence, radar control and Russian language, the latter at, among other places, the Joint School for Linguists in Cornwall, England. There, Polish teachers taught Russian from seven in the morning till six in the evening, leading to a 'Service Translator Certificate'. At an American station at Oldenburg, West Germany, in General Rommel's old headquarters, the syllabus consisted of monitoring and plotting of radar, including mobile radar.[14] In the meantime the Air Force High Command had to plan for buildings to house the new service. An application for funds from NATO's Infrastructure Programme was turned down. But the reconnaissance journey in the summer of 1952 had shown that Banak air base possessed modern buildings which were not being used. By some coincidence the Ministry of Defence had just decided that Banak was not to be developed as an air base.[15]

In a long note to Evang in September 1953, the chief of O IV section in the Air Force High Command appealed for his assistance in relation to the Americans:

> The circumstances that have been mentioned above show quite clearly that the development of the Air Force's warning service is confronting substantial and unforeseen difficulties and, as the situation is at present, it is impossible to continue with the work. The Air Force High Command is of the opinion that the delay has been caused by circumstances over which the Air Force has no control, and will therefore request that the Chief of the Intelligence Staff provide the necessary support *vis-à-vis* MAAG and any other American bodies ... and make it clear to the American authorities that a definite answer must now be given as soon as possible.[16]

The documents give no definite answer as to the reason for what the Air Force High Command clearly saw as delaying tactics on the part of the Americans. Internal American rivalry, with the CIA and NSA on the one side and USAF on the other, may have played a part, as could rivalry between the two major intelligence powers, the United States and Britain. It is also not entirely unlikely that Evang had exercised a certain amount of influence. He already had a nascent bilateral basis in which the Intelligence Staff and CIA/NSA were co-players, not the USAF. Co-operation at the highest possible level was always one of Evang's goals. Possibly he had put in a word or two indicating that the United States ought to wait with the delivery until a few internal Norwegian issues had been ironed out, including the initiative from NATO. Evang was, in addition, initially unsympathetic to allowing the armed forces to operate more or less untrammelled in an area he considered as the Intelligence Staff's territory. Even though, officially speaking, a co-operative effort in this matter existed between the Intelligence Staff and the air force, Evang would most likely have given precedence to his bilateral collaboration with CIA and NSA. In relation to this, the USAF and the Air Force High Command represented a side-track. Last, but not least, developments in the Elint field within the Intelligence Staff had, as we shall see, an effect on the plans in the air force. Haugland summed up his experiences in a later memorandum: 'The American material was, however, not delivered according to the programme, and did not start to arrive until 1954. In the meantime electronic intelligence in the Intelligence Staff was undergoing constant development, and came to embrace well nigh the whole of the field that was intended for the Air Force.'[17]

1954 – A BREAKTHROUGH FOR THE AIR FORCE'S ELINT

In the spring of 1954 the Air Force High Command discussed their predicament with the British Defence Secretary, Lord Alexander, during the latter's visit to Norway.[18] He lent a sympathetic ear, and through the British air attaché the air force now acquired both search equipment and a promise of special training. Shortly afterwards the UK Air Ministry declared that they would provide all possible support, both with regard to material, training and technical advisers. British experts were soon in full activity in Norway, and this new joint effort led to a certain alteration to the Norwegian plans, in the direction of the British 'Tactical Radio Warfare' concept.

As already mentioned, in the early 1950s co-operation as well as a certain form of rivalry existed between the United States and Britain about Norway as an intelligence area. To start with, Britain was a natural first choice for Norway, given the experiences and close comradeship of the war. But as the United States invested more and more in research and development, they gradually took the lead in technological developments. 'We use our heads, they use the instruments', the British said to comfort themselves, but where the British method was no longer up to the job, the American equipment took over. The air force in the meantime learnt that their supply problems had been a subject of discussion between the American and British authorities 'at a very high level'. This led to a detailed written offer from the US air force in June 1954 of equipment for two Elint installations, and special training for four officers for as many months in the United States. Again, optimism rode high. The offer meant that the air force would be able to start up much sooner, and it would also support directly the ongoing collaboration with the British. But Haugland saw one problem with the American offer, namely the request to receive regular intelligence reports directly from the air force. He therefore proposed to route such reports through the Defence Staff 'for the use of the Staff and possible forwarding to the UK and the United States, after the registered data have been assessed and analysed as well as possible by the Air Force High Command'.

The Chief of the Air Force, Major-General Finn Lambrechts, passed Haugland's memorandum to the Chief of Defence Staff. In a covering note he referred to a previous meeting between Evang and Major-General Tufte Johnsen of the air force, and assumed that the Defence Staff had no objection to the air force accepting the offer of equipment. At the same time he asked the Chief of Defence Staff to agree that the reports which the Americans were asking for be channelled through the Intelligence Staff, which goes to show that Evang had been successful in his efforts to retain control and have his staff hold the strings. Major-General Jakob A. Waage, replying on behalf of the Defence Staff, expressed his complete approval of Haugland's memorandum: electronic intelligence was one of the most important areas where Norway could not only acquire systematic knowledge of military and civilian developments in the most adjacent parts of the Soviet Union, but could also play a very significant role in the international intelligence work in NATO.

> It is with this in mind that the Intelligence Staff has so strongly supported the total expansion of this area, and has also been given significant support in this development work by the authorities. It is clear that important parts of the intelligence that can be gained in this way are of direct and immediate interest to the Air Force, but it is equally clear that the collected material is of decisive importance to the overall Norwegian defence effort.[19]

The American offer and the work carried out in the air force are here placed in a greater context, namely as an element in a united Norwegian intelligence service. The assumption for the future would be a fully joint effort throughout the whole of the electronic intelligence field, between the Defence Staff, the air force, and prospectively any other elements in the armed forces. Again we hear Evang's echo: firstly, the efforts on the part of the air force should not be seen in isolation from the total effort on the intelligence side, and, secondly, the work would have to take place

in close co-operation with the Intelligence Staff, through which all information to the American authorities should pass. Waage's proposed response
to the Americans on this latter point stated: 'The reports will be made
available to the CIA representative in Oslo through the Intelligence Division at the Norwegian Defence Staff.' This was subsequently amended
by Haugland, who underlined the initials CIA in ink, and added '*changed
to US Air Attaché*'. But this probably reflected internal procedures in the
American Embassy, and changed nothing in regard to the intentions of
the Norwegians.

The inauguration of such an important inter-Allied venture in
intelligence co-operation as the USAF–RNoAF Elint agreement of 1954,
was an event of political significance which clearly was a matter for the
Co-ordinating Committee. A note by the chairman, Andreas Andersen,
shows that the matter of Elint stations in Finnmark was first raised as an
issue for the committee at a meeting in August 1954, when State Secretary
Sivert A. Nielsen reported on a conversation with H. Freeman Matthews
of the US Embassy on the subject.[20] Andersen himself was clearly taken
aback by the proposal, which came on top of the plans for expansion of
the Comint service. Andersen thought it was bound to create political
problems 'if East Finnmark is filled with so many installations and
personnel'. Nielsen and Evang said that the matter would be subjected
to further study before it could be considered by the Ministry of Defence.
When the offer to the air force again came before the committee in October
1954, the issue was referred to as the 'tactical-electronic intelligence
service'. Then it was simply stated that the committee had discussed this
once before, and that the air force and the Defence Staff had reviewed
the budgetary consequences. Both parties had recommended that the
offer to supply material should be accepted. This time there was not the
least sign of disagreement in the Committee.

At this juncture the Ministry of Defence had already approved the
offer of equipment from the US for two permanent stations and one
mobile station. But the ministry had first requested a short description
of 'the intelligence benefits' to be gained with the equipment, as well as
a joint proposal from the Defence Staff and the air force on how the
collected information should be passed on to the US air force. The
response[21] emphasised that with the help of the right equipment, operated
by specialists, one should be able to uncover 'the control and warning
system of a potentially hostile air force' and also an enemy's 'order of
battle'. As far as getting the information to the Americans was concerned,

there was agreement that the intelligence should first be placed at the disposal of the Intelligence Staff, with the stations' comments. It would then be up to the Intelligence Staff to provide the required reports to the Americans. The Intelligence Staff would then in return receive the American assessments of the forwarded material, and inform the air force accordingly. At the same time the air force wished to keep its options open with regard to the technical collaboration with American experts. They wanted this to continue in the same way as when the air force had co-operated directly with the American and British air forces, with regard to the establishment of technically complex installations.

While all this was afoot, the air force carried out its first test of an Elint station. Asbjørn Thon together with two other specialists had gone to Finnmark in August 1954, and tests were carried out from Viksjøfjell and Nosfjell. With the assistance of sensitive mobile receivers, the intention was to reveal what types of alien signals could be intercepted on Norwegian territory. New tests were done in October, and a number of stations were registered. British equipment was used; among other things the air force had received a fully outfitted radio vehicle.[22] For the next stage, the analysis of the details of the registered signals, the American equipment would be needed. But delays and delivery problems were something the air force would have to put up with for some time to come.

CO-OPERATION BETWEEN THE RNoAF AND THE NIS

All through these early years one senses the struggle for competence and hegemony which the air force's Elint venture was destined to confront. The first effort to establish a division of labour between the Intelligence Staff and the RNoAF in this area was the report in 1952 from the 'Andersen Committee', which reviewed the whole organisation of the intelligence and security services. That committee seems to have felt that interception, direction-finding, analysis and assessment of the lower frequencies should be the responsibility of the Intelligence Staff, while the air force should be in charge of intercepting tactical voice or plain language traffic on very high frequencies among airborne aircraft, and between them and the ground stations.[23]

With particular regard to Early Warning, some co-operation between the two had in fact been established. We have seen that the NIS in 1952 had started sending EW reports to its partners at the American embassy, as an element of the joint Comint venture with the United States. The air force here played a major role in the collection effort, and in a 1952 memo Evang referred to that source as 'Early Warning section, the air force'. In 1952 'Air Force station, Vardø' became operational, and the intelligence section of the Air Force High Command began regular analysis and assessment of logs and reports emanating from the station. In March 1953 we find traces of an agreement between Evang and Haugland concerning a special assignment the station was to carry out for the Intelligence Staff. There was also co-operation regarding calibration flights, as well as *ad hoc* collaboration on a case-by-case basis.

This notwithstanding, the division of responsibilities and tasks of the two services was not clearly delineated. As the work that was being done by the air force progressed, the operators became aware of the fact that there was a large, uncovered area within Elint, namely interception, direction finding, analysis, and assessment concerning the higher frequencies used for the Control and Warning system, for navigational equipment, etc.[24] As the air force saw it, the Intelligence Staff was keeping them from entering this area. At a meeting between Evang and Haugland in December 1954, a preliminary arrangement for collaboration was established. Evang now gave the air force a free hand in the Elint area, but emphasised how important it was to avoid disclosing any information that might point back to and thus compromise Comint sources. Evang also said that the Intelligence Staff, as of February 1955, would be in direct contact with an American 'technical officer', and the air force would also have access to this officer in the event of 'technical questions'. The question of relations with the British was also brought up, and Haugland stressed the value of the air force being able to continue with this collaboration on the tactical level. Evang again made the distinction between Comint material and Elint, but had no objection to the air force co-operating fully with the British RAF in the Elint field.[25]

Summing up, Evang intimated that the air force did not need to take any more notice of the Andersen Committee; the agreement that had been formulated there 'has been outstripped by reality'. Moreover, it had been based simply on reason and common sense; the committee had not consulted foreign experts about how the service was organised in Britain and the United States. Even though he explicitly stated that the time was ripe for a concrete and formal agreement on the distribution of responsibilities and tasks, he still played for time on behalf of the Intelligence Staff in the hope, among other things, of their being able to establish their own

NIS Elint platform, so that the air force would not dominate the field too much.

Vardø radar station had since November 1952 registered increasing air-craft activity over the Kola Peninsula. Most surprising was the intensive flying in the winter in very bad weather conditions. This was seen as proof that the Soviets possessed a well-developed command, warning and navigational system. The excellent Vardø results were used in various reports from the air force to argue the great importance of developing an Elint service, not least because of the 'uncommonly suitable geographical position of Norway for running a tactical electronic intelligence service already in peacetime against a potentially hostile air force'. The long nights and the difficult weather conditions meant that the Soviet air force was obliged 'here more than in other places' to use electronic aids both in the air and on the ground.

> Foreign experts have alleged that in a short time, Norway will be the only NATO country in Europe from where it is possible to conduct effective electronic intelligence activity right up towards the Soviet Union. The reason is that the Americans and the British are gradu-ally pulling their electronic stations out of occupied areas which adjoin Soviet border areas. Norway and Turkey thus remain the only important sources that can provide information of the above-mentioned nature to NATO.[26]

Haugland, who was the author of this evaluation, was alluding especi-ally to Austria where the Americans had closed down costly installations in 1955. There is no doubt about the realities underlying the increasing interest in Eastern Finnmark, not only on the part of the United States. Britain had shown its interest by the visit of Mr Poulden in February 1955. NATO was also in the market. After a visit to Norway of the chief of the intelligence division at SHAPE, General Schweitzer, Evang told the members of the Co-ordination Committee that the general had shown considerable interest in SHAPE gaining access to the Elint material that was collected in Norway, and which was now only placed at the disposal of the United States.[27] Andreas Andersen thought this was a good opportunity to extract oneself from 'what he considered to be the unfortunate bilateral agreements with the United States in this area'. This view may have had some influence. At the Committee's next meeting, Sivert A. Nielsen said that the air force had been contacted by the Americans about a bilateral agreement on the exchange of certain types of intelligence material in return for deliveries of equipment. The Americans wanted a formal agreement, but Nielsen had advised the air force to be wary of any such deals.[28]

At the end of March 1955 Haugland and Thon met the American air attaché, Colonel Remington. The outcome was that the promised American Elint equipment was now to be delivered from Wiesbaden, and would be sent directly by plane to Bodø not later than 30 April.[29] But delays, and the inclusion of some equipment that was not quite suited to the purpose, meant that the timetable once again did not hold. Nonetheless, with the special equipment which the USAF and the Air Ministry had already supplied, the air force could with greater certainty than before 'record precise technical characteristics of Soviet Russian installations'. It was thus becoming increasingly possible to keep an eye on technical developments as regards Russian electronic equipment in the air and on the ground. One expected now to be able to cover the most important areas of the Kola Peninsula. In addition, it would be possible to monitor similar equipment on board naval units in the Arctic Ocean.

In August 1955 some American and British equipment was installed at Korpfjell near the Soviet border. In this second attempt with mobile Elint stations, a number of known and unknown stations were again registered. But the rapid technological development in this field meant that the equipment that had been received subsequent to the offer in June 1954 was already out of date. New special aerials were to be delivered in March 1956. In the meantime an offer from the British Air Ministry for supplementary special equipment was accepted, and most of that was in place before the end of 1955. In addition, promises by both the Americans and the British about special training for key personnel were honoured. The air force hence felt well equipped to commence the service as soon as the stations could be established.

The first station was now to be established at Vardø; a prefabricated house intended to make do as an operations centre was sent up north in the summer of 1955 and set up close to the existing 'remote warning' station. This was the start of HEKLA, one of the two permanent Elint stations of the air force, which eventually became fully operational on

1 February 1959. The installation of the equipment was scheduled for March 1956, and the intention was that testing was to start as soon as possible. In the meantime a simple cabin made out of planks had been erected as camouflage for 'the somewhat compromising aerials' that were on their way. The positioning of the other station was more doubtful. A technical adviser from the USAF, a Mr Decker, came to Norway for a fortnight from the end of August 1955 to lend a hand. He had been in charge of the establishment of American electronic intelligence stations in Japan and Western Europe, and his work in Norway was arranged in co-operation with Evang. Together with technical personnel from the air force, he set off on journeys to Vardø and to the Korpfjell region. According to the sources, Mr Decker was highly impressed with what he saw in eastern Finnmark. He thought that a station so close to the Soviet border would be of 'vital importance to the Norwegian air force, and to NATO as a whole'.

The work resulted in two proposals for speeding up the development of the electronic intelligence service in the air force, with two permanent stations interconnected by radio link. The plans included the establish-ment of a new American FPS-8 radar in a new bunker at Vardø. The air force lent its support to Decker's suggestion to make the electronic intelligence element at Vardø station operational at the end of 1955. HEKLA was to be the new name for this main station. Vårberget by Vardø had already been chosen as the location. Four alternatives for a so-called 'out station' near the Soviet border were considered: Viksjøfjell, which was considered the best, Korpfjell, Midtfjell and Reinsjøfjell. Evang gave his approval to Viksjøfjell, but with the reservation that the building must not have a 'provocative' appearance, but look like other towers along the border. The height could, if necessary, be extended to 20–25 metres. The cover name for the whole electronic intelligence service in the air force was to be 'The Air Force Radio Squadron'. The main station would be referred to as HEKLA, while the planned station on Viksjøfjell was to be designated BARHAUG. This is the first time this latter station name turns up in the sources, and we will return time and again in this and the following chapter to this project, which eventually became operational as a permanent station in 1964.

In a letter to the Ministry of Defence in February 1956 the Chief of the air force, Lieutenant-General Motzfeldt, gave strong support to Haugland's earlier arguments about the importance of the new stations. Several important electronic intelligence stations in Europe had now been closed down (Austria) or probably would be closed down (Germany). This increased the importance of the Norwegian electronic intelligence stations for the entire NATO organisation 'to a very significant degree'. The plan now was to accelerate the development of this service in the summer of 1956 and 1957. At the same time, Motzfeldt warned that the Air Force High Command would raise also the question of the establishment of an electronic warfare section, in which intelligence would be a necessary element.

THE NIS PUTS ON THE BRAKES

It is likely that the ambitious dimensions of the air force's plan – including the establishment of a whole new section with an intelligence element – have contributed to augmenting the scepticism which was already detectable among the Intelligence Staff, a scepticism which was often greater than Evang was wont to admit in his meetings with the air force. The chief of V Section, John K. Brynildsen, stated in a note to Evang that 'we in Norway still have too little experience in this particular area of intelligence to be able to defend "rushing in" and building an organisation such as the air force suggests'. The further argument was two-fold. Firstly, the familiar question turned up again concerning where the nub of the intelligence service was to lie. Secondly, a technical question had been raised about the strict separation of Comint from Non-Comint, another and perhaps more precise word for Elint, which the Intelligence Staff now chose to employ:

> According to the wish that all intelligence beyond the country's borders shall be the province of the Defence Staff, and that there is no real line of demarcation between 'Communications' and 'Non-communications', but that both of them are as two pieces from the same cloth, it does not seem reasonable that the air force alone should be awarded an establishment of these dimensions, unless that service is prepared also to do the work for the Navy, and the Army too, to the degree that these make use of electronics.

Brynildsen came to the conclusion that there ought to be a central body for Non-Comint either in V Section, at the Joint Signals Establishment, or in a completely new section under the Intelligence Staff. It was also advisable to proceed somewhat more slowly, gain experience and profit from that to achieve continual improvements.

Evang echoed those sentiments, but from a different angle, in a note summarising the meetings which had taken place between the Intelligence Staff and the air force in this matter. Among the several questions he raised concerning the prospective expansion was the political aspect, with particular reference to BARHAUG: 'It must be assumed that the construction of such a large station so close to the Soviet border will meet with considerable political opposition in Norway.' Evang had raised this matter with the State Secretary at the Ministry of Defence, Sivert A. Nielsen, and his reaction had been that it was not politically feasible to set up a station on Viksjøfjell. Any discussion of this matter in the Cabinet Defence and Security Committee would in Nielsen's opinion be a waste of time. Next came Evang's argument that 'the intelligence service in an external setting is the business of the Defence Staff and not of the armed services'. He intimated that agreements had been made with, and information given to, representatives of foreign countries in contravention of current directives. The air force had now had to guarantee that any contacts with foreign intelligence would proceed in strict accordance with instructions, and that they would have an open relationship with the Defence Staff. A final nail in the coffin was the suggestion that the Intelligence Staff probably could acquire the same information in other ways, and a lot more cheaply. Evang was thinking here of the operations the Intelligence Staff was already running in the Sigint area.[30]

There is a considerable difference between the views of Evang and Haugland about how open the co-operation between the two staffs actually was. Haugland attempts in one historical digest after the other to document how the Intelligence Staff, with Evang in the saddle, had known of and approved every step that had been taken, while Evang gives the impression of not being satisfied with the control the Intelligence Staff exercised over the situation. It is most likely that a number of motives have exerted their influence on Evang's attitude: basically, Evang did not like the idea of a powerful electronic intelligence service in the air force. Moreover, it probably represented a problem of some significance that Norwegian air force officers with close connections with the United States and Britain were more likely to consent to special arrangements which allowed the two great powers too much latitude. This Evang wanted to avoid at all costs; hence his insistence that foreign relations in the intelligence field had to be co-ordinated by the Intelligence Staff, including the forwarding of information to foreign services.

After Evang's interventions in the spring of 1956 the air force once again was obliged to reshuffle its plans. The Ministry of Defence ordered it to find a hilltop in the Kirkenes area for the second station. The air force investigated a number of sites, and Hill 212 south of Høybuktmoen turned out to be the only real alternative. Finn Lied, chief of the tele-communications section at the Norwegian Defence Research Establish-ment, said in an evaluation that even though Viksjøfjell from a radio-technical point of view was far more favourable than Hill 212, a compromise was not technically out of the question. On that basis the air force now requested permission to establish a test station at Hill 212, but with the addition of a small mobile forward station at Viksjøfjell. If the tests due in the autumn of 1956 should prove successful, one would then erect a permanent station by Høybuktmoen. Thus began the story of what was to become the air force's second permanent station, NABBEN, located on Nosfjellet outside Høybuktmoen by Kirkenes, which was completed and fully operational by February 1959. In regard to Viksjøfjell, Evang at another meeting with Haugland, in June 1956, took pains to convince him that it was not he but rather political considerations that stood in the way of building a station there. He agreed that an Elint station ought to be established there in due course, but it would have to be a step-by-step process.

TAKEOVER BIDS BY THE NIS

Air force station Høybuktmoen (LSTH) was established in the 'West Camp' at Høybuktmoen in July 1956, combined with an Elint installation in a tower on Nosfjell, which, in due course, was to become the permanent station NABBEN. All this took place with the co-operation of the Border Commissioner and the Intelligence Staff's element in Kirkenes. The station would operate four to eight hours daily. Soon after this a forward station was mounted on Viksjøfjell, as a prelude to a long-term project which by April 1964 would become the important BARHAUG station. A temporary test station on Strømbuktfjell near Høybuktmoen, proposed by the Norwegian Defence Research Establishment, also produced results indicating its location as favourable for a more permanent station.

In the meantime, co-ordination efforts between the Intelligence Staff and the air force continued. Talks were also held with the Americans about procedures for the transfer of data from the Elint collection activity. Evang conducted talks with the American air attaché in April 1956, and there were further discussions among the three involved parties in Wiesbaden in October. To enable a realistic evaluation of Elint raw material, the RNoAF declared its willingness to provide as much supplementary information as possible on activities in the north. Unprocessed operators' logs and tapes would be sent to the US air attaché by the Intelligence Staff twice a week. All voice recordings would be sent to the Defence Staff after having been translated by the air force.[31] In a parallel development, the Chief of the air force appointed a committee to report on the usefulness of an electronic service in the air force, and this was to be chaired by Captain Lars R. Heyerdahl of the Intelligence Staff – perhaps to avoid complaints that the NIS was not kept fully informed. The conclusion was unanimous that the electronic service, as organised in the air force, represented an important element in the Control and Warning system. On that basis, planning for construction of the two permanent stations could commence. In the meantime the temporary stations were proving their worth. This is shown by an evaluation from March 1957 by Erling Kruse, who at the time was acting chief of III Section at the Operations Staff, and later was to become a central figure in the Intelligence Staff.

> 20 Mobile Radio Squadron is effectively operational with the interception of the Russian Control & Warning system, and first rate results are arriving continuously at Air Force High Command 2–3 times a week. The results include electronic characteristics of most of the types of electronic equipment that are in use in the Eastern Bloc today. In addition, some unknown types have been registered which have not been heard anywhere else in the world.[32]

Perhaps it was precisely because of this that the Intelligence Staff needed to make haste to bring the whole of this complex under its leadership, in order to attain *one* intelligence service in Norway. Interest on the part of the other countries' services pointed in the same direction. In February 1957, Evang informed the Co-ordination Committee about urgent approaches from the British to obtain access to this Elint material, approaches that had been made directly to the air force. Once again Evang received backing for his view that contact with foreign countries in these questions ought only to go through the Intelligence Staff. He himself was willing to pass material on to the British, in return for help with analyses.

In March 1957 Evang, Haugland and the Chief of Staff of the air force, Major-General Waage, came together on the initiative of the latter. Evang at once took the bull by the horns, and declared that the tactical electronic service in the air force was now to be taken over by the Defence Staff. The issue of the transfer had been considered by the Ministry of Defence (State Secretary Nielsen), the air force (Motzfeldt and Waage), and the Defence Staff (General Bjarne Øen and Evang) and total agreement reigned. For political reasons it was now 'imperative' to gather the whole of this service under the Chief of the Intelligence Staff as the 'sole responsible head of all intelligence services in Norway'. There had been duplication of work, something Norway could not afford. It was even worse that the air force had started to operate on its own: 350,000 kroner had been used on the construction of a large installation at Høybuktmoen without Evang having been informed. Haugland tried to protest on this latter point, but was curtly ordered to present a proposal for a smooth transfer procedure.

In a long memorandum written after the meeting, Haugland made a valiant defence against accusations of the air force having gone behind the back of the Intelligence Staff in building up their intelligence effort: the air force electronics service 'was *established* and *developed* in close co-operation between the Defence Staff, the Ministry of Defence, and the Air Force. Every step of the development had been recommended by the Defence Staff and approved by the Ministry of Defence.' As for the relationship to the USAF, he asserted that all 'agreements between the Air Force and USAFE have been approved by the Chief of Defence Staff, and based on approbation by Ministry of Defence', and that all 'transfer of data to USAFE *has* taken place and will continue to take place in the future through the Defence Staff, as decided by Ministry of Defence'.[33] This may well have been the case. But Evang must still have felt that he did not have sufficient oversight and control over the *activity* engendered by the various arrangements. This applied not least to the collaboration between the air force and the USAF, probably also with the RAF. The air force probably lacked the mental 'brakes' which he instinctively applied whenever foreign countries' services presented their offers of co-operation. On this point, Evang wanted a no-nonsense approach, and could always find solid support for his stand in the political bodies which were kept informed about intelligence activities.

A POSSIBLE *MODUS VIVENDI*?

In their annual report for 1957 on the Norwegian armed forces, the British embassy commented that the 'air force function of intelligence has now been virtually absorbed by the Defence Staff'.[34] But this was not a process that could be completed overnight – in fact the formal transfer of the air force stations to the Intelligence Staff did not really take place until 1 January 1968. Already the day after Haugland had submitted his 'defence brief', he submitted a new report to Evang in which he detailed the consequences of the recent decision. Construction work at Vardø and Høybuktmoen had been stopped in abeyance of the transfer. A decision to proceed with the construction was therefore urgently required, independent of the administrative and financial arrangements that would have to be made in connection with the transfer. If not, then the intelligence service in particular would suffer by losing a lot of valuable information on the rapid developments in the field of electronics taking place on the other side of the border.

Four days later Evang informed the Chief of Staff of the air force that the construction work should not be stopped. He now agreed largely with the plans and had no objections to the work on Høybuktmoen or the projected tower on Strømbuktfjell.[35] In May 1957 Evang then gave the go-ahead to complete building the air force Elint station, using an old radar bunker as a foundation, and also to erect an 18-metre tower for mounting the aerials. Evang then turned his mind to the overall question of how to utilise the Elint service in eastern Finnmark to maximum effect, which meant satisfying the Intelligence Staff's need for a broad spectrum of intelligence as well as that of the air force for tactical warning, etc. So far the Intelligence Staff's own Sigint effort in Finnmark had mostly concentrated on Comint, and less on Non-Comint. But practice had shown that it was not possible to separate these categories from each other when the aim was to exploit available resources to the utmost. For the Intelligence Staff, the main goal was clear: the activity had to be co-ordinated and run by a single institution.[36]

Evang's May 1957 proposals had as their first point that the electronic intelligence service in Finnmark, with the stations HEKLA and NABBEN, ought to be organised as one unit and placed at the disposition of the Chief of Defence Staff. The Defence Staff should be in charge of missions, assessments, distribution of intelligence results, material, maintenance, etc. The air force would then deal with administration, wages, recruitment, etc. A unified leadership of the electronic Non-Comint service in eastern Finnmark should be established, in close co-ordination with the other Sigint activities in the region. As a final point it was emphasised that all contacts with foreign institutions and agencies should take place through the Defence Staff. There was so far little to indicate that these proposals would find approval by the air force. A pencilled note to that effect was quite categorical: 'The interests of the Air Force are by no means provided for by the proposal!' But at the same time, the service had to continue to provide important intelligence, so a *modus vivendi* had to be found. Not unexpectedly, concrete proposals emerged from the sections which were working with these problems on a daily basis. As the chief of Section III C in the Intelligence Staff admitted, it was inevitable that the planned co-ordination would have to be developed step by step, 'since the Defence Staff today lacks the necessary experience of the Non-Comint side to be able to lead this service on an ongoing basis'.[37]

US SELF–CRITICISM AND PRAISE FOR THE RNoAF

In July 1957 a two–day conference was held at the headquarters of USAFE in Wiesbaden to discuss 'Project COOKER', which appears to have been the code–name for USAF's activity in Norway. The purpose was to assess the situation so far with regard to this project, and to decide what sort of measures would be required to equip Norway with a sufficiently effective Elint capacity. No Norwegians were present at the conference. The report of the meeting shows that the USAF took self-criticism for deficiencies in planning, execution and co-ordination, something which had put the USAF in an embarrassing position. Since the Norwegians were now assessing the situation in order to determine how USAF could contribute, it was necessary to establish priorities regarding intelligence requirements. USAFE had by then fully understood the Norwegian unwillingness to install new equipment which could not be camouflaged in already existing buildings, etc. Nor could Norway afford a large increase in personnel. It was therefore important to establish an operational capacity based on existing stations rather than introducing new, far-reaching plans.

The conference concluded that a complete engineering overhaul of the project was required to equip Norway with 'the most efficient capability possible, consistent with the availability of equipment, space available and operating personnel'.[38] Most weight was placed on the two existing stations (HEKLA and NABBEN), less on the mobile capacity. But for the time being it was highly desirable that the mobile installation be completed by the spring of 1958. All these questions would have to be discussed with the Norwegians in the autumn of 1957. At new meetings in Wiesbaden and Washington, with the participation of Norwegian representatives, guidelines for co-operation and co-ordination were discussed. It was now becoming clear that the Intelligence Staff had both the clout and the connection with the Ministry of Defence necessary to carry the process through to completion. The weightiest argument was supplied by Martens Meyer in a comprehensive note which concluded as follows:

> It should be clear, given the above, that if Elint is to be efficient, then it must be co-ordinated under a *common* leadership. None of the respective defence services is in a position to satisfy all the requirements demanded by such activities ... Foreigners would then have a marvellous opportunity to infiltrate and take charge. That close co-operation with foreigners is necessary is one thing, but it must be co-ordinated. It should therefore be self-evident that the Intelligence Staff is the natural co-ordinator.[39]

Progress in the direction of a more unified service led by the Intelligence Staff would still meet many practical snags. But NIS personnel now had access to the air force Elint stations, and took part in all planning meetings as the co-ordinating partner. All recordings and logs from the stations were henceforth routed to a newly established analysis centre at Section VI of the Intelligence Staff. In the meantime, the work at the air force stations went on apace. In the summer of 1958, what the Americans called the 'rehabilitation' of both HEKLA and NABBEN began with a visit by Mr Decker and Mr Traugott of USAF. The main intelligence objectives were then determined. During a new visit in August by Mr Traugott together with key personnel from the air force, the objectives were transformed into detailed plans. In USAFE, preparations were made for the delivery of five plane-loads of equipment, and in the meantime most of the construction work had been done on the towers at NABBEN and HEKLA. Two other engineers, Mr Holter and Mr Bruce, had joined the working group in USAFE in August and came with Traugott to Oslo in the last week of September. Here the final conference was held, and in October the Americans proceeded to NABBEN and HEKLA together with air force personnel to start work on the installations. By February 1959 the stations were declared fully operational.

The air force now wanted a permanent station on Viksjøfjell, where they had operated the mobile station BARHAUG for the past six summers. The results at BARHAUG in the summer of 1958 were characterised as quite sensational by the Americans. After reports for the two first weeks had been processed, the Chief of the air force received a letter from the American air attaché with congratulations from the Deputy Chief of Intelligence, USAFE. The Americans had received 36 new signals of interest from BARHAUG, in addition to other valuable data related to other types of signals. This was 'beyond their greatest expectations'. The letter went on to detail the various radar and aircraft types, known and new, which the station had picked up. Moreover, BARHAUG was the only accessible ground station which could monitor this new Russian equipment on a continuous basis. For its part, the air force had conducted its own assessment and found that the electronic listening data here far outstripped the results from the radar at Vardø. The conclusion was that 'The electronic intelligence service provides the Air Force with steadily new knowledge about the electronic development within the Russian air force and its C & W system in the border areas in the North'.[40] To the Intelligence Staff, the results from BARHAUG were probably less sensational, since they had prior indication of many of the 'new' stations through Comint information, to which USAF and RNoAF did not have access. But there was no disagreement about the advantageous location of BARHAUG.

PRACTICAL CO-OPERATION – AND NEW STUDIES

The problems besetting relations between the air force and the Intelligence Staff were not limited to organisational turf wars. The air force also repeatedly complained that they were not getting the benefit of information collected by the NIS Comint stations which was relevant to their planning and operations. In particular, Comint could provide tactical information on the Russian air force and their C&W (control and warning) systems. Knowledge of Russian long-distance flights could be procured several days before takeoff. The air force's radar stations registered a certain proportion of the Russian air sorties, but it wanted more advance information from the Intelligence Staff. The Chief of Air Command North Norway, Tufte Johnsen, had participated in several conferences with Evang, and officers had visited the Defence Staff installations at Fauske and Vadsø to organise the forwarding of information. Nonetheless, Tufte Johnsen claimed that he was not receiving complete information. The air force also flew missions in the area to give the listening service a better chance of intercepting information, and the Air Force High Command had written to Evang proposing communications procedures for such tasks – apparently without results. Evang was probably not convinced that the air force's need for such intelligence outweighed the need to preserve the secrecy of Comint information.[41]

To ensure better co-ordination between the air force and the Defence Staff during the build-up of the Elint service in eastern Finnmark, the Chief of Defence Staff in October 1959 had decided to appoint a committee to review the problem and offer constructive solutions. The mandate was wide-ranging: the extent of the development; political considerations in connection with geographical positioning; equipment requirements; etc. The air force appointed Haugland as their representative on the committee. The others were Karl Holberg, Director of Research at the Defence Research Establishment, who was elected chairman, and Major Sigmund Nielsen from the Intelligence Staff. The report from the 'Holberg Committee' was presented on 8 January 1960. The committee noted that HEKLA and NABBEN were now in full operation as permanent stations, while BARHAUG was still at an experimental stage. They recommended additional testing on Falkefjell hilltop, and the continuation of operations on Korpfjell (METRO), a station established by the Intelligence Staff to which we shall return in the next chapter. They also stressed the value of supplementing the permanent stations with registrations from boat operations.

On the central question of allocating the main responsibility for Elint, the conclusions of the Holberg Committee did not favour the takeover bid pronounced by the Intelligence Staff in the spring of 1957. All permanent stations outside the immediate border zone ought to be built, owned, run and controlled by the air force as an element of the C&W system, albeit in close contact with the Defence Staff. BARHAUG ought to be constructed as a joint effort, so that the station could cover 'the absolutely essential needs of both services'. The special circumstances dictated that it would have to be camouflaged as a combined meteorological station and an air navigation station. A crew of 18 persons would be required. Concerning the channelling of data, or in other words the actual utilisation of the Elint information, the committee recommended that 'an air force tactical warning centre' be established in the area Vardø–Høybuktmoen, possibly combined with an NIS communications and co-ordination centre.[42]

In the meantime, and at the practical level, the USAF had come up with an offer of two trailers with Elint equipment to a total value of close to a million dollars. In November 1959 representatives of the Intelligence

Staff (Martens Meyer and Reiss-Andersen) and the air force (Lieutenant-Colonel E. Ulleberg) met with the CIA and USAF in the United States to co-ordinate planning. The various initiatives and plans had now to be presented for the authorities in Norway to determine, among other things, whether the new equipment was acceptable, and whether a permanent station was to be built at BARHAUG. In mid-January 1960 the air force and the Intelligence Staff finally agreed to recommend setting up the new equipment, and to start planning for the construction of a permanent station at BARHAUG to be operated jointly by the air force and the NIS. Immediately following that meeting Evang raised the matter with State Secretary Himle at the Ministry of Defence. The latter gave permission to continue with the work, but thought that it ought to be put before the Cabinet Defence and Security Committee, 'at least as an orientation'.[43]

TOWARDS FULL AGREEMENT

In 1960 a number of meetings were held, among the relevant Norwegian institutions as well as on the bilateral US–Norwegian level, to establish a programme for the continued development of Elint in north Norway. The goal was to arrive at some sort of concord about the Elint service and about American co-operation with the Intelligence Staff and the Air Force High Command. One important outcome of the meetings was that a major modernisation of HEKLA and NABBEN would be started during the summer of 1961. USAFE now stressed the importance of establishing a long-term plan for Elint, and asked the Norwegians to produce a study by the autumn of 1961. On the basis of such a study the Americans would then present their recommendations with regard to equipment. The timetable foreseen meant that they would submit a report to Norway by the autumn of 1962. After the Norwegians had had, say, three months in which to consider the report, yet another year would pass before the equipment could be in place. As the whole process would thus not be finished until 1964, the study would have to extend its perspectives to as far ahead as 1970.

In any event, BARHAUG would be the kingpin in all these plans, and it was therefore important to get that project going. The Americans were convinced, as were the Intelligence Staff and the air force, that the selection of BARHAUG was right. The question of finance had also been discussed. Martens Meyer, who reported on the meetings to Evang,

1. Vilhelm Evang, a science graduate from Oslo University, joined the intelligence service of the Norwegian government in exile in London in 1942. From 1946 he built up and led the postwar NIS. In 1966 the lack of co-operation between him and the chief of the security police, which came to a head with the Lygren affair, forced both to resign.

2. Colonel Alfred R. Roscher Lund, who laid the foundations for a Norwegian intelligence service during the Second World War.

3. Colonel Johan Berg, who served as Chief of Intelligence, 1966–70.

4. Jens Christian Hauge, leader of the military resistance in Norway during the war; as defence minister from 1945–52 he oversaw the build-up of the NIS.

5. Three photographs taken by agents on Norwegian merchant ships in Soviet ports
(a) Golf I-class diesel submarine, equipped with three ballistic nuclear missiles; (b) a
Foxtrot-class diesel submarine with reinforced bow for passage through the Northern Sea
Route; (c) a saw mill on fire at Igarka on the Yenisei River in Siberia.

6. CIA HQ, Langley, Virginia, in the mid-1960s.

7. U-2 spy-plane, of the type shot down over Sverdlovsk on its way to Bodø, northern Norway, 1 May 1960.

8. RB-47 aircraft in flight; the reconnaissance version, RB-47E, was shot down by Soviet fighter aircraft off the Kola Peninsula 1 July 1960.

9 and 10: Key persons in the development of NIS Elint activities in the 1950s and 1960s, above, Helge Reiss-Andersen and below, Knut Willy Kval.

FIGURE 7

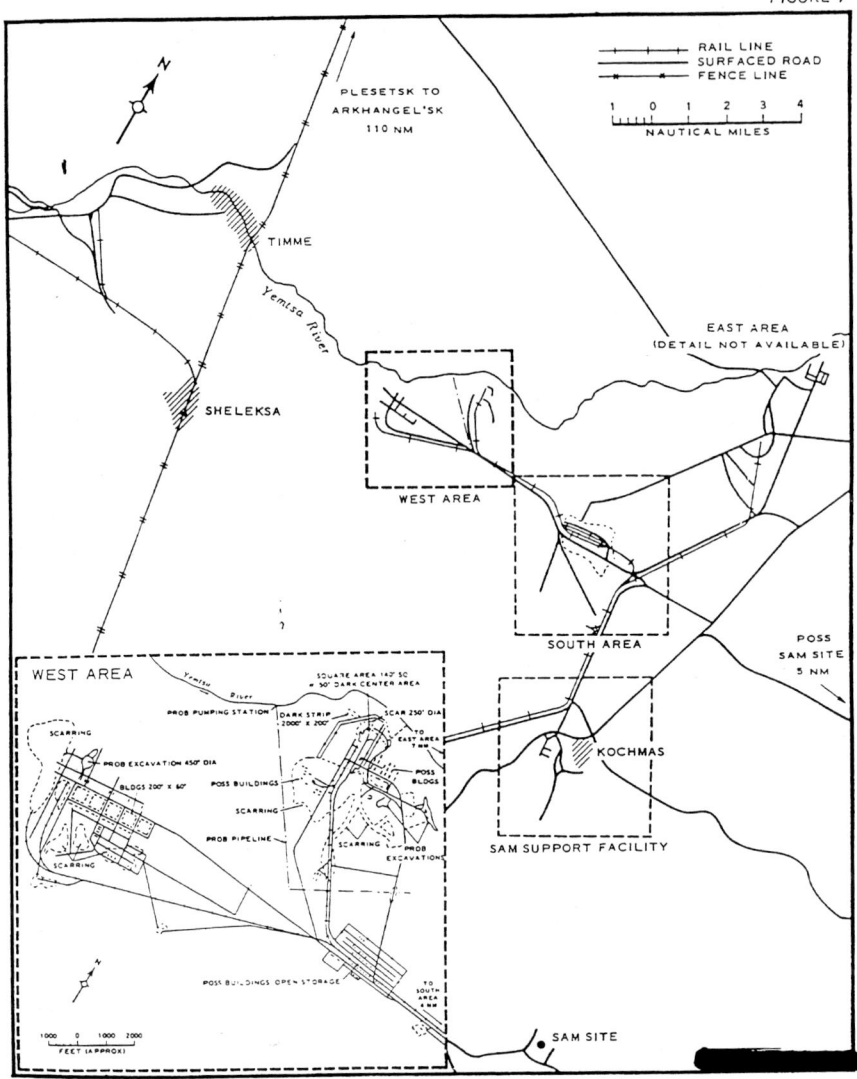

RAIL LINE
SURFACED ROAD
FENCE LINE

1 0 1 2 3 4
NAUTICAL MILES

PLESETSK TO
ARKHANGEL'SK
110 NM

N

TIMME

Yemtsa River

SHELEKSA

EAST AREA
(DETAIL NOT AVAILABLE)

WEST AREA

SOUTH AREA

POSS
SAM SITE
5 NM

WEST AREA

Yemtsa River

SQUARE AREA 142' SC
+ 50' DARK CENTER AREA

PROB PUMPING STATION

DARK STRIP
2000' X 200'

SCAR 250' DIA

TO
EAST AREA
7 NM

SCARRING

PROB EXCAVATION 450' DIA

POSS
BLDGS

BLDGS 200' X 60'

POSS BUILDINGS

SCARRING

SCARRING

PROB PIPELINE

SCARRING

PROB
EXCAVATION

SAM SUPPORT FACILITY

KOCHMAS

SCARRING

POSS BUILDINGS OPEN STORAGE

TO
SOUTH
AREA
4 NM

N

1000 0 1000 2000
FEET (APPROX)

SAM SITE

SUSPECTED ICBM DEPLOYMENT COMPLEX, PLESETSK, USSR. (Status in mid-1961)

11. Plan of ICBM launch site at Plesetsk, south of Archangel, recently made available by the CIA History Staff based on photographic reconnaissance up to 1961. The Norwegian Elint stations were among the first to detect launchings from Plesetsk, and the site remained a high-priority item throughout the 1960s.

12. Four founding members of the NIS: (a) Alf Martens Meyer; (b) Jon K. Brynildsen;
(c) Dag Falchenberg; (d) Erling Hellerslien.

13. The building on the right housed the first land station for the underwater sound surveillance system at Andøya in northern Norway at the end of the 1950s; established on an experimental basis by the Norwegian Defence Research Establishment, it became operational as a Royal Norwegian Navy station in 1963.

14. BRIDGE underwater sound surveillance system; 16 of the hydrophones shown in the top picture were anchored in pairs to triple-tube anchors (middle) lined up at great depth about 30 nautical miles offshore, and connected to the land station through a cable; for laying the cable through the shallows near shore a special barge (bottom) had to be built.

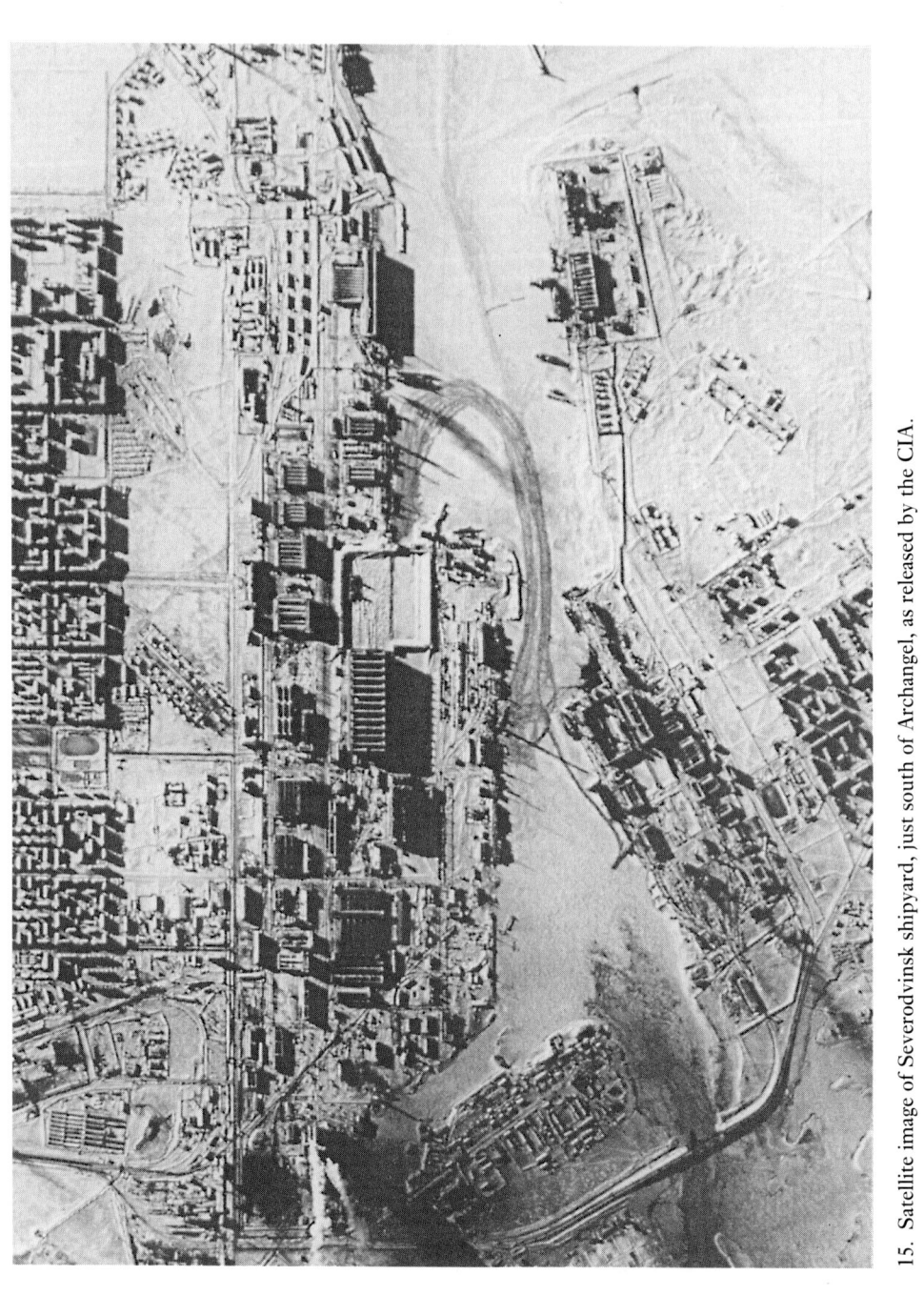

15. Satellite image of Severodvinsk shipyard, just south of Archangel, as released by the CIA.

(a)

(b)

16. METRO Elint station, two miles from the Soviet border: (a) in its earliest stages (note the special HAMILCAR aerial on the right); (b) as fully operational, from 1961.

17. Large Soviet aerial complex on Hill 220 near Luostari air base, as photographed by tele-lens from METRO in 1963; the wing-shaped aerial in the middle is a Tall King remote warning radar.

18. HEKLA Elint/Radint station at Vardø, on the Varanger Peninsula; the air force radar and early-warning station GLOBUS is in the background.

19. Interior of HEKLA, showing electronic equipment.

(a)

(b)

(c)

20. Three
generations of
vessels used
by NIS for
Elint missions:
(a) *Eger*;
(b) *Marjata I*;
(c) *Marjata II*.

21. The main Comint station, at Vadsø, on the Varanger Peninsula, with its array of special aerials.

22. The Fauske II (CODHOOK) station, established in the same area as the Fauske I Comint station east of Bodø in 1964 for the monitoring of Soviet satellite and missile activities.

23. The BARHAUG
Elint/Comint station in
Viksjøfjell, five miles from
the Soviet border: (a) the
first fixed installation;
(b) the station as completed,
1966; (c) section of the
aerial in the tower; (d) a
Comint 'position' or table.

(a)

(b)

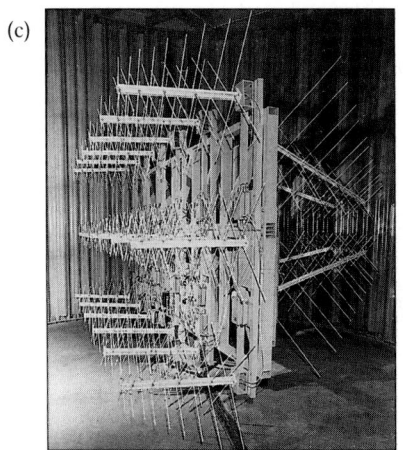

(c)

(d)

stressed the point that the United States should not finance the construction or part of the salaries, but only supply the equipment. In that way the Intelligence Staff would be in a good position to say that this was a Norwegian project under Norwegian control. He concluded his report as follows:

> It is my opinion that the meetings have been very satisfactory. The air force ... feel that they got it the way they wanted. The Defence Staff, as far as I can see, have got it the way we wanted. The CIA representative does not seem to have any objections (which he is not entitled to have anyway). In my opinion, then, they ought to feel satisfied as well. Colonel Jordan said: 'This is a prototype of how an Elint organisation ought to be.'[44]

Thus, all parties to this co-operation had for the first time attained a real consensus on the Elint service. Many factors may have contributed to this, not least the fact Martens Meyer was back in Norway after two years' leave and could take charge of this area. Also, new people, for example, General Wilhelm Mohr, were in charge in the air force. Martens Meyer found that the new men had a better understanding of the value of Elint as well as a will to work together. In a note before a new meeting with the Americans in June 1961, Evang put it this way: 'The main objective was that in the meeting with the Americans there had to be a Norwegian view and a Norwegian plan and that domestic contentions among Norwegians at the meeting would not be tolerated.' In this he received the whole-hearted support of General Mohr and Colonel Mehn-Andersen of the air force. As things looked now, a tenacious mutual scepticism between the Intelligence Staff and the air force was in the process of yielding to constructive co-operation.

NOTES

1. See NIE 11-4-1954 'Soviet Capabilities and Probable Courses of Action through Mid-1959' in CIA History Staff, *Estimates on Soviet Military Power 1954 to 1984* (CIA, Washington, DC, 1994), p. 35, and NIE 11-56 'Soviet Gross Capabilities for Attack on the US and Key Overseas Installations and Forces through Mid-1958' in CIA History Staff, *Intentions and Capabilities: Estimates on Soviet Strategic Forces, 1950–1983* (CIA, Washington, DC, 1996), p. 28.
2. On these air defence systems see Steven J. Zaloga, *Soviet Air Defense Missiles* (Jane's Information Group, London, 1989).

3. FO/E, binder 'Elektronisk E-tjeneste 1949–67', Chief of Defence Ole Berg to Air Force Chief, 28 May 1949.
4. Ibid., Naval High Command to Defence Staff, 14 Dec. 1949: 'Y-tjeneste og RCM' (Radio Counter Measures).
5. Ibid., Brynildsen to Evang, 22 Dec. 1949.
6. FO/E Box 'Historisk verdi', file 'VI. avd.', undated memo, 'Utbygging av den elektroniske etterretnings- og varslingstjeneste i Norge'. A possible explanation why electronic intelligence and not signals intelligence was used in Norway as a common term may be that both the word 'signals' and the word 'communications' would be translated as *'samband'*.
7. For these technical details we have largely relied on a study by RNoAF Lieutenant-Colonel L.W. Robertsen, annexed to a committee report from the autumn of 1960 on problems regarding reconnaissance flights in the Barents Sea area, in UD 33/6/14b.
8. FO/E, file 'Elektronisk krigføring 1949–1953', Falchenberg memo, 9 Oct. 1953.
9. Michael Herman, *Intelligence Power in Peace and War* (Cambridge University Press, Cambridge, 1996), p. 121.
10. FO/E, file 'Elektronisk krigføring 1949–1953./Y og RCM teneste'. Falchenberg to Evang, 6 Feb. 1952: 'Electronic Warfare Units. Ref. SHAPE/32/52 sig. 1460'.
11. Ibid., Evang note, 16 June 1952.
12. Ibid., L.W. Robertsen to Evang, 22 Sept. 1953.
13. FO/E, binder 'Elektronisk E-tjeneste 1949–67', Haugland's 'Memorandum. Avdeling for taktisk krigføring i flyvåpnet', 19 Aug. 1954, and author's conversation with Haugland, 31 May 1995.
14. Author's conversation with Frank Arnesen, 8 Jan. 1996.
15. On Banak air base see Håvard Klevberg, *Air Power in Finnmark: Banak air base in the Cold War, 1955–1970*, No. 4/1996 in the series *Forsvarsstudier* (IFS, Oslo, 1996).
16. See note 10.
17. FO/E, file 'Elektronisk E-tjeneste 1949–1967', Haugland memo for Major-General H. Mehre, 12 June 1956: 'Taktisk elektronisk etterretningstjeneste. Orientering. Mobil radioskvadron'.
18. Unless otherwise stated, the main sources for what follows are Haugland's 'Memorandum. Avdeling for taktisk krigføring i Flyvåpnet', 19 Aug. 1954, and his memo, 'Taktisk elektronisk etterretningstjeneste …' for Major-General H. Mehre, 12 June 1956, both in FO/E file 'Elektronisk E-tjeneste 1949–1967'.
19. FO/E, copy file H No. 6, Waage to Chief of the Air Force, 20 Sept. 1954.
20. SMK, KU, A. Andersen memo of 24 Aug. 1954, 'Møte i K.U. mandag 23. august 1954'.
21. FO/E, file 'Elektronisk E-tjeneste 1949–1967', Major-General E. Tufte Johnsen to the Defence Ministry, 2 Dec. 1954.
22. Ibid., note from Haugland to Chief of Staff of the Air Force, 23 Sept. 1955.
23. About the 'Andersen Committee', see Chapter 15 below.
24. FO/E, file 'Elektronisk E-tjeneste 1949–1967', Haugland Pro Memoria, 23 Feb. 1956, 'Forsert utbygging av Flyvåpnets elektroniske etterretningstjeneste. Generalplan'.
25. Ibid., Haugland note to L.W. Robertsen, 13 Dec. 1954, on future co-operation.
26. FO/E, file 'Elektronisk E-tjeneste 1949–1967', Haugland memorandum to air force

Chief of Staff, 23 Sept. 1955: 'Planlegging av forsert utbygging av Flyvåpenets elektroniske etterretningstjeneste'.

27. SMK, KU protocols file no. 5, meeting, 7 Feb. 1955.
28. Ibid., meeting, 14 Feb. 1955.
29. FO/E, file 'O IV/LST. 27.7.1954–18.3.1955', Haugland report of meeting with Colonel Remington, 29 March 1955.
30. FO/E, file 'Elektronisk krigføring 1954–60', Evang note of 11 April 1956.
31. FO/E, file 'Case 33.80, Folder 5. 'CREEK MAID/Elint'. Waage to Air Attaché, Oslo 27 Nov. 1956, 'USAF/RNoAF Agreement on Elint- and supplementary data'.
32. FO/E, file 'Elektronisk e-tjeneste 1949–1967', Kruse to air force Chief of Staff, 5 March 1957.
33. Ibid., Haugland memorandum, 'Angående overføring av 20. mobile radioskvadron fra Flyvåpnet til Forsvarsstaben', 13 March 1957.
34. Public Record Office, FO 371/135044, Annual Report on Norwegian Armed Forces.
35. FO/E, file 'Elektronisk e-tjeneste 1946–1967', Intelligence Staff to air force Chief of Staff 18 March 1957, with minutes by Waage.
36. FO/E, file 'Elektronisk e-tjeneste 1949–1967', Evang to air force Chief of Staff, 6 May 1957.
37. FO/E, file 'Elektronisk krigføring 1954–60', III c memo, 6 June 1957, 'Ad koordinering av Non-Comint og Comint tjenesten'.
38. FO/E, file 'Elektronisk e-tjeneste 1949–1967', Report of meeting 22–23 July 1957, submitted to NIS for information.
39. Ibid., Martens Meyer, note of 3 Dec. 1957.
40. FO/E, file 'Elektronisk e-tjeneste 1949–1967'. Chief of the Air Force to Ministry of Defence, 24 Nov. 1958.
41. On this problem see also Chapter 5.
42. FO/E, file '50.8': 'Innstilling fra utvalget til vurdering av den elektroniske e-tjenesten i Øst-Finnmark', 6 Jan. 1960.
43. FO/E, file 'Barhaug generelt I', Evang note, 13 Jan. 1960.
44. FO/E, file 'X-2 Elint–Comint drøftelser'. Martens Meyer's report of the meetings, undated.

7

Electronic Intelligence (2): The Norwegian Intelligence Service Takes Over

As we saw in the previous chapter, it was not the Intelligence Staff but rather the air force which led the way in the Elint or Non-Comint field. Some of the activities carried out under the auspices of the Intelligence Staff from the early 1950s nonetheless contained a strong Elint element. The central figure of VI Section, Alf Martens Meyer, was incessantly on the lookout for new methods to procure intelligence. The section therefore started to experiment with electronic intelligence early in the 1950s by means of boat operations in the Barents Sea during the summer months. A number of vessels were used, not least fishing boats, but also sealers. These types of boats provided good cover from inquisitive eyes, whether they happened to be Russian or Norwegian. These boats were also the cheapest and, 'for that matter, the only boats to be found'. The first such boat to be acquired for special operations was M/S *Harøysund*, bought by Martens Meyer in May 1952 and renamed M/S *Vinge*. Even though the price of 160,000 kroner was paid by the Intelligence Staff and Martens Meyer was only the formal owner, he arranged a loan from Bergens Privatbank in his own name. As to the purpose of the loan, he stated that he had plans to start fishing. But the bank director had already been informed of the circumstances, and the Ministry of Defence provided surety. An agreement was entered into with the shipping firm J. Evandt in Bergen, which accepted to act as the ship's manager. This boat was apparently mainly meant to be used in connection with border-crossing operations, and there is some doubt as to whether it ever did Elint missions.

The Intelligence Staff at this time had established good connections with the Bergen-based Radar Department of the Norwegian Defence

Research Establishment (NDRE). Of particular interest was the development of a radar search receiver or 'registration receiver' codenamed 'Forget-me-not' (in Norwegian 'Forglemmigei'), which was supposed to be able to search for, register and classify Soviet radar signals in the Barents Sea and on the Kola Peninsula. When this radar receiver proved viable, the Intelligence Staff asked to be allowed to use it for intelligence purposes. In July 1952 Martens Meyer carried out a mission with a rented 50-foot fishing smack in order 'to search for possible radar transmissions from the north Russian land mass'. The radar search was conducted along the Soviet 12-mile limit, and the NDRE recommended in their report after the mission that searching equipment be placed in the vicinity of Kiberg between Vardø and Vadsø. At the termination of the mission the equipment was, however, placed on a mountain-top near Fauske, for observation purposes during the big NATO exercise 'Main Brace' in the autumn of 1952.

After this, the development of 'Forget-me-not' was downgraded due to other engagements at the NDRE. But the Intelligence Staff did not forget. They approached the Radar Department from time to time, and Ernst Jacobsen, the man behind the design and construction, was given the task 'as an "in-between" job' of making a special version with a view to a new mission. He was given leave of absence from November 1954 to the summer of 1955 to work on the project. The apparatus was to be installed in the hold of an 85-foot Arctic fishing smack. Even though the archives are sparing on this enterprise, we know of the mission from several sources, both verbal and written accounts.[1] The vessel was the sealer *Godøynes*, the mission started in June 1955 and lasted 69 days. Typical for this activity was that Elint was only *one* element of the total objective. Comint signals were also intercepted, and this and later boat operations demonstrated the value of the combination of those activities. There was also close collaboration with the CIA which provided the electronic equipment. This was both wide ranging and advanced, and Jacobsen wrote modestly in the report about his own equipment that 'what this [...] was doing on board a ship which was already bursting at the seams with modern American searching equipment, operated by American specialists, is quite another question'. The Americans had been informed about 'Forget-me-not', and began to show interest in the project at the turn of 1954. By getting both the Norwegian prototype and their own equipment together on the same operation, they were probably able to compare efficiency and sensitivity.

The mission's cover name was SUNSHINE, and the leader was Lieutenant-Commander Bjarne W. Thorsen of the NIS. In addition to the ship's crew, five Americans and four Norwegians took part, among them Jacobsen himself. The mission's purpose was varied, with one of the tasks being to investigate conditions with a view to harbours, possible air bases, and other useful sites on Bjørnøya and Spitzbergen. Another task was to search for and locate Russian radar activity on Spitzbergen, Franz Josef Land, Novaya Zemlya, and along the Soviet Arctic coast. They were also to search for traces of radioactivity that might indicate nuclear testing. Water samples were therefore to be collected. In addition, the Norwegian Defence Research Establishment had found a method by which to determine nuclear traces in the jaw bones and muscles of seals. Hence seals were to be caught, and the seal heads salted and brought back for analysis. Some Comint monitoring was also to be undertaken.

The route for the voyage was Bergen–Tromsø–Bjørnøya (where the 'harbour and air base' personnel disembarked) – Novaya Zemlya. Here, the route took a turn to the southernmost point of Novaya Zemlya, then to the island of Kolguyev, Cape Kanin, the entrance to the White Sea, along the Murmansk coast, and then to Hammerfest in Finnmark for bunkering. Then back to Bjørnøya, to pick up the personnel left behind there, after which the trip continued to Spitzbergen where islands, straits and fjords were reconnoitred for ports, air bases, and radar activity. The special personnel disembarked once more, this time on Reinsdyrflya on north Spitzbergen, while *Godøynes* was to carry on to Franz Josef Land for more radar searches. But the ship was damaged in the Hinlopen Straits and had to be towed back to Bergen, where it arrived at the end of August. The Americans wrote a detailed report on the mission, and Bjarne Thorsen characterised the trip as successful: 'It was an expression of the thinking of that period: if NATO or the Americans were to move in, we would already know where the transmission conditions were good and where you could operate.'

From the available material it is impossible today to say whether these two missions in 1952 and 1955 were unique. The wording in some of the later reports, for example in connection with the evaluation of the activity and the issue about acquiring a special-purpose vessel, may indicate that such missions were carried out on an annual basis. There is also reason to believe that some of the DELFINUS operations performed Elint tasks. According to the Intelligence Staff, good results were at any rate obtained. The missions led to the identification of different types of

Russian electronic equipment. But even though fishing, sealing and whaling were plausible cover stories, the constant changing of ships was unfortunate. It caused problems related to installing the equipment anew each time, procuring of new crews, etc. The Intelligence Staff therefore concluded a long-term agreement in 1956 with the motor ship *Eger*, which was used for a number of years. The equipment could now be assembled in a container, and modified so that the installation procedure was easier, and costs associated with the operations were reduced. In addition, the Intelligence Staff managed to persuade the crew to remain on board for several years. Heightened requirements in regard to both equipment and results nevertheless made it necessary for the Intelligence Staff to acquire its own Sigint vessel in the 1960s. We will return to this later.

Boat operations for Sigint purposes

1952	*Vinge*
1955	*Godøynes*
1957	*Eger*
1958	*Eger*
1960	*Polartind*
1963	*Eger*
1964	*Eger*
1965	Purchase of whaler, *Globe 14*
1966–75	*Marjata* I (modified whaler)
1976	*Marjata* II (specially built)

Given the standards of the time, the Elint operations in the 1950s were deemed by the Intelligence Staff to be expensive. As time passed the size and amount of equipment grew, and the aerials became too large to be conveniently camouflaged. Also, as fishing activities in the Barents Sea suffered a sharp decline during the later 1950s, it became steadily more difficult to invent a reasonable cover story. As we have already seen, operations of this kind did have their weaknesses, in part due to their intermittent nature. Moreover, since one had to keep one's distance from the Russian coastline, interception of stations located further inside Russian territory, or operating on very high frequencies, was impossible.

ESTABLISHING A PERMANENT NIS ELINT STATION – METRO

With the experience of the first boat operations in mind, the Intelligence Staff in the summer of 1955 initiated a so-called passive, stationary electronic intelligence service from an observation cabin on Korpfjell, some two to three kilometres from the Russian border. This was the first step on the road to a permanent Elint station in east Finnmark for the Intelligence Staff. When the border guard cabin Korpfjell was rebuilt a couple of years later with a visual observation service in mind, the idea arose to use this building also for special electronic observations. The size of the tower and the layout of the operation rooms were designed, therefore, with an eye to 'Forget-me-not'. The construction work started in August 1957. Thus the groundwork was laid for the Elint station which bore the name of METRO. The station began operations in 1958, but changes had been made to the plans. It appeared that the first 'Forget-me-not' receiver was still not ready. Work was therefore limited to visual observations in addition to some tests with ordinary radio receivers to register special signals in the VHF band. In the autumn of 1958 the first 'Forget-me-not' was ready to be installed on Korpfjell. But Martens Meyer felt that the receiver did not satisfy requirements. The plan was therefore modified to include the installation of American search receivers and other necessary equipment for the analysis and recording of the signals.

In 1957 V and VI sections were also working on preparations for some stationary Non-Comint activity outside the METRO initiative. One of the first plans involved installing a receiver at Sæter on the outskirts of Oslo, for test operations, coincidental with the proposed visit of an expert from the Swedish Armed Forces Radio Division to hold a course on the subject. At the completion of the course, and depending on the results of the tests, the receiver was to be sent to Vadsø for test runs there and possibly at various other locations in eastern Finnmark. The starting date was to be 1 June 1958.[2]

The first search operations at METRO, codenamed ICEBOX, got under way in November 1958. This operation had three main objectives: (1) to provide a non–stop electronic surveillance of Luostari air base and the surrounding area; (2) to collect technical data as a basis for the technical planning to be carried out with a view to the further exploitation of this area; and (3) to exploit all possibilities to combine the gathering of Elint, Comint and visual observations. The operation was ended in December 1958, partly because the personnel were required elsewhere, and partly because a thorough analysis of the collected intelligence was needed before determining the further development of the activities. This analysis showed firstly that the stations covered a larger area than expected; secondly that signals had been registered which indicated the existence of hitherto unknown electronic equipment; and thirdly that the combination of different collection methods could furnish results which were hitherto impossible to achieve. A decision was therefore taken to resume the work as soon as circumstances permitted and, moreover, to supplement the station with more equipment for further registration and analysis of the newly observed signals.

Operation ICEBOX resumed in February 1959, and was carried on continuously for a period of six months, with three to five operators. The cover story was that the station was a combined weather forecast and air navigation station. The results again showed coverage of an area larger than expected, furnishing new and unknown signals such as a radar-type signal on a hitherto unused frequency in the S-band, possibly a new type data link, and – more curiously – television signals from Leningrad relayed through a repeater station in Murmansk. The station still suffered from a number of technical flaws, but the delivery of more new American equipment promised to rectify most of those. In addition, there were practical difficulties: bad roads, lack of water and power, and insufficient space for the aerials. At the same time, essential changes had to be balanced against the wish for as few breaks in the search activity as possible. Search operations began again in the late autumn of 1959, and proceeded without interruptions until 1 August 1960. Then operations were halted to enable, amongst other things, reconstruction of the tower with an aerial radome on top. But from the end of November 1960 search activity was resumed, from January 1961 on a 24-hour basis.[3]

In a meeting of the Control Committee for the intelligence service (28 May 1960) improvements of the observation tower, the power supply, and construction of an access road to Korpfjell were considered. The fact that this meeting took place at the height of the tension surrounding the U-2 incident may explain that the committee felt it necessary to refer the matter to the Cabinet Defence and Security Committee. A brief note from Evang to State Secretary Himle stressed the need to have a combined Elint and visual observation post very close to the border in order to monitor the activity on an important Soviet air base such as Luostari, especially 'now that the allied flights in the Barents region have stopped'. Himle also had a meeting with Martens Meyer where he interrogated him about all the details of the proposal. Probably as another sign of the heightened tension in the wake of the U-2 affair,[4] Defence Minister Nils Handal now decided to see for himself – without prior notification to Evang – the intelligence activity in Eastern Finnmark, before making his proposals to the Cabinet Committee. Armed with thorough briefing notes from State Secretary Himle, the minister visited Korpfjell, BARHAUG, and Høybuktmoen from 14 to 17 June.[5]

Evang seems to have been somewhat apprehensive about the minister's visit, which is not surprising in view of the current political reservations about the amount of intelligence installations and activities in that area. Quite apart from the air force EW radar and HEKLA Elint installations at Vardø and NIS Comint station at Vadsø, both on the northern side of Varanger fjord, there was now in southern Varanger, within ten miles of the Soviet border, the NABBEN air force Elint station and the MOEN NIS Comint station, by Høybuktmoen, and METRO and BARHAUG right next to the border. However, Evang was clearly relieved when the reports of the visit, both from the station chiefs and from the State Secretary, all indicated that Handal had been favourably impressed with what he had seen and heard. He had been particularly positive about the value of METRO, although he had some misgivings about the expansive character of the BARHAUG project.

In its memorandum to the Cabinet Committee's 20 June meeting, the Ministry of Defence gave the purpose of METRO as electronic mapping of the Russian control, warning and communications system, determination of the Soviet order of battle, studies of tactics and operational procedures for the Russian air forces and, finally, as a supplement to our own warning system: Elint was able to register changes in the military activity in the base areas, thus providing evidence of increased activity prior to an actual attack. The results so far of the Elint effort at Korpfjell were characterised as 'very good', especially after the station had begun to operate around the clock. On 20 June the Cabinet Committee then approved the proposed operational improvements for METRO. But in view of the proposals for a joint air force/NIS Elint station at nearby BARHAUG, it was decided to postpone consideration of improvements to the staff accommodation at Korpfjell.[6]

PLANNING FOR THE 1960s

While METRO was being developed, the organisation of Elint in the Intelligence Staff was undergoing changes. Helge Reiss-Andersen was now in charge on the operational side, and was also given the task of preparing the establishment of an Elint analysis and planning centre in

Oslo. At the end of 1959 Martens Meyer was called back from the Far East to become the NIS Elint chief. Through the efforts of Major Bjørn Egge, Elint was then being established as a separate section – Section VI – whereas Comint was renamed Section V. Martens Meyer obviously had far-reaching plans for his section. In spite of the expansion which we have seen occurred towards the end of the 1950s, the need for more and better intelligence was accelerating. A survey from the end of 1960 stated that the range covered by the Norwegian Elint stations on a regular, continuous, basis was probably no more than a 100 kilometre radius against targets on the ground. An upgrading of the stations with the technical facilities then available would mean the doubling of this range. For targets in the air, that is, emissions from aircraft, the range was much greater, depending on the altitude of the plane. For air targets at 30,000 feet, under optimal conditions, and with improved aerials at HEKLA and BARHAUG, it would be possible to cover most of the Kola Peninsula.[7]

In the autumn of 1960 the Norwegians and the Americans exchanged views and desires concerning further development of Elint activity in Norway. An 11-page unsigned Norwegian memorandum, which was submitted to the CIA, stressed among other things the need for better communications between the Elint stations themselves, between the Elint stations and the EW radar stations, and finally between Elint and Comint. In regard to the existing stations the memorandum pointed to certain shortcomings. The HEKLA station at Vardø had a 'black-out' sector to the north due to the location there of the Air Force EW radar station. NABBEN by Høybuktmoen was handicapped by mountains between it and the border. METRO, while its eastward and – particularly – southward range was excellent, had a 'black-out' sector to the north which was also due to mountains. All these stations were in the process of being re-equipped and improved. But – and this was evidently the main point of the exercise – BARHAUG was from all points of view the best site for a major Elint station, except that it would be very expensive to build.

At a three-day meeting in Washington in February 1961 a draft plan for a Norwegian Elint organisation was presented. The main points concerned collection work in East Finnmark and an analysis centre in Oslo. Both the Intelligence Staff and the air force were still bent on running their own Elint activity, in co-operation with the respective American organisations. In addition, there was a triangular project in which both the Intelligence Staff and the air force participated. There was complete agreement about the plans as they were laid before the Americans in 1961, and the expansion work continued.

The American interests in the Elint field were formulated in a 14-page memorandum[8] which the air attaché at the US embassy forwarded to the Intelligence Staff and the air force in November 1960. It was stressed that the memorandum merely expressed USAFE's interest, 'and not requirements levied on you. It is fully recognized that your Elint collection efforts are strictly a national program. Any requirements and recommendations made by USAFE through this office are merely in the form of guidance rather than direction.' As to which form the data to be delivered to the Americans should have, the air attaché wrote that they would like 'raw' data on new and unusual signals, and processed data, studies, and summaries for other signals.

The USAFE objectives for Elint were divided into five categories:

1. *Elint which might indicate present or future Soviet intentions to initiate hostilities.* This could take the form of a noticeable increase in the volume of signals, suggesting heightened activity or preparedness, or an abnormally low level of activity which might indicate major redeployment of electronics equipment. Other indications might be the appearance of many new or uncommon signals, unusual density of signals in the vicinity of bases for heavy bombers or missiles and, finally, jamming of Allied frequencies on such a wide geographical scale that it could indicate preparation for attack.

2. *Elint in connection with present and future Soviet capabilities to launch a nuclear attack.* At this point the main interest was in the characteristics, the location, and the operational patterns of all electronics associated with the launching and control of missiles of all categories, or offensive air operations.

3. *Elint which revealed Soviet bloc capabilities to defend against attack from the air.* This referred especially to anti-missile capabilities, and is an early indication of Western fears that the Soviet bloc might be developing an ABM (anti-ballistic missile) defence system.

4. *Elint which could say something about scientific and technical strengths or weaknesses related to Soviet military and economic capabilities.*

5. *Elint which was evidence of advances in the electronic field, such as utilisation of very low or extremely high frequencies.*

The memorandum went on to stress the importance of collateral information from other sources such as Comint. While Elint provided a type of information enabling the analyst to determine the characteristics of radiated signals, other intelligence would help to determine the function and capability of the radiating device. There followed a long and detailed list of the kinds of questions to which the Norwegian stations might look for answers in such collateral information, and then present in narrative or statistical form. As for the Norwegian Elint stations, their top priority should be searching for indicators of new or little-known equipment and, after that, on evidence of new locations for known radar or other equipment. New or unusual signals should be both audio-recorded and filmed.

Through this memorandum, and a series of expert meetings during 1960 and 1961, it was becoming abundantly clear that the Americans attached increasing value to the Norwegian intelligence effort targeted on Soviet air and nuclear activities in northern Russia and the Barents area. The Norwegian Air Force High Command put their own interpretation on this interest:

> Eastern Finnmark is one of the few places within the NATO area where ground-based Elint equipment can exercise surveillance over a militarily very important Soviet area. The electronic developments in this area dispel any doubts that the Soviet Union is here preparing the launch platform for an attack against NATO's most important partner – the United States of America – if war should come. The USA is totally aware of this, and cannot refrain from procuring for itself the necessary information on the military–technical developments in this area. If Norway can provide this information passively from Norwegian territory, then this Norwegian activity may very likely contribute to an easing of security–political tensions in the area, since it should cause a reduction in Elint activity by allied aircraft and ships.[9]

The purpose of this statement was to provide further argument for the development of a new major Elint station, BARHAUG, on Viksjøfjell close to the Soviet border. According to the air force this had been their choice already in 1955, but it had then been turned down for political reasons. While the Elint results from the existing stations had been good, they had clearly shown that no location measured up to Viksjøfjell. It was the only hilltop in Norwegian territory with a relatively free horizon in all directions of interest and which can be built up with reasonable efforts. It has such a commanding place that it not only covers a larger sea and air area than other stations, but will also make it possible to monitor electronic activity on the ground which cannot be picked up at other locations.

There was still the problem of financing. On 6 January 1961 the air force had written to the Defence Minister that the Americans, when reminded of this problem, had stated that they could not at the time find the extra millions for construction in addition to the 10 million already allocated for equipping the station. The proposal was now to approve BARHAUG in principle, and provide some modest Norwegian funds for the preparatory construction work. This the Defence Ministry accepted in September, after some skirmishes about the cost estimates provided. Work could then begin, with a projected completion date in early 1963.

SEARCHING FOR SOVIET SLBMs

While work continued on the BARHAUG project, other Elint operations were initiated. Among the tasks the United States wished to be carried out, the collection of technical and operational data on Soviet ballistic missiles came to play a major role. At a meeting between US and Norwegian experts in the autumn of 1961, the Americans said that Norwegian Comint intercepts had made it clear that the Soviet Union was performing tests with missiles launched from submarines in the Barents Sea. The missiles seemed to have a range of 200 nautical miles and to reach an altitude of 54 kilometres. But there were two important questions which could not be answered by Comint alone, namely whether the missiles were launched while the submarines were submerged or on the surface, and what type of fuel was being used. This was now a high priority project, and a search programme was agreed which would involve the Vardø radar station and METRO. New equipment would be needed, including infrared instruments to measure the burn intensity of the missile during launching. Hydrophones would be useful to determine possible submerged launchings.[10] A draft for a detailed plan for this project named it MAD CAT, as an acronym for Mobile Automatic Digital Collection and Analysis Trailers. Major Helge Reiss-Andersen was appointed as

Norwegian project officer and sent to America in January 1962 to participate in the planning.

In a report dated 10 May 1962 Reiss-Andersen informed the Intelligence Staff about the work in progress. The MAD CAT project was to consist of two land-based stations, Vardø and Korpfjell (METRO). Vardø would be equipped with a special tracking radar, and would also have Elint, infra-red, and optical equipment installed, in addition to serving as terminal for the hydrophone equipment. Korpfjell would receive Elint, infra-red, and optical monitoring equipment. Due to the short flight-time of the missiles, much of the measuring and registration effort would have to be automated.[11]

It was hoped to have the system in operation by 1 December 1962, but this was to prove wildly optimistic. Among other things the special tracking radar never materialised, and the replacement radar required major modifications. Not until November 1963 could it be said that the system was fully operational. In the meantime the project's 'nickname' had been changed from MAD CAT to SOUTH SEA (sometimes referred to as CORVUS, but more often as GLOBUS, in Norwegian documents). This was just the beginning of a profusion of nicknames associated with the project: in June 1965 SOUTH SEA changed its name to MAID MARIAN, and then to CREEK MAID well over a year later. The code name OLD AGE, which also crops up, appears to have been reserved for the air force Elint share in the project.

The main problem which MAD CAT/SOUTH SEA encountered was the installation of the new radar and radome at Vardø; difficult weather conditions also played their part. The project's first successful intercept of a Soviet SLBM occurred in January 1965, followed by four more intercepts through the spring and summer that year. In spite of ongoing modifications of the equipment, 1966 seems also to have been a fairly successful year, with seven so-called 'events' recorded, with four more 'events' having gone unrecorded. The system was then 'off the air' for most of 1967, but came on again with a single intercept in 1968. This was determined as an SL-4, which was a space-launch vehicle for satellites, although the data collected were unsatisfactory for a proper analysis. In 1969 and 1970 several successful intercepts of missile firings were made. At the same time a study was undertaken to see if the system could also be used to detect missile launches from Plesetsk, where the first land-based Soviet ICBM launch base was being built.[12] There we have to leave the story of MAD CAT/SOUTH SEA.

MOBILE ELINT OPERATIONS IN THE 1960s

We left the mobile boat operations as towards the end of the 1950s their cost-effectiveness was in doubt. Hence the NIS concentration on permanent land-based stations at METRO and later BARHAUG, as well as its co-operation with the air force on HEKLA and NABBEN. However, since different locations could serve different purposes, and close-range monitoring could serve to supplement or corroborate data from the permanent stations, there was still need for mobile operations both on land and at sea. Mobile operations on land in the Pasvik valley during the 1960s – the HAMILCAR/ORION operations – had as a main purpose to search for Soviet SA-2 and SA-3 ground-to-air missile installations. More was expected of the various boat operations which were carried out, known by a succession of code names such as ELINOR, CYKLUS, CATHERINE and CARMEN. The boat operations, some of which took the form of DELFINUS operations, often combined both Elint and Comint missions, and went eastward from Finnmark along the Soviet Arctic coast. Among the targets were Soviet radar stations, naval vessels and missile launchings. The actual and promised results of those operations persuaded the Intelligence Staff that, instead of relying on hired boats, it would be better to purchase a ship which could then be specially equipped for the purpose. This was approved by the Control Committee in 1965, and a whaler was bought with financial support from the United States. The boat was named *Marjata*, and an agreement was made with the Norwegian Defence Research Establishment which made them the formal operator of the vessel. *Marjata* carried out its first missions in 1966. The boat soon became the object of intense interest from Soviet aircraft and naval vessels, and some 'incidents' were reported. But the Intelligence Staff did not regard these as serious enough to discontinue the operations, since 'Soviet naval units play the same game all over the world, and specially against US units'.

In 1969 *Marjata* completed eight cruises. One of these was along the Norwegian coast for the purpose of listening in on Norwegian military traffic. The other seven went to the Barents Sea, using Ramfjordnes near Tromsø as a supply base. According to the Intelligence Staff's assessment, which comprises a report of more than 100 pages, the cruises had provided 'some very good results'. Among the most interesting finds were observations and pictures of exercises with landing troops from the sea, intercepted video transmissions of radar images from SS-N-3 missiles to the launch platform, and an unidentified platform with a new radar for anti–submarine warfare. A part of the mission had been to inspect the Soviet radars around the Barents Sea. The Intelligence Staff greatly prized *Marjata*'s performance: 'It is always reassuring to have CARMEN in the area [the Barents Sea] as our most advanced observation and warning post.' Major observations were reported immediately to the Intelligence Staff, and to the intelligence 'cell' at Defence Command Northern Norway, Reitan. To maintain an unbroken watch on whatever was going on, the Intelligence Staff were of the opinion that yet another vessel was needed. Thus, that very same year, they started to prepare a new boat acquisition; at the start of the 1970s, the curtain could thus be raised on *Marjata* II.

NIS TAKES CHARGE OF ELINT

While the air force's station complex at Vardø became heavily involved in the MAD CAT/SOUTH SEA project concerning Soviet SLBM launches, it still had important functions to perform in the ongoing Elint and Radint programmes, largely for Early Warning purposes. Basically, the interaction between the two programmes was that the Elint stations were able to assist the radar by intercepting aircraft before they entered radar coverage, provided the aircraft's radars were transmitting. But this required continuous 'sweeping' of a wide frequency range. The radar, in its turn, could assist the Elint stations by alerting them about 'silent' aircraft within radar range. The advantage of radar for Early Warning purposes was its ability to cover an area quickly, since an FPS-8 radar displayed a two-dimensional picture of the area every 15 seconds. Analysis of the joint effort had three stages. First came a basic on-site analysis, for quality control and programming of searches. Then there was the thorough intermediate analysis, done jointly by the Oslo analysis centre and USAFE according to their different requirements. Here the Oslo centre would correlate the Elint information with information from other sources, for Norwegian consumption, whereas USAFE would integrate the information into the wider European picture for NATO purposes. A third and final stage would then be performed by specialised, professional USAF analysts in case of unknown or unusual signals which needed correlating with information from all other sources.[13]

USAF support for the Norwegian air force's Elint activities at HEKLA (Vardø) and NABBEN (Høybuktmoen) was formalised in a programme first called OLD AGE and then – from 1965 – ROCKY MOUNT. By 1965 it also included BARHAUG; a projected communications centre nicknamed EUREKA which eventually became the Sigint 'cell' at Defence Command North Norway; the airborne Elint equipment on board SA-16 aircraft, and the so-called TIPSEY analysis centre in Oslo. The collaboration was formalised in a detailed Memorandum of Understanding signed in Oslo on 6 December 1965 by Evang together with representatives of USAFE and RNoAF. This stated, among other things, that while USAF would provide all the equipment and logistical support, the Norwegians would provide land, installations, operations and support personnel, and operating expenses.[14]

While equipment at the stations was continually being updated, the rapid growth of activities brought into focus the difficulty for the air force in providing qualified personnel to operate the equipment. This again brought to the fore the slumbering plan about the NIS takeover of the Elint stations of the air force. During 1965 the military members of the Control committee repeatedly suggested that the time had come for the air force to pull out of Elint and leave the operations to the NIS. As a preliminary measure the Chief of Defence in November 1965 said that he and the Chief of the Air Force now agreed that BARHAUG should be transferred to the Intelligence Staff, 'in a way which does not reflect unfavourably on the Air Force'. One might for instance state that as the air force had built and established BARHAUG, it might now be possible to close down METRO and thereby save on personnel.[15]

A committee was now appointed to study the modalities of the transfer – or 'merger' as it tended to be called in order to spare the air force's feelings. To ensure that RNoAF should continue to get the benefit of the Elint effort, it was decided to reinforce the intelligence element of the air operations centre at Defence Command Northern Norway, and to give BARHAUG a central co-ordinating function for all intelligence collection in the area. METRO had been closed down, and the equipment there transferred to BARHAUG next door in 1966. In regard to the air force station at Vardø, which combined the Early Warning radar establishment with the HEKLA Elint station, it was decided to separate the two so as to let the air force retain the EW function.[16] Finally, on 10 August 1967 the Ministry of Defence instructed the air force that their station Høybuktmoen with BARHAUG be transferred to the Intelligence Staff as from 1 September, and that HEKLA, as well as the Elint elements at Defence Command Northern Norway, likewise be transferred as from

1 January 1968. Of the 132 posts required for Elint at those establishments – 90 at BARHAUG/Høybuktmoen, 30 at HEKLA, and 12 at Reitan – 100 were to be manned by the personnel transferred from the air force, and the remaining 32 would be filled by NIS personnel.[17] A long process had thereby been brought to its conclusion. In the Intelligence Staff the Elint and Comint sections had been joined together in an electronic intelligence division two years earlier. With the addition of the Elint personnel now transferred from the air force, this division now counted over 800 employees.

The Intelligence Staff towards the end of the 1960s felt the need to assemble and formalise the various projects which had been the subject of more or less formal MOUs or agreements with the United States. With 800 personnel already covered by the projects, and with plans for hiring another 120 during the coming years, it is understandable that the Defence Staff wished for confirmation from the United States of the agreements on which this joint effort was based. Without the approximately 80 per cent of the expenses covered by the United States, the present level of activity could not be maintained. So far there was no indication that the United States was considering reducing its involvement. The total investment on the part of the United States, in addition to new plans and current agreements, mitigated against such a development. Added confirmation of this could be found in a memo from Richard Helms, who was to take over as the new CIA chief, to the Intelligence Staff. The memo had been sent via the American contact in Norway. The perspective was there expanded to include the whole of the Sigint service. Helms availed himself of the opportunity to underline that the intelligence services of the United States also were interested in a reorganisation of the Norwegian signals intelligence set-up, because they wanted to ensure a continued association with the NIS in the area of Sigint.[18]

In meetings with their Norwegian opposite numbers – in particular Colonel Erling Kruse, who since 1966 was head of the Electronic Intelligence Division, and Helge Reiss-Andersen as chief of the Elint section – the Americans now also felt a need to formalise the various bilateral arrangements in the Elint field. In particular, they found it 'difficult to explain to higher authorities the details of this relationship in terms of number of personnel required, and equipment and facilities necessary for you to properly conduct the activity in accordance with the level of operations deemed necessary to accommodate our mutual interest in this field'.[19]

By 1970 Elint, while still employing less than half the number of people engaged in Comint, had grown into a very important part of the Norwegian intelligence effort. This new status became formally acknowledged through an assembling of the various projects in a new Memorandum of Understanding, referred to as NORUSA II, which was signed on 1 August 1970.[20] Its general clauses conformed closely with the first NORUSA agreement, and included the mutual assurance against the provision of intelligence material to third countries, except to the United Kingdom and Canada. The Elint stations which by that memorandum had in a sense 'come home', were: BARHAUG (64 personnel), HEKLA (34 personnel), CARMEN (13 personnel), further the new telemetry station at Fauske, CODHOOK (42 personnel), and the analysis and administrative units at Reitan (12 personnel) and at Sæter (37 personnel).

NOTES

1. Documentation on 'Forglemmigei' and the two boat missions is in both the archives of the NDRE (file 663, 1970, with reports from Ernst Jacobsen), and in FO/E, file 'Forglemmigei'. Also authors' interviews with Bjarne Thorsen and Frank Arnesen.
2. FO/E file '33.04.3 METRO historikk (1957–1967)', Klungsøyr to Evang, 17 Dec. 1957 'NonCominttjenesten'.
3. Ibid., Reiss-Andersen status report to head of E VI, 19 Aug. 1959, and unsigned nine-page report on METRO improvements, dated 26 May 1961.
4. FO/E, file 'Kontrollutvalget, notater m.v. 1958–1961': Protocol of meeting 28 May; Evang to Himle 31 May; and Martens Meyer note to Evang, 7 June 1960.
5. Ibid., Himle memo, 'Oversikt …', 10 June, and Evang note, 'Statsråd Handals besøk …', 17 June 1960.
6. SMK, Defence Ministry memo, 7 June, and RSU protocol of meeting, 20 June, 1960.
7. UD, 33/6/14b, Annex 3 to the report from a committee to review the problems regarding reconnaissance flights in the Barents region, autumn 1960.
8. FO/E, file 'Hist.matr. Grønn Ringperm'. US Air Attaché to NIS and RNoAF, 22 Nov. 1960.
9. FO/E, file 'Elektronisk e–tjeneste 1949–1967', RNoAF to Evang and Defence commands, 22 March 1961.
10. FO/E, file '33.51 Rakettutskytninger'. Evang's note of conference, 30 Nov. 1961.
11. FO/E, file '33.00 mappe 5. CREEK MAID/Elint'; 'Prosjekt 'MAD CAT' status rapport pr. 1. mai 1962'.
12. FO/E, collection of documents from Vardø station. 'GLOBUS. Introduction.'
13. Ibid., 'HEKLA. Technical description of the Norwegian air force sites, Hekla and Nabben'.
14. FO/E, file '33.00 Mappe 4. CREEK ROCK/Elint', MOU of 6 Dec. 1965.
15. FO/E, file 'Barhaug generelt I', Evang note, 9 Nov. 1965, 'Barhaug–Metro'.

16. FO/E, green file 'Overføring av Elint fra LOK til FST/E', committee report dated 7 March 1966.
17. FO/E, file 'O IV/LST. 27.7.54–18.3.68'. Chief of Air Staff to Air Command North Norway, 19 Aug. 1967: 'Overføring av Luftforsvarets elektroniske etterretning-stjeneste til Forsvarets Utenriks- og Etterretningstjeneste'.
18. FO/E, Red cassette No. 6, note from Helms to Evang, 27 June 1966.
19. FO/E, file 'MOU–E-B 01.11', note to Kruse, 30 Dec. 1969.
20. Ibid., MOU signed 1 July 1970.

8

Sound Waves in the Seas:
BRIDGE/SOSUS/CANASTA

As submarines gradually began to deploy long-distance nuclear missiles in the 1950s and 1960s, their role in the area of strategic planning in the Cold War became increasingly important. They constituted an element of a combined deterrent capability which rested primarily on their ability to conceal themselves when out on patrol. Given this state of affairs, none of the parties to a war could count on neutralising the enemy's potential in this area. But even prior to this, when submarines were conventionally powered and carried conventional weaponry, great efforts were made in military research establishments to come up with methods and devices to counteract submarine warfare, generally rendered as ASW (Anti-Submarine Warfare). One of the most important aspects of this effort was the development of a submarine detection system. If one could keep tabs on where the submarines happened to be at any time by means of a system like this, then it would represent an important supplement to the intelligence picture.

As we have mentioned several times, nuclear weapons were a central element of the arms race which was gaining pace between the Soviet Union and the Western powers in the 1950s. Just as important as the weapons themselves were the so-called 'means of delivery', of which there were three types: intercontinental ballistic missiles (ICBMs), strategic bombers, and submarines. Scientists and the weapons industry in the Soviet Union were extremely active within all three areas, though which of them was most important varied from time to time. In one important phase, from around 1957 to 1961, the development of ICBMs was clearly a top priority. At that time the Soviet submarine force possessed mostly diesel-powered boats of the Zulu, Foxtrot and Golf types, equipped with nuclear torpedoes and short-distance missiles. But from 1961 the development of nuclear-powered, missile-bearing submarines moved to centre-stage, with the Hotel-class boats as the first type to see operational service. This was the Soviet Union's answer to the Kennedy administration's defence budget increase, where the focus was on a seagoing strategic force in the form of Polaris submarines and massive aircraft carriers. These types of mobile weapon platforms were the most likely to survive the initial nuclear phase of a major war, and were therefore seen as constituting what was called a 'second-strike capability'.[1]

On the Western side there were good grounds to keep a very watchful eye on what was going on in this area. An invisible fleet of Soviet submarines in the western Atlantic, loaded with nuclear warheads pointing at targets in the United States, added a new dimension to the threat as it was perceived from the United States. From the point of view of Norway and Western Europe, this development represented primarily a threat to the transoceanic deployment of all forms of military support from the United States to Europe. The development of methods by which to register the passage of Soviet submarines to and from bases on the Kola Peninsula could give Western intelligence an idea of the Soviet navy's operational pattern, and a forewarning of any potentially offensive moves.

The results of research and development in this field formed the basis of the various acoustic intelligence systems, Acoustint or Acint. The system is based on the simple fact that submarines emit noises, and that sound waves propagating in water have the ability to travel very far indeed. There are, however, many obstacles that have to be tackled by a system of this nature: one is that sound waves travel at differing speeds depending upon salt content, temperature, etc. of the water; different layers of the water have different sound propagation characteristics; and the sound of a submarine is only one of many in a variegated world of sounds beneath the surface of the oceans. In practical terms, the way such a system works is that sounds are intercepted by hydrophones which are attached to moored buoys in the sea and connected by cables. The deeper the hydrophones, the better the result. Cables are stretched from the hydrophone systems to a station on land. This station contains electronic equipment to record and analyse the sound signals, and the 'decryption' requires breaking down the sound spectrum and examining every individual frequency interval. The result is printed out, and the sounds can be identified on the print-out as produced by propellers, engines, pumps, etc.[2] Along the way this method was supplemented by dropping sonar buoys into the sea from aircraft. A cable was attached to the buoy with a hydrophone on the other end, 60 or 180 feet under the surface. The plane carried a special system for submarine detection which intercepted the signals made by the hydrophones. Even though these hydrophones could not be sunk to such great depths and were less sensitive than the anchored hydrophones, this method had its advantages, as we shall see.

After the war a separate section embracing ASW was incorporated into the Norwegian Defence Research Establishment (NDRE), with the collection of hydrographic data as one of its major tasks. This type of data included such things as the characteristics of the water, i.e. the proportion of salt, its temperature, circulation, etc., and information needed to allow the drawing of sea charts, the characteristics of particular stretches of water, timetables for the tides, etc. American and British interest in such analyses led to a trilateral collaboration in oceanography from 1951 onwards. For the detection of submarines, the institute focused its efforts on the registration and identification of submarines passing through the Norwegian Sea. An arrangement which was entered into in 1957 as part of the Mutual Weapons Development Programme (MWDP) – initially for two years, but subsequently extended – was supposed to complete a project whose aim was the collection of as much information as possible on submarine traffic, with a view to the establishment of a long-range, underwater listening station in the north. The programme included operating an experimental station in the area.[3]

This project was called BRIDGE, later also referred to as BRIDGE I, and the US navy was the partner on the American side. Andøya had been selected as the best location, and a temporary testing station was built at Stave. A hydrophone antenna was placed offshore at a depth of about 1,000 metres. According to the NDRE, the first results suggested that it would be possible to 'close' the gap between North Norway and the island of Jan Mayen in this manner. This was probably aiming too high. But the optimism engendered by the efforts was sufficient basis from which to launch a proposal to extend BRIDGE with a BRIDGE II project, which was to last from 1 July 1960 to 31 December 1962.[4] During this second project period the NDRE developed LYDIA, a listening system centred on a specially made digital processor for the correlation analysis of aural signals, with a short range but of high precision in establishing the actual *position* of the submarine. In fact, the aim was to be able to determine the position of the sound source with such accuracy that weapons could be fired towards the target from land. The system never matched the aspirations, but for a while the Americans demonstrated great interest in it and shared the costs. In the meantime the Americans were also developing their own systems, commonly referred to as SOSUS (Sound Surveillance System), and more specifically, LOFAR (Low Frequency Analysis and Recording). The range of these systems was much wider, but did not give accurate positions.

BRIDGE I had indicated the existence of a relatively stable deep-water stratum which covered large parts of the seascape between North Norway and Jan Mayen. By placing a number of hydrophones in this layer with the aim of intercepting signals on very low frequencies, it was assumed that the existing listening system would be improved. According to the NDRE this represented a logical extension of BRIDGE I. At the same time, investigations were to be carried out to determine whether this layer could also be used as a communications channel between the buoys moored in the sea and the station on land. In such a case the detection zone could be expanded to several hundred kilometres. In a Ministry of Defence memorandum the new project was referred to as a logical continuation of the desire to determine how far it would be possible, by passive means, to locate submarines passing between North Norway and Jan Mayen. The Norwegian and the United States navies as well as NATO felt there was an 'urgent' need to cover northern waters. Registering not only the *passage* of submarines but also *where* these occurred was a part of the project, although this was rather optimistic. The memorandum divided the plan into an oceanographic part, 'continuing to chart the sea from Andøya to Jan Mayen', and a signals part. Of the expenses to the tune of 6.3 million kroner, the United States would cover about 4.5 million, and the NDRE would bear the rest.[5]

On 5 January 1960 Defence Minister Handal presented the project to the Cabinet Defence and Security Committee. He reported the Naval High Command's opinion that the tests might make possible 'an efficient passive, defensive location line for submarines from Andøya to Jan Mayen'. He also emphasised that the project was in the nature of a scientific experiment. The question of permanent installations and running expenses would only arise at a later stage. The Cabinet Committee had 'no objection against the NDRE's entering into agreements with the American authorities about continued economic and technical support for an extension of the test project'.

TESTING THE BRIDGE SYSTEM

In the NDRE's annual report for 1962 the outcome of the project so far was characterised as follows:

> Bridge (passive location of submerged submarines) has during testing attained maximum ranges of 225 nm [nautical miles] (400 km) in experiments with the two Norwegian submarines *Kaura* and *Kyra* acting as target vessels. The station at Andøya will be manned on a permanent basis as of March 1963, and exercises and tests will be conducted in the near future to assess the operational capabilities.

Up to 1963 the installation at Stave had been run by the NDRE on a purely experimental basis with their own men and equipment, under the code name of BRIDGE, and with co-operation and support from the US navy. In the spring of 1963 the station was fitted out with a permanent listening system, including measuring and direction-finding devices of the LOFAR type (Low Frequency Analysing Recorder). This appears to have been the first time that the United States allowed the use of LOFAR by another country. In contrast to LYDIA, LOFAR did not employ digital analysis, but was based on a direct frequency analysis, the results of which would then be compared with the characteristic sound 'signatures' of different classes of submarines, which were logged in the system's electro-magnetic 'library'. During the previous summer both systems had been in operation at Stave, and each of them had its forte: as we have seen, LYDIA was best at locating, while the LOFAR system was better at characterising the various contacts, such as the submarines, and also ranged much further afield.[6] The station was now put under the military command apparatus, and named the Royal Norwegian Navy Station Stave (Sjøforsvarets Stasjon Stave – SSS). The navy recruited staff locally, while training was carried out at Håkonsvern with final courses in the United States. In addition to providing a good education, these courses provided the opportunity to forge useful connections within the American expertise environment. The Norwegian participants were given a great deal of important information in their daily contact with their American colleagues, information which could be put to good use when back on service in Norway.

Early in 1963, the NDRE had requested the Commander-in-Chief Northern Norway to participate in arranging an exercise or a demonstration at the Stave testing station, to be carried out in the period 24–28 June of that year. The military subsequently asked the Intelligence Staff, which so far had had little or nothing to do with BRIDGE, to despatch observers to the exercise, and this coincided with an American initiative. The United States was also displaying interest in utilising BRIDGE in exercises, but now specifically with a view to what was happening on the Soviet side. Evang was asked to agree to the stationing of three aircraft for about a week on Andøya during an impending Soviet naval exercise during July–August. Between 60 and 70 individual flights were planned over the waters west of Andøya. One of the elements in such a joint operation with aircraft was to have them trying to locate Soviet submarines on the basis of a tip-off from BRIDGE.[7] Generally speaking, using aircraft in direct conjunction with such contacts was regarded with some reticence. The danger of interactive exercises such as this was that they could compromise the listening system which the Soviets allegedly were unaware of in the period up to 1970.[8]

Two of the prerequisites of this second exercise, which was now apparently scheduled to follow immediately after the Norwegian exercise planned by the NDRE, was the existence of a well-functioning communications channel BRIDGE–Andøya–Bodø–Oslo, and that the observations were sent to the Americans without delay. The Americans wanted to train Norwegian crews, and desired the presence of an American officer and two non-commissioned officers at BRIDGE during the exercises. Another precondition laid down by the United States was that this very secret 'special project' must be kept apart from all other joint arrangements with the British and Americans during the exercise. Reading the writing on the wall, Evang noted that his American contact, Captain Pew, 'assumed that future financial support for BRIDGE would depend on the results obtained during the exercise'. Evang thought it likely that the Russians knew about BRIDGE already, and that the submarines would therefore keep further out to sea, while Pew assured him that the scheme would not reveal to the Russians that BRIDGE had become operational.

In May a meeting was convened at the Intelligence Staff concerning the BRIDGE project, and the purpose of this meeting was precisely to obtain permission to base a certain number of American planes in North Norway, to operate together with BRIDGE during this exercise. The BRIDGE equipment would, if it performed up to expectations, be very important in giving forewarning of Soviet 'submarine deployments'. In addition to direction-finding, it could tell the distance to the contact within a range of about 30 nautical miles, and possibly also identify the type of submarine. To achieve this, as many submarine types as possible would have to be studied in order to build a 'database' for comparisons every time a new contact showed up. An excellent opportunity to conduct such a collection of data would be the Soviet naval exercise, of course. But to make the most of it one would need aircraft which could be steered to certain positions. Norwegian naval aircraft lacked the requisite instruments and were therefore unsuited to the task. The US navy hence wanted two of their planes in North Norway in addition to the three US/UK aircraft which had already been allowed to participate in the foregoing exercise.

It is clear from the minutes of the meeting that an agreement had been entered into in connection with the BRIDGE project between the United States, the UK and Norway, to the effect that the results which had been achieved should be placed at the disposition of all three countries. The agreement was signed on behalf of Norway by Chief of Research Henrik Nødtvedt, Section for Underwater Warfare, Norwegian Defence Research Establishment. As was generally the case with such arrangements, the results would not be channelled directly to NATO, but NATO's intelligence base would, of course, be strengthened indirectly.

The results emanating from BRIDGE during the various exercises and tests in 1963, especially from LOFAR, were sufficiently promising to warrant operational use of the information from Stave. In a detailed orientation from Naval Command North Norway (MKN) to the Naval High Command (SOK) that autumn, operational plans, experiences and future requirements for the listening system are explained in greater detail.[9] The goal was four-fold: (1) the registration of acoustic signals from Soviet submarines which passed through the control zone; (2) the registration of these submarines and, in addition, surface vessels, so as to establish strategic scenarios by surveying the frequency of passages and find the normal traffic pattern; (3) registration of extraordinarily large amounts of traffic which could serve as a warning of the deployment of the Arctic Fleet for purposes of war or exercises; and (4) the registration of the sound 'signatures' of individual submarines on tape for later comparison. To carry out identifications and classifications at greater distances, the station had to rely on naval aircraft to the extent that this was practically feasible and operationally expedient. The planes would then have to be directed along the relevant bearings from Stave for a closer investigation of contacts. So far, American and Norwegian aircraft had only been used in general searches in the area. The use of aircraft in a manner that could compromise the very system had to be avoided. But in an agreement on operational procedures for BRIDGE, dated 18 October 1963 and seemingly meant for an operation of some duration – operation COLD ROAD – aircraft on routine maritime patrols over the Norwegian, Barents and Greenland Seas would report, and further investigate if requested, any submarine contacts.[10]

Practical experience so far, based on feedback from American analysts, suggested that in the short time the station had been up and running the number of valuable contacts exceeded all the corresponding American contacts in the same period. Nonetheless, the lack of aircraft had complicated their verification. The need for underwater warning in the northern waters was substantial: CINCNORTH (Commander-in-Chief Northern Europe) calculated that about 134 submarines – some 80 per cent of the Soviet's force in this area – would have the task of executing missile attacks on the United States and attacks against the Strike Fleet and shipping in the Atlantic. Since one had to assume that the submarines would be obliged to sail to their starting positions before D-Day, a very unusual increase in traffic would provide a valuable warning to both American and Norwegian authorities, and, thereby to NATO as well. American national interests would be particularly implicated with respect to early warning, and the same applied to SACLANT (Supreme Allied Commander Atlantic).

The actual detection zone would additionally cover the passage of vessels with missions along the Norwegian coast and in the North Sea. The warning would therefore be of vital importance also for the Norwegian armed forces. On the whole, then, North Norway was particularly suited for warning about Soviet maritime activities. This would represent crucial support for NATO, which was important because Norway, as the navy saw it, would otherwise have little to contribute militarily speaking. The orientation ended with these words:

> The great interest with which warning is associated make any investments in the detection area profitable. Permanent stations are independent of the weather, and, with a warning capacity at significant depths, the station can hardly be replaced by surface vessels. One cannot achieve the same results with a comparable investment of *matériel* and personnel. A national effort costing moderate sums will be appreciated not least by the United States

and NATO. At the same time, it represents an indirect effort to protect our own merchant fleet.[11]

The Andøya project was examined by the Control Committee for the first time at a meeting on 11 March 1964. Since the system was becoming operational, it was only natural that the Intelligence Staff should now become more directly engaged in the project. The activity would still be under the administration of the Naval High Command, but policy, planning and operations would be under the direction of the Defence Command.[12] Two weeks later, hydroacoustics, and with it, the station on Andøya, were specially mentioned at a meeting in Washington between the Intelligence Staff, represented by Evang and Trond Johansen, and the various intelligence organisations in the United States, represented by the Office of Naval Intelligence (ONI) and NSA. Admiral Rufus L. Taylor chaired the meeting for ONI, while Evang made known his views on the project, especially the benefits the intelligence service saw in it, and also the improved intelligence product which could be gained as information from other sources was fed into the system. The Americans planned to send their experts at regular intervals, one at a time, to check that the instruments were functioning as they should.[13] Taylor expressed a wish to have a similar station in Vadsø, but lacked available funds, and would have liked to put hydrophones on Norwegian fishing boats as well. He also said that the information coming from Stave had to be kept within 'the family': this kind of information could not be allowed to be fed into NATO channels because it could very quickly compromise the station's position and capacity. Admiral Shaffer, Assistant Chief of Naval Operations with special responsibility for ASW, said that he did not believe the Russians possessed a similar system – they were no doubt conversant with the theory, but were unable to realise it in practice.[14]

A memorandum written by Bob Porter, the American Sigint contact person, in April 1964 and addressed to Evang, detailed the points on which agreement had been reached at the meeting. The US representatives were agreed that 'Bridge' had passed the research and development stage, and was now operational and producing intelligence. Both parties also agreed that the project must be kept secret as long as possible, and the number of people who had to be informed must be kept at a minimum. The Norwegian navy would have to formulate procedures to receive and disseminate feedback. It was also suggested that visiting American technicians ought to be disguised as Norwegians! This was not always easy, and the problem was often solved with the Americans finding themselves locked up in a room for the whole of their stay in Norway, without leave to gallivant around and about in the local community. Porter's memorandum went on to say that the Intelligence Staff should ask the US navy to supply basic literature on the Soviet navy, and to arrange equipment and training for the Intelligence Staff's photo interpreters. The suggestion about hydrophones on Norwegian fishing boats could be carried out if the US navy secured the equipment and left the camouflage and cover story to the Intelligence Staff. This idea never materialised, however. Technically, the operation could have been carried out by hanging buoys over the sides of the boats, and recording the sounds on tape for subsequent analysis. But it would have been an extensive operation, and it was important that no more people became involved than was strictly necessary.[15]

'BRIDGE' BECOMES OPERATIONAL – BUT WHO HAS THE 'NEED TO KNOW'?

Immediately after the meeting in Washington, the Norwegian navy and the US navy formulated a document entitled 'Agreement on Operational Procedures for Project Bridge', signed by Rear-Admiral Tore Holthe for the Norwegian Navy, and Rear-Admiral Buie on the part of the US navy. In a written commentary on the agreement, Evang was particularly concerned with securing access to information and ensuring that the NIS should maintain control. He had secured backing for this in a preparatory meeting with Minister of Defence Handal and Chief of Defence Bjarne Øen. The minister had emphasised that the operational leadership and control of all intelligence operations had to be co-ordinated within the Defence Staff, even when administered by the armed services. Taking this as his cue, Evang said that current proposals by the Naval High Command seemed to be in violation of that arrangement. He also referred to the meeting in Washington at which he and the chief of the US navy's intelligence service had agreed that all information should go via the Intelligence Staff. Only in 'certain situations, such as when the station on Andøya had made a contact which the American Navy had operational interests in acquiring without delay, could this be done directly (but with information to the Intelligence Staff)'.[16]

This seems to be a clear parallel to the kind of difficulty the air force was creating for the Intelligence Staff in the Elint field. One might well gain the impression that whenever the individual services got a chance to conduct anything approaching independent collaboration with their counterparts in the United States, they had a tendency to overstep the strictly delineated border marks of national control which Evang had made Norway's official line. He was then obliged to put his foot down, sort out the unfortunate constellations, and gather the reins where he believed they ought to belong, namely in the hands of the Intelligence Staff. There were clear instances of injudicious decisions being made both within the navy and the air force in respect of what was handed over to other countries.[17] Hence the navy and the air force had to be restrained.

It is very likely that this attempt on the part of Evang, to draw a line with regard to the navy's collaboration with the US navy, had reached the ears of Admiral Taylor at the US navy's Office of Naval Intelligence. This would explain why the latter wrote Evang a letter in August expressing disquiet that misunderstandings seemed to have arisen over what the United States wanted from BRIDGE. He was of the opinion that the many and sometimes diverging American interests might have obscured the essential US purpose in supporting the project. Seen from Taylor's viewpoint, the purpose of the station was relatively straightforward: here was a means by which, if it was handled properly, tactical intelligence for US operational objectives could be procured regarding Soviet submarines, as well as technical information on Soviet detection systems, and last, but not least, strategic intelligence on Soviet deployments. He admitted that the first type was of far more importance to the United States than to Norway, but had noted the increasing interest in anti-submarine warfare shown by the Norwegian Intelligence Staff. It was evident that Admiral Taylor went as far as he could to placate Evang, accentuating Norwegian needs and Norwegian control, and welcoming all suggestions about how he could be of assistance.[18]

Replying in September to Admiral Taylor, Evang outlined three main reasons for the difficulties regarding the BRIDGE project. Firstly, it had taken 'some time before the real importance of the information has been understood in this country'. Secondly, the feedback from the United States had been much too slow. Thirdly, which was the main reason, 'too many cooks spoil the broth'. There had now been discussions between the Intelligence Staff, the NDRE, the navy and the station chief. All stressed their great interest in a continuation of the project, but felt that it was important that feedback from the United States arrived within a reasonable time. What remained now was to conclude the formal agreement.[19]

In the meantime, Naval Command North Norway (MKN), following an order issued by the Chief of the Navy, had formulated a briefing on and an assessment of Stave after a year in operation. This report shows that as of 1 June 1964, 20 diesel and four nuclear submarines had been registered. All of them were positive contacts. Among them was a submarine which had been tracked for 86 hours, with results considered by Washington to be the most rewarding intelligence yet achieved in the area of Soviet submarine speed capabilities. The detection area had turned out to be larger than expected. With a bit more experience, it ought to be possible to detect submarines also east of the line Tromsø–Bjørnøya, so that within a six-month period Stave would be providing all information on the submarine patrols carried out by the Russians north of the North Cape. The navy concluded that 'Project Bridge' had shown capabilities far beyond all expectations in detecting Russian diesel and nuclear submarines in the Norwegian Sea and from the coast of Norway to the coast of Greenland. Furthermore, BRIDGE was able to provide information on target positions, early warning of submarine operations in the Norwegian Sea and the North Atlantic, and important information on the acoustic 'signature' of the new submarine types.[20]

As we have seen, the original agreement as signed by the NDRE provided for UK access to results emanating from BRIDGE. But in April 1965 Captain C.E. Olson, from the Office of the Chief of Naval Operations in the US navy, sent a letter to the Chief of Defence, Vice-Admiral Folke Hauger Johannesen, reminding him that Evang in February 1964 had stated that these data were to be earmarked for Norway and the United States on a bilateral basis. However, since BRIDGE produced 'extremely important and, in some cases, unique material on the operational characteristics of Soviet submarines, their tactics and transit routes', and since this was 'of exceptional interest to the UK, especially in the vicinity of the British Isles', the US navy felt that the Chief of Defence ought to revise present procedures with the aim of supplying certain data to the UK 'on a Limited Distribution basis'. Both technical data on the identity and location of Soviet submarines, and the final product emerging from the analysis, would be of immediate and direct interest to the British.

This 'need to know' issue was raised on a broader basis in an eight-page report from the US navy to the UK and to Norway on BRIDGE and SOSUS. The report began with the observation that, while the Soviet submarine force – the largest in the world – had hitherto demonstrated a high degree of caution in its operational patterns, it seemed now to be becoming more expansive and adventurous. With the submarines venturing out more often they were also more difficult to track. Since BRIDGE and SOSUS represented the only reasonably reliable way of keeping tabs on them, the system had to be kept secret. The US navy was of the opinion that the United States, Norway and the UK ought to work towards an extensive exchange of information on submarine detection, but with one interesting restriction: there would be no exchange of intelligence about the movements of their own submarines unless required for the safety of their operations. Finished intelligence analyses based on BRIDGE and SOSUS would be exchanged on a case-by-case basis.[21]

Information from SOSUS sources about American submarines was thus only channelled to Norway in extraordinary circumstances, such as when the danger of operational 'collisions' loomed large. What is more, the United States and the Intelligence Staff had agreed on a code word which could be used if one of their submarines was in distress and needed Norwegian assistance.[22] The fact is, however, that the stations did register submarines of nationalities other than those belonging to the target group, as a matter of course. These were then formally classified as 'unknown', whether they were American, British or French, and nothing more was done about it.

A trilateral meeting to establish guidelines for the exchange of intelligence was held in June 1965. The basis was a draft Norwegian–British–American agreement on the distribution of information from BRIDGE and SOSUS. The representatives agreed to have another meeting in the middle of July to formulate a final agreement. On the Norwegian side, one of the issues to be decided was whether the most important information and the operational reports from BRIDGE ought to go directly to the Defence Staff and be distributed from there, or if the exchange could be made between the operational British and American authorities and the headquarters in Bodø. The latter had practical advantages, such as reducing the volume of communications, but it would allow the British and the Americans greater leeway to dominate affairs.

While the exchange of information under the 'need to know' principle may have been the most thorny matter under discussion, there was no disagreement about the importance of the BRIDGE project and the need to get the fullest benefit from the whole field of submarine detection and surveillance. During the meetings it had become clear that the Americans were in the process of building their own BRIDGE–type system on Iceland. Plans to involve Bergen in this project had been dropped; they would probably use a harbour in Scotland instead. Evang, in his report[23] of the meeting, termed these American plans 'warning lines of extremely significant dimensions', and saw them as 'a new sign' of the increased importance of the sea area west of Norway. Reading between the lines, it is however possible to sense a certain degree of disquiet on the part of Evang about developments he, or Norway for that matter, was not in a position to control. It was important for the Norwegian side to find 'a person or an institution able to keep abreast of these considerable expansion efforts as far as possible. Has Iceland been told? What about the likelihood of keeping such things secret in Iceland?' In his report he added that 'it is not apparent that the Commander in Chief North Norway or the Naval Command North Norway entirely comprehend the international consequences the operation might give rise to in the eventuality of unfortunate circumstances'. This may well have been the 'U2 syndrome' rearing its head in the background, together with Evang's general dislike of too intimate a contact with foreign intelligence bodies on the part of Norwegian military chiefs.

Following a proposal from one of the Norwegian participants at the meeting, what Evang called 'the affair' was now baptised 'Canasta'. Thus, Operation CANASTA saw the light of day, a co-ordinated trilateral ASW surveillance operation with coverage of the Norwegian Sea, especially aimed at exploiting the full potential of the navy's station Stave in this area. The Naval High Command stressed in a draft immediately thereafter that no efforts should be spared to avoid compromising the operation. All material would be classified 'Secret CANASTA' and access to it would require a special CANASTA clearance. The number of people awarded such a clearance would have to be kept at a minimum. It is evident that this was taken rather literally: just before a projected trip to the north in 1970 by the Control Committee for the Intelligence Staff, the Chief of Intelligence, Johan Berg, was in doubt as to whether he ought to apply to have the whole committee cleared. Erik Himle, the Committee's chairman, was automatically cleared in his capacity as Permanent Under-Secretary in the Defence Ministry, and Berg thus recommended that he should visit the station instead of the committee.

CANASTA: REHABILITATION AND EXPANSION

We gain an impression of BRIDGE's capabilities from a target analysis dated 2 May 1966, in which are notified 36 contacts made between 20 June and 19 August 1965. The analysis specified the types of vessel involved, provided comments on every contact, often supplemented with the time, position, direction, signature characteristics, and whether the contact was a new one, etc. A breakdown of the observations shows nine surface vessels, ten Soviet nuclear submarines, 15 Soviet diesel-powered submarines, and – curiously enough – one certain and one possible British submarine.[24] That analysis seems to provide ample confirmation of a somewhat understated Norwegian evaluation, carried out a year later, which characterised the station as 'a significant component of the Norwegian and allied surveillance of UVB manœuvres in the Norwegian Sea'. There was, however, a problem which was in need of a solution: as time went by, the *matériel* was becoming obsolete. There were also problems with the sea cable. In March 1966 Chief of Defence Folke Hauger Johannessen asked the anti-submarine warfare section of the US navy for technical assistance to conduct a prognostic analysis of the Norwegian station's capacity in this field in the 1970s. It was probably a combination of this request, on the one hand, and the need to modernise Stave's instruments and increase its efficiency, on the other, that created the opening for the United States to recommend an expansion of the operation.

In May 1967 the question of future operations and a possible expansion of activity was raised in a letter from the chief of the Operations Staff, Commodore Hans B. Gundersen, to the Chief of Defence Staff, Major-General Herman F. Zeiner Gundersen. This referred to a plan with five options proposed by the US navy. Options 1–4 concerned rehabilitation and modernisation of the present system, and could be carried out through national efforts. Option 5, however, was that the US navy, to supplement submarine surveillance in the Norwegian Sea, wanted a new cable system laid from the coast of Finnmark, but terminating on Andøya. The cable would be about 100 nautical miles long, the laying process would take one to two days, and the Americans were not interested in doing this themselves. Chief of Intelligence Johan Berg, and the Chief of the Operations Staff, stressed the great value of SOSUS in both a national and an international perspective, and clearly favoured the rehabilitation plans, but without any economic burden falling on Norway. The risk entailed by the increased activity on Andøya ought to be accepted, since the alternative was the discontinuation of the station altogether. But there were nevertheless 'strong reservations' with regard to the laying of a new, permanent underwater system from the coast of Finnmark. The same reservations did not apply to the proposed oceanographic measurements in that area, as long as it was made clear that they did not imply a commitment to the proposed new cable system.[25]

These recommendations were accepted by the Chief of Defence, and formulated as his own proposals in a letter to the Minister of Defence. In respect of the surveillance system on the coast of Finnmark, he advised not taking a standpoint as yet. In his response, dated 29 May 1967, the Minister of Defence gave his agreement to go ahead with the rehabilitation of Stave and the oceanographic work off the coast of Finnmark. The Norwegian navy, in close co-operation with the Norwegian Defence Research Establishment, now spent the summer months on a review of the past history, current status, and future prospects for CANASTA. The result was a 12-page assessment put together by the navy and the NDRE in concert. Here, five alternatives were mapped out, one of which was then recommended and approved by the chief of the navy, Vice-Admiral Aimar Sørenssen. This involved replacing the LOFAR *matériel* with new equipment analogous to what was being used in the United States. The new equipment, referred to by the initials DSA, had been developed in cooperation with NDRE, and appears to have been a digitised version of LOFAR built around a digital frequency analyser. By moving the station from Stave to Andøya air base, benefits would accrue both operationally and in relation to security.[26]

Vice-Admiral Sørenssen took this occasion to raise the question of financing the operation. The entire rehabilitation would, according to an American estimate, cost around five million kroner. Sørenssen objected to the Americans having to pay everything, and maintained that if Norway were to cover some of the costs, for example 10 per cent, then it would be in a much freer position. The Chief of the Operations Staff concurred in this, emphasising that a Norwegian financial contribution would reinforce demands for a full 'exchange of information which is necessary for our surveillance of the northern sea areas'. NIS chief Johan Berg appended his approval with the following note: 'I agree completely with the above and feel also that we should participate in the funding – as suggested – to ensure our right to co-determination.'[27]

As it happened, Vice-Admiral Charles B. Martell, director of ASW programmes in the US navy, brought up the question of finance in a simultaneous letter to the Chief of Defence, in which he also put the issue of rehabilitation into a wider context. The letter opened with the statement that shared knowledge of the Soviet navy, especially its submarine capacity, had increased immeasurably as a result of the joint investment in BRIDGE and CANASTA. It was in this context that Martell wanted to discuss the future support from the United States to Norwegian planning and development of fixed passive detection stations.[28] The collaboration so far between Norway and the United States had shown that the cable systems could be made more productive if coupled with, or supported by, a complementary system of aircraft, submarines and surface vessels. Moreover, as far as Norway was concerned, the surveillance of Soviet submarines in the Norwegian Sea north of the North Cape would become more efficient if it could be supplemented with a fixed passive system of detection covering also that particular area.

The United States was of the opinion that Norway was in need of such an extended system, and would lend its support in whatever ways it could. In the earlier talks there had been agreement that BRIDGE needed an overhaul. Proposals had been tabled for a new station on Andenes, a few kilometres northeast of Stave, which was also where the new PB–3 Orion aircraft were to be stationed, equipped with modern analytical instruments for the detection of submarines. Included in the proposal was a new submarine cable. The United States would be willing to foot the bill for the cable and equipment and provide technical assistance for cable-laying and installation. The rest ought to be taken care of by Norway. While the United States would gain a strategic advantage from all these improvements, Norway stood to win more in the tactical area than the United States, and would thereby further improve its strategic situation.

It was only a matter of a few days afterwards that the chief of the air force, Lieutenant-General Wilhelm Mohr, presented a proposal to establish a joint navy–air force unit at Andøya air base for the purpose. Mohr drew attention to the fact that new equipment would be installed into two of their Albatross aircraft enabling them to register submarine sounds. This would also be included as standard equipment in the new Orion aircraft which the air force was hoping to get in 1969. It was therefore very important that the post-operational analysis could be conducted wherever the planes happened to be, namely on Andøya. Vice-Admiral Sørenssen replied to this by describing what had taken place thus far in the matter. There was all-round agreement on the basics, the use of the new equipment, and close co-operation with the air force. But the Naval High Command could see no need for the establishment of a joint unit. On the other hand, Sørenssen had appreciated the co-operation of Lieutenant-Colonel Hauge of the air force, and hoped that it would be possible to continue in the same vein. While awaiting a removal to Andøya, which might well take a year, the navy would prepare the ground for joint efforts to commence 'the day the aircraft are ready to start testing'.

ROYAL NORWEGIAN NAVY STATION ANDØYA

The move of the SOSUS station from Stave to Andenes, including erection of new buildings and installation of new equipment, was carried out during 1968. The actual cable-laying process took place in the autumn of that year, and was divided into two phases. The first was PATIENCE, which was now the operational codename for the Andøya project, and involved laying a cable from the new station building at Andenes to connect with the hydrophone array cable outside Stave. This operation was accomplished without mishaps or problems, and the installation was functioning immediately thereafter. While the cable was in the process of being laid, Lieutenant-Colonel Sven Hauge and Director of Research Erik Klippenberg of the NDRE were despatched to the United States to learn more about submarine warfare from aircraft. There was already concern about apparent significant advances made by the Soviets in reducing the sound level of their nuclear-powered submarines. Steps to meet this development were discussed, and, in addition, an orientation on the further development of ASW equipment in the US navy was given. For Hauge, this collaborative effort paved the way for a future career in the intelligence service, culminating in the post of Chief of Intelligence from 1 May 1975.

The second cable operation, codenamed POKER, involved laying an experimental cable from the Finnmark coast. A cable vessel belonging to the telecommunications company *Televerket*, K/S 'Telekabel', was used for this part, and the purpose of the cable was stated as being measurements of background noise in the western Barents Sea. An initial series of measurements was concluded in April 1970. When testing was to be resumed in November that year, however, it was discovered that the cable had been badly damaged, probably by trawlers fishing in the area.

Subsequent attempts to lay new cables, in that area as well as further east, lie outside scope of this book.[29]

The installation on Andøya has been described as 'a new generation of analysis systems'.[30] Given the marked increase in the number of hydrophones, which, moreover, were to be found in relatively deep waters, the station's coverage area was considerably extended. At the same time it became possible to exploit fully the co-ordination of findings by the station on land, sonar buoys dropped from aircraft, and the modern analysis instruments on board the Orion planes. These instruments, named Jezebel, had already been tried on two Albatross aircraft, and were a kind of airborne LOFAR. After the sonar buoys had been sunk into the water at intervals of about ten nautical miles, the aircraft could intercept the sound signals from the buoys in sequence and, on this basis, calculate the direction of, and distance from, the various submarine contacts. An aeroplane could also follow a contact and search through an entire network of distributed buoys over an expanse of several hundred nautical square miles. It was this information that would later be transferred to the British, not the final SOSUS information. We will return to this later.

The available archive material is scarce concerning the actual intelligence results obtained with these new systems during our period. But a report from May 1969 stated that the new Norwegian P3B Orion aircraft in recent weeks had achieved good results by detecting and classifying Soviet submarines operating in the Barents Sea, using Jezebel equipment. One contact with a Soviet Y class on 15 May and two contacts with a C class on 23 and 28 April were of 'exceptional interest' from a LOFAR point of view. This seemed to provide ample confirmation of the expectations contained in the 1967 study already referred to:

> The new maritime patrol aircraft with their equipment for submarine surveillance and anti-submarine operations will give the defence establishment a much greater potential in those sectors than before. Their primary missions in peacetime will be surveillance of the ocean areas where the fixed installations at least for the time being have little effectiveness, that is the Barents Sea and the areas over the continental shelf in the Norwegian Sea. In contrast to the fixed installations, the coverage area and probability of detection may in a crisis situation be augmented by increasing the flight frequency. Their coverage area can easily be moved from the Barents Sea to supplement the fixed installations in the deeper parts of the

Norwegian Sea or to the extensive areas of the continental shelf along the Norwegian coast which the fixed installations do not cover.[31]

The increasingly 'interservice' character of the CANASTA/PATIENCE operations from the end of the 1960s provided a natural opening for the Intelligence Staff to establish itself as the co-ordinating agent. For that purpose the Staff in the autumn of 1969 established a separate Sonar Section, E–12.

THE FUTURE OF PATIENCE

At the end of 1969 and in 1970, in what may have been a part of an economising urge on the part of the Americans, the question arose concerning funding of PATIENCE and connected developments. In the Control Committee for the Intelligence Staff, it was agreed that under-secretary Himle should discuss the issue with the American embassy. In their reply the Americans stressed that precisely the principle that stations such as PATIENCE were owned and run by Norway had been a corner-stone of the extensive co-operation between the two countries in this area. It had never been, nor would it ever be, the case that the United States would cover all expenses. The United States had contributed equipment to the value of a million dollars in addition to about 100,000 dollars in annual expenses. From now on, this latter sum must cover all expenses to be met by the Americans in connection with the project. This meant that running expenses would have to be paid over the Norwegian budget.

In a preliminary comment, the Chief of the Intelligence Staff never-theless wrote that he viewed the project as so important that he would strongly urge that the search activity should be retained at the present level, in spite of a reduction in the American support. He raised this issue again in February 1970 in a meeting at the Ministry of Defence where the Chief of Defence, the Director of the Norwegian Defence Research Establishment and Himle were present.[32] The project was now estimated at a cost of about a million kroner in running expenses, of which 800,000 would cover personnel expenses for 17 officers and men. The 100,000 dollars from the United States would be used on investments, which meant that the total expenses for the Norwegian state would be a million kroner.

The direct value of the project, as the Intelligence Chief saw it, lay primarily in its contribution to the larger strategic picture, of particular relevance to the United States and, thereby, for the whole of the NATO Alliance. For Norway, PATIENCE was not that important, but Berg emphasised that the project provided us with a certain form of warning, at the same time as he set great store on the value of participating in the wider network the Americans had devised. Political implications were also mentioned, and the Chief of Defence pointed out that they were 'two-sided'. The activity could lead to irritation and undesired interest from the Soviet Union. At the same time, it would engender corresponding American interest and support. All agreed that there was an evident trend, not least in the Soviet Union, towards greater weight on submarines for strategic deterrence, which meant that the sea waters off Norway were gaining in importance. The Chief of Defence, in summing up, reviewed the Norwegian benefits ensuing from the intelligence as follows: As background information Norway now received on a daily basis a good survey of the activity of the Soviet submarines in the Norwegian Sea, with the value this had for defence preparedness as an indication of a possible crisis or attack. A by-product was the information provided about other vessels, and, lastly, and perhaps the most important of all, there was the more indirect warning which such a close-knit collaboration with the Americans could give.

The Defence Ministry, as evidenced by Erik Himle's statements at the meeting, had reacted negatively against the American proposal to 'consign large parts of the project PATIENCE, which must be assumed to be of interest primarily to the United States, over to us'. If the United States withdrew its support, the project ought be discontinued. At the same time, one had to take into account the strong indications in the United States signalling reductions in the defence budget, and its wish that the Allies should contribute more to the common defence. Further developments in this matter lie outside the scope of this book. However, we note that a formal MOU was signed in June 1972, signalling that the problems about finance had been solved, and that the co-operation between Norway and the United States in the field of submarine surveillance continued. From a recently published history of the Norwegian Defence Research Establishment we also learn that a hydrophone array cable was laid off the coast of Finnmark in the summer of 1972. That particular cable ran into a succession of problems, but another cable system, laid in 1974 at a location further west, apparently was a great success.[33]

ALIEN SUBMARINES IN NORWEGIAN WATERS: THE NIS VIEW

Apart from tracking the movements of Soviet submarines to and from their Kola bases, Norway had a long-standing concern about alien submarines using Norwegian fjords for hostile purposes. By a Royal Decree dated 13 October 1916 the Norwegian government had banned submerged foreign submarines from Norwegian waters, but in the years of the Cold War there were recurring suspicions that the ban was being violated. The debate on possible alien exploitation or penetration of Norwegian territorial waters, not least our fjords, has generated what might be called two schools of thought in Norway. On the one side there are those who insist that the phenomenon is grossly overrated, and that, in fact, it is as good as non-existent. On the other hand there are those who are of the opinion that this has been going on all the while, and that there is more than enough evidence of it. What, then, was the view of the Intelligence Staff in the period we have dealt with? What could CANASTA/PATIENCE contribute here, and could LOFAR technology, for instance, be adapted for such use in Norwegian fjords? Taking as a point of departure some sources dating from the end of our period, we shall, as an epilogue to this chapter, take a closer look at this.

From time to time in reports to the Intelligence Staff we read about 'unknown submarines and other objects' observed in Norwegian waters. Generally, there appears to have been very little organised processing of this type of information, largely due to lack of qualified personnel on the staffs of the Commander-in-Chief North Norway, Naval Command North Norway, and Section IIIb of the Intelligence Staff, which were the authorities primarily concerned with such questions. At the same time, it is apparent that when the Intelligence Staff did spend time on the issue, the assessment of the observations differed slightly between, for example, the Naval Command North Norway and the Intelligence Staff. A general impression was that 'Naval Command North Norway is more inclined to classify observations as *certain*, while the Intelligence Staff, after a thorough investigation of all the material, ends up with *possible* observations'. In spite of that, the 'joint conclusion is that border violations may have occurred'. By 1964, however, when that report was produced, there was no material in the III Section which could fully substantiate or prove reported violations. The Intelligence Staff found then that it was 'meaningless to make lists and attempt to evaluate' all the so-called submarine observations in north Norwegian waters. Only increased surveillance efficiency, together with a concomitant co-ordination of all reports at one centre, preferably within Naval Command North Norway, could produce more substantial conclusions.[34]

It seems therefore that the Intelligence Staff was inclined to turn the whole problem over to the Navy. This may explain why the 'alien U-boat' alarm of 1966 has left no apparent trace in the NIS archives. While observations in the earlier 1960s had been from zero to three each year, a series of observations in the autumn of 1966 saw the number for that year rise to 13. In one of them there was clear indication that a frogman had been put ashore. The Defence Chief took the observations very seriously, and urged the political leadership to go public with the information, both to increase people's awareness and as a warning to Moscow. Foreign Minister John Lyng was against such action, since there was no proof that the submarines were Russian. Defence Minister Grieg Tidemand nevertheless raised the issue during his visit to Moscow in 1967, only to be told by the Chief of Staff of the Soviet navy that their vessels had never violated Norwegian waters.[35]

In March 1968 the III Section submitted a short summary of reports on submarine contacts in North Norway in the second half of 1967. The Intelligence Staff did not pretend to have an independent analysis based on any observations of their own, but, based on the assessment of Naval Command North Norway, III Section concluded that most of the reported sightings were 'figments of the imagination'. Only two were deemed certain: one in the Porsanger fjord, where the nationality of the submarine is not mentioned, and one in Måsøy, where it must be 'considered certain that the said submarine was Russian, possibly of type "N"'.[36]

In 1969 the Intelligence Staff got a naval officer, Commodore Odd-mund Åkenes, as the new Deputy Director. He reacted against the way submarine reports were handled. That the reports which came in to the Defence Staff were simply registered and filed was not deserving of 'the efforts made regionally and locally to secure material substantiation'.[37] Åkenes appealed for a more thoroughgoing study to be undertaken, and III Section was ordered, in addition to registering and plotting the observations with all available methods, to assess the material with a view to discovering indications, interconnections and patterns. This should lead to an annual report to the Chief of Defence. In Norwegian material there are no such annual reports. But in 1970 the Intelligence Staff did study four episodes that occurred within the space of a week in May–June, all in the Vestfjord area in North Norway. The conclusion was that alien submarines had penetrated Norwegian territorial waters, and that this ought to be reported to the Ministries of Defence and Foreign Affairs. Two of these episodes were 'to all intents and purposes' factual, and in a third case a submarine was not ruled out. Available data could not positively determine that the submarines were of Soviet nationality, but the naval section of the Intelligence Staff were of the opinion that this was most likely. To rule out any suspicion that Western submarines might be operating without giving prior notification, the Intelligence Staff urged an inquiry to be carried out by the Chief of the Operations Staff, Commodore Hans B. Gundersen. But Gundersen poured cold water on the suggestion. If the submarines had been Western, which he thought was unlikely, he saw 'no chance of obtaining any confirmation'.[38]

With the new generation of detection and analysis systems operating from 1969 in the CANASTA/PATIENCE project, there was an increased possibility of detecting unknown submarines operating near the north Norwegian coast. In one such instance, in November 1970, a target near the Norwegian coast was analysed with regard to number of engines, operational mode and calculated position. An immediate inquiry to COMASWFORLANT, the NATO commander in charge of ASW in the region, produced only a negative reply: 'No known submarines in area of position'. The next day a Norwegian Orion aircraft registered and photographed a French submarine in the area, and the Chief of the Sonar Section (E 12) was crystal clear in his evaluation:

> The class is said to have three twelve-cylindered engines and is also otherwise in complete accordance with the acoustic signatures received from PATIENCE. There is no doubt that this is the submarine with which PATIENCE had contact. In light of this, it can be ascertained that French submarines operate along our coast without either us or COMASWFORLANT knowing anything about it.[39]

The new Chief of Intelligence, Colonel Reidar Torp, thought that the case was interesting in more ways than one. Firstly, it showed that Norwegian sonar capacity and combination of various methods of collection could give 'reliable results', and, secondly, Western operations were going on not far from the coast of Norway without the knowledge of the Norwegians. It is likely that this once again started the process of achieving a more systematic analysis of these foreign submarines, Western submarines included. It seems also that the Intelligence Staff, to a greater degree than the navy and the Operations Staff, were concerned about operations by 'possible Western submarines' near Norwegian waters.

At about the same time as the Intelligence Staff was taking those new steps to increase efficiency of the analysis effort, a concrete suggestion for a mobile LOFAR system for use in precisely this type of situation was presented. The reasons were apparent: 'Seen from the intelligence point of view there is no doubt that there exists a need to devise uncomplicated means which can contribute to the acquisition of intelligence on any possible alien submarine's movement in Norwegian waters.' The suggestion was based on the rewarding experiences one had made with the Jezebel system on board Orion aircraft which, it said, 'guaranteed detection of any submarine type whatever at distances up to 1,500 metres', while the submarine was moving at what was called 'a slow, quiet pace'. The proposal reviewed the weaknesses of that system when used in fjords or narrow waters, and provided a simple, concrete recipe for a 'home-made' LOFAR version for use in such environments. The Chief of the relevant section of the Intelligence Staff characterised the idea and its outlined solution as so good that it deserved to be pursued.[40] We now also know that the Norwegian Defence Research Establishment from the end of the 1960s was engaged in an intensive research and development programme, precisely with the aim of improving possibilities for detection of submarines in coastal waters.[41]

NOTES

1. An excellent survey of the nuclear arms race at sea is Michael MccGwire, *Military Objectives in Soviet Foreign Policy* (Brookings, Washington, DC, 1987).
2. FD, file '101.5 Lydforplantning ('Bridge'-programmet, 1959–1961)', *passim*, and author's interview with former intelligence chief Sven Hauge, 10 Oct. 1996 (hereafter referred to as Sven Hauge).
3. On the NDRE's work in this area see Olav Njølstad and Olav Wicken, *Kunnskap som våpen: Forsvarets Forskningsinstitutt 1946–1975* (TANO Aschehoug, Oslo, 1997), pp. 201–17.
4. FD, file '101.5 Lydforplantning …': 'Project proposal to MWDT/Bridge II – Development of a long-range sonar detection system'.
5. Ibid., memo from Section III, 22 Dec. 1959.
6. FO/E, file series 33.81.
7. Ibid., folder 'BRIDGE–SOSUS–CANASTA', meeting of Captain Pew with Evang, 3 April 1963.

8. Sven Hauge.
9. FO/E, file '33.81 Stave', MKN to SOK, 25 Nov. 1963: 'Orientering om Stave'.
10. FO/E, CANASTA papers, undated, 'Operational procedures for project Bridge'.
11. Ibid.
12. FO/E, Control Committee protocol for 11 March 1964.
13. Apparently the American visitors also would be looking for recordings of US submarines in order to remove them. These had, however, by then already been registered by the Intelligence Staff under the label 'unknown submarine'. (Sven Hauge in conversation with the author.)
14. FO/E file '40.04 Tjenestereiser utenlands'. Report of meeting 23–27 March 1964.
15. Ibid., Porter memorandum, 10 April 1964.
16. Ibid., 'Agreement ...', dated 1 April 1964, and Evang's commentary, dated 29 May 1964.
17. Sven Hauge in conversation with the author.
18. FO/E, file '33.81 Bridge (Stave), SOSUS, Canasta', Taylor to Evang 11 Aug. 1964.
19. Ibid., Evang to Taylor, 21 Sept. 1964.
20. FO/E, file '33.81 Stave', MKN to SOK, 8 June 1964, 'Orientering om Stave'.
21. FO/E, file '33.81 Bridge (Stave), SOSUS, Canasta', undated memorandum, probably from April 1965.
22. Information from Sven Hauge.
23. FO/E, file '33.81 Bridge (Stave), SOSUS, Canasta', Evang Pro Memoria, 29 June 1965.
24. Ibid., memorandum to Chief of Defence Staff for Colonel Evang's attention.
25. FO/E, CANASTA papers, SJO to STSJ, 5 May 1967: 'Sjøforsvarets stasjon Stave – videre drift og evt. utvidet virksomhet'.
26. Ibid., annex 2 to letter from SOK to FSJ, 4 Sept. 1967: 'Vurdering av Sjøforsvarets stasjon Stave – videre drift'.
27. Ibid., SJO to FSJ, 9 Sept. 1967.
28. FO/E, file CANASTA, letter dated 3 Aug. 1967 and included as enclosure to a memorandum of 9 Sept. from Chief of Operations in the Defence Staff.
29. Olav Njølstad and Olav Wicken, *Kunnskap som våpen*, gives some further information on the fate of that system.
30. Author's interviews at Andøya Station, June 1995.
31. As note 26.
32. FO/E, red file 'SJE Notater 1970 I'. Note 45/70, 18 Feb. 1970, SJE–FSJ: 'Oppsummering av møte i FD mandag 16. feb. om Project Patience'.
33. O. Njølstad and O. Wicken, *Kunnskap som våpen*, p. 407.
34. FO/E, collection 'Dokumenter i retur fra saksbehandlere', FST/E/III to FST/ E/II, 13 May 1964, 'Ukjente ubåter og andre objekter observert i Nord-Norske farvann'. An interesting recent analysis of the whole postwar period, based precisely on material from Defence Command North Norway, was published in 1995 by the Norwegian Institute for Defence Studies as IFS Info 1/1995: Fred O. Nilsen, *Sovjetisk ubåtvirksomhet i nord – behov og tradisjoner*.
35. Cf. Rolf Tamnes, *Oljealder. 1965–1995* (Vol. 6 in the series *Norsk utenrikspolitikks historie*), (Universitetsforlaget, Oslo, 1998), p. 42.
36. FO/E, file 'SJE Notater Inn-Ut 1967–68'. Sjef FST/E III to FST/O, 8 March 1968: 'Kort resymé over meldinger om ubåtkontakter i Nord-Norge'.

37. FO/E, file 'SJE Notater 1969', SJE to E III, 4 July 1969.
38. FO/E, file 'SJE Notater 1970 I', SJE to FSJ, 28 Aug. 1970; and SJO to STSJ, 2 Sept. 1970.
39. Information from the Intelligence Staff to the author, June 1997.
40. FO/E, file SJE Notater 1970 I', FO/E to FO/O, 14 Dec. 1970.
41. O. Njølstad and O.Wicken, *Kunnskap som våpen*, pp. 399–404.

9

Monitoring of Nuclear Tests

In the early postwar years all the Western powers were carrying out sweeping defence cuts in both manpower and funding, with the United States in the forefront: while the number of servicemen in the US armed forces as of August 1945 was 12 million, by the time demobilisation was officially completed, on 30 June 1947, this number had been cut down to 1.6 million. The army and the marine corps were reduced from 97 to 12 divisions. Of 1,166 vessels, the navy only retained 343 in operation, and by the end of the war the air force, which once boasted 213 'operational groups', had been shrunk to 63, of which only 11 were fully equipped for operational deployment. The defence budget had slowly dwindled from 42 to 14 billion dollars in step with these other reductions.[1] At the same time, American estimates over the size of the Russian forces stated that there were 4.1 million servicemen who were divided mainly among 175 army divisions and large tactical air units. That these estimates were later shown to be exaggerations is another matter.

Under the impression of such a glaring Western deficit in conventional military manpower, as far as their own defence capability was concerned the Western powers had little else in which to put their trust than the American atomic bomb monopoly. And while it had to be conceded that this monopoly would cease to exist one day, the United States would have a head start in the development and manufacture of nuclear weapons and 'means of delivery' – bombers that could reach targets on enemy territory. A memorandum from the CIA dated 20 September 1949, reviewed their impression of the Soviet atomic bomb programme as follows:

> The USSR has an atomic energy program which started in late 1945 and which is being vigorously pursued under a top priority. The current estimate of the Joint Nuclear Intelligence Committee is that the earliest possible date by which the USSR might be expected to

produce an atomic bomb is mid-1950 and the most probable is mid-1953.[2]

This was a few days *after* the Soviet Union had conducted its first nuclear detonation in the steppes of Kazakhstan northwest of the city of Semipalatinsk. Western knowledge of this explosion remained distinctly patchy for some time. President Truman publicly announced the detonation on 23 September 1949, assuming it to have taken place some time between 19 and 21 August, 'somewhere in central Siberia'. It is only recently that we have been able to substantiate the correct date: 29 August. Uncertainty also prevailed as to whether it really was a bomb or not; samples of rainwater from contaminated clouds on 14 September provided positive indications, but were not definitive. All this doubt and uncertainty underlay a central point in a memorandum presented by George Kennan, Chief of the Policy Planning Staff the American State Department, immediately prior to all this. In that memorandum the heaviest emphasis was put on acquiring the best possible information on the Soviet atomic bomb programme. The State Department could not say 'whether scientific techniques or equipment can be developed to detect the explosion by the USSR of an atomic bomb. It is clear, however, that *only if a high degree of certainty can be placed on systems of detection, would this Government be warranted in basing policy decisions on intelligence derived from them.*'[3]

There were several different ways of registering atomic bomb detonations. Firstly, it could be done by means of the analysis of combined Comint and Elint material. Possibilities existed especially in the field of Comint to ascertain and, therefore, to recognise procedures that were utilised in each case prior to an impending nuclear detonation. We shall see that in this area the Intelligence Staff early on developed particular expertise. Secondly, a chemical analysis of fallout material in the atmosphere, on the ground and in the sea could be conducted. We have previously mentioned that the Norwegian Intelligence Service collected samples (of water, seal heads and fish) with a view to this type of analysis. A third method was seismic, basically using the same principles that were used in the registration of earthquakes. Registering acoustic waves travelling through air or water represented a fourth method, while the measurement of electromagnetic radiation in the atmosphere was a fifth. All of these methods were important in the acquisition of knowledge about Soviet nuclear tests, and the United States early on felt in need of assistance from the Norwegian Intelligence Service in the matter. The capability accurately to determine both the time and place of detonations would be important in relation to early warning (EW) and to future agreements on nuclear test bans. And by measuring the force of the explosion and analysing the fallout particles one could establish how far the Soviets had got in their atomic bomb technology At the same time, this was an area of particular interest to Norway. The facts of geography, meteorology and topography meant that Norway, and especially eastern Finnmark, was highly exposed to radioactive fallout, while its proximity to the Soviet Union rendered it particularly suitable for stations to register Russian nuclear activity.

Thus it was that as early as 1951 a request arrived on the table of Director Fredrik Møller of the Norwegian Defence Research Establishment (NDRE) from the US air force, signed by Colonel McDuffy, asking if an American team could travel around in Norway to find suitable sites for detection stations. The letter does not exist in our material, but in light of Møller's reply we may deduce that McDuffy envisioned stationing an American staff element in Norway for 18 months. Møller's preliminary reaction had been that this would have to depend on the number of personnel involved. The reconnaissance activity itself should not cause any problems, and all necessary help and assistance would be given. In a handwritten letter to Minister of Defence Hauge, Møller informed him of the American initiative. His choice of words indicates that Hauge must already have been aware of the plans. 'The matter is *acoustic* and *seismic*, not nuclear', Møller underlines. But 'the enterprise is of no mean size', envisaging at least five stations. Nonetheless, there was one aspect about which the Americans nurtured unrealistic hopes: 'They still entertain the hope of maintaining a full American complement for a period of about 2 years, after which we will be able to take over.' At this point, Hauge wrote with heavy strokes of pencil in the margin 'Sic!!!'. The letter was also seen by 'H.L.' (Foreign Minister Halvard Lange) and 'E.G.' (Prime Minister Einar Gerhardsen).[4]

In a later letter from Møller to McDuffy in the beginning of January 1952, Hauge's exclamation marks were put into words: 'I should like to state to you that our Minister of Defence demands that part of the staff should be Norwegian from the very beginning. He cannot agree to an entirely American staff.' He adds that 'the concern in this matter is for political reasons only'. There is no trace of the Intelligence Staff in the material emanating from this early initiative by the USAF, but that does not mean that Evang had not been informed.

The original plans for five stations were transformed into plans for two so-called micro-meteorological research stations, for which Hauge gave his stamp of approval. For some reason the stations did not materialise this time round. In the meantime the Intelligence Staff began by other means to amass intelligence on the Soviet nuclear programme. Determining the time and place of explosions was not the only factor of interest to Norwegian and American intelligence services: the analysis of radioactive fallout could furnish indications of the actual device used. As the 1950s wore on, Norwegian boats on combined intelligence cruises were often instructed to take seawater samples in areas exposed to radioactive fallout following detonation of a Soviet atomic bomb. (We have previously noted that NDRE carried out this type of analysis on the jaw bones of seals, and that seal heads were collected and brought to Norway on board the Intelligence Staff's boats.)

In September 1955 Evang wrote to a naval officer employed by the NIS, Commander Sverre Aas, about a nuclear detonation in the Barents Sea in the previous month. The letter contained a special assignment from 'X', that is, the United States, to collect 25 litres of seawater from the area. The assignment was a matter of high priority, and two precise locations were given. Evang asked Aas if he could procure such samples 'by hiring a vessel or by other means'. Aas replied the following day that he had been promised a boat and would sail from Vardø to collect the samples on 4 or 7 October. Later that autumn Aas reported to Martens Meyer on further missions to collect samples of fish, as well as seawater, partly in collaboration with naval vessels. All in all, the sources[5] suggest a relatively systematic collection under the guidance of the Intelligence Staff with respect to nuclear activity and waste.

The Intelligence Staff's Comint stations also participated in efforts associated with the detection of nuclear detonations, and, in the specific case of the August 1955 explosion, queries from the United States were relayed by Evang to the stations concerning possible restrictions on traffic and unusual observations or activity in the southern or eastern Barents Sea after 1 August. Brynildsen, head of the Comint section, subsequently examined the entire radio activity for the period 1 to 20 August 'to see if it was possible to detect any activity which could be put in connection with the assumed nuclear blasts in the NORTH'. Nothing untoward was discovered as far as radio traffic from Soviet ships was concerned, but in regard to aircraft there was a certain amount of activity the purpose of which V Section was so far unable to comprehend. The same thing occurred after a detonation near Novaya Zemlya on 21 September of that year.[6] As step followed step these Comint stations became expert at discovering the radio procedures that came into use in the run-up to a nuclear detonation. Just to give one example, they discovered that a specific teleprinter was activated each time.[7] The manner in which such forewarning gradually became something of a Norwegian speciality will be addressed later.

After a break from early 1952 – as far as the sources inform us – the USAF entered the fray once more in 1955, this time with a proposal to establish a seismic registration station to measure vibrations in the ground after a nuclear detonation. Once again the idea embraced several measuring sites: three with automatic registration equipment, plus one manned assembly station, not unlike the 1951 project. The matter was deemed of sufficient importance to be put before the Cabinet Defence and Security Committee. The Committee Secretary, Andreas Andersen, had beforehand consulted Evang, who had recommended setting conditions about the presence of Norwegian personnel at the station, and access to the results of the measurements. At the meeting the Committee was informed that a *Note Verbale* on the subject had been received by Minister of Foreign Affairs Halvard Lange, who had thought that Norway ought to consider the proposal in a positive light, but had wished to defer taking a decision until the matter had been discussed with the Prime Minister. Fredrik Møller, representing the NDRE, explained that the station was intended to work in conjunction with similar installations in Germany and Turkey, and that to achieve the necessary cross-bearings the installation would have to be in North Norway. He was of the opinion that the proposal would meet a NATO requirement, but was also of direct interest to Norway. The Cabinet Committee were in favour of allowing the station, but suggested, for consideration during the negotiations with the Americans, various conditions regarding Norwegian administration and a gradual replacement of American personnel by Norwegians. The Prime Minister also queried whether one should not, from the Norwegian point of view, stipulate access to the results as a precondition. But Møller felt that 'the general results' should suffice. Minister of Justice Jens Haugland thought that the results would be placed at the disposition of NATO, and that otherwise 'one would just have to take the chance that our own people at the station would be able to put two and two together and learn from the co-operation'. The Cabinet Committee concluded by leaving the negotiations to NDRE, in consultation with the Intelligence Staff.[8]

From 5 to 12 September a US delegation now travelled from place to place carrying out a so-called 'granite reconnaissance' of southern and northern Norway. In charge of this delegation was Mr J. Allen Crocker, an electrical engineer from George Washington University. He had been a member of the first group of 75 men who had initiated the Los Alamos atom bomb project. The delegation's purpose was to find a suitable place to establish stations which could register nuclear explosions. The type of rock in the area had to be as homogeneous as possible, giving 'maximum sound velocity', and be fissure-free. Four areas were selected for trials in October and November. These were Bodø–Fauske, Rygge–Fredrikstad, Drammen–Hurum and Gardermoen.[9] Only one would be selected as a site for a permanent station.

There is no material directly relating to these trials, but in a note from Evang, dated August 1956, we read that the geological conditions were not considered suitable for seismic measurements because rock formations in Norway were too heterogeneous. On the other hand, conditions for electromagnetic measurements were good. Two Americans had recently carried out investigations in that respect in collaboration with the NDRE and the Intelligence Staff. What they proposed was the establishment of an electromagnetic measuring station in the vicinity of Rygge air base southeast of Oslo. Neither the station itself nor the number of personnel was likely to attract unfavourable attention. Of a total of 12 men, half would be Norwegian, the other half American civilians. Evang stressed that the Defence Staff saw a 'considerable Norwegian interest' in playing a part in this effort. The measurements could determine the precise time and direction of a nuclear detonation, and by taking cross-bearings with other stations the location of the blast could be pinpointed. Norway would gain access to the information and would be able to launch necessary countermeasures in case of radioactive fallout, something which would otherwise remain beyond the bounds of feasibility. The Ministry of Defence, however, was unwilling to approve such a project, so the idea had to be put aside for the time being.[10]

OPERATION CROCK POT

At the end of 1957 a new proposal was put forward by the Americans. At a meeting with State Secretary Sivert A. Nielsen of the Defence Ministry, Ambassador Frances Willis returned to the question of setting up an electromagnetic observation station on Norwegian territory. She had been instructed to raise the matter again, since both the USAF and the US State Department saw it as a matter of some urgency to keep track of Soviet missile and nuclear weapon experiments on Novaya Zemlya. The question was whether Norway would be willing to operate a small station on the Varanger Peninsula for that purpose. The personnel would be Norwegian, but the United States would supply the *matériel* and train the operators. In the event of a go-ahead the Americans would despatch a couple of officers from Washington in January 1958 to review the technical aspects. Nielsen promised a reply within a week, and saw no major problems in the project in the form it had now been presented.

Nielsen now summoned Evang to a meeting at the Ministry of Defence on New Year's Eve to discuss the project. At the meeting it was revealed that Norway had not only rejected the previous proposal for an electro-magnetic station at Rygge, but also an American proposal for a major radar station near Ørland air base in the county of Trøndelag, with a personnel of 350. Evang viewed the new American offer, not surprisingly, as 'of great interest from a national point of view'. The existing NDRE stations for registering nuclear detonations were only capable of analysing radioactive fallout, and could not ascertain the time and place of the detonations. The Defence Staff had already considered the construction of installations with a view to keeping tabs on Russian missile and nuclear weapon experiments on Novaya Zemlya. The American offer could satisfy that requirement. The condition was that the entire matter must remain a wholly Norwegian affair, even though the Americans supplied the *matériel* and saw to the training of personnel. Evang felt that this endeavour was so important that it warranted 'sacrificing other undertakings if neces-sary'. Moreover, the United States considered the station to be of such great importance that if Norway said 'no', then they risked an increase in American air activities between Svalbard and North Norway. This could prove to be more of a political cross to bear than the proposed electronic observation post.[11]

Agreement was reached to inform Ambassador Willis that the Nor-wegian authorities would welcome the arrival of two American officers for technical discussions. The American offer would be given the most sympathetic consideration, but it was impossible to give any binding consent at the present moment. The precondition was in all events that the station must be run by the Defence Staff as a purely Norwegian set-up. The salaries of the personnel were to be paid by Norwegian authorities, and Norway ought also to be ready to fund the construction work. The

station ought, if possible, to be established within existing military installations. The project, which was electromagnetic, was given the cover name
of CROCK POT or CP – possibly in honour of Mr Allen Crocker who
was its leading American expert on the project.

On 2 January 1958 Evang received a memorandum from Air Attaché
James I. Flanagan at the American embassy which outlined the arrangement. The equipment would be installed in a van-type 10-ton trailer, and
the requisite number of operators was between six and ten. Thirty days'
training would suffice if the operators were of high quality, and it was
hoped that operations could begin in April. After a series of meetings with
American intermediaries, people from the Intelligence Staff and Fredrik
Ramm from the Defence Ministry, an MOU was ready for signature on
1 March 1958. The secrecy of the operation was emphasised, and even
in the MOU the project was called 'a weather research station'. Contrary
to the assumptions in the New Year's Eve meeting, the project would now
be entirely funded by the Americans. Evang himself had now apparently
concluded that the operation was of only minor value to Norway, but
important to NATO. In the meantime Allen Crocker had made a
reconnaissance trip to find a suitable site for the station. It turned out that
Høybuktmoen satisfied virtually every single requirement. The Cabinet
Defence and Security Committee had considered the project at the end
of February, and Defence Minister Handal had stressed that while the
analysis of the measurings could only be done by experts in America the
results would be communicated to Norway. In approving the project the
Committee had noted that controlling nuclear weapon tests was
important, and Norway was the only NATO country in the proximity of
the Soviet test sites at Novaya Zemlya.[12]

REGISTRATION OF THE FIRST SOVIET TEST SERIES

Preparatory work on the site at Høybuktmoen started on 7 March 1958,
and the station became operational on a 24-hour basis from 18 April. It
was therefore in full operation during a series of Soviet nuclear tests in
September–October that year. Initial results were reported in a memorandum from the Intelligence Staff dated 14 October. The last analysis
mentioned in this report was registered 30 September. Signals had been
intercepted at 0750 hours GMT which showed that an A-bomb between
700 and 7,000 kt, probably 1,000 kt, had been detonated in the vicinity

of Novaya Zemlya. Two hours later on the same day another A-bomb of between 700 and 7,000 kt (more likely 2,000) was detonated in the same place. Both detonations were later confirmed by other sources. Later registrations, five in all, the last one being on 12 October, had not yet been analysed. These results were communicated to the Cabinet Defence and Security Committee on 7 November by the Defence Minister, who added the information that the total number of Soviet nuclear tests, up to and including 30 September, was 57. Of those, 12 were in the Novaya Zemlya region, 43 near Semipalatinsk, and two in other regions. For Novaya Zemlya the dates were 21 September 1955; 7 and 25 September 1957; 6 and 10 October 1957; 23 and 27 (two that day) February 1958; 14 and 21 March 1958; and two on 30 September 1958.[13] A later report of the completed Soviet test series noted 12 further detonations at Novaya Zemlya in the period 1–25 October, thus bringing the total to 69.

On 20 November 1958 Evang was informed by the Americans that it had been decided to shut down the CROCK POT operation. The reasons were technical: the analysis of the results had shown that very little of the kind of desired information had been obtained, most probably due to the limitations of the equipment. Out of concern for the personnel employed the official termination date was set at 1 April 1959. The US air force still wished to retain the option of reactivating the project at a later date. Further analysis work undertaken during the winter and spring of 1959 suggested that the poor performance of the equipment was in reality mainly due to the physical environment in which the station had been operating. In July 1959 Evang received a forewarning that the operation might be resumed after further site testing.[14]

Given the poor results of CROCK POT I, it may not be far-fetched to say that the greatest advances in the monitoring of nuclear tests that autumn was made by the Norwegian Comint stations. We have already touched on the role that Sigint could play in this regard. It can now be revealed, due to intercepts by the Norwegian Comint stations, that the Soviet nuclear tests in 1957 and 1958 were conducted by employing strategic aircraft based at Olenya air base on the Kola Peninsula. Vessels from the Arctic Fleet had also been operating in the area, possibly on security and reconnaissance missions. After having registered extensive reconnaissance flights over the Barents Sea and the Norwegian Sea, at the same time as transport aircraft activity at Belushya air base and Novaya Zemlya increased significantly from early in September, it was noted that the Olenya aircraft, which had performed the characteristic flight pattern on the occasion of previous tests, were now on the wing to the testing site on Novaya Zemlya. Again, a number of trial flights to the testing site were carried out prior to the first detonations, in addition to several 'dummy runs' during the tests themselves.

By keeping track of this traffic, especially that of the aircraft, and comparing it with the detonations, the Comint side had managed to establish an operational pattern which would enable them to sound the alert when new detonations were impending. Thus far, the aircraft operations prior to the sortie itself could be divided into two stages. Initially, about two hours before the test planes started, a Badger (TU-16) would take off from Olenya, aim for the radio beacon at Belushya air base (Novaya Zemlya), continue in a northerly direction, making a turn over each of the testing sites. The plane then returned to Olenya via Belushya. It was assumed that this was some form of reconnaissance. Then, during the actual testing flight, two or three planes flew along the same route as the reconnaissance plane. While over testing site A it was usual for the plane to make a 'dummy run' before the 'bomb run'.[15] In addition to all this Comint could register another success when their own data, compared with data subsequently released by the US Atomic Energy Commission, showed that they had correctly registered at least five detonations which CROCK POT had missed. The only drawback for the Comint stations was that their timing of the explosions diverged by up to plus or minus three minutes from the atomic clock signal available to CROCK POT.

PLANNING CROCK POT II – PLUS AN ACOUSTIC STATION?

In December 1959 the Americans notified Evang of their plan to reactivate CROCK POT, with a possible start in the late summer of 1960. A suggestion to build permanent housing for the personnel indicates that a long-term operation was contemplated. Plans also existed for an acoustic station in the immediate neighbourhood, to complement and work with the CP station. A station of this type would consist of four unmanned outposts in the corners of a rectangle, the sides of which varied between 7 and 11 km. Evang stated in his reply that the location of the original CP station was not suitable for a permanent station. In addition he nursed some disquiet concerning both the short time schedule and the idea of a new acoustic station on the same site as CP. He therefore suggested getting a project officer to Oslo before making any final decisions.[16]

The project now began to suffer delays, one of the reasons probably being the political turmoil following the ill-fated U-2 flight on 1 May. In July 1960 the US air attaché had turned to Martens Meyer to find out if a reactivation of CP would be possible. Martens Meyer replied that this might be difficult given the political situation, but they were prepared to meet with a representative from Washington for technical discussions. In the ensuing talks later that month it transpired that the Americans were planning a gradual development of CP, over a two-year period, towards a permanent station which by 1963 would be linked with a world-wide net. The acoustic station ought to be located on the same spot, or at least with perfect communications to the CP station. Norwegian personnel would man both stations, with about 14 men each. But they would like to have one American – 'of Norwegian descent and speaking fluent Norwegian' – at each station for a longer period. The minutes of the meeting give a detailed account of all aspects of the planning, with Martens Meyer especially concerned about what he called 'the grave political situation'. All in all, the Intelligence Staff for their part seem to have had no real objections to the establishment of the stations, although they feared that it would be difficult to find enough men with the requisite expertise in electronics.

Evang now began a new round of consultations with the Ministry of Defence through Himle, in which he seems to have made an effort to present the proposal as a natural continuation of CROCK POT I after merely a temporary halt. Himle's preliminary reaction to the plan was positive, but the matter would need the approval of the Cabinet Defence and Security Committee. The Cabinet Committee discussed the project on 18 August 1960. According to the minutes of the meeting, Defence Minister Handal called the planned acoustic station 'similar' to CP, except that it should also 'register possible acoustic waves'. He also said that the system might become a link in 'an international control system for registration of nuclear weapon tests', and stressed the passive character of the activity. The committee thereupon approved the project, with the usual proviso that the personnel had to be Norwegian, and the station to be under complete Norwegian control.[17]

In September 1960 three American experts arrived to reconnoitre suitable locations for the new stations, the acoustic station now being referred to by the codename JACK FROST. The Americans had beforehand selected Karasjok as the only feasible area, while Martens Meyer thought that Kautokeino, Porsanger and Pasvik were worthy of consideration as well. The point of the acoustic station was to register atmospheric pressure changes resulting from nuclear explosions in the earth's atmosphere. An important factor in selecting a site for the acoustic station was of course to avoid interference from the natural environment, particularly windy conditions. The survey resulted in the selection of Pasvik, Kautokeino and Karasjok, in that order. For the CP station Høybuktmoen was again the preferred location, except that the trailers would have to be placed some distance away from the radio aerials of the air base and of the Sigint station.[18]

RENEWAL OF CROCK POT, AND BRITISH INTEREST

As it turned out, the plans for an acoustic station were shelved before the end of the year. This meant falling back on a reactivation of CROCK POT, although with improved instruments. Official approval was given by the Ministry of Defence after a few changes had been made to the tendered Memorandum of Understanding from the USAF. One of the changes aimed at limiting the presence of American experts during the period of testing and initial operations. Another alteration was made under the section called 'Security'. Contrary to the proposal of the Americans to let the station officially be known as a 'weather research station', it was decided to let the station appear as part of the Defence Experimental Station Kirkenes/Moen (FFSK/M). A new CROCK POT Memorandum of Understanding was dated 24 January 1961. Target date for the station to become operational was set as 'during the third quarter of calendar year 1961', and the agreement was made for a period of five years. Funding would be from American sources by way of reimbursement through the 'Fund', and would include a substantial sum for the construction of permanent housing for the personnel. Norwegian operators would undergo a 23-week course of instruction in the United States, starting in April 1961 at the latest.[19]

Long before the training of the operators for CROCK POT was completed, and before even the equipment for the station had arrived in Norway, alarm signals about an impending resumption of Soviet nuclear tests sounded, not only in Washington, but also in London. Khrushchev had announced a voluntary moratorium on testing after the completion of the autumn 1958 series, but some time in the summer of 1961 American and British intelligence must have picked up indications that a new series was being prepared. At NIS headquarters the alarm was sounded on 1 September by the Comint section. In a note to Evang that day, Erling Hellerslien of V Section confirmed their weekly report, issued on the previous day, that ship and air movements in the Novaya Zemlya area presaged a new series of detonations. There were also indications that air-to-surface missiles would be test-fired – perhaps already that same day. Flight patterns of TU-95 aircraft, and weather reports for the Novaya Zemlya sites from Belushya air base were the most important indications.[20]

On the same day the British entered the arena. In the morning of 1 September the local British representative in Oslo, Mr Bosley, had got in touch with Evang requesting permission to establish a 'CP-Y' in North Norway as quickly as possible – the 'Y' designating, as usual, Britain – using four British civilians. Equipment was ready to be flown in, and timing was urgent. Evang's own reaction was positive, but the British had to clear it also with the Americans, since there was a bilateral Norwegian–American agreement about such activity. Evang also informed the Defence Ministry through State Secretary Erik Himle. The next day saw the arrival of Mr Newman, the British top-ranking man in the field, who gave his assurances that the situation *vis-à-vis* the Americans had been taken care of. Defence Minister Gudmund Harlem was now also brought in, and the proposal received his approval, subject to the arrangement being a temporary one, and that the British would have to fit in with 'any decisions whatever made by the Norwegian authorities'. The CP-Y trailer and personnel arrived by plane in Bodø on 5 September. Newman and Martens Meyer boarded the plane here and the journey continued to Banak the following day. From there a Twin Otter aircraft brought the two men to Høybuktmoen, while trailer and operating personnel went by road. Two days later, Friday 8 September, the instruments had been set up and were operating, about 48 hours before the first nuclear detonation near Novaya Zemlya.[21] The Soviet Defence Ministry had in the meantime – on 3 September – officially announced that they would be testing different types of modern weapons in the period 10 September to 15 November in the Barents and Kara Seas, and warned all ships and aircraft to keep away from a large area around Novaya Zemlya.

On 8 September, Colonel Chapman of the USAF called on Evang with an urgent request for permission to send about 40 tons of equipment and 17 men to Kirkenes, to establish a temporary measuring station. Evang's immediate response was to suggest that the data collected by the British station ought to be good enough. He also worried about the political repercussions of an influx of 17 Americans to Southern Varanger, in addition to the presence of an American naval vessel in Kirkenes, bringing the equipment which was too heavy for transport over land. The Americans then returned on Sunday 10 September with a proposal for two separate stations. Eight men and 30 tons of equipment would be flown to Bodø, and transported from there to Kirkenes by a chartered civilian vessel. The remainder, 14 men and 40 tons of equipment, would be set up in the Bodø–Bardufoss area. This final proposal was laid before Harlem, who got in touch with Prime Minister Gerhardsen, and at 4 p.m. on 11 September permission was granted.[22]

NEW SOVIET TEST SERIES, AND NORWEGIAN ANALYSES

The four first detonations in the new Soviet test series were carried out over Semipalatinsk 1–6 September, while the fifth, also on 6 September, took place at Kapustin Yar. Most of the rest of this massive series, lasting until 4 November, were over Novaya Zemlya, interspersed with some smaller detonations at Semipalatinsk. In all, 45 tests were conducted, of which 14 were not publicly announced. Apart from one underground detonation and one underwater, the detonations occurred in the atmosphere; one of them at an altitude of 12,000 feet was estimated to have had the massive yield of 58,000 kt.

During October and November both V and VI Sections of the Intelligence Staff submitted preliminary analyses of the tests, based on the material available at that time. The report by VI Section paid particular attention to the question of possible prior warning or 'tip-off' about detonations. The analysis suggested that the Americans were unable to predict a detonation. The British had been successful in this area a couple of times, and it seemed possible that the British at one stage had penetrated the communications associated with the test series. Nevertheless, it concluded that 'NORTHERN HOPE [the American station] and CP-Y were unable to give advance warnings'. Regarding Norwegian Comint, the analysis showed that a *distinct* increase in activity occurred on the special network on days when detonations took place. This might provide the basis for an early warning. 'There appears to be a connection between the forewarning of aircraft to Novaya Zemlya and the detonation sites, but the trend is insufficiently consistent to draw definite conclusions.' V Section submitted its own analysis at the end of November 1961. This one is especially deserving of interest because of its suggestion that the 'means of delivery' for one or more tests might have been missiles fired from ships. The Comint service had tracked extraordinary ship operations in the western Barents Sea from 19 to 21 October, with two or three unidentified ships using highly unusual call signs. Communication was partly with each other and partly with the fleet headquarters in Severomorsk and the fleet base Belushya. Particularly on the 20 October a number of short calls were made. 'It cannot be dismissed that a missile launch may have been conducted from one of the above-mentioned vessels.' This has lately been confirmed from Russian sources.[23]

A final summary report, marked 'for Norwegian eyes only', was compiled and distributed to Ministers and military chiefs on 3 January 1962. This repeated the suggestion, albeit still unconfirmed, that at least one of the detonations might have been delivered by a ship-borne missile. In addition, the NIS stations had identified two missiles – probably SHYSTER (T-1) – launched from the Archangel area towards an area in the Kara Sea, and one air-to-surface missile, probably type AS-2, fired from a Badger aircraft over the White Sea. Development of the AS-2 had in fact been noted in a CIA estimate as a new missile, likely to become operational by 1961, and capable of carrying a nuclear warhead.[24]

POLAR REIN AND PINE FOREST: LINKS IN A GLOBAL CHAIN

The intensive Soviet testing of nuclear devices seemed to continue unabated during 1962. As recorded by the NIS, the first Soviet nuclear test that year was registered on 2 February in the Semipalatinsk area. The level of activity rose after 27 July, and by the end of the year 70 tests had been registered, of which 37 were in the Novaya Zemlya region. The explosive power varied between 10 kilotons and 30 megatons. Altogether, the equivalent of about 180 megatons exploded in this area in 1962. The Soviet Ministry of Defence announced on two occasions that exercises would be taking place in the Barents Sea and the Kara Sea, and that modern weapons would be deployed: on 24 July for the period 5 August to 20 October, and 13 December for the period 15–25 December. The operational pattern echoed that of previous years. Apart from two missile tests and one in which the means of delivery remained unknown, aircraft were employed. The NIS intelligence report No. 1/63, dated 30 January 1963, concluded that the way in which the tests had been carried out indicated that their main purpose had been to test explosive power, radioactive radiation, fallout, etc. 'Only in a very few cases do the means of delivery appear to have had any significance.'

The ongoing tests also meant that American interest in keeping track of Soviet developments in the nuclear weapons field, not least up north where the heaviest yields had been registered, was undiminished. In the meantime, the second CROCK POT station, intended for long-term use and installed near Høybuktmoen during the autumn of 1961, was completely destroyed by fire in November, just days before it was to begin regular operations. Shortly thereafter the USAF and the Intelligence Staff decided to re-establish the station under the name POLAR REIN (PR). While awaiting the completion of that station, on the same site as the old CP station, a provisional station – also under the cover name POLAR REIN – was to be operated by the Intelligence Staff in a garage building at nearby Høybuktmoen, commencing if possible in mid-April 1962. The permanent station was supposed to be completed the same year. An MOU to that effect was signed on 9 May 1962.[25] Work started on the station buildings and personnel quarters at Hesseng in June. On 4 June three mobile units for the temporary station, named CP-3, CP-4 and CP-5 in Norwegian documents, arrived accompanied by eight Americans. The British were also again active in the area. Three experts arrived on 12 May, and on 10 November CP-Y was operational. In addition, a small seismographic station was established and run by the Intelligence Staff in co-operation with the University of Bergen, to find out what contribution seismic data could make to the detection of nuclear detonations.[26]

The permanent POLAR REIN facility, called the Central Recording Station (CRS), was finally established in the spring of 1963. But despite being continually updated with new and improved equipment, the station as well as its temporary predecessor seem to have been plagued with a series of problems, some due to technical malfunctions, and others having to do with the Norwegian operators. Norwegian labour laws and holiday regulations, which meant that only a skeleton crew would be working during the summer holiday period, were a source of annoyance to the American project officers.[27] It is indicative of the importance of the station and its mission that the project nevertheless was continued. At one stage a resurrection of the plan to build an acoustic station was also suggested.

Again, however, plans were changed. By 1964 the idea was to view the entire detection problem in a wider perspective, taking into account all the various instruments, aids and facilities that were becoming available. There was a connection here to the trilateral moratorium on nuclear tests in the atmosphere, in outer space and under water from the autumn of 1963. The chief interest of the United States focused on the degree to which it would be possible to detect breaches of the test ban. At a Senate hearing prior to the ratification of the agreement on 10 October, the American administration gave its assurance that it would be possible to detect all types of infringements with the measures it was planning on carrying out during 1964 and 1965. Current efforts were concentrated on achieving an improved registration of detonations in outer space and smaller detonations on or just below the earth's surface. In this connection the Intelligence Staff received a memorandum from the American military authorities on 7 January 1964 carrying a proposal to expand the existing control system in Norway.

Evang raised this question in a note to Defence Minister Harlem a few days later, explaining that the expansion was three-fold: firstly, the existing POLAR REIN station would have to be given new instruments to enable better registration of detonations in outer space, measuring frequency variations in the lower frequency bands; variations in cosmic noise; variations in atmospheric fluorescence; as well as carrying out air filtration to detect fallout substances. This part of the work was estimated by the Americans to require a personnel of 20, but Evang thought the number too high and in need of reconsideration. Secondly, an acoustic system was proposed at Karasjok, which would register nuclear explosions in the atmosphere and just beneath the surface of the earth by measuring air-pressure fluctuations. Thirdly, a search for a suitable location for a seismic system was to be launched. The desired schedule for these sundry measures was 1964 for the filtering apparatus, December 1965 for the other installations in Sør-Varanger, June 1966 for the acoustic station at Karasjok and December 1966 for the seismic station.[28]

Evang clearly favoured a participation by Norway in efforts to ensure compliance with the test moratorium. He was aware of a 'certain amount of concern' in higher military and political quarters about the relatively large number of persons in eastern Finnmark actively collecting data on Soviet military deployments, but felt that the significance of the effort that Norway could contribute in this area quite outweighed the potential elements of risk inherent in the arrangement. Evang suggested that the expansion in Kirkenes be approved in principle, but that the number of operators be reconsidered. As far as the acoustic and seismic stations were concerned, no decision should be taken before there had been further studies and consultations with the American authorities.

The political concerns which were surfacing at this juncture will be dealt with in greater detail in Chapter 13. In the context of the new American proposals for improved detection of seismic tests it only needs to be noted that they came on top of the expansion of Comint activities in the area near the Soviet border. Persons in both the military and the political leadership were of the opinion that a ceiling had now been reached. Defence Minister Harlem, who was in favour of the new plans, therefore decided to take the matter to the Cabinet Defence and Security Committee. This was the backdrop to the account given by Evang to the Committee on 31 January 1964, covering not only the current proposals but the whole gamut of Sigint and other activities in eastern Finnmark. At this meeting, the new plans concerning control measures in connection with the nuclear test moratorium were reviewed, as an aspect of a totality, and approved with the usual caveats.[29]

After a prolonged series of further bilateral discussions, another Memorandum of Understanding was signed on 12 March 1965 between the Intelligence Staff and the USAF. This was for the establishment of a station at Karasjok, nicknamed PINE FOREST. This project was now designed to include not only an acoustic station, but also the elements proposed in January of the previous year for installation at POLAR REIN, except for the air filtration unit. The suggestion of a major seismic station appears to have fallen by the wayside, possibly on account of the NDRE's initiatives in that field. As usual, the United States was to foot the bill for the construction of the station and for lodgings for the staff, in addition to the total investment costs and running expenses. The Intelligence Staff was to oversee the provision of a suitable location and adequate manning. The station was planned to start operations in August 1966, and the agreement, signed by Colonel Lester J. Johnson and Evang, was made to cover a period of ten years.[30] Recruitment of personnel began in the autumn of 1965, and the station in fact became operational in September 1966.

It seems that the problems at POLAR REIN were in the meantime gradually ironed out. In May 1965 Evang reported to Harlem, and probably not without a glimmer of pride, 'The second Chinese nuclear test, which was carried out on the 14 inst. at 0200 hours, near Lop Nor, was accurately registered by our station.' The intermediate analysis had indicated that the fission substance was uranium 235 and 238, and that the magnitude was 40 kilotons.[31]

With both POLAR REIN and PINE FOREST in operation, Norway now had two stations connected to the global network operated by the USAF, the Atomic Energy Detection System (AEDS). There remains to be considered what sort of routines existed with regard to Norway's access to the information acquired by the stations. It is clear that Norway received data on every detonation registered, including the time down to the nearest minute, the site and the power of the detonation. But it is equally clear that the Intelligence Staff considered the routine feedback from USAF to be inadequate, considering the level of sophistication of the equipment at the stations. They therefore approached the United States requesting more information, and in December 1967 a positive response was forthcoming in a letter from US Ambassador Margaret Joy Tibbetts to Defence Minister Otto Grieg Tidemand. From now on Norway would also receive raw data, such as films and tapes, produced at the AEDS stations in Norway. The information would also include timing and altitude of 'nuclear clouds' approaching Norway in the aftermath of Chinese and Soviet detonations.[32]

From 1962 onwards the Managing Director of the Norwegian Defence Research Establishment, Finn Lied, had taken several initiatives to get Norway and his institution involved in seismic research related to nuclear tests. The NDRE's efforts were further stimulated when in the autumn of 1966 the first underground Soviet nuclear tests were carried out, followed by new tests in 1967 and 1968. And in 1967, this time on the initiative of the US Defense Department's Advanced Research Projects Agency (ARPA), the NDRE became a partner in the establishment of NORSAR, a very extensive project for the monitoring of nuclear detonations composed of one central and 22 subsidiary seismic installations around Lake Mjøsa in south Norway.[33] At the same time the activity of the Intelligence Staff in the field of registering and monitoring nuclear tests was gradually being concentrated on the PINE FOREST station at Karasjok. At POLAR REIN work still proceeded in the important new field of electromagnetic pulse technique, recording radiated energy in the VLF (Very Low Frequency) spectrum from nuclear detonations at very high altitudes. Such detonations, if sufficiently powerful, had the potential to paralyse communications and weapon systems over great distances. But in 1970 the USAF decided to deactivate this facility, possibly because satellite systems had made it superfluous. This left fall-out sampling by means of air filtration as the only remaining activity at POLAR REIN.

NOTES

1. Historical Office, Office of the Secretary of Defense: *History of the Office of the Secretary of Defense.*, Vol. 1, Steven L. Rearden, *The Formative Years, 1947–1950* (Office of the Secretary of Defense Washington, DC, 1984), pp. 4–13.
2. 'Intelligence Memorandum o. 225. Subject: Estimate of Status of Atomic Warfare in the USSR', in CIA History Staff: Michael Warner (ed.), *The CIA Under Harry Truman* (CIA, Washington DC, 1994), p. 319.
3. PPS 58: 'Political Implications of Detonation of Atomic Bomb by the USSR', in T.H. Etzold and J.L. Gaddis, *Containment: Documents on American Policy and Strategy, 1945–1959* (Columbia University Press, New York, 1978), pp. 364–5.
4. FD, file 'Koordineringsutvalget for 1950–51', Møller to Hauge, 10 Sept. 1951, Møller to McDuffy, 21 Nov. 1951 and 4 Jan. 1952. FFI central archives file 032, Møller to Hauge, 25 Sept., and Møller to McDuffy, 29 Sept. 1951.
5. FO/E, file 'Radioaktivt nedfall', *passim*.
6. Ibid., Chief FST/E/V to Chief FST/E, 6 and 26 Oct. 1955.
7. Author's interview with Tormod Næss, 20 June 1995.
8. SMK, RSU Protocol, meeting of 29 July 1955.
9. FO/E, file '33.04.4 Polar Rein. Historikk (1955–1963)'. Tour Report of 16 Sept. 1955.
10. Ibid., Ramm to Evang, 28 Dec. 1957.
11. Ibid., Ramm P.M., 31 Dec. 1957.
12. SMK, RSU protocol, 26 Feb. 1958.
13. Ibid., RSU protocol, 7 Nov. 1958, and FO/E file '33.04.4 Polar Rein', memo of 14 Oct. 1958.
14. FO/E, file '33.04.4 Polar Rein', letters to Evang, 20 Nov. 1958 and 27 July 1959.
15. FO/E, file '33.50 Kjernefysiske prøver – våpensystemer'. Memorandum of 11 Nov. 1958.
16. FO/E, file '33.04.4 Polar Rein', letter to Evang, 8 Dec. 1959, and Evang to US air attaché, 28 Dec. 1959.
17. Ibid., Evang memo, 30 July; and Evang to Himle, 10 Aug. 1960. Also SMK, RSU protocol, 18 Aug. 1960.
18. Ibid., Martens Meyer memo, 29 Sept. 1960.
19. Ibid., Ramm memo of 28 Dec., and Ramm to Evang 30 Dec. 1960; FO/E, file 'Sak 33.00 Mappe 14. CROCK POT/Elint' minutes of meeting 29 Dec.; and 'Mappe 15. POLAR REIN/Elint', MOU dated 24 Jan. 1961. For the 'Fund' see Chapter 13 below.
20. FO/E, file '33.04.4 Polar Rein', Hellerslien to Evang, 1 Sept. 1961.
21. FO/E, file '33.50 Kjernefysiske prøver – våpensystemer', Evang note, 14 Sept. 1961.
22. FO/E, file '33.04.4 Polar Rein', Evang note 'Amerikanske målestasjoner ...' 14 Sept. 1961.
23. FO/E, file '33.50 Kjernefysiske prøver – våpensystemer'. VI Section to Evang, 26 Oct. 1961, and Brynildsen to all section chiefs, 27 Nov. 1961. For confirmation of a ship-to-air missile shot on 20 October, see T.B. Cochran, R.S. Norris and O.A. Bukharin, *Making the Russian Bomb: From Stalin to Yeltsin* (Westview Press, Boulder, CO, 1995), p. 48.
24. FO/E, box 'E-rapporter', Report No. 25/61; CIA NIE 11-8-59, as published in

CIA History Staff, *Intentions and Capabilities: Estimates on Soviet Strategic Forces, 1950–1983* (CIA, Washington, DC, 1994), p. 88.

25. FO/E, file '33.04.4 Polar Rein', MOU, signed 9 May 1962.
26. Ibid., E VI to SJE, 15 Nov. 1963.
27. Ibid., Staff Visit Report, 2 Aug. 1962.
28. FO/E, file '33.86', Evang memo, 10 Jan., and Evang to Defence Minister, 15 Jan. 1964.
29. SMK, RSU protocol, 31 Jan. 1964. But see also Chapter 13.
30. FO/E, file 'Sak 33.00. Mappe 16. PINE FOREST/Elint'. MOU, 12 March 1965.
31. FO/E, file '33.52 Kjernefysiske prøver', Evang to Defence Minister and Chief of Defence, 28 May 1965.
32. Ibid., letter to Grieg Tidemand, 20 Dec. 1967.
33. O. Njølstad and O. Wicken, *Kunnskap som våpen*, p. 420.

10

Telemetry: Surveillance of Space, Missiles and Satellite Activity

A speciality within the field of signals intelligence is that which intercepts and analyses telemetry, the latter term signifying that portion of the sum of signals that contains technical information on, for example, missile launches. From the beginning of the missile age it was important from an intelligence point of view to follow developments in regard to new missile systems bearing either conventional or nuclear warheads, charting their technical characteristics, where they had been manufactured, the location of the testing places, or whether the launches took place from land, from surface vessels or from submarines. As developments in space technology gave rise to the launching of space probes into outer space, surveillance of space from ground-based stations, in order to monitor the space probes and their orbits, was one of the elements in determining the potential military threat this represented. The Norwegian Intelligence Service came to play a role in both these areas.

In the 1950s the Soviet Union was, to all intents and purposes, a closed realm. There was, within the confines of Western intelligence services, a sense of near desperation at the lack of exact knowledge of what might be going on behind the Iron Curtain. One of the consequences of the dearth of information in the area we are dealing with here was the mistaken assessments produced by the CIA in its 'Estimates on the Soviet Union', which created the phenomenon known as 'the Missile Gap'. Precise knowledge of Soviet developments in the field of missiles became an urgent priority, and here Norwegian Sigint stations were well placed to make a contribution. Comint could cover many activities related to missile firings or space launches, but interception and analysis of technical signals from missiles or satellites were the province of Elint.

The importance of Norwegian Elint collection grew as the Soviet navy from 1960 onwards began to test submarine-launched ballistic missiles. Unfortunately the Americans were late in realising the importance of feedback from their telemetry analyses, and were also reluctant to supply the necessary equipment. This became a topic for discussion at a meeting between the Intelligence Staff and the NSA/CIA in Oslo in February 1962. The Norwegian participants had come to realise that the Intelligence Staff had been registering telemetry signals from missile launches from submarines in the Barents Sea for some considerable time, but without having been able to decipher them. Was the Intelligence Staff in the process of turning into a supplier of raw data without the capacity to decipher what it was handing over? Evang raised this issue during the meeting, and wanted to know why they had not been informed earlier about the probable nature of those new signals. The explanation forthcoming from Dr Louis Tordella, representing the NSA, was that the United States had not been able to discern a pattern for the launches until the end of 1961. They then went back to scrutinise the 1961 material which, in fact, showed that the missile data had been there all the while.[1]

From then onwards Norwegian telemetry became increasingly important as a source of knowledge about Soviet SLBM developments. For example, in an annual evaluation report for 1964 it is stated that five intercepted telemetric signals included data on ballistic missiles fired from submarines located in the operational area of the Soviet Northern Fleet. They supplied quite unique and extremely useful information on both the characteristics and the capabilities of these missiles in an important Soviet area of operations. One CIA expert has later described the Norwegian stations as 'crucial' in this respect.[2] We have seen, moreover, that one of the tasks of the MAD CAT (SOUTH SEA/GLOBUS) project was to collect technical and operational data on Soviet ballistic missiles, and that this also constituted a part of the mission of 'Marjata' and its predecessors.

When the satellite age got off to a flying start with Sputnik on 4 October 1957, this was a sobering warning of the high technological level which Soviet rocketry had attained. Developments in Soviet space engineering continued apace, as witnessed by three moon probes which transmitted images of the other side of the moon (1959), probes to Venus, the first manned space ship (1961), and the Mars probes (1962). A third aspect of the space age and its effect on the world's intelligence activity was the countermeasures initiated by the United States in its attempts to respond to the Soviet challenge. Besides a heavy engagement in its own space programme, in a race which for a time was led by the Soviets, the United States initiated a programme for space surveillance with a direct reconnaissance objective. The aim was to develop a surveillance system which could supplement and in due course perhaps replace photography from aircraft of the U-2 type. Satellites would provide vastly extended coverage, and would be perfectly compatible with international law since objects in outer space would not be violating the territory and sovereignty of nation-states.

CORONA – which was the name of the first US satellite project – gained the approval of President Eisenhower in February 1958, and from August 1960 the United States had access to what was gradually becoming a well-stocked supply of satellite images. Even though the quality of the pictures in the early stages could not be compared with images taken by the U-2, this represented, nonetheless, the start of a new era in which satellite surveillance would play a steadily more important role. The project was so secret that Norway had not been informed, and, although the existence of such images became known after a while, the Intelligence Staff was denied access to them. Not until 1978 did the United States publicly acknowledge its use of satellites for photo reconnaissance.[3]

But the usefulness of space satellites was not exhausted by using them for 'overhead reconnaissance'. Satellites also had the potential of becoming platforms for space-based weapon systems. In a National Intelligence Estimate of April 1963 – NIE 11-4-63, Soviet Military Capabilities and Policies – the CIA wrote that 'the USSR is almost certainly investigating the feasibility of space systems for military support and offensive and defensive weapons.' As part of a national programme to strengthen defence against a potential threat from Soviet spacecraft, the United States worked out a plan of electronic space surveillance, the Space Surveillance System (SSS), rendered in Norwegian simply as ERO. The idea was to establish a network of ground-based stations capable of monitoring the Soviet space programme. Sigint was already able to monitor what went on at the missile bases Kapustin Yar and Tyuratam from which satellites were being launched, by intercepting signals created by such activity. But new stations, with new equipment, would be needed to collect information on the activity and purposes of a given space capsule, determine the type of data it was gathering, and give technical details on guidance and control functions.

It was thought that five such SSS stations would suffice: two in the

Middle East, one in the Far East, one in North America, and one in northern Europe, preferably in Norway. A location in Norway would be particularly advantageous, in part because it was expected in 1963 that the Soviet would start placing satellites in a 'polar orbit', a trajectory passing over the North Pole, and also because a station here would lie close to 'potential data dump areas' in the northwestern Soviet Union. Underlying these considerations was something which did in fact turn out as predicted, namely that the satellites would transmit, or rather 'play back', their data to a receiving station from a position liable to interception by the Norwegian Intelligence Service.

US INITIATIVES FOR A NORWEGIAN STATION

The first US approach about a Norwegian space surveillance station came in October 1962. In a memorandum dated 30 October Evang detailed the proposal and its background:

1. As part of a national programme to strengthen the defence of the United States against current and possible threats from Soviet spacecraft, the USA has made a plan for electronic space surveillance. The purpose is to listen to and analyse radiations from Soviet space vehicles. In that context there is a need for collection possibilities in the neighbourhood of the northwestern part of the Soviet Union. It is estimated that adequate coverage can only be obtained from Norwegian territory.

2. A collection station in North Norway will obtain electronic information impossible to acquire anywhere else outside the Soviet Union. It is assumed that it will be possible to obtain information both at an early stage and at a late stage from spacecraft ascending from or returning to the Soviet Union following a trajectory that is polar or approximately polar. ... In addition to supplementing other means as part of the coverage of the Soviet perimeter, and to intercept radiations and data transmissions from the northern Soviet Union to satellites in polar orbits, a Norwegian station will also provide early information about polar orbit satellites before they pass over the United States, and make it possible to eavesdrop on satellites returning over the northern Soviet Union.[4]

It had been made clear to Evang that to secure maximum coverage of targets in the northern USSR, the station ought to be located in Finnmark. On the other hand, any position in Norway north of 65° would afford unique and extremely valuable information, even if range and quality of coverage would be reduced in proportion to the distance from the Soviet border.

Presumably due to the apprehensions about overcrowding eastern Finnmark with intelligence installations – with a projected two-storey tower topped with a radome, the station would hardly blend into the landscape – the search for a suitable location had pointed in the direction of Fauske. If Fauske lived up to expectations and requirements, there would be obvious advantages in linking up with Fauske I in such a way that Comint, Elint and space surveillance could complement one another.

In November four American experts, together with Evang and another person from the Intelligence Staff, travelled to Fauske to survey the area. The outcome was a decision to build a station bearing the operational name of CODHOOK, and a draft for a formal agreement was drawn up by the United States.[5] The wording of the agreement did not diverge to any great degree from other bilateral agreements of the same kind. The personnel, as usual, would be Norwegian nationals. As it was not expected that Norway would have the analysis capacity for such a complex field, the collection results would go the United States. The Intelligence Staff would therefore send reports by electronic means and in the agreed fashion directly to the United States through established channels. In addition, all tapes, logs and other material issuing from the collection would be despatched to the American embassy in Oslo. But there was a clear understanding that any information of significance would be fed back to Norway forthwith. Evang briefed the Control Committee about the project at a meeting on 26 June 1963 where Defence Minister Harlem was present. Since CODHOOK would be engaged in a passive collection of intelligence it was felt unnecessary to put the matter before the Cabinet Defence and Security Committee, but Harlem would inform Prime Minister Gerhardsen.[6]

Consultations with American specialists on concrete aspects of the developments continued through the spring and summer of 1963. The CIA and NSA were both represented by Mr Bernard of the NSA, functioning as 'project officer' with wide-ranging authority. The Norwegian side was concerned to preserve the secrecy of the project and evidently feared that the configuration of the aerials might reveal the purpose of the station, thus provoking questions as to why Norway took such interest in satellite monitoring. The aerials ought therefore to be mounted inside – and thus covered by – the radome.[7] Norwegian project officer during the initial stages was Martens Meyer, but it was Helge Reiss-Anderssen who gradually became the mainstay and station chief. Fifteen operators and technicians, mostly engineers, were hired for the project during the autumn of 1963, receiving their training in the United States from February to July 1964. They then participated in dismantling and packing the equipment in California. Large crates of equipment were loaded on board a small Norwegian cargo ship in San Francisco, and the journey – via the Panama Canal – took two months. The personnel then reassembled and tested the equipment together with specialists from the American supplier.

FAUSKE II BECOMES OPERATIVE

The construction period for the station – officially designated as Defence Station Fauske II (Forsvarets Stasjon Fauske II, or FSTF II) – lasted for two years. The official starting date for regular operations was 1 January 1965, but in fact it had already carried out its first assignment on 30 November the previous year. This was the surveillance of a Mars probe, number 83 in the Soviet Sputnik series. As it turned out, the commencement of CODHOOK's operations coincided with a period of sharply increased Soviet satellite launchings, going from 35 in 1964 to 64 in 1965, and rising to 92 in 1970. The majority were either photo or communications (Molnyia) satellites, but soon a number of other types were identified, such as Elint, Radint, navigation and meteorological satellites. In 1966 CODHOOK tracked what was thought to be the precursor of a military fractional orbit bombardment system (FOBS), and two years later the first Soviet test of an anti-satellite system with important military implications. The intensified activity which all this generated created an urgent demand for more personnel, particularly operators with experience from the Comint/Elint stations.[8] Starting with 15 operators, the station by 1968 had twice that number, in addition to ten persons in administrative and maintenance functions.

In practical terms, as the pattern of operations developed, the station's main tasks would be specified as follows:

1. coverage of satellite passes;
2. reception and collection of radio transmissions from the same;
3. searches for possible new/unknown signals;
4. presentation of data in readable form;
5. collection of orbit data;
6. analysis and processing of telemetry/command/sensor data;
7. reporting of results to the Intelligence Staff and collaborators;
8. despatching of tape-recorded data.

As of 1967, the registration of launches of missiles and satellites from the northwestern Soviet Union was added as a secondary duty, since Plesetsk near Archangel had become the main launch site for satellites as well as for new generations of ICBMs. From then onwards until the end of the period covered by this book, the surveillance of missile and satellite projects was given top priority by the United States in the Sigint field. This concentrated investment resulted in three large and expensive re-building operations of CREEK MAID (CORVUS) and the incorporation of a telemetry component at HEKLA, in addition to upgradings at Fauske. The way the Intelligence Staff viewed the situation, none of these three telemetry projects could function single-handedly. They were inter-dependent, but also depended on a complex Comint 'tip-off' system; improved data communications; and on an effective control centre in Oslo. Such a centre – called OCC, Operational Control Centre – was thus established at Sæter in Oslo.[9]

As we have seen, the procedures for CODHOOK entailed the trans-ference of raw data to the United States via Oslo. Telemetry was an extremely labour- and computer-intensive field, as it involved the hand-ling of very large quantities of data, and personnel with the necessary experience and expertise had to be on hand before Norway could have a chance of analysing this material at home. However, as the operators gained experience through identifying and monitoring an ever larger number of missiles and different types of satellites, they were increasingly able to carry out operational analyses. A substantial upgrading of the station in 1968, including the installation of advanced computers and 'training of site analysts in new techniques to be employed with the upgraded systems', took this development still further. A plan for further upgrading from 1972 described the situation in this respect in more technical terms: 'For those signals which can be "decommutated" in the field, site analytic personnel provide "quick look" analysis for timely vehicle identification and electrical reporting to the intelligence community.'[10]

With the assumption that the accelerating development of ICBMs would lead to attempts to devise defence systems against the same, intelligence on Soviet experiments with anti-ballistic missile (ABM) systems was a high priority task for Norwegian Sigint. Both Elint and telemetry were in the forefront of these efforts. In a note of 1967, the Intelligence Staff summarised what it assumed was the current state of Soviet developments in the area: Two advanced warning radars of the type 'Hen House', at Olenya on the Kola Peninsula and near Skrunda in the Baltic area, seemed intended to give early warning of any incoming ballistic missiles before handing them on to a 'Dog House' phased array battle management radar at Kubinka close to Moscow. The 'Hen House' installation at Olenya had been registered for the first time in August 1966, its activities suggesting that equipment was undergoing tests. The Skrunda installation was registered in March the following year. 'Dog House', near Moscow, had not been registered carrying out trials up to then. The ABM missile itself, of the 'Galosh' type, had been shown in a parade in Moscow in 1964. Some 'Galosh' sites around Moscow appeared to be ready, while others were under construction. It was thought that this ABM defence system might be complete within six to 18 months.[11]

The note also included a paragraph about what was called the 'Tallinn system', which was believed for some time to be an ABM chain under construction along the Soviet's western border from the Baltic states to the Leningrad district. If this was in fact the case, then a large question mark would have to be placed on the ability of the Western powers to reach targets in the Soviet Union with their missiles in the event of a war. But the assessment of the Intelligence Staff was that the short range of the radar installations and missiles in this system pointed more in the direction of it being an air defence system against attacks by strategic bomber aircraft. After a while this view was adopted by the Pentagon, but it was not until the concluding work on the ABM agreement in 1972, which imposed strict limits on the construction of such systems, that this view was adopted as the basis for negotiation.[12]

SATELLITE INTELLIGENCE AND NORWAY'S INTERESTS

It is not the purpose of this book to delve into technological details about missile and satellite telemetry. In practical terms, however, the intelligence product that CODHOOK provided was to answer the following sort of questions: A satellite is launched, what sort of satellite is it? Is it another launch in an established series, or is it a new or modified type? Then there were the questions of the satellite's function, capability and operational pattern. Of special interest in the Norwegian context was the mapping of Soviet satellite coverage of Norwegian territory – what might they be looking for? In the case of major military exercises in Norway, action could then be taken to pre-empt satellite coverage or intercepts by going under cover or imposing signals silence. In the final analysis, CODHOOK's product would then become an input in attempts to assess development trends in Soviet military space activities.[13]

The most numerous and most important satellites launched during the 1960s, both from the Soviet Union and the United States, were photographic reconnaissance satellites. Each satellite carried one or several cameras on board, and when one or more of them was activated this sparked off a certain pattern in the telemetric signals that were intercepted by the stations. By comparing the time of this particular activity with the satellite orbit, it was possible for the Norwegians to determine the area over which the satellite was moving, and, thereby, what it had been photographing. The actual films, however, were either ejected as capsules with parachutes attached, and retrieved in flight by specially equipped aircraft, or they came down with the spacecraft as it returned to earth. Digital transmission of the images in near real time from the spacecraft to ground stations – much like television transmissions – only became possible in a much later period than that covered by this book.

As we have already mentioned, the use of satellites for overhead reconnaissance was surrounded with particular secrecy on both sides of the iron curtain. The existence of the special institution established for this activity in the United States, the National Reconnaissance Office (NRO), was not officially acknowledged until 1992. As for the images collected by the American CORONA photographic satellites, it would take many years before they were released to the Norwegian Intelligence Service. The main reason for keeping the pictures secret was of course to avoid revealing the rapidly improving technology, which made it possible to photograph installations of military value in amazing detail. Whenever the Intelligence Staff requested release of the images, the Americans attempted to get round the problem by assuring Norway that it was receiving all information of any value contained in the images which could have relevance to its area of interest. Since this did not satisfy the Intelligence Staff, they asked for special studies from the Americans on topics of particular interest to Norway in which information derived from photo satellites was included. Such studies began to arrive towards the end of the 1960s, and provided background information on the Soviet forces in Norway's area of interest. They were characterised as extremely important and confirmed with 'a great degree of certainty that we are as close to the correct picture as it is possible to come', as Chief of Intelligence Johan Berg put it. In regard to tactical or operational intelligence of an 'order of battle' character, there was still not much to be gained from satellite images. But the Intelligence Staff was assured that they would receive whatever information the United States could provide also on this point. Berg concluded that 'We have examples indicating that we really would be given this [information] in a critical situation.'[14]

ESRO AND THE SVALBARD TELEMETRY STATION

The European Space Research Organisation (ESRO) was founded in 1964. Its purpose was to prepare and co-ordinate a civilian scientific and technological joint effort in the area of space research by European states. Norway was accredited with observer status and took part in research projects. In our context it is of interest to see how the Intelligence Staff assessed the question of the construction of a telemetry station on Svalbard, under the auspices of ESRO. The intention was that the station would be one of a quartet in a network. A request to permit the erection of such a station, addressed to the Ministry of Foreign Affairs, arrived in January 1964. Although the Cabinet's original inclination was to view the request in a positive light, a few months with rounds of talks and negotiations were nevertheless required before it pronounced its approval in principle in September. Further complications then arose in 1965, in the shape of Soviet protests that such a station could be used for intelligence purposes. Given Svalbard's treaty status as a territory under Norwegian sovereignty, but with special restrictions on the use of the archipelago 'for warlike purposes', and a ban on the construction of fortifications, this was not entirely unexpected. The Russians were the only other nation maintaining a substantial presence on the islands, in the form of an active mining community, and they felt that this gave them a special position in regard to Norwegian activities there.

In his dealings with this point of contention, Evang was inclined to give the Soviet Union the benefit of the doubt, finding it 'reasonable that the Russians will pursue this matter'. In an earlier assessment of

Svalbard's strategic significance, formulated in June 1963, the Intelligence Staff had pointed out that both East and West had intensified their military activity in the northern areas, and this produced 'strategic tension with associated incidents'. But since the Soviets had air bases around the Barents Sea as far as to Franz Josef Land, ice stations in the Arctic Ocean as well as the constant presence of Elint vessels in northwestern waters, the conjecture was that they would not 'take possession [of Svalbard] under normal international conditions'. If the military balance should change, or if too many factors weighed in NATO's favour, then one might expect political or military responses on the part of the Soviet Union to restore the balance.

At first, when asked for his opinion in regard to an ESRO station on Svalbard in March 1965, Evang had argued that since the telemetry station was fairly basic, it would not intercept other signals than what it was intended for unless provided with extra equipment. In a lengthy memorandum in July, however, entitled 'Theoretical possibilities for a Soviet military reaction on Svalbard', Evang warned that the Russians might see the matter differently. Seen in isolation, the construction of the station was 'possibly not a substantial factor to provoke a military reaction by the Soviet Union'. But viewed in connection with other factors, such as the plans to build an airfield on Svalbard, one should not exclude the possibility that the Soviets would believe that Norway was acting on behalf of NATO, and that plans were being made for military use of the island. Evang concluded that the Soviets, if it came to that, would be able to carry out a controlled action against Svalbard and withdraw before Norwegian authorities were able to intervene.[15]

In another, more or less concurrent, note written by Evang to Defence Minister Harlem during the summer of 1965, and again to State Secretary Arne G. Lund in October the following year, he discussed the ESRO station on Svalbard in greater detail. He pointed out that the Norwegian line of reasoning was firstly based on the presumption that the arrangement would not include any military objectives, and, secondly, that any such assertions by the Russians amounted to incitement and were built on deliberate misinterpretations. Against this, Evang indexed the *Soviet* questions: (1) whether the equipment could be used to collect data on Soviet defence capabilities; (2) whether the Soviet had a guarantee that the seven NATO members in ESRO could not misuse the station without the Norwegians being in a position to control such misuse; and (3) if the landing of small aircraft on the planned airfield would require the installation of security equipment of potential military significance.

After a closer study of the plans for the ESRO station, Evang had now concluded that 'the construction of the station and the choice of matériel is such that it would NOT present technical difficulties to install supplementary equipment which would render the station able to carry out surveillance.' Targets could be Soviet reconnaissance satellites and space stations, Soviet tests on intercontinental missiles, and Soviet air and sea communications. From a purely intelligence perspective it would in fact be 'extremely desirable for the Intelligence Staff to gain access to certain positions at the station'. One could also not disregard the possibility that the Soviets might wish to build their own telemetry station on Svalbard, something which would probably lead to an American initiative for countermeasures. He concluded that this could lead to an 'electronics race on Svalbard' which would not be in Norway's interest.[16]

In spite of Evang's apprehensions the ESRO station was established on Svalbard, and was operational until 1974 when it was closed down. The personnel were Norwegian, but the station was open to scientists from many countries, and Russian scientists visited the station in 1968.

NOTES

1. FO/E, file 'X-2 Elint/Comint drøftelser'. Minutes of meeting 6 Feb. 1962.
2. FO/E, file '33.92. Elint-konferanser', report dated 10 April 1964; author's interview with Sidney Greybeal, 19 Oct. 1964.
3. On CORONA and its background see CIA History Staff, *CORONA: America's First Satellite Program* (CIA, Washington, DC, 1995) and Robert A. McDonald (ed.), *CORONA between the Sun and the Earth: The First NRO Reconnaissance Eye in Space* (American Society for Photogrammetry and Remote Sensing, Bethesda, MD, 1997).
4. FO/E, file '33.04.5 ERO – Historikk'. Evang memorandum, 30 Oct. 1962.
5. FO/E, file 'Sak 33.00. Mappe 6. CODHOOK/Elint'. Draft 'Norway & United States Agreement on Establishing a Space Surveillance Installation in Norway'.
6. FO/E, Control Committee protocols, meeting of 26 June 1963.
7. FO/E Sæter, collection of documents on CODHOOK/ERO.
8. Collection of viewgraphs prepared at Fauske. It is not known whether Fauske's designation 'sambandssatellitt' – communications satellite – also included Comint satellites. The United States apparently had a highly secret Comint satellite programme from the mid-1960s.
9. FO/E Sæter, E-E to SJE, 12 Dec. 1968: 'Etablering av Sigint senter på Sæter'.
10. FO/E, file '33.87 Fauske II. Prosjekter', memo to Kruse, 30 Dec. 1968; file '06.25 CODHOOK': 'Headliner' updating 7 Feb. 1972.

11. FO/E, file '33.99 ob. Kruse', unsigned memo of 24 Aug. 1968, 'Sovjets ABM-system'.
12. On Soviet AMB developments see Steven J. Zaloga, *Soviet Air Defence Missiles* (Jane's Information Group, London, 1989), in particular the section 'ABM role' pp. 103 ff.
13. Fauske viewgraphs.
14. FO/E, file 'SJE Notater', SJE to FSJ, 13 Oct. 1969.
15. FO/E, file '60.70 Svalbard', Evang memo, 2 July 1965.
16. FO/E, file '33.82 ESRO', Evang to Harlem, 23 June 1965, and Evang to Lund, 31 Oct. 1966.

11

'Sets of Professional Bargains': The Foreign Relations of the Norwegian Intelligence Service

Contact and co-operation with the secret services of other countries was from the first of great importance to the NIS. Norway was hardly a special case in that respect – no country, with the possible exception of the United States, can maintain an intelligence service on a self-sufficiency basis. But there was the additional consideration that a small nation like Norway could not possibly obtain satisfactory intelligence coverage of its surroundings when those surroundings mainly consisted of the closed and secretive society of the Soviet Union. Exchange of information was therefore both desirable and necessary. Moreover, a service which in many respects was in its infancy had a great need both to learn from others and to gain access to modern equipment. In all these respects it was a question of what a British intelligence veteran has called 'sets of professional bargains'.[1] It was to a great extent a question of bartering or trading, where what one got depended on what one could give in return. The other limiting factor was the need to protect one's own sources. The wider the circle sharing the information, the greater the risk of compromising sources.

The full extent of the network which gradually got established cannot today be traced in detail. Still the main contours seem reasonably clear. In many ways the choice of countries to co-operate with was self-evident: primarily the Nordic countries which shared the same area of interest, subject to the limitations imposed by the neutrality of Sweden and Finland, and our closest allies in NATO – first and foremost the great powers the United States and the United Kingdom, but also Western Germany. When mapping the NIS network one has to bear in mind that co-operation also embraced the military security service until, in 1965, the security section was established as a separate staff. A point to remember in this respect is Evang's uncompromising insistence that the Intelligence Staff should control all co-operation with foreign services, even in questions of security which otherwise would have been the concern of the Security Police.

Security and counter-espionage seem in fact to have occupied a major share in the co-operation between the NIS and its foreign counterparts during the early postwar years. This was certainly the case for co-operation with the various services working on German territory – the British and American secret services, and eventually the Gehlen organisa-tion, which began as a satellite of the CIA but later became the BND (Bundesnachrichtendienst) of the German Federal Republic. Information from Germany was important to the NIS for two special reasons: the security of the Norwegian occupation forces in the British sector, and investigations connected with the judicial settlement of cases of col-laboration with the German occupiers during the war. The Gehlen organisation, moreover, being the successor of the wartime Abwehr section 'Fremde Heere Ost' was considered to have unparalleled know-ledge of – and presumably also agents and contacts in – the Soviet Union and the Soviet military.

Co-operation with the United States, being by far the most important aspect of NIS foreign relations, is reflected throughout this book in considerable detail and so need not preoccupy us in this chapter. Instead we shall look at relations with some other countries. We have seen in Chapter 5 how the NIS already in 1946 established fruitful contact with the Swedes in FRA (Försvarets Radioanstalt). Through that organisation Sweden during the Second World War had created an advanced service for Comint and cryptology. This became very useful when the NIS in 1946 began developing its own radio control section, with TORKEL as the first out-station in Finnmark. At the same time Evang seems to have cultivated a close friendship with Thede Palm who until the late 1960s ran the Swedish Humint agency. This was known by insiders as the 'T-byrån', and seems to have been particularly active in surveillance of the Baltic, partly through agents on Swedish merchant ships and fishing vessels. Evang and Palm had met in Sweden during the war, and we have it in Palm's own words that 'we got on very well and have done so ever since'.[2]

As time went on, co-operation with both Sweden and Denmark took on a pattern of regular and routine exchange of information which for obvious geographical reasons was of mutual interest. The information was partly transmitted through established wire channels, and partly through fairly frequent meetings of section chiefs on a bilateral or tri-lateral basis – the latter known as the 'triangle co-operation'. From the Norwegian side there was a particular interest in information thus acquired concerning the Soviet, Polish and East German navies. Until the early 1960s the Baltic Fleet was still an important part of Soviet naval strength.

In the early years co-operation with the United States and the UK was largely one of exchange of information, supplemented from 1950 by the close ties developed around the Stay Behind network. From 1951 the co-operation between the Royal Air Force and the Royal Norwegian Air Force in the Elint field was added. Concrete co-operation with the United States 'took off' as we have seen in 1952, specially in the Comint sector, and from 1954 the United States was firmly ensconced as Norway's main intelligence partner, with Comint as the groundwork. One reason for this was that the United States and the UK, whose close collaboration in the intelligence field was developed during the war, decided in 1954 to 'divide' Scandinavia between them as regards Comint. The United States, with NSA, took over Norway, whereas the UK, through GCHQ which was their special agency for Comint, took care of Sweden.[3] In the 1960s, as the Intelligence Staff took over more and more also of Elint activities, both the United States and the UK shared in the collaboration, with the CIA's 'Chief of Station' in Oslo in some kind of co-ordinating capacity.

There seem also to have been quite regular meetings for exchange of information and consultation with British agencies, notably with GCHQ representatives in Sigint matters, but also with the intelligence sections of the British navy and air force. A memorandum from 1963 has a reference to an 'agreement for mutual semi-annual exchange through meetings alternating between Norway and the UK'.[4] The trilateral US–UK–Norwegian relationship in the Sigint field was otherwise arranged in the way that information which wholly or partly came from Norwegian Comint stations would be relayed to GCHQ through the Americans, as specified in the 1954 NORUSA agreement. In addition there existed a special bilateral agreement about direct, mutual and immediate exchange of information about 'new and unknown signals'. Over and above this there was the direct bilateral co-operation on a project to project basis, as explained in the relevant chapters of this book.

In Anglo-Norwegian intelligence chiefs' meetings the topics were generally policy matters, as was also the case in Evang's meetings with senior American representatives. In those cases Evang did not mince his words if he had reason to criticise his Great Power allies. One example of this is Evang's meeting in May 1963 with the head of GCHQ, Sir Clive Loehnis, and his deputy. Evang opened by referring to the quickening development of the intelligence picture in the north. The NIS now had four major targets in their collection effort: missile-firing from submarines, nuclear tests, underwater detection of U-boat movements, and indicators suggesting Soviet development of ABM weapon systems.

> The current problems were a lack of US–UK coordination, and that US or UK collection by other means, such as aircraft or naval vessels, which in one way or another involved Norwegian territory, might give the Russians cause for countermeasures. It was therefore necessary to have a joint review of activities, and above all that Norway had to be informed in advance of such other activities.[5]

Similar criticism, with the added remark that he did not believe the British had told him the whole truth about the reconnaissance flights in question, was voiced by Evang at a meeting on the following day with the head of MI6, Sir Dick White. Perhaps to make amends, representatives of the British Admiralty then offered detailed information about a curious recent incident involving a British submarine. The boat had been on an Elint mission in the Barents Sea when the skipper apparently found himself in the middle of a Soviet anti-submarine exercise 16 nautical miles off the Kildin island near the mouth of the Murmansk inlet. Having been detected by a Soviet helicopter, the submarine was then pursued westwards by Soviet surface vessels. Eventually the boat had to surface to charge its batteries, and then discovered that it had wandered into Norwegian waters. The Admiralty assured Evang that he would be given all the intelligence material gathered under that eventful cruise.

On the whole it seems that the exchange of information between Norway and its two main co-operating partners, the United States and UK, was of mutual benefit. British and American willingness to provide information can hardly be interpreted otherwise than that they in terms of such 'professional bargains' also received important information; that Norwegian, American and British intelligence officers mostly met as professionals on an equal footing who could learn from each other;[6] and also that the Allies felt confident that the information given would be safeguarded, without danger of leaking. On that score the NIS had more reason to hold back in view of recurring revelations of betrayals by members of the US and British services.

The existing material is insufficient to describe the co-operation with the Germans beyond stating that it existed and was apparently quite extensive and mutually satisfactory. After a meeting in Germany in 1965 the deputy chief of the NIS, Colonel Lars R. Heyerdahl, quoted the head of BND as having 'repeatedly referred to the good relationship between the NIS and BND, and emphasised that the NIS was one of the first foreign agencies with which BND had established co-operation. He had given assurances that there would never be any demand for full mutuality in regard to the amount of information supplied. What was most important was the complete trust that prevailed between the two parties.' This might suggest that the Germans gave more than they got in that exchange, quantitatively, but that the quality of the intelligence they received from the NIS was highly valued. Germany in fact seems to have been the only country apart from Finland where the NIS maintained a more or less permanent representation – for long periods by way of two officers, including one in the port city of Kiel for the purpose of the shipping operations.[7] The strong presence in Germany may also be explained by the need to be in contact with the extensive American and British intelligence activity in that country, targeted towards central and Eastern Europe. One of the NIS officers in Bonn also on one occasion ran a year-long secret operation in Czechoslovakia for American intelligence.

Another interesting collaboration partner was Yugoslavia, which after the break in relations between Tito and Stalin sought secret contact with Western countries. Relations between Norway and Yugoslavia had a certain basis in wartime experiences – both had been occupied by the Germans, and Yugoslavs in German prison camps in Norway retained good memories of the efforts by Norwegian civilians to give them food and to help those who managed to escape. From the intelligence point of view, co-operation with Yugoslavia was of great potential interest. The Yugoslav elite's intimate military and political relationship with the Soviet Union both during and after the war had provided them with uniquely valuable knowledge of the way of thinking of the Soviet elite, and of Soviet military capabilities.

The initiative for such contact came from the Yugoslav envoy in Oslo in February 1953. He approached a Norwegian with good connections in government circles, Mr N.N., a couple of days before the latter was due to go to Belgrade, and asked if the Norwegian side might be interested in an exchange of intelligence. With approval from the Defence Minister, Nils Langhelle, Mr N.N. replied in the affirmative. In Belgrade he was then approached by Deputy Foreign Minister Alois Bebler and Vice President Edvard Kardelj. Kardelj expressed interest in an exchange, and Mr N.N. then delivered the following statement:

> I replied that the initiative had come from the Yugoslav side, and the Norwegian attitude was that a certain exchange of military intelligence material would be of interest to both countries. It was however necessary to realise that our membership of NATO of course imposed certain limitations on us in such an exchange. Apart from exchanging information about the military situation around our countries' borders and assessments of the strategic situation, we would be particularly interested in information about agents in the service of the Russians. We imagined that the Yugoslavs possessed special information in that regard, and would greatly appreciate their assistance. I further stressed that the eventual contact would have to be established between the intelligence services of the two countries at a very high level, and should be of a purely technical nature.[8]

In the middle of May Evang himself then travelled to Belgrade to establish contact. During the four days he spent there he was given detailed information about Yugoslav assessments of the security situation in Europe. Although relations between Yugoslavia and the Soviet Union were strained, they did not expect an isolated attack, but thought the Russians would use every means short of open war to destroy Yugoslavia. Referring to Tito's recent official visit to Britain it was said that such contacts 'were primarily aimed to ensure that their country should not become a bartering object in a peaceful East–West settlement. They assumed that Norway's membership of NATO was based on similar reasoning.' Evang was also given detailed information about how the Soviet Union through its embassy and other channels sought to infiltrate and subvert the regime. The meetings concluded with an arrangement for the exchange of information between Evang and the Yugoslav intelligence chief by the diplomatic bag via the Norwegian Legation in Belgrade.[9]

A partner of a somewhat more exotic nature was Israel. Fragmentary sources suggest that Israel took the initiative through its embassy in London in 1959, proposing an exchange of intelligence material. In 1962 the chief of Israeli intelligence and two other officers visited Oslo, and gave Evang a briefing on the organisation of the secret services in Israel. It would have been no surprise that the NIS had an interest in the area: Norwegian military officers had since 1956 served as observers in supervising the truce between Israel and the Arab states, through UNTSO – United Nations Truce Supervision Organisation. From the same time there was a Norwegian military presence in UNEF, the United Nations Emergency Force, which had been stationed in Sinai after the Suez affair in 1956. It seems nevertheless as if the interest in and initiatives for contact came from the Israeli side. After the Six-Day war between Israel and Egypt in 1967 the situation was different. Israel had taken a lot of Soviet arms and equipment as war booty. Then the Defence Staff sent a five-man study group to Israel in November 1967, and two of the men were from the Intelligence Staff.[10]

Bilateral co-operation with NATO countries other than those already mentioned appears to have had a more sporadic character. The Netherlands and France are cases in point. As regards multilateral intelligence collaboration in the NATO framework, it is well known that NATO does not have its own intelligence service. The intelligence material on which the organisation bases its plans and assessments is therefore composed of information from member states' intelligence services. The central NATO documents in this area – the SG 161 series, later MC 161 – hence are committee products to which the national intelligence services have contributed. A problem in this respect is the risk of leaks or at least uncontrolled dissemination of sensitive information when so many countries are involved. This makes many of the member states wary of divulging the basis for their intelligence, and particularly their sources. Norway is a case in point. When for example NATO in the mid 1960s wanted to create its own set-up for Sigint, Evang told a meeting of NATO officers of his strong reservations:

> Evang expressed strong doubt about the appropriateness of the Sigint plan, and stressed that the western great powers and SACLANT were already receiving all the information which Norway possessed, in the most secure manner possible. From the Norwegian point of view this plan would only mean duplication of effort paired with increased security risks.[11]

On the other hand it was obviously important for Norway to influence the Alliance's threat perceptions, so that Norwegian views could prevail in the defence planning in relation to the northern flank. This was done through what a veteran of British intelligence has called 'a second, elaborate, but unofficial system of national cells ... to give private briefings'.[12] In that manner the Intelligence Staff in the 1950s made determined efforts to provide special information to SACLANT. With his two hats, as Commander-in-Chief for NATO's Atlantic Command and as Commander-in-Chief of the US navy in the North Atlantic, SACLANT had the main responsibility for the waters around Norway. The extent to which such special intelligence could prevail depended of course on the quality and reliability of the information. But Colonel (later Lieutenant-General) Wilhelm Mohr, who served for a period in the 1950s in Standing Group, NATO's highest military organ, has stated that Vilhelm Evang had a very high reputation in those circles.

To sum up, we would refer again to the British intelligence veteran Michael Herman, whose book *Intelligence Power in Peace and War* contains a thoughtful chapter specifically devoted to intelligence co-operation:

> National intelligence systems are not self-sufficient. Intelligence on some subjects (the USSR in the Cold War; international terrorism and nuclear proliferation now) has become a kind of international knowledge system, a partial and undeclared replica of open systems such as the World Meteorological Organisation. The result is a patchwork of bilateral and multilateral arrangements of all kinds and all degrees of intimacy.[13]

Herman also underlines the high degree of professional specialisation in such co-operative networks. This has to be kept in mind when considering the so-called 'liaison group' – LG – which was established in the 1960s to supervise and control liaison with foreign agencies. LG functioned partly as a policy-making organ for such co-operation, and partly as an executive body for the more clandestine Humint collaboration. In relation to co-operation in the Sigint field, however, it served mostly as a co-ordinator, making sure that no lines were crossed or that duplication of effort was avoided. A clear indication of this is the organisation proposals from the 'Kaldager Commission', in 1965, which allotted only two officers to the office for foreign intelligence agencies. A later organisation proposal from Reidar Torp, who in 1968 became head of a 'special section' with *inter alia* responsibility for policy analysis, divided liaison with the Americans into four separate functions: (1) The Chief of NIS – then

Colonel Johan Berg – would handle policy matters and matters of special urgency which required his attention; (2) the head of the electronics section would handle all contacts in his field, except that feedback from Comint material could go directly to the chief of that particular section; (3) questions of operational intelligence and general background information would be dealt with by the civilian veteran intelligence officer Trond Johansen; and (4) finally, all questions relating to Stay Behind would be handled by Sven Ollestad.[14]

This would appear to confirm that only specialists could take an active part in the work within each particular field of Sigint, exchanging data, holding meetings where results of analyses were discussed, etc. The reason was partly that the different aspects of technical intelligence, like other scientific or technological disciplines, had become fields in which only the specialists understood each other. Even more important, because the 'need to know' requirement of secrecy sets strict limits on the number of people who are able to talk about the work, the tried and well-established collaborative channels across national borders had become the best and probably the only forum for the advancement of knowledge.

NOTES

1. Michel Herman, *Intelligence Power in Peace and War* (Cambridge University Press, for the Royal Institute of International Affairs, Cambridge, 1996), p. 218: 'Overseas liaisons are ultimately sets of professional bargains.'
2. See the minutes of a meeting with Thede Palm in the collection of documents made available in photocopy by the Swedish Commission on Neutrality Policy (Neutralitetspolitikkommisjonen) in 1996.
3. Author's conversation with Louis Tordella, 25 May 1995, and with the GCHQ veteran Michael Herman on 28 December 1996. See also for Sweden the papers of the Neutrality Policy Commission, in particular the meetings with Gunnar Smedmark, Bengt Wallroth and Lars Ljunggren.
4. FO/E, 'Skuff 15 – 40.04 Tjenestereiser utenlands'. Memo, 10 May 1963 from the head of Section VI to Chief, Intelligence Staff entitled 'General Communications Headquarters – GCHQ'.
5. Ibid., Evang note of 20 May 1963: 'Møte London'. A sign that the British took the criticism seriously is a meeting three months later between Major Sveinsson from the Intelligence Staff and representatives of the British Air Ministry. The British then made a point of informing the Norwegians that they had just postponed some planned reconnaissance flights since 'one does not wish to irritate the Russians while the test ban talks are going on in Moscow' (ibid. note to Chief of NIS, 16 Sept. 1963).
6. See for example FO/E, file 'Skuff 5 – 8.00 SIS'. SIS here stands for 'Special

Intelligence Studies' and contains memoranda and critical commentaries exchanged between the services.

7. As alluded to in Chapter 5, the NIS periodically maintained liaison officers in important ports for briefing and debriefing of agents in shipping operations. In addition to Kiel there were for long periods representatives in London, Singapore and Hong Kong.

8. SMK, KU protocol, unsigned annex dated 16 March 1953 on 'Utveksling av etterretningsstoff med Jugoslavia'.

9. UD, unregistered papers relating to KU. Evang note of 30 May 1953 'Besøk Beograd 15–19 mai, 1953', and UD 38.5/53B, Foreign Ministry to Minister Braadland, Belgrade, June 1953.

10. FO/E, file 'Skuff 13. Løse dokument. Ad Israel'. A more detailed account of these contacts can be found in Odd Karsten Tveit, *Alt for Israel: Oslo–Jerusalem 1948–78* (Cappelen, Oslo, 1996).

11. FO/E, file 'Skuff 15 – 40.05 Utenlandske besøk'. Evang note about Sigint meeting with Captain Harrel and Commander Pierucki, 3 July 1964.

12. Michael Herman, *Intelligence Power in Peace and War*, pp. 364–5.

13. Ibid., p. 203.

14. FO/E, file '1968 SJE-A Notat Inn/Ut', note 8/68. For the Kaldager Committee see Chapter 15.

A State Within the State?
Controlling the Intelligence Service

It is a well-established part of the Norwegian parliamentary system that expenditure of public funds is subject to control by the Storting, which also decides on the budget. Control is exercised on the Storting's behalf by the Auditor-General's Office. This is a time-honoured system with very strict rules and routines. For a secret service this poses obvious problems: even when the Storting meets in secret session and approves secret annexes to otherwise public expenditure accounts, this is no guarantee against leakage of information. And with knowledge of budgetary allocations an agent will be well on his way to finding out the kind of activities underlying.

During the first postwar years this was not a serious problem. The cost of the very modest intelligence activities was small enough to be easily camouflaged in secret or relatively unspecified budget items. What did create some difficulties was the continued existence of unused moneys collected from state or private sources for wartime resistance activities – funds which had not been allocated by the Storting (which of course was not in session during the occupation) and which therefore were outside the normal field of concern of the Auditor-General. The requirement of control over the use of the funds still applied, however. And we have seen that Evang as early as December 1946 proposed setting up a special committee to control the secret budget, and to act as adviser whenever large amounts of money were to be expended.[1]

In the spring of 1947 Defence Minister Hauge took the initiative for a meeting with the Auditor-General, Hans T.H. Lütken. Thor Sire, the head of the division auditing the accounts of the defence establishment, was also present. 'I took it upon myself to audit the secret accounts of the intelligence service', wrote Sire in a later memorandum. But he made it a condition that he should be assisted by a control committee with the Defence Minister and Chief of Defence – or their representatives – as members. This was then approved, with the addition that the committee would have as secretary the head of the finance division of the Defence Ministry.[2]

Partly as a consequence of this the expenditures on intelligence were divided into three parts. Funds voted by the Storting, which mostly covered the salaries of the personnel, were included in the regular defence budget under Chapter 901: 'Joint expenses – the Defence Staff'. Initially it was there specified, year by year and quite openly, how many new positions for officers would be allocated to the 'intelligence and foreign liaison' staff: five in 1950; 16 in 1951; another 16 in 1952; and three in 1953. Some routine office expenses, and travel and transport, came under the same chapter without further specification. Temporary appointments to the Radio Section were included in the Army Signal Corps budget allocations. From 1948, however, the Defence Ministry was given an extra budget for 'extraordinary preparedness measures'. Allocations for intelligence and security work could then be divided between two budgets – in the extraordinary budget camouflaged as 'security measures'. The third, secret, budget could hence be limited to cover expenses directly connected with secret intelligence activities, such as the cipher service, the shipping operations and Stay Behind.

The expansion of the intelligence service 'took off' in the financial year 1953–54, when the total sum of allocations became tripled from the previous year – over four million kroner compared to one and a half million in 1952–53. As the total defence budget was then about one thousand million kroner, the intelligence service's share went up from 0.15 to 0.4 per cent. The Defence Ministry had then already submitted secret proposals for a reorganisation of the intelligence and security service. While based on the proposals of the Andersen Committee, about which more will be said in Chapter 15, the ministry stated that developments 'have shown the proposed plan as quite insufficient. The intelligence and security service has grown in size and importance, and has in recent years been given a series of new tasks which cannot properly be dealt with by other elements of the defence establishment.' The Storting's Military Affairs Committee accepted the ministry's proposals, but refused to go along with the proposition to free the service from the shackles of the Defence Staff. They also appended a curious rider to the effect that the service 'ought not to be expanded beyond what the work demands'.[3]

The main cause for the budgetary increase was the increase of personnel, primarily for Comint. For 1953–54 it was proposed to increase the number of military officers to 80. The greatest increase was, however, in the number of civilian posts – to 211. This would give the Intelligence Staff a total personnel strength of 291, as against a total of 203 in October 1952. With such an increase the Defence Staff found it necessary to request 'that expenditure for the intelligence and security service be covered up as much as possible'. It was necessary to avoid discussion in the Storting and in the media about the number of personnel employed by the service, or about the individual budget posts. Henceforth the personnel complement for the intelligence service would have to be excluded from the general statement of personnel in the defence establishment, which normally circulated as Secret Annex No. 1 to the budget proposal. A large part of the allocations should also be transferred to the special preparedness budget.[4] The solution, put into practice from the 1954–55 budget, was to let the Intelligence Staff operate with two personnel lists, one covering regular personnel which could be included in the 'Secret Annex No. 1', and one which was kept separate from it. The budget allocations were then divided into two parts, one which formed part of the regular defence budget, and one – amounting to about two million kroner or about half the budget for salaries – subsumed under the special preparedness budget, where it was included in a section for 'various expenditures' at the disposal of the Defence Ministry.

As far as can be seen, both those parts of the budget were presented for approval by the chairman of the Storting's Military Affairs Committee. That left the funds for special secret purposes, which at least from 1948 were partly provided from foreign sources. This was in particular the case for Stay Behind, which was financed one-third by the Americans and one-third by the British. This must also have covered the border-crossing operations, the funding of which does not otherwise emerge from the source material. Finally there were the shipping operations, where the identity of the agents required special protection, and compensation paid to a few so-called 'protected persons', such as special consultants to the cipher section. Controlling and approving all these expenditures was then the task of the Control Committee.

From a constitutional point of view there remained the problem that the Storting was not kept in the picture, since the funds were not voted by the Storting and hence escaped the formal control mechanisms of the Auditor-General's office. Up to the end of the 1950s this was, however, a question of 'small change', relatively speaking.

REORGANISING THE CONTROL COMMITTEE

The task of auditing the secret accounts was becoming increasingly burdensome for Thor Sire as the years went by, and the Control Committee was not functioning according to intentions.

> The number of problems and the mass of bills and vouchers steadily increased, and I had to spend evenings and weekends to cope with the work. The meetings of the Control Committee became more and more irregular, and often ground to a halt because of lack of time by some members. Stand-ins were also used. As the activity increased, the accounts system became inadequate.[5]

At the end of 1955 Evang decided to act to get the control work more properly organised. The impetus was somewhat unusual: the financial contributions to intelligence activity from foreign sources had evidently produced a surplus, and the Norwegian Defence Research Establishment (NDRE) needed to obtain an electronic computer which had become available abroad. Evang brought the matter up at a meeting with Defence Minister Nils Handal. Present also were the Auditor-General, Lars Breie and Christian von Krogh as head of the finance division of the Ministry. 'After some discussion it became clear that it would not be possible to obtain Storting approval of funds for such a machine for the time being.' Evang was therefore asked to consult with the Director-General of NDRE to find 'a practical solution' which could be acceptable to the Control Committee. The NDRE somehow did get their computer about a year later, and gave it the nickname 'Fredrik' or 'Frederic' – Ferranti Rapid Electronic Defence Research Institute Computer.

With that as the impetus, the rest of that December 1955 meeting was devoted to the problems concerning the Control Committee, and it was decided to 'resurrect' the committee and establish it on a more regular basis. Members would be the State Secretary and the head of the finance division, from the Defence Ministry, and the Chief of Defence Staff or his deputy, together with Thor Sire and Evang – the latter presumably as a non-voting member. The committee would be formally charged with reviewing and approving the secret accounts, and would meet at least once every four months.[6]

In March 1956 the Intelligence Staff proposed an arrangement for budgeting, accounting and auditing, worked out after consultation with the Auditor-General's office. At this time the Defence Staff had achieved status as a separate accounting unit under the budget of the armed forces. This meant that the Intelligence Staff, or G-2, budget share had to be specified under the various headings for salaries, travel, *matériel*, etc. But approximately half the expenditure for intelligence and security purposes would still be covered by largely unspecified items in the 'Special Preparedness' budget. Both 'halves' were, as far as we can see, submitted for review by the Storting's Military Affairs Committee. But it is doubtful whether that committee was given all the secret annexes, such as personnel lists. The procedure was explained in the following terms in the budget proposals for the Intelligence Staff for 1954/55:

> According to confidential information from the Defence Staff, last year's procedure was that the total defence budget was presented to the Finance Minister. Having been approved by him the matter was then passed on to the chairman of the Military Affairs Committee of the Storting, whereupon the sums were apportioned between the ordinary and the Special Preparedness budgets. The Defence Staff recommends a similar procedure this year.[7]

There still remained the problem, in relation to the Storting, of the secret annexes, particularly personnel lists. From 1958, if not before, this was solved by giving the chairman of the Military Affairs Committee specified lists of all personnel with regular appointments in the intelligence service. 'This is to be regarded as constituting approval by the Storting', wrote von Krogh after a meeting in April 1958. Regarding personnel outside the regular lists, the chairman would be given 'the principle and the numbers', but no names. At that April 1958 meeting, which was attended by the Auditor-General and by Thor Sire, the chairman was informed about the arrangements, and apparently gave his approval.[8]

That left the secret budget, which up to 1958 mainly comprised two categories: 'protected persons', which were a small number of persons employed on a part-time basis as special consultants – for cipher work, for example – and 'protected operations'. This latter category is not defined in the sources, but seems in the main to have been offensive intelligence operations abroad – particularly DELFINUS or shipping operations – and also special courses or other activities within the framework of Stay Behind. Lists, plans, and descriptions as regards all such activities were submitted to the Control Committee for review and approval, whereas the accounts were audited by a representative of the Auditor-General's office, now posted to the Defence Staff on a permanent basis and reporting to Sire as his superior in all intelligence matters. It seems clear that the chairman of the Military Affairs Committee was also informed about these arrangements.

Looking at the total budget for the Intelligence Staff, for the last year before the start of the new era with rapid expansion of Comint, we find a sum of just over six million kroner. Closer scrutiny reveals that the 'protected operations' required fairly modest sums, less that half a million. Norway's one-third of the Stay Behind costs covered about an additional quarter of a million. All such costs were then scrutinised by the Control Committee, in considerable detail. In the minutes of the committee's meeting on 20 October 1958, for example, we find that they questioned the running costs of the modest car fleet of the Intelligence Staff, and approved an allocation of 15,000 kroner for refurbishing an office building.

A NEW ERA: THE HP AND CP PROJECTS

In the chapter on Comint we characterised the supplementary NORUSA agreement of August 1958 as the opening of a new era for the NIS. This is also true in the economic sense. The greatly expanded Comint and Elint activity was to be fully financed by the United States, and the sums were not modest: a memorandum for Evang from October 1959 shows an investment programme for buildings and installations under the HP – High Priority – project of about ten million kroner. Most of that would be completed by the end of 1961. In addition came running costs which would amount to some six to seven million a year once the build-up was completed. Evidently, neither the Norwegian nor the American authorities wanted it known that such a massive expansion was afoot, and with US funds.

The solution was a major increase in the secret budget, with the so-called 'Fund' as a central feature. This special fund was kept outside the public accounts, deposited in the Bank of Norway, and put at the disposal of the Defence Ministry. But this did not mean a 'free for all' with regard to the Intelligence Staff's use of the money. The requirement of control and audit was maintained, through the machinery of the Control Committee and the Auditor-General's representatives. This special fund was first reflected in the minutes of the Control Committee's meeting of 15 April 1959, when Sire gave the following explanation of how finances from abroad were handled:

> All direct expenditure for operation, construction and installations, and refunds concerning the projects in question are kept outside the national accounts. All payments from such non-national sources – which are not included in the national accounts – go to the end user through the Defence Ministry via the Bank of Norway. The Control Committee shall oversee the use of such funds, and the Auditor-General's representative in the Intelligence Staff will perform the day to day audit.

In practice, the NIS would from 1959 operate with a number of different budgets and accounts. First came its share of what may be called the regular 'national budget', one part of which was unspecified as it covered the salaries of the permanent staff officers. Next came the Special Preparedness budget, which contained the ordinary budget for salaries and running costs of the intelligence service – part of which was again unspecified under a chapter for 'various expenditures'. Since that chapter had a maximum limit of five million kroner, some of the running costs had to be covered by the 'Fund'. On top of all this came what was variously called 'the foreign budget' or 'the projects budget'. This was special, not only through its size, but also because it had to follow the American 'fiscal years' from July to July. The main post in this 'project budget' was the HP or 'High Priority' project, with its Comint and Elint activities. Next in importance came the CP or 'CROCK POT' project, which came to include a number of activities concerning registration and measuring of Soviet nuclear tests. Later would be added the BRIDGE/CANASTA/SOSUS projects for the surveillance of Soviet submarine activity.

It is difficult with so many components to get an overall view of expenditures in the framework of the NIS during the 1960s. The total costs must also have varied greatly from year to year, since capital costs would diminish and running costs increase as construction was completed and regular operations got under way. A first – and we must assume – fairly representative estimate may be found in the budget for 1966, when the long era of Labour governments had come to an end, and Defence Minister Otto Grieg Tidemand of the new non-socialist Government decided to make a full report to the new chairman of the Military Affairs Committee. The 'national' budget was then a little over 18 million kroner, of which half was subsumed under the regular budget of the Defence Staff. Of the remaining nine million, about one half could be entered as 'various expenditures' under the special preparedness budget. But as that item had a limit of five million, the rest had to come from the 'Fund'. The Defence Minister then explained the 'Fund' as 'coming mainly from the activity financed by the Americans, owing to the Americans providing a full refund for pension and social security payments, plus a charge for administrative expenses'. This means that pension and social security payments, being covered by expenditure under the regular national budget, were then refunded by the Americans and deposited as a special fund. Finally, Grieg Tidemand stated the amounts provided by the Americans under the projects budget, which for the fiscal year 1966/67 came to nearly 49 million, with 20 million for capital costs and the rest as running costs.[9]

In practical terms, what all this amounted to is that the United States paid the capital costs of constructing and equipping the stations built up under the expansion programmes included in the NORUSA agreement of 1954 and subsequent supplementary agreements. The personnel, being Norwegian citizens, and enjoying the normal social security and pension scheme benefits for civil servants, had their salaries paid by the Intelligence Staff and paid normal taxes. The net salary expenses were then refunded by the United States to the Norwegian Government. It has been estimated that about 70 per cent of the total personnel employed by the NIS were indirectly paid by the United States. Refund of pension scheme and social security payments, however, were paid into the 'Fund'. The 'Fund' hence served as a reserve which occasionally could be used to cover unexpected outlays in relation to the various projects, but which otherwise, and mainly, was kept as a 'cushion' for future needs. If for example major changes of a political or economic nature should force a cessation of US funding for ongoing projects, the personnel would still be entitled to unemployment benefits, etc. under the social security network which covered all Norwegian citizens. As of 30 September 1969 the 'Fund' represented an asset of over 32 million kroner.

The Americans obviously felt that the results of this large investment, in terms of the intelligence product, justified the cost. Only towards the very end of the period covered by this book did some reservations appear. The cost to the United States of the war in Indo-China was beginning to squeeze public funds, and savings were called for. The issue arose at a conversation in January 1971 between Erik Himle, then Permanent Secretary in the Defence Ministry, and John Ausland, no. 2 in the American embassy. In connection with a proposal to use part of the 'Fund' to finance the purchase of new maritime reconnaissance aircraft for the Norwegian air force, Ausland aired his reservations about the arrangements for financing the Norwegian intelligence effort:

> It was his personal opinion that the arrangement providing for general support outside the individual projects was unfortunate, and that he would not be able to recommend such arrangements. He was also against the close connection between such support and ongoing intelligence activity. Such arrangements could in certain circumstances give rise to serious political problems.

Ausland's reference to political problems may have been addressed both to Norwegian internal politics, where revelations about US subsidies to the Norwegian intelligence effort would stir up a heated debate, and to American concerns about the consequences if it should become known that US military assistance to Europe, while officially ended, was continuing to Norway. This might engender demands from other NATO countries for similar financial support from the United States. But Himle in his reply chose to emphasise Norway's special situation:

> We have taken upon ourselves to build up stations and carry out intelligence activity which is of major importance to the Americans, to NATO, and in some degree to ourselves. To the extent that such activity is important to the Americans it is bound to irritate the Soviets. The heavy concentration of such activity in northern Norway, and particularly Finnmark, has increased the military 'sensitivity' of the area. This needs to be compensated through an increase of armed strength in the region. This will however require an economic effort which we have so far not been able to muster. We

have found it natural that the Americans should make a financial contribution in this respect, for the purpose of achieving a better balance between the sensitive intelligence activity in the area and our military preparedness at key points. Our strengthening of the southern Varanger garrison is based on such considerations. And even if the general financial assistance from the US formally goes to the purchase of Orion and Hercules aircraft, the indirect result is that it has freed funds which we can use to improve our defences in northern Norway.[10]

THE QUESTION OF CONSTITUTIONAL AND POLITICAL RESPONSIBILITY

Over and above the control functions exercised by the Control Committee for the intelligence service, major projects such as HP and CP were also subject to political oversight through being submitted for approval by the Cabinet Defence and Security Committee.

The need for this oversight was emphasised when such project proposals coincided with periods of political sensitivity regarding US and British reconnaissance flights in the North. The U–2 and RB–47 incidents in 1960 did not directly concern the NIS. The same goes for the issue of LORAN-C stations on Norwegian territory, with its implications for Norway's stand against nuclear weapons, and also for Norway's part in the establishment of NATO's NADGE chain of warning radars. But they all had implications for Norway's security policy stance, with its particular combination of integration in the collective defence system and screening against activities deemed provocative towards the Soviet neighbour.

As for the Government's general position towards expansion of NIS Sigint activity in the North, we have seen how the Cabinet Committee in 1958 approved the 1958 NORUSA extension with the Prime Minister's statement that Norway, given its special geographic position, ought to perform such special services for the common defence as long as they had a clearly defensive character. The same stance lay behind the committee's approval, in 1960 and 1961, of the BRIDGE/SOSUS projects, the monitoring station at Korpfjell and the BARHAUG station. But new American proposals for further expansion, put before the committee in January 1964, were met with some reservation by certain Cabinet ministers.

The subject this time, which Evang had discussed beforehand with Defence Minister Harlem,[11] contained several elements. First there was the issue of adding 40–50 operators to the personnel at the Comint stations in eastern Finnmark. Then there was a wish to expand the system for monitoring Soviet nuclear tests, not only with new equipment and an increase of personnel at the existing stations, but also building a new acoustic intelligence station at Karasjok and possibly another seismic installation elsewhere in Norway. Evang's explanation to the Cabinet Committee had as its point of departure the determined personnel limit of 624 under the NORUSA agreements. Another 40–50 persons could be accommodated within that maximum. Evang for his part stated that 'an increase was by itself undesirable in areas so close to the Soviet border. On the other hand the electronic intelligence service was of major importance to both Norwegian and NATO interests, and Britain and the USA set great store on its being carried on to maximum effect.' In regard to stations for seismic and acoustic monitoring of nuclear tests, Evang advised further talks with the Americans before any decisions were taken.

Trygve Lie, the former Secretary-General of the United Nations who had just joined the Government as Minister for Shipping and Trade, opened the discussion in the Cabinet Committee by asking whether the stations in question, being financed by the United States, could be characterised as the kind of foreign bases which Norway had banned through previous public policy declarations.

> *Prime Minister Gerhardsen* thought the answer was no. The personnel was Norwegian, and the activity had a purely defensive character. It was partly aimed at a control function which would contribute to a lessening of tensions. The Prime Minister was of the opinion that we ought to provide this service to the Alliance. Nationally it was to our benefit since we shared in the results of this intelligence activity.
>
> *Minister Gundersen* saw it as important that the limits of international law were respected, and that activity and operations were clearly defensive. Sharp Russian reactions had to be expected if certain limits were transgressed. He could accept the plans as proposed, on the assumption that they were kept within the limits he had indicated.
>
> *Minister Lie* said he agreed with the views of Minister Gundersen.
> *Minister Himle* also agreed with this. He suggested that it was unfortunate to have such a concentration of personnel in the border areas. He asked that it be considered whether some removal of

activities to western Finnmark or to Troms/Nordland was technically feasible.

Minister Lange agreed that it was important to provide these services
to the Alliance. But we had to be aware that the Russians did not
accept our definition of a base.

Minister Gundersen proposed for consideration possible changes in
the form of American financial support, for example that we took
over more of the personnel costs against compensation in the form
of increased deliveries of *matériel*. The minister also mentioned in
this context the question of informing parliamentary bodies in one
form or another about the financial arrangements concerning the
building and operation of the stations.

Minister Harlem intimated that it was usual to inform the chairman
of the Military Affairs Committee.

The Prime Minister determined that the Cabinet Defence and
Security Committee had no objections against the matter being
proceeded with in the manner proposed by the Defence Minister.[12]

Two years later, in January 1966, the intelligence service again appeared
on the agenda of the Cabinet Defence and Security Committee, this time
as the first item. The point of departure was a lengthy paper from the
Defence Minister, and there were good reasons for its detailed nature.
After being led by Labour governments ever since the Second World War,
the country now had a non-socialist coalition government with Per Borten
as Prime Minister. The new Defence Minister, Otto Grieg Tidemand,
opened the meeting by declaring that he wished to give a survey of 'the
manner and extent of the collaboration which had been established
between the Defence Intelligence Service and American military authorities on the basis of our membership of NATO'. As he had himself been
informed by his predecessor and by senior military and civilian officials,
he now felt that the Cabinet Committee ought to be aware of the situation,
'in order to determine whether they were prepared to take the constitutional responsibility for the continuation of the activities, to the
extent and in the fashion in which they had been conducted under the
previous government'.[13]

The brief minutes of the meeting make it difficult to determine if
Grieg Tidemand's statement covered all aspects of the work of the NIS.
He appears to have laid primary emphasis on the Sigint activities,
including their financing and the control mechanisms. He called those

activities 'one of our most important military contributions to the co-operation within NATO', and underlined 'their defensive character'. Prime Minister Borten was the only one to query the statement. He asked whether the intelligence service received other financial support beside what had been explained about the 'Fund'. This Grieg Tidemand denied. The conclusion of the meeting has the following wording:

> *The Prime Minister* declared that no one of the members of the Cabinet Committee had any objections against the activity explained by the Defence Minister being continued in the main to the same extent, along the same lines, and with the control arrangements which had been explained.

As far as can be seen, this was the last occasion within the period covered by this book that the intelligence service as such was discussed in the Cabinet Committee. This reinforces the impression that the Government was satisfied that the control mechanisms that were in force, at least during the 1960s, given the need for secrecy, were satisfactory both from the constitutional, political and financial points of view. The problem that remained was that of parliamentary control, where strict rules of procedure were circumvented. Here the Government from 1958 instituted the chairman of the Military Affairs Committee – later supplemented with the vice-chairman, and still later with the President of the Storting – as a sort of parallel to a well-established practice whereby an extended parliamentary committee for foreign and constitutional affairs functioned as a secret consultative organ for the Government. What we cannot be certain about is the extent to which the various bodies outside the Defence Staff and Defence Ministry were given all the details about the more clandestine activities of the NIS, such as the Stay Behind activity, or the shipping operations. Such operations are not mentioned in the written version of the meetings where the chairman of the Military Affairs Committee or the Cabinet Committee were informed about the activities. But it is quite likely that they were only described orally on account of their extreme secrecy.

NOTES

1. See above, Chapter 1, p. 10.
2. RR, undated memorandum (probably from 1969) by Thor Sire.
3. Ibid.

4. FO/E, copy file H, Chief of Intelligence to Defence Minister, 1 Oct. 1952: 'Etterretnings- og sikkerhetstjenesten i Forsvaret. Budsjettforslag for FST II 1953–54'.
5. RR, Thor Sire's memorandum.
6. FO/E, Evang papers, memo of 6 Dec. 1955.
7. FO/E, file 'Skuff 2. Budsjettforslag FST/E 1954/55'. Chief of Defence Staff to Defence Minister, 1 Sept. 1953.
8. RR, report of meeting by von Krogh, 19 April 1958. The Military Affairs Committee's chairman, Henrik Svensen, was then new to the job. The sources give no indication as to whether his predecessor, Alv Kjøs, had been similarly informed.
9. RR, von Krogh memo, 6 Oct. 1966: 'Etterretnings- og utenriksstaben'.
10. FD, record group 34 'Etterretningstjeneste'. E. Himle memo of conversation with Ausland, 15 Jan. 1971.
11. FO/E, file 'Skuff 5. 10.01 FD–Forsvarsministeren–Statssekretær'. Evang notes of 7, 15 and 23 Jan. 1964.
12. SMK, protocol of Cabinet Committee meeting, 31 Jan. 1964.
13. Ibid., protocol of meeting, 21 Jan. 1966.

13

The Uses of Intelligence

The need for knowledge about a potential enemy's capacity and intentions is the main purpose of the considerable intelligence activity of states and alliances. This need has both a long-term and a short-term perspective. In the longer term, the political leadership needs information on which to base guidelines for the size and structure of its armed forces. Based on the information fed into the defence establishment by the intelligence services, the political leadership has to achieve its primary task: to plan, build up and maintain, within the limits set by the country's economic strength, a credible defence which can serve the purpose of deterring a possible enemy from armed aggression. In the short run it is the task of the intelligence services to give timely warning of an adversary's preparation for aggressive action against the country. Political scientists analysing the problem of warning in relation to 'strategic attacks' here tend to distinguish between 'strategic' and 'tactical' warning. Strategic warning is then taken to mean more long-term indications that a potential enemy is planning or preparing aggressive action, whereas tactical warning is information that an attack is about to be launched.

In a Pro Memoria from 1962, Evang summed up the most important tasks of the national intelligence service in the military and foreign policy field. They were:

- to keep the political and military leadership abreast of developments in the countries of the Eastern bloc;
- to be the collecting agency in the strategic intelligence community;
- to act as the staff element for intelligence within the Defence Staff;
- to look after Norwegian intelligence interests in NATO;
- to build, maintain and develop bilateral relations with the national intelligence organs of other countries;

  • to be in charge of the central security service of the armed forces
    as well as their cipher service.[1]

The production of intelligence reports by the Intelligence Staff began in
a very modest way in 1945. Those early reports tended to be very general,
based largely on open sources, summarising available information on
individual countries' armed forces, or with a thematic content such as
'The Bikini nuclear tests', 'The atom bomb and the war at sea' and the
like. But from 1948 onwards there is a clear turn towards the Soviet Union
as the centre of attention, interspersed with incursions into matters
regarding the Nordic countries, other Eastern Bloc states, national and
international communism, etc. The first report preserved in the archives
which deals exclusively with the Soviet Union is a fairly comprehensive
study, filed as No. 1/1948, of the merchant navy of the Soviet Union as
of July 1947.

    As the Co-ordination Committee through 1949 developed a pattern
of more or less regular meetings, the first item on the agenda was
the consideration of a 'Survey of the most important military–political
developments', which was produced specially for the committee. This
may be seen as an attempt to live up to Defence Minister Hauge's intention
to have the committee as some kind of joint intelligence committee. The
practice soon died down, however, probably because Evang found the
discussions unproductive. Intelligence items thereafter tended to come
up only when Evang needed the support of the Committee – and particularly of the member from the Prime Minister's office – for new initiatives
or proposals.

    A survey[2] shows that 18 fairly comprehensive intelligence reports
were produced during 1948–49. During the 1950s and 1960s the number
of reports issued annually varied, with an average of 15 to 25 reports.
Their distribution was initially highly restrictive, with only the Defence
Minister and the Chiefs of the armed services as regular customers. From
1955 onwards the list was expanded somewhat, but was still very limited,
although with considerable variation according to recipients' special
interests in the subject-matter. A kind of 'revolution' occurred from 1964,
after which some reports had as many as 60-odd recipients.

    Looking at topics we find that most of these special reports – called
'E-rapporter' – were devoted to one or more special themes. Aspects
of the situation as regards the Soviet Union's army, navy and air forces,

as well as its merchant navy and fishing fleet, are most frequently covered. Finland seems to have been at the centre of attention in 1950, probably because the Norwegian Legation in Helsinki was the first such station to be provided with an attaché posted there from the Intelligence Staff.

In addition to those special reports, the Intelligence Staff from the early 1950s produced and distributed a monthly intelligence digest – 'Månedlig Etterretningsrapport', or MER. Recipients were in the beginning the same as for the special reports, but distribution – and the sheer volume of the individual reports – increased considerably from 1956. This may have been inspired by a positive evaluation from the Army High Command, recommending that 'for reasons of preparedness all active units should have the opportunity to study the information contained in the MERs'.[3] The MERs began with a brief summary, followed by a 'general' chapter which regularly opened with a one-sentence threat assessment. Separate chapters on the different armed services followed, country by country, beginning with the Soviet Union, East Germany and the other satellite states, reporting 'order of battle' news, information about major exercises, new weapon systems, etc. Other chapters might be on 'Communications and Logistics', and on economic and political developments. Often special studies were appended to the reports, on such topics as 'Soviet submarines in World War II: An assessment of their performance', 'Guided missiles in the Soviet Union' or the like. Intelligence items were graded as to their reliability, with sources classified in a range from A to F, and the reliability of the specific item graded from 1 to 6.[4]

It has to be said that the reports of the kind so far mentioned, whether special or monthly, were of the 'static intelligence' variety. They took time to produce, and mostly reflected developments over time, intending to give the addressees an overall picture of the strategic situation. They therefore need to be distinguished from the daily reporting of special events, or intelligence of a strictly operational or tactical nature intended for the operations staffs of the armed services. But they had one major purpose in addition to keeping the Norwegian defence and military community abreast of the situation: they were meant to influence Alliance assessments of the relative importance of the northern flank of NATO, and thereby to push Norway and the northern areas higher up on the priority scales for NATO's defence planning.

NATO, SG 161 AND NORWEGIAN THREAT ASSESSMENTS

In a report from December 1951 entitled 'Intelligence survey 1951. Possibilities of a Soviet attack against Scandinavia', the Intelligence Staff made this concluding assessment:

> There are no indications that the Russians are seriously considering military moves against the West in the near future. But their capabilities for offensive action are steadily increasing, as evidenced by their build-up of air forces with jet-propelled aircraft and their atom bomb tests. The Russian naval forces in the north have been considerably strengthened, hence their offensive potential is greater than before.[5]

Clearly, one aim of reports of this kind was to raise consciousness in NATO about the security problems of the northern flank. Right from the beginning of the Alliance, and through most of the period of this book, Norway was fighting an uphill battle against the dominance of the central front of the European continent in NATO defence plans. As NATO had no independent intelligence service, the assessments on which planning was based was the product of inputs from the intelligence services of the member states. The NIS was of course fully aware of this, and their wish to make an impact on Alliance assessments was an important factor in the effort to improve the quality of their product. In the early 1950s this led to the build-up of a special military analysis section, with qualified professional officers from all three armed services.

Initially the NIS sought to make its influence felt at SHAPE as well as in AFNORTH, the Allied Forces Northern Europe Command in Oslo. But Evang soon realised that the ultimate arbiter of NATO strategy was the Standing Group in Washington DC, and – for naval planning – ACLANT in Norfolk, Virginia. SG 161 was the document which laid down the Alliance's assessment of the threat from the Soviet Union and its satellites, and the main tenor of that document from 1953 onwards was that the Scandinavian peninsula ranked low on the list of possible targets for a Soviet offensive.[6] Initial efforts by Evang to change this assessment, at a special meeting in London in December 1952 under the aegis of Standing Group, and also in conversations with ranking SHAPE officers in January 1953, were fruitless. But in September 1953 a request from Standing Group for a Norwegian evaluation, coinciding with the start of work towards a new Norwegian defence plan, set the ball rolling. An interservice Intelligence Assessments Committee under the guidance of the Intelligence Staff was established, with the dual aim of producing an intelligence basis for the Norwegian defence plan and an assessment to serve as Norway's input into Standing Group's next SG161 revision on 'Soviet Strength and Capabilities'. In fact the document would serve a four-fold purpose: as a joint national view of the strategic position of Scandinavia; as a common basis for the military's advice to Norwegian political authorities and to the Allies; as Norway's view and contribution to SG 161/3; and as a framework for a more specific analysis of Soviet possibilities for attack against Scandinavia.[7]

The Assessments Committee produced its report, entitled 'Norwegian Assessments of Soviet Bloc Strength and Possibilities of Attack against Scandinavia 1955–60', in June 1955. It was a voluminous document, in six parts and with 59 annexes. Part One contained an introduction, and Part Two considered 'Factors influencing Soviet strategy', with the following conclusions:

> The Soviet Bloc, as controlled by the government of the Soviet Union, possesses considerable military strength which is based on a continually improving economy and increasing labour resources. In the period 1956–60 the ability of the Soviet Union to wage war will steadily increase. The strategic shortcomings which the Soviet Bloc is faced with, are not so serious that they in themselves will prevent them from going to war. The shortcomings will gradually be reduced during the coming years.

The third part of the document, on the presumed basic strategy and aims of the Soviet Union, stated that the Soviet Union would possess a sufficient arsenal of strategic and tactical nuclear weapons for that to constitute the decisive factor in their strategy. But since they had to assume that the adversary would have superiority in atomic weapons, surprise would be all important. Part Four, considering 'Soviet capacity to achieve eventual operative aims in Scandinavia', began with the assertion that a military threat against Scandinavia had to be considered in the wider context of a large-scale aggression against the whole of Western Europe. In regard to the other Nordic countries it was assumed that Sweden would remain neutral, but would resist if exposed to attack; that Finland would not resist the passage of large forces but would not take part on the Soviet side; and that both strategic and tactical nuclear weapons would be used by both sides. The main conclusion of the report was that 'Scandinavia stands forth as an important strategic target area for the Soviet Union.' They had the necessary resources, and the forces were deployed so as to be able to launch an attack without re-grouping, and the importance of Scandinavia was seen as warranting the launching of armed aggression aiming at conquest of the whole area. Defence plans would have to assume that no warning would be possible, so Allied mobilisation would have to take place during the initial main Soviet assault.[8]

It is clear that the Norwegian threat assessment differed from the official NATO planning estimate, both about the importance of Scandinavia in Soviet planning and about the size of the forces which might be employed against the area. Norwegian intelligence, and the planners, would therefore have a difficult job to influence Allied assessments and plans. Evang had in the meantime continued his efforts to convince Standing Group of the validity of Norwegian intelligence assessments, but without noticeable success. The SG 161/3 assessment, from the summer of 1955, was still very different from the Norwegian estimates of the threat against Scandinavia. The main thrust of a possible Soviet attack was expected to be directed towards the European continent and the UK, and the Scandinavian peninsula would be bypassed.

In the spring of 1956 this began to change – a fact which the Intelligence Staff took to be a direct result of the more solid assessments contained in the Norwegian document from June 1955. In April Evang reported to the Co-ordination Committee that SHAPE had accepted Norwegian estimates of the air threat against the area, and would support Norway's views in the Standing Group. A few weeks later, a memorandum from the Intelligence Staff to the Cabinet Defence and Security Committee was positively brimming with self-confidence:

> In the course of the last three years the Intelligence Staff has by its own efforts reached a clear view of the military threat against Norway from the northwestern parts of the Soviet Union. That view has now in the main been accepted by the military authorities in NATO. Together with other intelligence organs we have established corresponding estimates of the threats from the Baltic, Northern Poland, and the northern parts of East Germany. Those views have also been accepted by NATO. The major part of the information has been

supplied by electronic intelligence, supported by shipping information and special intelligence. An increased effort in the electronic
field is now required in order to maintain the favourable position
which Norway has attained in this matter.[9]

It is fair to assume that such professional optimism was strongly
coloured by a desire to strengthen the Intelligence Staff's efforts to
convince political quarters about the importance of their work, and the
need to provide them with more resources. So, although Norway's
struggle to raise Allied consciousness about the importance of the
Northern flank did produce results, perhaps particularly with regard to
the growing interest of US intelligence services in the area, and in general
the attention which the US air force and the US navy were beginning to
pay to the region, the meagre Allied commitment of forces for the
reinforcement of Norway's defences indicated that the Northern flank
was still a sideshow in relation to the Central Front.

Further estimates from the Intelligence Staff, which from 1960 tended
to be more frequent, did not waver from the earlier assessments about
the assumed importance of the Scandinavian peninsula to Soviet strategy
and planning. If anything, that importance was thought to be increasing.
But the NIS consistently declined to go along with those who thought
that the threat of a Soviet attack was coming nearer. However, while 'the
possibility of a limited attack against Norway cannot be regarded as very
likely in the present situation, even small changes in the political situation
may alter that assumption'. This sentence, which with minor variations
was a regular feature of the assessments, brings up the question of the
two elements that threat assessments are traditionally based on: capability
and intentions. If the capability, or the military strength, of the Soviet
Union and its satellites was throughout seen as sufficient for an armed
attack, and such an attack nevertheless was seen as unlikely at least in the
short run, then logically this could only mean that the Soviet Union's
intentions were generally peaceful. However, a recurring item in the
estimates is a reference to the innate trend of Soviet communist ideology
toward expansion. This points to an endemic weakness in predominantly
military intelligence services, namely the tendency to concentrate on
'bean-counting' in order to measure capabilities, and a corresponding
lack of attention to, or inability to assess, an adversary's intentions as a
function of politics. We shall return to this in the concluding chapter of
this book.

GETTING THE PRODUCT TO THE CONSUMERS

An adage about intelligence which has become something of a banality, but still raises an issue of fundamental importance, is that the best intelligence is useless if it does not reach those quarters – military and political – which make the decisions about defence and security. With the NIS, and the Intelligence Staff, being part and parcel of the military side of the defence establishment, the first question to be considered is whether the intelligence product reached those elements of the military that were concerned with planning and operations, and also, whether the presentation of the product in form and content was seen as relevant to their needs.

A general impression from the 1950s and early 1960s is of fairly frequent complaints from military quarters that what they got from the Intelligence Staff was meagre and unsatisfactory. Some of the complaints reflect a feeling that Evang and the Intelligence Staff tended to isolate both themselves and their information from the military. Demands for more and better intelligence often came from the Commander-in-Chief North Norway, who had particular responsibilities for preparedness in the areas bordering on the main adversary. Part of the problem may here have been that the military commanders with operational responsibilities were mainly interested in short-term tactical intelligence, whereas the NIS product tended to emphasise more long-term strategic intelligence. On the other hand, alarms or alerts of an 'Early Warning' nature, which called for quick military responses, were few and far between, and the Intelligence Staff presumably saw no need to waste time in producing and disseminating intelligence about Soviet military activity of a more or less routine character. Hence the military commanders in the field most of the time had to be satisfied with the regular series of intelligence reports, supplemented with institutionalised forums for the exchange of views and information. On this latter count Defence Command North Norway did get special treatment, with the institution, in 1951, of an intelligence committee for North Norway.[10] There the intelligence officers of the three services met, sometimes also a representative from the Security Police. The impression is that a main purpose of that committee was precisely to consider matters of security and counter-intelligence. Only towards the end of the 1950s was an intelligence committee established at the national level, in Oslo, to serve as an organ of co-ordination, exchange of information, and advice in the field of military intelligence. This committee was composed of the deputy chief of intelligence and the intelligence officers – G-2 – of the three services.

In a major long-term planning exercise undertaken by the Defence Staff in 1964, the question of the military's use of the product of the intelligence service, and the usefulness *per se*, was taken up on a fairly broad scale.[11] The conclusion was that the situation in those respects was not satisfactory, but the blame was divided in equal portions between producer and consumer. The operational commanders were blamed for having an inadequate understanding of what the Intelligence Staff could be expected to provide, and also for not having formulated their requirements in a satisfactory manner. The Intelligence Staff, for its part, was urged to make more effort toward anticipating the needs of its customers and adapting its product accordingly. For both purposes, the study stressed the need for better contact and communication between producer and user. One result of this may have been the institution, later in the 1960s, of a wider forum for contact and exchange of views between the services and the Intelligence Staff.

On a more practical level, the latter part of the 1960s saw major improvements in the working relationship between the Intelligence Staff and the military. Of particular importance were the initiatives taken by Major-General Herman F. Zeiner Gundersen, first as Chief of Staff to the Defence Chief, and then as Commander-in-Chief North Norway. He started with a 'strong impression that much of the intelligence about the forces on Kola which ought to reach C-in-C North Norway, or at least pass through his HQ, never got to him'. A first step was the establishment of a Sigint 'cell' at his HQ at Reitan, under his command, but operated by the Intelligence Staff. Through that unit would pass, in particular, all electronic intelligence collected by the stations in North Norway. Intelligence of a more tactical or operational nature would be assessed in place before being passed on to Oslo for further analysis. The presence of such an element at his headquarters, under his command, also enabled the Commander-in-Chief North Norway to communicate his requirements directly to the stations, and to pass on the resulting information to his subordinate commanders.[12]

The other side of the same coin were complaints by the Intelligence Chief, Colonel Johan Berg, about insufficient feedback from Defence Command North Norway to the Intelligence Staff. He felt that information of intelligence value collected by the military in the North in the course of their daily activity, did not reach the NIS. But he also criticised the way the Defence Command handled the information received from the Intelligence Staff, such as unauthorised distribution of highly classified intelligence. Colonel Berg therefore insisted on, and Zeiner Gundersen accepted, the appointment of an officer from the Intelligence Staff to head the intelligence 'cell' at Reitan.[13]

At the same time as those rearrangements were being put into place at Defence Command North Norway, efforts were under way to achieve a better working relationship between the Intelligence Staff and the central Defence Staff. The latter was then about to be reorganised into a Defence High Command, with greater power and authority over the armed services, and with particular responsibility for planning. This new set-up would be equipped with an 'Operations Room' with continually updated information about the military situation in and around the country. Since the Intelligence Staff would not be housed in the new Defence High Command's headquarters, the NIS would maintain a strong element attached to the Operations Room, providing a continuous intelligence update based on information supplied from intelligence headquarters through specially secure communications links.[14]

As the final item in this reform process concerning 'the uses of intelligence', some modest steps were taken to enable the Intelligence Staff to provide more of the kind of analysis that would be of use to security policy planners in the Defence and Foreign Ministries. For that purpose Colonel Berg brought in Colonel Reidar Torp as chief of a 'Special Section' with among other things special responsibilities for military–political analysis. The further fate of that element lies outside the time-frame of this book, but we shall return to the wider problem of military–political intelligence in the Conclusions.

1968: INTELLIGENCE PUT TO THE TEST

In June 1968 the border areas between the Soviet Union and Norway witnessed a Soviet force demonstration without precedence. Presumably timed to coincide with a NATO exercise POLAR EXPRESS/POLAR ICE further west – all NATO exercises in North Norway were as a matter of policy prohibited from coming within 500 kilometres of the Russian border – the Soviet Union carried out a major preparedness exercise in their Leningrad military district. In the final phase of that exercise, on 6 June a motorised infantry division lined up in battle order within sight of the border, guns facing west towards Norwegian territory. Tanks moved into Boris Gleb, the small Russian enclave on the western bank of the frontier river, and airborne units were landed at an airbase in the region. The forces were not withdrawn until four days later.

This provocative act evidently caught the NIS napping. In a 'post-mortem'[15] on the affair, the Intelligence Chief had to admit that the event, having taken the intelligence service by surprise, painted 'a dark, but in my opinion realistic, picture of our ability to provide warning of an attack across the border'. With the means available, it had to be realised that there were 'limited possibilities for registering, from the Norwegian side, a line-up and preparation for attack over land from Kola against Norwegian territory, prior to the attacking force being within sight of the border'. The rapid transition from an exercise pattern to a march-up towards the frontier also showed that preparations for attack could to a great degree be camouflaged as exercise activity. In mitigation, it was stated that in case of an actual assault, one might expect to have strategic warning through a build-up of tensions, in which case intelligence from our own sources, bilateral contacts, and NATO, might be expected to provide some indicators.

It was in fact clear that the demonstration had a purely political purpose, intended to intimidate Norway in relation to the staging of NATO exercises in North Norway. For one thing, with the presence of considerable and fully prepared NATO forces further west, the days in question would seem the worst possible time for aggressive Soviet action. At the same time there is no doubt that the demonstration was an impressive show of the Soviet army's readiness for combat, its mobility and the flexibility with which it had moved from one operational pattern to another.

The later weeks of the summer of 1968 were to prove even more eventful, however, as the crisis in Czechoslovakia began to unfold. How did the Intelligence Staff, with its recent addition of a military–political unit, measure up to that challenge? A central document in that respect is an analysis, put together by section chief Colonel Reidar Torp and circulated one month before 21 August 1968.[16] There it was stated that 'the means we may expect the Soviets to use in the present situation will in all likelihood be of a political nature. For political reasons it is most probable that a military intervention will not occur, even though Soviet forces remain in the country, and strong units are in position on the East German and Polish side of the Czech border.' The scenario outlined in the analysis was that psychological pressure, by political and military means, would continue until there were adequate assurances against an unacceptable outcome of the crisis. On the face of it, that analysis was to prove wrong. But we also know, from recently available material, that a political and not a military solution remained the preference of several major decision-makers in the Kremlin up until the last moment.[17]

At a meeting with the NIS's American partners in Washington DC in November 1969, Colonel Berg brought up the issue of timely indicators of activity that might suggest Russian troop movements in the Kola Peninsula. The connection to the experiences of June 1968 is obvious. Berg specified three concrete requirements: registration of all traffic on a highway curve east of the town of Pechenga (which could be seen from the Norwegian side but which became obscured on days of bad visibility); registration of heavy traffic on other main highways in the area; and selective registration of landing craft passing through the Pechenga Fjord. Berg said he was aware that such equipment had been developed for the American army, and wanted to try it out in the North. The main idea was to place such instruments on Norwegian territory, but if this did not work then the equipment might have to be placed clandestinely on the Russian side, for automatic operation. The American representatives at the meeting expressed their willingness to comply with the request, but the results, if any, lie outside the framework of our study.[18]

To round off this consideration of the 'uses of intelligence' from a strictly Norwegian perspective, it seems reasonable to conclude that the NIS's greatest strength lay in keeping the military abreast of events and activities in an intermediate time perspective, leaning towards what we have defined as 'strategic warning'. As regards tactical warning, although the June 1968 experience was an eye-opener, it was hardly conclusive evidence of an inability to give tactical warning of activity on a scale which suggested preparations for an actual attack. Thankfully, the capabilities of the NIS in that respect were never put to the test.

NOTES

1. FO/E, file 'Organisasjon og virksomhet. Del I', Evang PM, 22 March 1962: 'Forsvarsstabens etterretnings- og utenriksstab. Arbeidsformer og organisasjons- messig plassering'.
2. FO/E, box 'Mikrofilmer – E-rapporter 1948–69 ...': 'Oversikt over utgitte E- rapporter i perioden 1948–69'.

3. FO/E, file 'Dokret', Army High Command to Intelligence Staff, 24 Feb. 1956, requesting 14 additional copies of the reports.
4. FO/E, 'MER' files, *passim*. While reports of this nature may in earlier years have been issued at more irregular intervals, it seems that this regular monthly routine began in 1954.
5. SMK, Co-ordination Committee papers, 1950–51.
6. The issue of Norway and the Northern Flank's place in Allied strategy, which can only be touched on here, is extensively analysed in the standard work by Rolf Tamnes, *The United States and the Cold War in the High North* (Ad Notam, Oslo, 1991).
7. SMK, Co-ordination Committee protocol, meeting of 23 Sept. 1953. The material concerning the interservice committee is in FO/E, box 'E-vurderinger/Trusselvurderinger', file 'E-vurderings-utvalget 1953'.
8. FO/E, box 'E-vurderinger/Trusselvurderinger 1954–61'. Report dated 7 June 1955.
9. SMK, RSU papers, Evang memo of 26 April 1956.
10. Ibid., Co-ordination Committee protocol, meeting of 19 March 1951. ˙
11. FO/E, red box 'E-tjenestens organisasjon og virksomhet' No. 2. LPG report 'Studium av FST/ES organisasjon, ansvarsområde og virksomhet', May 1964.
12. FO/E, collection 'Dokumenter i retur fra saksbehandlere'. I.a. ØKN to FST 6 March 1968 and 23 Oct. 1969, ØKN to FST/E, 16 April 1968, and author's interview with Zeiner Gundersen, 9 Jan. 1997.
13. Ibid., SJE to FSJ, 6 Sept. 1969, and interview with Zeiner Gundersen.
14. FO/E, file 'SJE Notater 1969', SJE to SJO, 24 May 1969, and STSJ to SJO and SJE, 16 Oct. 1969.
15. FO/E, box '1969 E-rapporter', Report No.3/69, dated 28 Sept. 1969. See also FD file 342, FD to UD, 20 June 1968.
16. FD, file 344. FST/E to FD,. 20 July 1968.
17. A useful survey of recent research on the events in Czechoslovakia in 1968 is a report by Mark Kramer in *Cold War International History Project Bulletin*, 2–3 (Washington, DC, 1993).
18. FO/E, file '1969. SJE/A Notat Inn/Ut', memo, of 12 March 1969.

14

'Square Pegs in Round Holes':
Organisation and Personnel

In a study of the NIS as an organisation, two problems in particular need to be considered: its place within the Norwegian official establishment, and the recruitment and composition of its personnel. The two are connected. First of all, should the NIS be a part of the military establishment, and if so, should the personnel be military officers? Or should it be a separate entity, under the Defence Ministry, the Foreign Ministry, or the Prime Minister's office, with a mainly civilian staff? Many of the troubles experienced by the NIS in the period considered by this book can be traced back to an inability to devise a proper place for it in the structures of Norwegian officialdom. In the early years, as we have seen in the two first chapters, this hardly mattered: the service was very small, and was expanding very slowly in an almost experimental manner. Then, when the rapid expansion began, especially from 1954 onwards, the window of opportunity for reorganisation had passed, as all energy went into managing the professional challenge of new tasks. The unsolved problems, perhaps best summarised under the broad concept of civil–military relations, in the end were to lead to the chief's downfall.

The first clear sign that the NIS had outgrown its harness came in May 1952, in a ten-page document sent to the Defence Minister by the Chief of Defence Staff, Lieutenant-General Ole Berg, but probably based on a draft from Vilhelm Evang.[1] A growing number of tasks and missions, and a corresponding increase in the number of personnel in a bewildering array of categories, had resulted in a 'flat' organisation with ten different activities placed directly under the Chief of Intelligence Staff. The professional military officers in the central staff were mostly on short-term secondment from their service, which made advancement in grade difficult if not outright impossible. Civilian staff had had to be given civil service grades with ill-fitting job descriptions and little chance of promotion. The time had surely come for a thorough review of the whole set-up.

General Berg listed five preconditions for such a review. First, the service would have to remain firmly national. The burgeoning trend towards internationalisation of the armed services, through our membership of NATO, should not affect the Intelligence Service. Secondly, there had to be a centralised service for strategic intelligence, not one spread among the armed services. And the service should be militarily organised. Although there might be practical advantages in a unified civilian intelligence service placed under the Defence Ministry or directly under the Prime Minister, this was not feasible in the circumstances. Fourthly, the service should be placed directly under the Chief of Defence Staff, with direct access for the Chief of Intelligence at all times. The fifth precondition was a properly functioning co-ordinating organ, with representatives from the Prime Minister's Office, the Foreign and Defence Ministries, and the Security Police. This was a reference to the existing Co-ordination Committee, but that committee needed to be put on a firmer footing, with clearer authority.

THE ANDERSEN COMMISSION

1952 was a year marked by reform planning in the Norwegian defence establishment. The shape of Norwegian postwar defence had been subjected to a thorough review by the 1946 Royal Commission on Defence. But its report, issued in 1949, had been overtaken by events, namely Norway's membership of NATO, which altered the basic premises on which the country's armed forces would be based. The central structure of the military establishment, which in 1946 had changed from the wartime set-up of a Defence High Command to the less centralised Defence Staff, with a Chief of Defence Staff as not much more than a figurehead, was again in the melting pot. It was known that the Defence Ministry was leaning towards the British model of a Chiefs of Staff Committee, and this was one of the parameters when the ministry in the spring of 1952 asked Andreas Andersen to head a committee to review the place and structure of the military intelligence and security service. The other terms of reference were contained in General Berg's ten-page document.

The Andersen Commission, which reported in September 1952,[2] accepted General Berg's basic premise of a national intelligence service, recognising that Norway's special geographic location required a national institution which could evaluate the strategic situation on NATO's northern flank, and inform the Allied planning and command authorities accordingly. The commission also agreed that the chief of the service needed direct access to the top of the defence hierarchy, but wavered as to whether the proper place of the service was in the military or civilian sector. Two solutions were considered: either a directorate under the aegis of the Defence Ministry, or a service responsible to the Chiefs of Staff Committee – if that should be the shape of things to come. The commission did not come down in favour of one or other arrangement, but the chairman, in a subsequent memorandum to the Permanent Under-Secretary of the Defence Ministry, seemed to lean in the direction of placing the service under the COS. He also touched on a third possibility, which would have meant suborning the service under the Cabinet Defence and Security Committee and administratively attaching it to the Prime Minister's office. But he found that such a solution raised a series of political and constitutional difficulties which made its consideration untimely. Oddly enough, another memorandum, which although unsigned and undated bears the marks of coming from the same author, saw a more independent service under the Ministry of Defence to be the best solution. Co-ordination of the work of the three secret services – intelligence, military security and secret police – would then be the task of the Prime Minister's office. It is not irrelevant in this context to mention that Andersen was in line to become the Prime Minister's representative on the Co-ordination Committee for the secret services.[3] Yet another unsigned memorandum, which bears the marks of having been written by Evang, suggested the form of a directorate under the Defence Ministry as a solution.[4]

In December 1952 the Ministry of Defence presented its proposals for the organisation of Norway's defence. A central feature of the proposals was the replacement of the Defence Staff by a Chiefs of Staff Committee. However, in an unusual twist, the Military Affairs Committee of the Storting rejected that idea, proposing instead to strengthen the authority of the Defence Staff over the armed services. As a natural consequence of that, the Committee had the intelligence and security service remain as part of the Defence Staff.[5] The Intelligence Staff, now with the abbreviation FST/E – Defence Staff/Intelligence, or in full 'the

Intelligence and Foreign Liaison Staff' since it included liaison functions with other countries' armed forces – hence would continue as a specialised staff under the Defence Staff.

In regard to the internal organisation of the Intelligence Staff, the Andersen Commission proposed to have six sections. Apart from sections for administration and security, the actual intelligence work would be organised into four sections. The collection of intelligence would be the task of V Section, as the Radio or Sigint section, and VI Section, whose duties included such special intelligence work as the shipping service, the handling of other agents abroad, and the Stay Behind organisation. The cipher section, IV Section, would be responsible for protecting the country's own ciphers as well as code-breaking, and III Section, the military section, subdivided into bureaus for the army, navy and air force, would collate, analyse and produce reports based on the collected intelligence. The Commission foresaw an Intelligence Staff with a total personnel of 289, three-fifths of which, or 173 persons, would man V Section. This would have two sub-sections, one to direct and run the listening and monitoring stations at Vadsø (ex TORKEL), Fauske, Trondheim (Heimdal), Stavanger (Randaberg) and Oslo, and one for analysis of the material.

EXPANSION – AND ITS PROBLEMS

The rapid growth in the activities of the Intelligence Staff towards the end of the 1950s, and the concomitant personnel increase, was not accompanied by any major change in the way the Staff and the service was organised. Internal restructuring to fit the unequal growth of different sectors hardly affected the overall organisational pattern, where once again a great number of separate and almost watertight compartments reported directly to the chief. No hierarchic structure was established which might have facilitated co-operation and co-ordination among different but related activities, and which might even have solved internal problems before they could fester to the extent that Evang himself had to be the peacemaker. In a broader perspective, some of the problems were obviously due to the peculiar character of the activities of the intelligence service, and to the veil of extreme secrecy which surrounded most of them. A number of watertight compartments enclosed within one large and nearly as watertight compartment was hardly conducive to a tidy and transparent organisational structure.

The heterogeneous character of the personnel was another complicating factor. Most of the men in the mid–range management category had been recruited through personal acquaintances, in the majority of cases going back to wartime comradeship. They often had officers' grades without having gone through the schools and training required for regular commissioned officers. Any advancement had therefore to be arranged on a personal basis, with the chief interceding on their behalf with the Chief of Defence Staff, instead of being more or less automatic, as was the case when regular officers were appointed to positions in the armed services which carried a particular grade. The sprinkling of regular officers serving in the Intelligence Staff, mostly in the Military Section which was charged with analysing and evaluating information about the Soviet armed forces, mostly stayed only for the normal three to four years' tour of duty before returning to the fold of their own armed service. Then there were the operational personnel, particularly the radio operators, more often than not recruited from telegraphists in the merchant navy. Once inside they, like the middle-management veterans, tended to make intelligence work a lifetime occupation. All this resulted in an NIS which was largely staffed by highly experienced specialist personnel, but which was at the same time a closed society, communicating more easily and freely with its opposite numbers in collaborating intelligence services than with its fellow countrymen in other parts of the defence establishment.

In a memorandum to the Chief of Defence Staff towards the end of 1961,[6] Evang admitted that the situation within the Intelligence Staff gave cause for concern, but blamed the rigid structure imposed by the need to conform to the overall Defence Staff organisation – again, the 'square peg in a round hole' syndrome. To the extent that the Intelligence Staff had undergone changes in previous years, they had to be seen as 'an adjustment to the outer framework determined by the organisation of the higher defence leadership'. It was now high time to reconsider the place of the Intelligence Staff, so as to achieve a better conformity between framework and content. At the same time Evang seems to have realised that the room for change was limited. In particular, the Intelligence Staff would have to remain within the Defence Staff. The same realisation imbued the report of an internal study group which had been appointed to review the organisation. Drawing conclusions from that report, Evang in March 1962 presented two memoranda to the Defence Chief with a series of proposals for reorganisation.[7]

In the first of these memoranda, Evang listed four major reasons why a reorganisation had become necessary:

1. Due to the country's geographic situation, the Norwegian collection effort, particularly in the electronic intelligence field, had within a few years grown to become an essential element in Western efforts to gain knowledge of new Soviet weapon systems.
2. The situation with regard to evaluation and analysis had changed considerably. After many years when the main effort had gone into getting the various collection efforts off the ground, the current task was to achieve a better co-ordination of efforts.
3. The operative collection of intelligence had changed character. Sharp Soviet reactions against Western collection methods meant that not only the operational environment but also the possible political repercussions had to be taken into account.
4. The demands on the Intelligence Staff to provide G-2 services to the Defence Staff had over the years seen a strong increase, and the Chief of Defence Staff's new directives had taken this development still further. This was expected to augment the difficulty of making the Intelligence Staff fit into the regular activities of the Defence Staff.

This diagnosis by Evang was hardly remarkable for its clarity. And the second memorandum, purporting to propose solutions, seems in retrospect both superficial and inconsequential. In Evang's defence it should be said that with the urgent demands for expansion of the Comint effort, and so many new activities coming on stream, there was a not unreasonable fear that any in-depth reorganisation might severely damage current projects. His one major reform proposal was to suggest organising the various intelligence functions into three divisions, each with a division head to whom the section chiefs would report. With three division chiefs instead of a multitude of section chiefs reporting directly to him, Evang hoped to gain more time and breathing-space for central and long-term planning. One of the three divisions would concentrate on military intelligence, one on Sigint (or what he still tended to call electronic intelligence), while the third division would concentrate on evaluation and analysis.

THE DEFENCE STAFF'S 1964 LONG-TERM PLANNING EXERCISE

The mention in Evang's 'diagnosis' of the Chief of Defence Staff's new directive referred to what was to become the first step in a major reorganisation of the Norwegian military leadership. It had become increasingly clear that the weak position of the Chief of Defence Staff hampered the efficient functioning of the military establishment, both internally and in relation to being able to speak with one voice in Alliance contexts. The new directive gave the Chief greater authority over the separate armed services, and a stronger position towards the Defence Staff. The second step was to appoint a new Chief who was willing to use the new powers. That came in the person of Vice-Admiral Folke Hauger Johannessen, who took over the top job in January 1964. To mark the new authority of the position the title had been changed to Chief of Defence.

The third step came in the shape of the Defence Staff's 'Long-term Planning Group', commonly referred to as LPG, which in May 1964 produced a series of proposals for organisational changes in the military hierarchy. In their recommendations about the Intelligence Staff, the group took as their point of departure the fact that the evaluation and analysis functions were lagging behind the collection effort, and recommended efforts toward a better balance. They also proposed strengthening the leadership functions, and, in particular, wanted close and daily cooperation between the Intelligence and Operations Staffs. Suggestions to divide the NIS into a staff element with planning and analysis functions, and a separate institution for intelligence collection, were however put aside.[8] Evang was dismayed by the LPG report, which he saw as another push in the direction of making the intelligence service a mere servant to the military. In a meeting with Defence Minister Harlem and the new Chief of Defence, followed by a memorandum to Hauger Johannessen, Evang now put the finger on the fundamental problem: the Intelligence Staff's double role as an independently functioning intelligence service and as an element in a military staff. The more the military insisted on the staff functions of the service, the more difficult it would be for the Intelligence Staff to perform its functions as the national intelligence service. For his own part, Evang 'regarded it as not possible to lead an active service with over 800 employees in ever-changing activities concurrently with having to participate fully in the work of the Defence Staff'. It seems in fact that the real purpose of his earlier proposal about the three division chiefs was to let them handle the staff functions, leaving him free to run the intelligence service. However, the new Chief of Defence showed no understanding for Evang's predicament, and insisted that the Intelligence Chief himself would have to participate fully in the work of the Defence Staff.[9]

Largely as a result of the LPG report, the Chief of Defence in the spring of 1965 decided to convert the security section of the Intelligence Staff into a separate Security Staff/Inspectorate within the Defence Staff. This move probably had Evang's approval, and led him to renewed attempts to convince the Chief of Defence of the need to give the intelligence service a more self-contained status inside the defence establishment. In a new memorandum he reiterated his firm conviction that an intelligence service whose personnel was 90 per cent civilian could not be run on military staff regulations.

> The power struggle between the Soviet Union and the United States is now and in the years to come the main factor exposing Norway to military aggression in any form. The most important danger elements are the testing of new weapon systems in the vicinity of Norwegian territory, and the increasing intelligence effort which the Soviet Union and the United States are mounting against each other. This demands a Norwegian military intelligence effort which can follow this development, see the trends, and have an apparatus to evaluate and interpret the events. This also requires a leadership which is entirely focused on that task, and this can in my view not be done by a chief who at the same time has to fulfil the functions of head of a regular staff element.[10]

In the middle of the discussions about the place and role of the Intelligence Staff, murmurings about personnel problems in the Intelligence Staff had come to the surface. Without going into details, it seems that the problems arose because certain regular officers, on secondment for periods of varying duration, had complained about being passed over for promotion to positions of leadership within the Intelligence Staff. In September 1965 the Chief of Defence responded by appointing a committee to look into personnel management within the Intelligence Staff. As chairman he appointed Major-General Chr. R. Kaldager, who as his Deputy Chief of Staff had had oversight of the Intelligence Staff since April 1963. Since the timing of the Kaldager Committee and its report made it a central element in the process that led to the removal of Evang from the Intelligence Staff, it will be dealt with in the next chapter.[11] Here we shall limit ourselves to a brief look at the organisational changes proposed by the Committee and acted upon by the Government. Mainly, these went in the direction of 'militarising' the Intelligence Staff, by appointing more regular officers, and by transferring the Intelligence Staff's personnel administration to the Defence Staff. In sum, this meant closer integration of the Intelligence Staff with the Defence Staff.

TOWARDS A NEW DEFENCE HIGH COMMAND

There is no need here to go into the details of the internal changes in the organisation of the NIS after Evang's departure, as materially they did not affect the functional intelligence work of the NIS. What remains to be considered here is the fourth and final step in what we have referred to as a major reorganisation of the Norwegian military leadership structure. Already in 1963, when the first steps in that process materialised, a high-powered commission with former Defence Minister Jens Chr. Hauge as chairman was appointed 'to analyse, evaluate, and propose guidelines for a possible reorganisation of the defence leadership'. This commission, referred to as 'Hauge I' since it would later be followed by a 'Hauge II' commission to review the organisation at the regional level, found that the directives giving the Chief of Defence greater authority had not provided him with a staff apparatus which could enable him properly to exercise that authority. Various models were reviewed. The 'British model' with a Chiefs of Staff Committee was glanced at and quickly discarded. But a related arrangement, with the Chief of Defence and a Defence Staff organisationally incorporated within the Ministry of Defence, seemed to offer many advantages in terms of simplifying and reducing the dimensions of the overall leadership of the nation's defence. Better co-ordination of the military, the administrative and the technical/ scientific defence-related activities was seen by the commission to be one of the main benefits.

The uniformly negative reactions from the military against this proposal, which they alleged would not give the Chief of Defence the necessary freedom and powers, led the Defence Ministry to ask the military leaders to work out an alternative. The result was a proposal characterised by a strong interservice centralisation of staff functions, and this the ministry now put forward in a proposition to the Storting in 1966. The new organisation would take the shape of a Defence High Command [Forsvarets Overkommando] wherein would be 'integrated all military functions that were suitable for integration'. This would be 'a joint staff under the Chief of Defence's indisputable leadership and in line with his status as command authority for operational activity and force production'. This new organisation eventually materialised in 1970, simultaneous with the construction of a new defence headquarters – Huseby, nicknamed Norway's Pentagon but in fact an H-shaped building – to accommodate both the new Defence High Command and the Defence Ministry.[12]

For the intelligence service, the decision to re-establish a Defence High Command was accompanied by the resurrection of a proposal to single out a staff element – somewhat akin to a liaison group or perhaps an intelligence 'embassy' – which would be housed at Huseby. Its function would be to keep the Chief of Defence continually updated on the situation in the military environment, and to feed any special intelligence requirements back to the service. The NIS itself would remain at its own established headquarters somewhere else in town, and run the various stations and activities from there. This idea, which the LPG study had considered but rejected, appears in fact to have originated with Evang. But this time the proposal came from the Chief of Defence.[13] Initially Hauger Johannessen wanted a fairly sizeable element, including an 'estimates' or assessments unit, to be installed at defence headquarters. But faced with yet another proposal, this time from the Military Affairs Committee of the Storting, which now suggested reuniting the intelligence and security services in a directorate separate from the military, the Chief of Defence and Intelligence Chief Johan Berg worked out a compromise: a small staff element of about 16 officers at Huseby, with the assessment function ensconced within intelligence headquarters. That, then, was the organisation with which the Norwegian Defence High Command and the Norwegian Intelligence Service would meet the challenge of the 1970s.

NOTES

1. FD, file 'H–O.2. Forsvarets øverste ledelse og Forsvarsdepartementet 1951–1952'. Berg to Defence Minister, 7 May 1952.
2. FO/E, file 'Diverse utvalg'. Undated draft report 'Innstilling fra utvalget for koordinering av E- og S-tjenesten i Forsvaret'.
3. SMK, file 'KU', Andersen memos on 'Forsvarets Etterretnings- og Sikkerhetstjeneste', one dated 3 Oct. 1952, the other undated.
4. Ibid., memo dated 20 Sept. 1952: 'Forsvarets Etterretnings- og Sikkerhetstjeneste. Plassering i fred og krig'.
5. *Stortingsforhandlinger*, 1953 (Parliamentary proceedings), *Innst. S. nr. 6*; and *Stortingstidende*, pp. 1906–58.

6. FO/E, file 'Organisasjon og virksomhet, del I, avsluttet 1963', Evang to Chief of Defence Staff, Dec. 1961.
7. Ibid., PM 'Forsvarsstabens etterretnings- og utenriksstab. Forslag til foreløpig organisasjonsendring' and PM 'Forsvarsstabens etterretnings- og utenriksstab. Arbeidsformer og organisasjonsmessig plassering', both dated 22 March 1962.
8. Ibid., LPG report 'Studium av FST/ES organisasjon, ansvarsområde og virksomhet', May 1964.
9. Ibid., Evang note of meeting 5 June; Evang to Chief of Defence, 11 June 1964.
10. FO/E, Evang papers, SJE to FSJ, 22 March 1965.
11. See Chapter 15, pp. 277–8.
12. This brief account of the process that led to the establishment – or perhaps the re-establishment – of the Defence High Command, is based on Reidar Godø, *Forsvarets ledelsesordning etter 1945* (FHFS Notat No. 4/1983, published by the Norwegian Institute for Defence Studies).
13. RR, memo, FSJ to Himle, 2 Nov. 1968.

15

Final Act for Evang

On 10 October 1965 the Labour Party in Norway had to give up the reins of power and give way to a non-socialist coalition government, with the Centre Party's Per Borten as Prime Minister and Otto Grieg Tidemand, from the Conservative Party, as Defence Minister. In view of Vilhelm Evang's identification with the Left in Norwegian politics, particularly because of his membership of the communist 'Mot Dag' movement in the 1930s, it would not have been surprising if the new government had sought a change in the important post of chief of the NIS. There was also a fair amount of accumulated dissatisfaction with Evang's management and leadership style both within the intelligence staff and in the military establishment. Most of those with insight into the service seem to have respected his intellectual capabilities and expertise in intelligence matters, as well as his way of handling the relationship with Allied services, although there were some who found him too adamant and dogmatic in his defence of national interests.

There was in particular dissatisfaction with the way in which he handled organisational and personnel problems. He seems to have found it difficult to delegate responsibility to the extent necessitated by the rapid expansion of the service from the end of the 1950s, and tended to surround himself with an inner circle of persons whom he liked and felt comfortable with. Externally his relations with the military officers were particularly difficult. Many military career officers found it hard to accept that someone without a military background or training had the grade of colonel, and headed a special staff several times larger than the Defence Staff of which it was formally a part. Evang's political background also undoubtedly came into this. While the relationship between the Intelligence Staff and the military establishment may have worked reasonably well on the surface, there seems all the time to have been a distance which was not only due to the special nature and particular secrecy with which an intelligence service is inevitably surrounded.

Far more problematic was Evang's relationship with the head of the Security Police, Asbjørn Bryhn. They seem to have fallen out with each other already in the early 1950s, which explains why the Co-ordination Committee never functioned as intended. At the organisational level the two secret services tried to establish a working relationship in matters of security and surveillance, partly through a special interdepartmental control committee where the NIS was represented by an officer with the title of security inspector, and partly through that officer's direct contact with Bryhn. This appears to have taken care of the co-operation as long as Andreas Lerheim held that post – from 1953 to 1960. But his two successors during the next five years, until the security section became a separate staff under the Defence Staff, do not seem to have established the same personal relationship with Bryhn.[1]

THE LYGREN AFFAIR

The final breach in relations between Evang and Bryhn, and between the NIS and the Security Police, came in the sensational and much-debated Lygren Affair. Ingeborg Lygren had served in the secretariat of the Intelligence Staff for most of the time since the Second World War, as well as spending a brief period as Russian language interpreter for the Border Commissioner in eastern Finnmark. In 1956 she was posted to the Norwegian embassy in Moscow as a secretary. During the three years she spent there she also – with Evang's approval – performed 'postman' services for the CIA, posting a total of 15 letters from the CIA to their agents in the Soviet Union. Back in Oslo from 1959 she worked in Evang's secretariat.

In November 1964 Asbjørn Bryhn visited Washington DC, and was then invited by the FBI to an interview with the Soviet defector Anatolyi Golitsyn. A KGB officer, Golitsyn had been serving in the Soviet embassy in Helsinki when he defected to the Americans in December 1961. The information he provided about the KGB, its methods and its agents in Western countries during his initial interrogations led to a number of major spy trials, such as the Vassall case in the UK. Hence the FBI, and the principal spy-hunter in the CIA, James Jesus Angleton, apparently placed full confidence in Golitsyn's revelations.

In an extensive after-action memorandum to Justice Minister Elisabeth Schweigaard Selmer, dated 29 December 1965, Bryhn gave this account of his meeting with Golitsyn:

> Golitsyn stated that it was known to him that the CIA had a joint operation with the Norwegian Intelligence Service, and that a female secretary in the Norwegian embassy, who had been sent to Moscow by the Norwegian Intelligence Service, was an American agent. The KGB in one way or another got to know that she had been charged with posting letters to American agents in the Soviet Union. She was then approached, and recruited. Golitsyn continued: 'This I know for a fact. And a group in the KGB were rewarded for that recruitment. I know further that when she was recruited, she gave information not only about the American operations, but also handed to the KGB the cipher, the code, of the Norwegian ambassador, whose secretary she was. Besides I heard in 1958 that she was unwilling to work in Norway. She expressed her willingness to work anywhere, only not in Norway. This is what she said to the KGB.[2]

Two months later, on 14 January 1965, Bryhn again visited Washington, and had new meetings with Golitsyn 'wherein his information was expanded and confirmed'. On 8 February Bryhn briefed O.C. Gundersen, then Minister of Justice, about the matter. Gundersen had been Norwegian ambassador in Moscow for part of Lygren's sojourn there, and supposedly retorted to Bryhn that he was 'not surprised by my account'.

Bryhn had instigated surveillance of Ingeborg Lygren during the period between his meetings with Golitsyn, but without any results that could be of value for the investigation. Apparently due to pressure of work related to the espionage case against Kristen Gjøen, an air force captain who in June 1965 was convicted of passing on secret documents about Rygge air force station, the Security Police could only resume the Lygren investigation some time during June. But with the summer holidays looming the work had to be postponed yet again. 'I returned from holiday on 29 August, and on one of the first days of September we reviewed the case and decided to arrest her in the beginning of the week of 6–12 September.' But the Defence Chief had first to be informed.

> On Monday 13 September in the morning I called on the Defence Chief and briefed him about the case, and said that we had decided

to arrest her the next morning, Tuesday 14 September. In view of the circumstances of the case, and particularly since we were aware that Miss Lygren had also done work for the Intelligence Staff, which it was essential to clarify as soon as possible through questioning of Miss Lygren, I said that we found we could not for the time being inform Colonel Evang. The Defence Chief stated that it was 'obvious that Colonel Evang could not be informed'.[3]

Ingeborg Lygren was arrested on the morning of 14 September. Not until four days later, Saturday 18 September, did Bryhn inform Evang about the case. The chief of the newly formed Security Staff of the Defence Staff, Colonel Carl Ruge, was also present.

As could be expected, Evang reacted sharply against the way the Security Police had proceeded in this matter. And on 12 October, when he was finally questioned as a witness in the case, he was particularly critical of the failure to inform him immediately, which he called a breach of a prior agreement between the police and the Intelligence Staff about mutual and immediate information in such matters. He could not disregard the possibility that what had happened was a plot against the Intelligence Staff, aiming 'to paralyse our service'.[4] The matter had leaked to the newspapers at about the time when Evang was first informed, and for a whole week the press had been full of attacks against Evang and the Intelligence Staff. This had gone so far that the Chief of Staff in the Defence Staff, Major-General Herman F. Zeiner-Gundersen, felt it necessary to issue a press statement warning against prejudging Evang on account of suspicions about a member of his staff.

In the period between her arrest and the end of November the police conducted 20 interrogations of Ingeborg Lygren. During questioning on 10 November she made a sort of 'confession', on which the police tried to build. Early in December the Defence Staff became aware of rumours that the police still had insufficient evidence. And on 8 December, when Colonel Ruge met with one of the district attorneys on a different matter, he was told that their office had that day submitted the case to the Attorney-General with a recommendation that the case be dropped and the suspect freed.[5] Accordingly, on 15 December the prison gates were opened for Ingeborg Lygren's exit. She was first looked after by friends and relatives, and later – visibly marked by what she had gone through – came back to work in Section V of the Intelligence Staff.

Bryhn himself, and two or three of his closest associates, continued to believe in Lygren's guilt. Evang, and most of the people in the Intelligence Staff, were equally convinced of her innocence. Trond Johansen, a section chief in the Intelligence Staff and one of Evang's close collaborators, submitted the case to thorough analysis in January 1966, and found several weak points in the material from the investigation and interrogations. Together with Lars R. Heyerdahl, Evang's deputy, he also visited Washington, and the material and interviews they had there – including a meeting with James Angleton, strengthened their conviction that the accusations against Lygren were groundless. It does indeed seem remarkable that the Security Police could proceed to arrest someone for espionage on no other grounds than four-year-old information from a Soviet defector about what supposedly had happened in Moscow six to eight years previously. Their visit to Washington also reinforced Johansen's and Heyerdahl's suspicion that Golitsyn's information was a case of mistaken identity, and that a different female embassy clerk, Gunvor Galtung Haavik, was the one who had been recruited by the KGB. But when they tried to begin an investigation against Haavik, they were told to keep off the case by the new Intelligence Chief, Colonel Johan Berg.[6] In the Security Police, police inspector Ørnulf Tofte apparently put a couple of their men on surveillance of Haavik for a month or two, based only on the fact of her having also been in the Moscow embassy in the 1950s. But no results were obtained.[7] It was not until January 1977 that Gunvor Galtung Haavik was arrested in the eastern suburbs of Oslo while handing documents to a KGB officer from the Soviet embassy. During her interrogation – she died in prison before she could be brought to trial – she confessed to having worked as a spy for the Soviet Union since 1950.

The Lygren case, seen in isolation, had not reflected badly on Evang. But the dissatisfaction of the military with Evang, which had been smouldering since the beginning of the 1960s, began to burn brightly when the Defence Chief, at the same time as Lygren was arrested, appointed a committee to review urgently organisation and personnel administration in the Intelligence Staff. The committee got its mandate on 15 September, and it contained the following clause: 'Investigate whether personnel who have made criticism and complaints against the leadership of the Intelligence Staff have real grounds for their utterances. This should include both persons whose complaints have been transmitted to the committee and persons whom the committee encounter during their work.'[8] As chairman of the committee the Defence Chief selected Major-

General Chr. R. Kaldager, who as Deputy Chief of Staff had been charged with overseeing the NIS since April 1963.

The Kaldager Committee reported on 17 December 1965, after only two months. The short time did not stop them from very sharp criticism of Evang:

14. The Committee thinks fit to assert that a crisis of confidence has arisen between the personnel and the personnel administration. The crisis includes both military and civilian personnel, but is strongest among the military. On the out-stations, which contain the largest number of the Intelligence Staff's employees, dissatisfaction seems to be significantly less than in the central elements of the institution.

15. In the Committee's opinion there is a feeling among the personnel that this is more due to the leadership of the Staff than to its personnel administration, and that the leadership remarkably often disregards the recommendations of the administration. Personnel administration is today clearly the responsibility of the leadership in all institutions and staffs. In the Intelligence Staff this responsibility appears at times to have been discharged in a direct and highly personal fashion, and not always with due regard to formality. This has contributed to the personnel sensing a lack of consistency in policy as well as in practice.[9]

One direct and concrete result of the report was the transfer of personnel administration for the Intelligence Service to the Personnel Staff of the Defence Staff. This was done despite the committee's awareness of the counter-arguments, which were partly rooted in the problem of having the NIS, 'with its very large civilian component and the number of different categories of civilian employees', put under military administration. There was also the problem of the special financing of a large part of the activity.

It is not for the author of this book to judge between Evang and his critics. It seems clear that the critics represented both traditional military grievances, for having been passed over for promotion, and suspicions about political favouritism based on Evang's leftist past. But it seems equally clear that Evang's personnel policy deviated from military regulations and routines. Yet the Intelligence Staff was a very special institution, whose insertion into the Defence Staff – as we have suggested

– had to give rise to the sort of problems which occur when trying to 'fit a square peg in a round hole'.

THE MELLBYE COMMISSION

The aftermath of the Lygren Affair inevitably put a sharp searchlight on Bryhn and the Security Police. Bryhn had earlier stuck his neck out with public statements that were branded as a kind of 'McCarthyism'. Voices were now raised in the Storting about the need to investigate 'the secret services', and the Government responded by asking a highly respected lawyer, Johan Chr. Mellbye, to lead a commission to 'consider various aspects of the preventive security service'. We have seen that the Lygren case by itself did not put Evang in a particularly bad light. But it was known that Evang and Bryhn did not work well together, and as the Mellbye Commission got to work there soon appeared a broad consensus that both had to go. One of the first to advocate this was the Defence Chief, Vice-Admiral Folke Hauger Johannessen, who wrote to the Defence Minister that the Lygren case had shaken public confidence in both the security and intelligence services, and that this loss of trust would not be dispelled as long as the two chiefs remained in their posts.

A change in the post as head of the Security Police was in fact decided already before the Mellbye Commission had reported. Bryhn accepted a post as police chief in Bergen, and Gunnar Haarstad came back to become chief of an institution which he had only nominally left when he became chief of police in the border district of south Varanger in 1958. Information which has since come to light suggests that Bryhn demanded that Evang should be removed at the same time to avoid being a lone scapegoat. This must have seemed unfair to Evang, since both dismissals would then be seen as the result of the Lygren case. But in a long-term perspective, against the background of the difficult relationship between the Security Police and the Intelligence Staff, this may not have been such an unreasonable demand.

Defence Minister Grieg Tidemand was questioned by the Mellbye Commission on 24 February 1966. In his statement he said that the antagonism between Bryhn and Evang was 'the heart of the matter', pointing in that connection to the Lygren case. But he added:

> The conditions within the Intelligence Staff are not satisfactory, and it will be reorganised. The difficulties may in part be due to Evang's

special position, with direct access to the Defence Minister. That
has now been stopped. But there are also indications that not all
information of significance is passed on from the Intelligence Staff
to the Defence Chief.[10]

Since the Defence Minister had been in office for only four months, we
must assume that those complaints had come to him from the Defence
Chief. One month later it was the turn of the military chiefs to meet the
Commission, and the Defence Chief was first on the list. He introduced
his statement with somewhat faint praise of the work of Evang and the
Intelligence Staff:

> Much very valuable intelligence work has been performed within
> the Intelligence Staff, and the intelligence produced there is highly
> valued in NATO. This may be partly on account of our country's
> geographical position, but there is no doubt that Colonel Evang is
> a very able intelligence officer.[11]

The Defence Chief's criticism of Evang was that he did not take a
sufficient interest in security matters, and that personnel matters tended
to be neglected. Since the security service had already been taken away
from the Intelligence Staff, and personnel matters would go the same way
after the Kaldager Committee's recommendations, those were hardly any
longer sufficient grounds to dismiss Evang. But the Admiral then turned
to the Lygren Affair, which had convinced him that the problems between
the two services 'might endanger national security'. His precise complaints in that connection were insufficient information to the military
authorities before the arrest of Miss Lygren, and the leaks to the media
– for which Evang could hardly be blamed! It seems clear therefore that
the Defence Chief had already decided to get rid of Evang.

There are indications that Hauger Johannessen's dissatisfaction with
Evang may have had its roots several years back. In his memoirs, now
at last published, he states as his impression from a previous tour of
duty in the Defence Staff that Evang 'regarded the intelligence service
as self-sufficient, and saw his organisation as on the side of and not an
integrated part of the defence establishment'. He had also noticed that
Evang very seldom showed his face in the Defence Staff: 'It surprised me
that he himself chose, and that the chiefs allowed him, to isolate himself
from the Staff. It seemed as if he had acquired a special position, which
had then been accepted both in political and military quarters.'[12] On his

appointment as Chief of Defence from 1 January 1964, with extended powers, Hauger Johannessen was obviously determined to change matters in that respect. That much seems clear from Evang's report of a meeting between them in March 1964:

> The Defence Chief, evidently well prepared, brought up the question of the relationship between the Chief of Defence and the Chief of the Intelligence Staff. He was aware that the Intelligence Staff had developed into what was in reality a fully independent institution, and that this was probably in part due to the way the Defence Staff had evolved and to the attitude of the earlier chiefs of Defence Staff. Since there now was a real Chief of Defence this would have to change. Formerly the task of the Defence Staff had been limited to a sort of kind uncle's function of knocking the service chiefs' heads together when they disagreed. Now the pyramid had at last been built, and the Chief of Intelligence would hence be under full and real command of the Defence Chief.[13]

Evang's response, as he has rendered it, was that 'he was glad that the issue had now been clearly formulated'. He also pointed to the proposals already put forward by the Intelligence Staff about organisational changes. 'He stated further that the previous Chief of Defence had not wished to be kept abreast of current important matters, and thus also had avoided taking responsibility. The Intelligence Chief's real master had therefore for many years and in most crucial matters been the Defence Minister, a situation which Evang fully realised was untenable in the long run.'

The reorganisation proposals which Evang here referred to had just beforehand also been sent to the then Defence Minister, Gudmund Harlem. One of those proposals – from 1962 – had somewhat surprisingly advocated that the place of the intelligence service ought still to be within the Defence Staff. Evang had in that context recalled earlier proposals to make the Intelligence Service a kind of directorate within the defence establishment, something which would entail greater freedom from the Defence Staff and a more direct relationship with the Defence Ministry. 'This option', he continued, 'remains open. But it should be stressed that as the Chief of Defence Staff has been given an independent, national and operative responsibility, it would be illogical and damaging to partition the responsibility for strategic intelligence among several institutions.' But for the proposed location to be compatible with the special demands of such a special service, one condition had to be fulfilled: 'The precondition for that is [that] the Chief of the national intelligence service has delegated to him such powers as are necessary to satisfy the demands of flexibility and freedom of action.'[14] But that would have required a flexibility and willingness to compromise which neither the new Defence Chief nor Evang possessed. Hauger Johannessen in later years summed up his view of Evang in the following terms:

> It was apparent from his attitude that he regarded himself as the independent head of an organisation of major national importance. He wanted no direction or oversight from any quarter, and very seldom turned up in person at staff meetings. It became clear to me that he was in closer contact with the political side than with the military during the time that the Labour Party was in power.[15]

In reality the relationship between the two seemed early on to be marred by mutual distrust. Evang's direct relations with Defence Minister Harlem, which was one of the complaints made against him, may in fact have been both cause and effect. In a conversation with Harlem in February 1964, Evang reported himself as having said that 'from the sort of leadership so far shown by Admiral Johannessen as Defence Chief, Evang had concluded that the Intelligence Staff ought to convert to some kind of civilian status, the sooner the better. Evang went on to express deep concern for future developments in the armed forces in view of the kind of rigid bureaucracy and hidebound thinking which reigned.'[16]

The next military witness before the Mellbye Commission was the Chief of Staff of the Defence Staff, Major-General Herman F. Zeiner Gundersen. He was rather more eloquent in his praise of Evang as 'an exceptionally able intelligence officer'. But he added that Evang was no administrator, and that it was impossible to live with the lack of trust and will to co-operate between the chiefs of the two services. More specific criticism of the state of affairs in the Intelligence Staff was forthcoming from number three in the military hierarchy, Major-General Christian R. Kaldager. As Deputy Chief of Staff he had chaired the committee which had reviewed the personnel and organisational problems in the Intelligence Staff. His primary complaint was reported as follows:

> Kaldager thought that Evang had a tendency to envelop his affairs in an unnecessary veil of secrecy. He also tended to keep incoming intelligence to himself. Not even his second in command has been

kept informed. The failure of communication may partly be due to Evang's lack of a military education, whereas others in the Defence Staff expect business to be conducted in a military fashion.[17]

It seems clear from this that the dissatisfaction with Evang, as suggested above, was particularly directed at his way of running the Intelligence Staff, and in particular his handling of personnel matters. He seems to have had difficulty delegating matters to his staff, or co-operating with those with whom he did not get on at a personal level. To some extent this may be explained as a kind of 'culture collision' between a civilian chief with in many ways a clear intellectual bent, and an apparatus which may have been a civil–military hybrid but still formed part of a military set-up. But the dissatisfaction may also have had political overtones. When a military officer in 1964 complained to the Protocol Committee of the Storting about being passed over for promotion, the members from the Conservative Party expressed suspicion that this was a case of party political favouritism. The strongest criticism came from the later Prime Minister Kaare Willoch, who in a meeting of the Conservative members of the Storting 'suggested that the Intelligence Service needed an overhaul, and that he for one found it difficult to accept that it should be led by a former communist'.

This is not to say that doubts about Evang in political quarters was confined to the non-socialist opposition. Even inside the Labour Party there were many who mistrusted him. The Foreign Minister from 1946 to 1965, Halvard Lange, seems to have felt after the U-2 affair that Evang had not been entirely frank with the Government, and that he may have known and been part of more than he was willing to admit. Lange was not the kind of person to engage in personal intrigue. But he had clashed with Evang on a different occasion, in the spring of 1961, when Evang in conversation with a member of the parliamentary opposition had expressed criticism of the Foreign Ministry's handling of a particular case. Lange and others had then hit back at Evang with a vengeance.

EXIT EVANG

The Defence Chief must have decided early in the spring of 1966 that Evang would have to go. The problem was to find a suitable alternative post. Not until the summer did a solution appear, when the position as National Military Representative at NATO Headquarters was becoming

vacant as from 1 October. Johannessen wrote a personal letter to Evang
– who was then on holiday – in the middle of July, suggesting that he
should apply for the post. He reminded Evang of an earlier conversation
about a change at the top of the Intelligence Staff, and added that the
main problem since had been 'to find something suitable for you, both
for your own benefit and for the sake of appearances'. He stressed that
the post in question was an important one, which had on occasion been
filled by officers of the grade of General. 'What is more important, however, is that it is a position which carries great trust in relation to national
as well as NATO authorities.' The post would of course have to be
announced in the usual way. But the suggestion was that this was more
or less a formality, and the letter made it clear that the Defence Minister
had given his preliminary approval. If Evang should decline the offer,
there would still have to be a change at the top of the Intelligence Staff,
and Evang would have to be placed 'at the disposal of the Defence Chief'.
Evang then accepted the offer.

The Defence Chief now appointed the 49-years-old Colonel Johan
Berg as the new head of the Intelligence Staff. Berg had had a long and
varied career as an army officer, but with only brief tours of duty in
intelligence. He could therefore not be said to fulfil the need for continuity
in the leadership of the service which the Defence Chief had stressed in
his statement to the Mellbye Commission. Continuity at the technical
and professional levels was not a problem, since most of the senior or
specialist staff had spent many years in the service. But in the realm of
oversight and professional co-ordination, and particularly as regards the
'foreign relations' of the service, a new and inexperienced chief might
find it difficult to step into Evang's shoes. At the level of organisation one
major change had already been carried out, in that security matters had
been placed in a new, separate Security Staff in the Defence Staff, with
Colonel Carl Ruge as head.

What remained was to establish a new organ of liaison and collaboration between the secret services to replace the practically defunct
Co-ordination Committee. The Mellbye Commission had recommended
setting up a committee of co-ordination to include the chiefs of the
Intelligence Staff, the Security Staff and the Security Police, together
with a senior civil servant from the Ministry of Foreign Affairs. An
independent chairman would then be appointed by the Justice Minister.
For some reason or other this was not followed up at once. Instead, an
advisory committee for security had been instituted as a temporary

measure, which then gradually grew into an informal forum for the heads of the secret services to meet. By 1968 this had in fact developed into a version of the proposed advisory committee on security, in which intelligence matters were also handled. But another ten years would elapse before this arrangement was officially sanctioned as the 'Co-ordination Committee for the Intelligence, Surveillance and Security Services'.

In the autumn of 1966 Vilhelm Andreas Wexelsen Evang was appointed as national military representative at NATO Headquarters, and served there – first in Paris, and then in Brussels after the Headquarters had been expelled from France by de Gaulle – until 1969. Back in Oslo he was put 'at the disposal of the Defence Chief', with an office at Defence Headquarters. Together with an official from the Foreign Ministry he was given the task of producing a review of the strategic situation with regard to North Norway since the war. In the formal mandate it was stated:

> Colonel Evang's investigation should concentrate on the intelligence/ military aspects, with sidelight on the field of military policy.
>
> The purpose of Colonel Evang's study is to search for possible patterns in the attitude and activity of the superpowers in relation to North Norway.
>
> The Colonel will further attempt to identify possible indicators/ signals which the countries appear to be utilising in the intelligence/ military field that are relevant to the area in question and that may be useful also for the future.[18]

The assignment bore all the hallmarks of being invented in order to give him something to do. Senior officers who served at Defence HQ at the time do not remember him being there.

On 29 January 1970 Evang presented a preliminary study of only nine pages, noting that 'this does not include essential sources of information and is intended as a basis for discussion'. What later happened with this special assignment is unknown. Evang resigned on reaching retirement age in 1974. He died in 1983 at the age of seventy-four.

NOTES

1. These issues are well documented in the files in the Ministry of Justice relating to the 'Mellbye Commission', a commission whose report led to the separation of the security service from the Intelligence Staff.
2. FD, file 'Lygren-saken', Bryhn PM to the Minister of Justice, 29 Dec. 1965. It is

not clear in the available material when and how the name of Lygren actually turned up in the case.

3. Ibid.
4. Ministry of Justice, Mellbye Commission papers, report on interrogation of Evang, 12 Oct. and acknowledged by him on 1 Nov.
5. Ibid., Defence Staff to Minister of Defence, 4 Jan. 1966: 'Forsvarsstabens befatning med Lygren-saken – hendelsesforløpet'.
6. FO/E, Trond Johansen memorandum, 14 Jan. 1966, 'Lygren-saken'; and author's interview with Heyerdahl, 16 Aug. 1995.
7. Interview with Ørnulf Tofte, 15 Nov. 1994.
8. FO/E, file 'Diverse': 'Innstilling fra Kommisjon vedrørende personell- forvaltningen i FST/E', p. 2.
9. Ibid., p. 16.
10. Ministry of Justice, Mellbye Commission papers. Minutes of meeting, 24 Feb. 1966.
11. Ibid., meeting of 21 March 1966.
12. F.H. Johannessen, *Erindringer 1948–1973* (Norse, Oslo, 1998), pp. 43, 141.
13. FO/E, Evang papers, note of conversation 12 March 1966 'from 10.00 until 11.05'.
14. FD Record Group 34. Folder marked 'Lygren-saken'. Evang to Harlem, 4 March 1964 enclosing 1962 proposals.
15. F.H. Johannessen, *Erindringer 1948–1973*, p. 78.
16. FO/E, file 'Skuff 5. 10.01 Forsvarsminister – Statssekretær'. Evang note of conversation with Harlem, 3 Feb. 1964. Also note of Evang–Harlem conversation, 6 Jan. 1964, and Harlem–Hauger Johannessen meeting, 13 March 1964. It should be noted that the Andersen Committee in 1953 stressed the need for the Intelligence Chief to have direct access to the Minister of Defence.
17. Ministry of Justice, Mellbye Commission papers, Kaldager testimony, 21 March 1966.
18. FO/E, Evang papers. Unsigned and undated memorandum 'Langtidsplanlegging. Oppdrag for oberst V. Evang'.

Conclusion

In the previous chapters we have seen how the NIS, during the course of 25 years, grew from practically nothing to a multifaceted and comprehensive enterprise. By the turn of the year 1945–46, about 80 people in all worked in the combined intelligence and security service of what was then the Second Bureau of the Defence High Command. A little more than 20 years later, the number had increased to around 1,000. The budget, which in 1946 was probably not more than a million kroner, amounted in 1966–67 to about 70 million. All this was known to only a tiny minority of the people: intelligence in Norway was, as in all other countries, a 'secret service'. And the reason for secrecy is, quite simply, that intelligence is in the business of acquiring knowledge which the adversary – an actual or potential enemy – desires to keep under lock and key. If an adversary gets to know what the people on the other side know, and how they got to know it, then it will try to take effective countermeasures to ensure that this knowledge is rendered more or less useless. Here it must be said that a great deal of what goes by the name of intelligence in reality has little to do with 'espionage', being knowledge which has been collected and systematised from relatively open sources. But because the sum of the information, as a rule, will include elements of secret intelligence, not only must the methods and modes of operation be kept secret, but also the final analysis.

The activity of the secret services will, in the nature of things, always and everywhere be fertile ground for speculations, suspicions and conspiracy theories. This concerns primarily those who are on the outside because they cannot look in and must, therefore, use their imagination as an aid to create a picture of what is going on within the fenced perimeters. Moreover, fancy and mystification have, down the ages, received inspiration from a copious number of spy stories. But also those who are on the inside will, in most cases, have strictly circumscribed knowledge about those aspects of the service with which they personally do not work. This is a necessary consequence of the so-called 'need to know' principle, which stipulates that each employee shall only know as much as he needs to know to get his job done. Thus, speculations, suspicions and conspiracy theories will find fertile soil also on the inside, and especially among those people who, for various reasons, are dissatisfied with their wages or conditions of work, or lack of advancement. The secrecy, and the fact that adversary services will always be looking for ways and means to penetrate the veil, will in given circumstances also take the form of venomous suspicions of dishonest servants.

Extreme demands for secrecy had to be applied to the different parts of the special occupation preparedness called 'Stay Behind', an institution which had been placed under the Intelligence Staff, but which, strictly speaking, had nothing to do with the actual sphere of activity of the intelligence service. During the period of time we deal with in this book, this secrecy worked unbelievably well. It was not until later that it started to crack. And because the secrecy surrounding Stay Behind was so tight and extensive, the room for mystification, for speculations and conspiracy theories was correspondingly large. A corps of less than 300 men became, in fantasy, a Norwegian 'secret army': stories about activities in which one or another over-zealous person in the service might have been involved in on a personal basis, and without instructions or the knowledge of the leadership, inspired theories and insinuations about an even more secret network – sometimes called 'a fourth service' – which is supposed to have operated 'on the fringes of' or 'in connection with' the organised occupation preparedness. Our study of the archive material and conversations with centrally placed persons have, to put it briefly, fully confirmed the unequivocal rejection of these imaginative speculations by the 1996 Parliamentary Commission of Investigation.

In this concluding chapter we will not attempt to summarise the insight the previous chapters have provided on the various aspects of the multifarious and widely divergent activity of the NIS. Instead, we shall try to paint something like an 'ideal picture' of such a service, and offer our impressions of the degree to which the NIS was able to meet or approach such an ideal.

The starting point here would have to be that Norway is a small state with strictly limited resources, but positioned at a geostrategic focal point. A state such as this will never on its own be able to develop and maintain an intelligence service which can provide adequate answers to questions about the threats facing the country. A state such as this will therefore always have to rely on co-operation with friendly or allied states, especially those which can mount greater resources aimed at common goals. For Norway, the choice of partners was not difficult, as we have seen. In general, ideology, interests and traditions all pointed in the same direction: the Anglo-Saxon Great Powers, and the Nordic neighbours. Co-operation can be organised on different levels. It can take the form of a straight forward 'buying and selling' of information between two relatively independent services, in which the 'trade balance' is not totted up in the quantity of the goods, but the quality. Without having pursued this further, we would be of the opinion that co-operation with the Nordic neighbours was of this latter type.

But co-operation can also be of a more integrated kind, the kind we know of from the defence co-operation in NATO. This takes the form that each partner country, instead of building up an allround and nationally based defence, concentrates on what it has particular qualifica tions to do. In such cases there will be no question of a complete integration, since that would make the countries totally dependent on one another. Each country in the partnership will therefore combine specialisation with a certain degree of allround competence. To cite an example: there was never any question of abolishing the Norwegian navy in the 1950s, even though the main responsibility for naval defence of the Norwegian area lay with the British and American navies. But Norway gave less priority to the navy in order to develop the land and air forces' defence capability, primarily because an air force and an army which are familiar with the terrain and climate have to be in place from the first moment, while naval assistance is mobile to quite another degree.

Co-operation between the NIS and the corresponding American services – and, partly, also the British – was characterised relatively early on by this type of integration model. What Norway had to offer was, first and foremost, its geography. As initially the only, later on one of only two NATO countries sharing borders with the Soviet Union, there was the great advantage, in the context of intelligence, that from Norwegian territory one could gain a more direct and immediate insight into Soviet military activity in important areas. This geographical advantage was primarily of interest for 'intelligence collection'. In relation to an intelligence service's two main fields of activity, namely *intelligence collection* and *analysis*, it was therefore natural that a Norwegian service should concentrate on the former. And because the value of this distinctive

Norwegian geographical advantage was more or less inversely propor-
tional to the economic resources which the country could spare for such
purposes, the United States, with its enormous resources, was willing to
foot most of the bill, while accepting that the work was carried out by
Norwegian personnel and under Norwegian control.

Another and more singular form of intelligence collection was also to
become something of a Norwegian speciality, namely, the collection of
information with the help of people on board Norwegian merchant
ships plying transport routes to and from ports in communist countries.
Observations, taking photographs and reporting are, in this connection,
key terms for an activity which, intelligence-technically speaking, lay at
the intersection between so-called 'Legal Travellers' and agent activity.
That this should be an important Norwegian speciality may at first sight
seem surprising. It has its justification, nonetheless. It was not the
geographical position of Norway that represented the starting point here,
but its standing as the homeland of one of the largest merchant fleets in
the world. In addition, there was a coincidence of circumstances, such as
Norwegian shipping's long experience in freight transport to the north
Russian ports, and the fact that Norway was one of the first Western
countries formally to recognise the People's Republic of China and,
thereby, was given permission to traffic Chinese ports. But these are
explanations which suit another country with an even larger merchant
fleet, namely Britain. When Norway nevertheless achieved such a dominating position in this field, it is difficult to find any other reasonable
explanation than that which several veterans in Norwegian intelligence
have spoken of: namely that Norwegian seamen – 'many of them were, of
course, wartime sailors' – generally speaking managed these tasks better
than others. Perhaps they were better trained and had better photographic
equipment, too.

The analysis of the collected intelligence was much less dependent on
geographical factors, and could, therefore, be carried out to a greater
degree in the co-operating countries' agencies with their extensive personnel and knowledge resources. So far, this does not relate to the often
discussed issue of national control, but to *realpolitik* and rational
specialisation. But there is a limit: just as Norway could not leave the
whole of its sea defence to the Allies and dismantle its navy, so the NIS
was obliged also to build up an analysis competence, to avoid becoming
too dependent on what the Americans and British could find out and were
inclined to divulge. The NIS leadership was acutely aware of this, and

reacted quickly in those cases where there was a danger that Norway could become a mere 'supplier of raw material'. An ideal picture of the NIS during our period hence requires possession of an analysis capability of high quality within areas of significance to the Norwegian threat assessment. To some considerable degree, the intelligence service will here be subject to the same conditions as all other international knowledge-based activities: only a minority of countries have the capacity to be on the cutting-edge in several areas at once. But there must exist, within the country, the expertise to understand, critically evaluate, and eventually exploit that knowledge which must be 'imported'. Without such expertise one would be reduced, in an intelligence context, to either swallowing hook, line and sinker – or categorically rejecting – analysis results originating from the outside. In that situation, the NIS would have been what in the debate of recent years has been called 'beyond national control'.

It will be apparent from this presentation that the NIS gradually succeeded in acquiring qualitatively high standards in several – in fact, most – areas. This happened first in the Comint field, where the Norwegian specialists appear to have acquired an international top-level competence relatively early on with respect to locating, identifying and characterising stationary and mobile Soviet radio transmitters. With this as a foundation, the NIS seems also to have come a long way in the field of analysis and interpretation of more distinctly Elint material, especially in the context of radar installations in the northwestern regions of the Soviet Union. The combination of Comint and Elint expertise could, in turn, be exploited in the analysis of telemetric data from Soviet missile launches and satellite activity. The limitations here lay in the obvious fact that Norway neither constructed nor possessed missiles and satellites and, therefore, lacked the basic knowledge which this would have given. Last, but not least, Norwegian operators and analysts developed, towards the end of our period, and with good help from the Norwegian Defence Research Establishment, expert knowledge of Acoustint in the surveillance of Soviet submarine capacity and patterns of operation. In all these fields there are clear examples of Norwegian experts meeting especially their American 'opposite numbers' as equals, exchanging opinions and analysis results, receiving praise and offering criticism.

There was however one area – as we have seen – on which the NIS never got a good grip; decryption, 'code-breaking' – popular things have many names – was the service's Achilles' heel. In spite of certain ambitions during the 1950s, this was an activity which never really 'took off' in the

Intelligence Staff, and which, from 1965, was given the *coup de grâce* in that the crypto unit followed in the wake of the detachment of the security section. From then on, the Norwegian crypto service was reduced to being a question of technology and protection of its own ciphers. What took place in 1965 might well have been an element of the 'wing-clipping' of Evang, as one of the service's veterans views it. But it is difficult to imagine that so important an operation as decryption would have been levelled if the unit had given the impression of being a vital and well-functioning activity.

The reason for the failure in this area must be sought even further back in time. It is not without relevance here to mention the extensive resources demanded by decryption at a high level, both as regards person-nel, especially those with high mathematical competence and mechanical equipment, especially computers. Anybody with any knowledge of the suspense-filled literature on 'the boffins' at Bletchley Park during the Second World War, and their intense efforts to transform the cryptic signals from the German 'Enigma' machines into plain language for the Allies' top-secret 'Ultra' network, will know how demanding this kind of work is. The development of such a capacity, on top of the extensive collection activity performed by the Intelligence Staff, was clearly beyond the capabilities of a small country. It may still be argued that the NIS should, nevertheless, have made the effort to develop a small core of specialists who, through concentrated effort, could have managed to perform tasks of special interest to Norway. When this did not happen, one of the reasons *may* have been collaborative difficulties between the Comint unit and Nils Stordahl's crypto unit.

A well-known but still fundamental axiom for all intelligence is that even the most comprehensive quantity of information is useless if it never gets through to the users. Organisation and communication are involved here. We dealt in Chapter 13 with the communication problems which from time to time arose between the Intelligence Staff and the military staff units which were meant to convert information into the production of forces and operative planning. At this juncture we shall limit ourselves to establishing that the difficulties that arose never seem to have been of a serious nature, and that communication gradually seems to have 'found its feet' – also in the relationship between the Intelligence Staff and the Commander-in-Chief North Norway which was at times troublesome.

We have already dealt with the organisational aspects within the NIS in Chapter 14, as well as touching upon them in Chapter 15. The organisational placing of the NIS has, nonetheless, another side from the one which concerns the relationship between the Intelligence Staff and the military. International 'intelligence' literature often distinguishes between, on the one hand, military intelligence and, on the other, what is frequently referred to as 'all source' intelligence and analysis. This means that a balanced threat analysis must also include an intentional element and, on the whole, a broader perspective than generally charac- terises the analysis of an enemy's military capacity. And such a more inclusive analysis needs, firstly, material from other sources than the more narrowly focused military intelligence service and, secondly, opinions and ideas from resource personnel in other surroundings.

The most important advantage of a more varied, allround composition of those bodies which are supposed to analyse the collected material is that there is a greater chance that unconventional views will be heard. Ideas from contrasting environments will at least reduce the likelihood of strategic preconceptions dominating the floor. An Israeli intelligence expert said it in the following way in a book published some years ago: 'When the entire analysis process is in the hands of one organisation, the number of alternative hypotheses is necessarily limited. The climate of opinion within that organisation may lead to the elimination of all hypotheses except the prevailing one.'[1] According to a former director of the CIA, an important reason behind the establishment of the CIA was the desire to liberate the intelligence process from the 'institutional prejudices' of military intelligence units. A former head of the US Board of National Estimates – the body which produced the finished national intelligence assessments – expressed himself in the following way in his testimony to a Senate committee:

> Thus decision-making on major foreign policy and national security issues requires intelligence support which draws on a variety of collection methods and analytical skills. This fact generated the concept of a *national* intelligence, and led to the designation of a single officer, the DCI [Director of Central Intelligence], who is also advisor to the NSC [National Security Council], to produce it.[2]

These concerns raise the question of the optimal organisational placing of the NIS, which we have touched on earlier. As part of the Defence Staff? As a separate institution within the defence establishment? Under the Office of the Prime Minister? All these alternatives had their benefits and drawbacks, and, as we have seen, the solution was that the service remained as an element under the Defence Staff.

The need for a more versatile or multifaceted service, less confined to the military apparatus in regard to both information collection and analysis potential, could still be satisfied in other ways than by the dissociation of the service from the Defence Staff. Taking the cue from a model used in Britain, and, partly, the United States, a co-ordination and analysis unit could have been established on an interministerial and 'interagency' basis, in which specially selected high-level representatives from various quarters – primarily from the Intelligence Staff, the Security Police, the Ministry of Foreign Affairs, the Ministry of Justice and the Office of the Prime Minister – could meet on a regular basis as a committee, perhaps with its own little secretariat, to discuss the intelligence situation and formulate a national intelligence assessment. Such a committee, which we understand exists today in the form of the so-called 'high-level group', was missing throughout our period. We have reasons to believe that Jens Chr. Hauge wanted something of this sort with his 1947 prototype for a co-ordinating committee for the secret services. But the Co-ordination Committee as instituted became something quite different. We see the direct contact which became established between Evang and – particularly – Defence Minister Gudmund Harlem, as an indirect result of this lack of a national intelligence committee, an arrangement which in one way or another may have found its successor in the personal contact between Deputy Director Trond Johansen and subsequent ministers of defence and foreign affairs. It is also possible to see the somewhat haphazard communication between the different institutions during the U2 affair in the light of the lack of such a 'Joint Intelligence Committee' – which is the British variant – or the 'Board of National Estimates', which is the American version.

Why was this type of 'high-level group', or national intelligence committee, not established in Norway during the 25 years that we deal with? As far as we can see, no proposal in this direction ever emerged from the Intelligence Staff or from the military. This might be understandable given that *they*, in such an eventuality, would lose control, and that secrecy could be endangered. But it has also been vociferously pointed out by Intelligence Staff people that on several occasions they appealed for closer contact especially with the Ministry of Foreign Affairs, but received no answer. And the Ministry of Defence, which would have been the natural initiator of such a reform, was during this time relatively weakly equipped to conduct security policy analysis. Besides, the high-level persons of that ministry who took special interest in intelligence, such as the State Secretaries Sivert A. Nielsen, Erik Himle and Arne G. Lund, had, as far as we can see, adequate direct contact with the service without having to go through a new unit.

What about the Intelligence Staff's own contribution to the analysis of that aspect of the intelligence picture which more concerned the military or security policy situation? As long as Evang was in command this seems to have been his own 'shop'. And he had, in many ways, the intellectual capacity to handle such an assignment. After his period was over, Reidar Torp initiated the creation of such an analysis capacity within the Intelligence Staff when, in 1968, he became the head of the newly established 'Special Section'. We are probably not far off the mark when we link his initiative to the Czechoslovakian crisis of that year, and the wish to be better prepared for similar occurrences in the future. The development in this area after Torp had left the Intelligence Staff he was head of intelligence from 1970 to 1975 – is outside the time-frame of our study. But we have reason to believe that this new analysis element did not enjoy particularly fertile growth conditions, either because it would have duplicated existing security policy expertise in other quarters, or because the best experts were not interested in being sequestered among the Intelligence Staff's secret fellowship, without the scholar's freedom to communicate with unauthorised colleagues beyond the barbed-wired enclosure. It is probable that conditions in this area have improved during the course of the most recent years, since the unstable and inscrutable political situation in the former Soviet Union and in Eastern Europe placed the political rather than military developments in those countries at the centre of interest. But it was probably not without cause that the Minister of Defence, Jørgen Kosmo, as recently as 1995 demanded that the service had to 'become better at political analysis of the countries in Eastern Europe'.

With the reservations we have taken – about the lack of decryption expertise and a national analysis and assessment unit – there are grounds to characterise the NIS as a national asset at a high qualitative and quantitative level, and possibly as Norway's most important contribution to the Western Alliance's security and strength during the 25 years we have surveyed here. Some will, no doubt, still claim that Norway, in developing such a comprehensive intelligence service and such a close co-operation with the American superpower, unnecessarily exposed land

and people to the risk of war. In response to this it needs first to be said that the archives of the Soviet Ministry of Foreign Affairs, which are now becoming accessible, reveal a remarkable lack of complaints about Norwegian intelligence activity. Sharp protests were reserved for instances of US intelligence activity involving Norway, such as the U-2 incident. It is also necessary to consider the alternative to a nationally controlled NIS: an extensive intelligence activity by the Allied great powers themselves on or around Norwegian territory, in which consideration for the Norwegian 'low-tension profile' would have had to yield to urgent needs for Western knowledge about the adversary's constantly increasing military activity in the north. The geostrategic focal point which Norwegian and especially northern Norwegian areas represented during the Cold War was an established fact, independent of Norwegian policy. For this reason, a Norwegian intelligence service, in close co-operation with Allied powers, but with Norwegian personnel and under Norwegian control, was both the best alternative and the best Norwegian contribution to the Western Alliance's common defence.

NOTES

1. Ephraim Kam, *Surprise Attack: The Victim's Perspective* (Harvard University Press, Cambridge, MA, 1988), p. 255.
2. John H. Huizenga, 'Statement to the Senate Intelligence Committee', p. 2 (MS in author's possession). It is often overlooked that the DCI is not only Director of the 'Agency' but Director of Central Intelligence, with a national co-ordinating responsibility.

Operations and Code-Names

ALICE	Cancelled Humint border-crossing operation.
ANITA	Elint search operation.
ANNY	Humint border-crossing operation.
ARGUS	Special communications network organised as part of the Stay Behind occupation preparedness.
ATUB	Training scheme for shipping agents. See DELFINUS.
BABYFACE	The first US U-2 reconnaissance operation from Bodø air station.
BAMSE	Humint border-crossing operation.
BARBARA	Humint border-crossing operation.
BARHAUG	Elint station in south Varanger near the Soviet border.
BETTY	Cancelled Humint border-crossing operation.
BLUE MIX	A network under the Stay Behind occupation preparedness scheme, for the reception and repatriation of Allied military personnel.
BRIDGE	Acoustint operation for surveillance of submarines.
CANASTA	A further development of the BRIDGE operation.
CANOPUS	Elint boat operation.
CARMEN	Elint boat operation with the special vessel *Marjata*.
CAROLINE	Elint search operation.
CATHERINE	Elint boat operation.
CATHINKA	Elint search operation.
CODHOOK	Telint operation by the Fauske II telemetry station for satellite and missile surveillance.

COOKER	USAF codename for Elint co-operation with Norway in the late 1950s.
CORONA	US 1960s programme for photographic intelligence by satellites.
CORVUS	Elint programme, see MAD CAT.
CP	See CROCK POT.
CP-Y	British operation for nuclear test registrations.
CREEK MAID	Elint programme, see MAD CAT.
CREEK ROCK	Elint programme, see MAD CAT.
CROCK POT	Operation for the registration of Soviet nuclear tests, especially on Novaya Zemlya. Often called just CP.
CYKLUS	Elint boat operation.
DELFINUS	Shipping operation, where selected officers of the Norwegian merchant navy observed, photographed and registered items of possible interest in Eastern Bloc waters and ports.
DINA	Plans, apparently abandoned, for landing agents on the Murmansk coast by boat.
DOROTHY	Humint border-crossing operation.
DREAMBOAT	US plan for a series of air reconnaissance operations by C-130 aircraft, using Bodø air station.
DUE	Humint border-crossing operation.
EFRAIM	Comint search operation for Soviet KGB radio station in the Svalbard archipelago.
ELINOR	Elint operations by DELFINUS agents.
ERO	(Elektronisk RomOvervåking) Norwegian acronym for the equivalent of Space Surveillance System (SSS).
EUREKA	A communications and analysis centre, first planned for Finnmark but later established at Defence Command North Norway near Bodø.
FILTER	Humint border-crossing operation.
GJEDDE	Humint border-crossing operation.
GLOBUS	Norwegian nickname for the MAD CAT Elint system.
HAMILCAR	Mobile Elint operation, see ORION.
HAVANA	Humint border-crossing operation.

HEKLA	Elint/Radint station at Vardø, operated by the RNoAF.
H(igh) P(riority)	Norwegian nickname for the expansion of Comint operations from 1959 onwards.
ICEBOX	Elint search operation at the METRO station.
JACK FROST	Planned but cancelled seismic operation as part of CROCK POT.
JUPITER	First plan for industrial protection as part of an occupation preparedness, subsequently included in Stay Behind.
KORNELIUS	Air reconnaissance and 'ferret' operations operated by the RNoAF along the Soviet border.
LINDA	Humint border-crossing operation.
LINDUS	Intelligence collection element of the occupation preparedness scheme Stay Behind.
LOFAR	Low Frequency Analysing Recorder – for acoustic intelligence operation against Soviet submarines.
LOG CABIN	Humint border-crossing operation.
LYDIA	An NDRE digital processor for correlation of acoustic signals from submarines (see BRIDGE and LOFAR).
MAD CAT	(Mobile Automatic Digital Collection and Analysis Trailers) – a joint Elint operations system established in Finnmark by the RNoAF and NIS in co-operation with USAF. Also known by other nicknames such as SOUTH SEA, MAID MARIAN, CREEK MAID, CREEK ROCK, CORVUS and GLOBUS.
MAIBLOMST	Elint search operation.
MAID MARIAN	see MAD CAT.
METRO	NIS Elint/Comint station at Korpfjell, eastern Finnmark.
MINERAL	Air reconnaissance operations by the RNoAF in the 1950s.
MULDVARP	A co-operative operation by the NIS and the Security Police for eavesdropping on Soviet ship-chartering offices in Oslo.
MYGG	Mobile Comint operation in eastern Finnmark.

NABBEN	RNoAF Elint station near Høybuktmoen by Kirkenes.
NILSEN	Humint border-crossing operation.
NORUSA	'Communications Intelligence Agreement' between the United States and Norway, the first one dated 10 December 1954.
OCEAN	Humint border-crossing operation.
OLD AGE	USAF–RNoAF agreement for the establishment and operation of Elint stations, nickname later changed to ROCKY MOUNT.
ORION	Mobile Elint operation as part of the CANOPUS system.
PATIENCE	Acoustic intelligence operation for surveillance of submarines, based on Andøya.
PEDER	The first RNoAF air reconnaissance operation along the Norwegian–Soviet border, in August 1952.
PEGGY	Planned but abandoned Humint operations involving landing agents by boat on the Murmansk coast.
PINE FOREST	Acoustint etc. station at Karasjok for registration of nuclear tests.
POKER	Operation to lay a 110-nm cable with hydrophones northwards from the coast of Finnmark.
POLAR REIN (PR)	Operation for electromagnetic registration of Soviet nuclear tests from a station near Høybuktmoen.
RENA	Humint border-crossing operation.
RENOVATE	Norwegian submarine patrols for surveillance of Soviet maritime activities in the Barents Sea.
RETARDATION	NATO plans for guerrilla operations to delay enemy advances.
RETINA/FOKUS	RNoAF photo reconnaissance operations along the border.
RITA	Humint border-crossing operation.
ROC	(Originally ROCAMBOLE) A Stay Behind organisation for sabotage operations behind enemy lines under an occupation of the country.

ROCKY MOUNT	Elint, see OLD AGE.
SATURN	The initial plan for an intelligence Stay Behind organisation as part of an occupation preparedness scheme.
SOSUS	Sound Surveillance System (United States) for detection of submarines.
SOUTH SEA	Elint operation, see MAD CAT.
SUNSHINE	Multi-purpose boat operation 1955.
TIPSEY	Defence Station Oslo, analysis centre.
TORKEL	The first Comint operation in Finnmark, which eventually grew into the main Comint station FFSV, Vadsø.
TRULS	Mountain cabin in central south Norway intended as back-up command post for Stay Behind.
UPPSALA	Humint border-crossing operation.
URANUS	Intelligence expedition to Svalbard in 1947.
VEGA	RNoAF air reconnaissance operation along the Soviet border.

MAP 1: ACTIVE NORWEGIAN INTELLIGENCE STATIONS, 1945–72

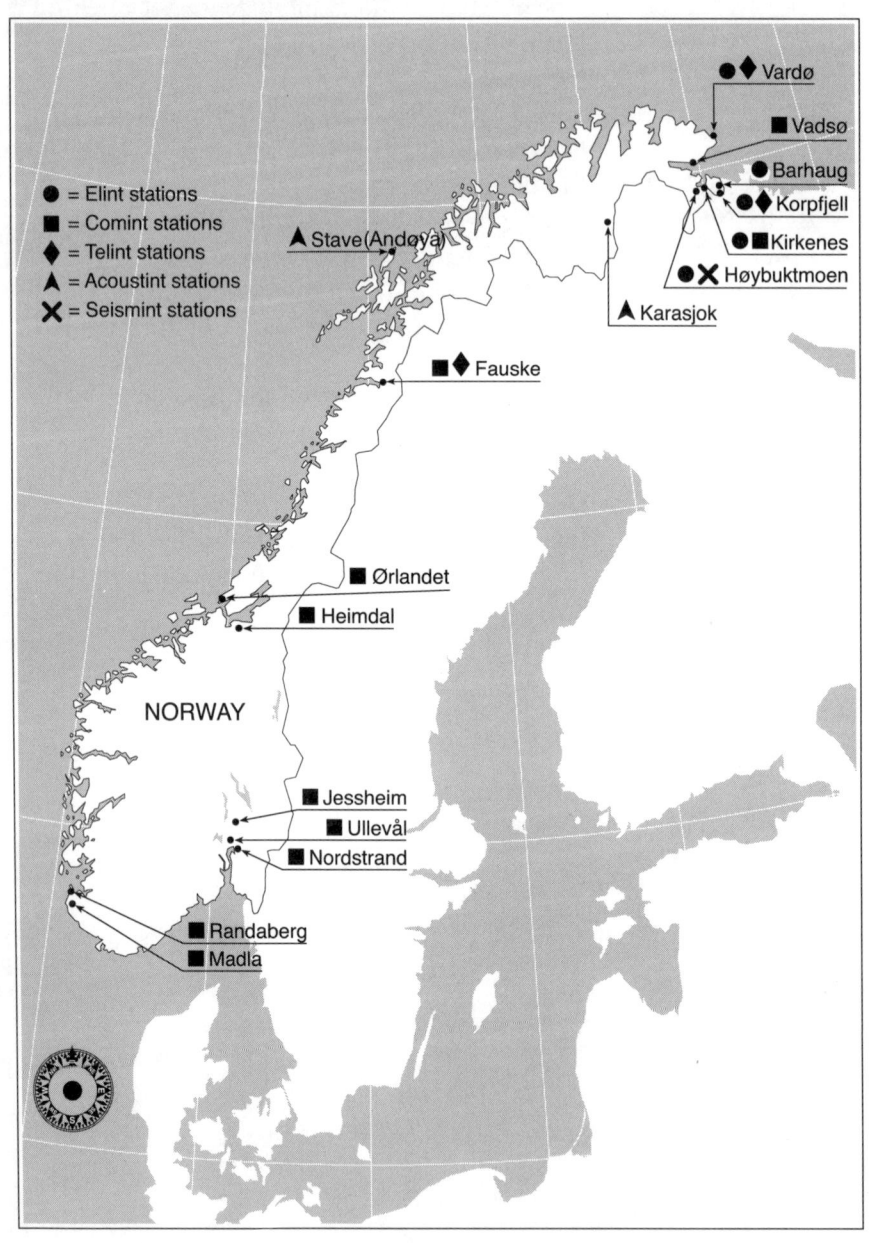

MAP 2: THE NORTHERN SOVIET UNION AND ADJOINING AREAS

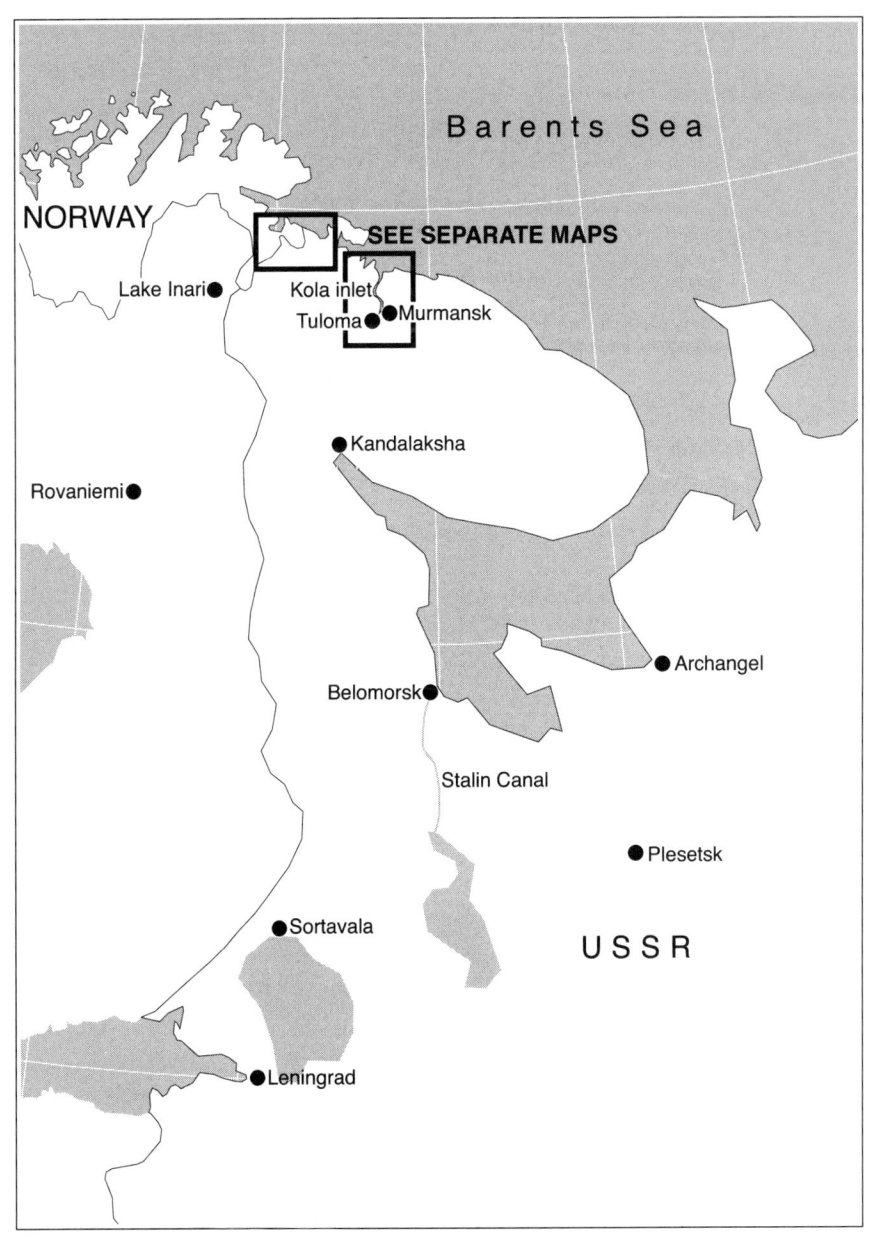

Barents Sea

NORWAY

SEE SEPARATE MAPS

Lake Inari●

Kola inlet

Tuloma● ●Murmansk

● Kandalaksha

Rovaniemi●

● Archangel

Belomorsk●

Stalin Canal

● Plesetsk

● Sortavala

U S S R

●Leningrad

MAP 3: THE SOVIET–NORWEGIAN BORDER REGION

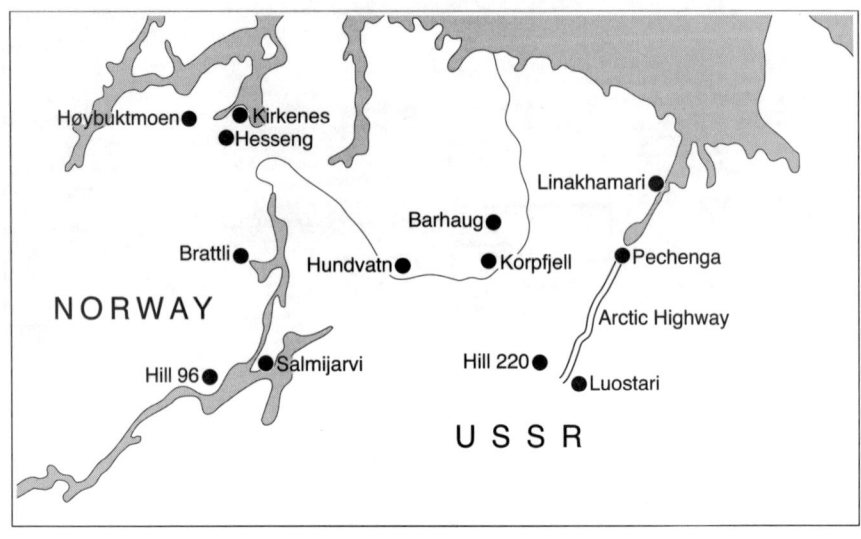

MAP 4: SOME INTELLIGENCE TARGETS IN THE KOLA INLET

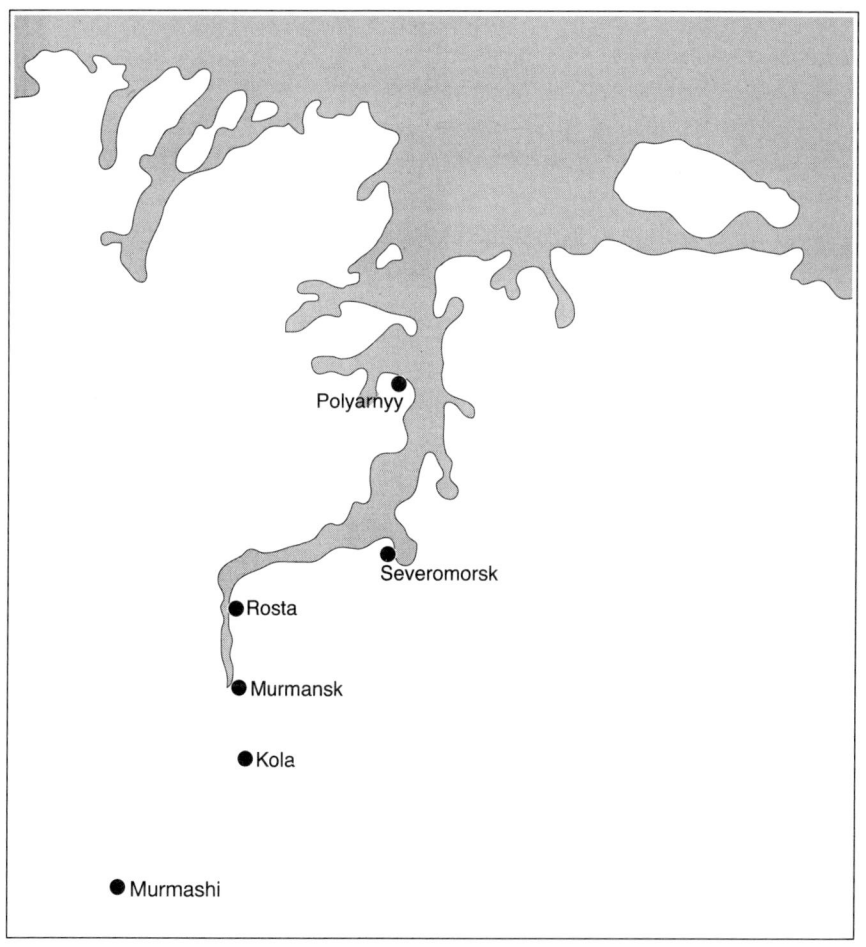

Bibliography

ARCHIVE COLLECTIONS

Norway

FO/E: Archives of the Norwegian Intelligence Service.
FO/S: Archives of the Security Staff, Defence High Command.
FO/Adm: Central Archives of the Defence High Command.
FD (Forsvarsdepartementet): Defence Ministry Archives.
Ministry of Justice, Mellbye Commission Papers.
RR (Riksrevisjonen): files of the Auditor General's Office.
POT (Overvåkingssentralen): Archives of the Security Police.
SMK (Statsministerens kontor): Archives of the Prime Minister's Office.
UD (Utanriksdepartementet): Foreign Ministry Archives.

United Kingdom

PRO: Public Record Office, London.

United States

National Archives, Washington DC.
Lyndon B. Johnson Library, Austin, Texas.
John F. Kennedy Library, Boston, Massachusetts.

Sweden

Documents of the Swedish 'Neutralitetspolitikkommisjonen', 1994.

OFFICIAL PUBLICATIONS AND REPORTS

Stortinget

St. meld. nr. 18 (1980–81): *Om visse spørsmål innenfor overvåkings- og sikkerhetstjenesten.*

St. meld. nr. 39 (1992–93): *Om overvåkingstjenesten.*

Dokument nr. 15 (1995–96): *Rapport til Stortinget fra kommisjonen som ble nedsatt av Stortinget for å granske påstander om ulovlig overvåking av norske borgere* (Lund-rapporten).

NOU 1994: 4: *Kontrollen med de hemmelige tjenester.*

'Inberetning fra utvalget til å undersøke påstander om ulovligheter eller irregulære forhold med tilknytning til Forsvarets etterretningstjeneste (Nygaard-Haug utvalget), 30. juni 1994'.

CIA, History Staff

CIA Documents on the Cuban Missile Crisis 1962 (CIA, Washington, DC, 1992).

The CIA under Harry Truman (CIA, Washington, DC, 1994).

Estimates on Soviet Military Power 1954 to 1984. A Selection (CIA, Washington, DC, 1995).

'Corona': America's First Satellite Program (CIA, Washington, DC, 1995).

Intentions and Capabilities: Estimates on Soviet Strategic Forces, 1950–1983 (CIA, Washington, DC, 1996).

National Security Agency

Various publications concerning the VENONA project (NSA, 1995).

SECONDARY SOURCES
(INCLUDES ONLY LITERATURE USED IN WRITING THIS BOOK)

Aldrich, Richard J. (ed.), *British Intelligence, Strategy and the Cold War 1945–51* (Routledge, London, 1992).

Andersen, Roy, *Sin egen fiende: Et protrett av Asbjørn Bryhn* (Cappelen, Oslo, 1992).

Bamford, James, *The Puzzle Palace: A Report on America's Most Secret Agency* (Houghton Mifflin, Boston, MA, 1982).

Berdal, Mats R., *The United States, Norway and the Cold War, 1945–60* (Macmillan, London, 1997).

Bergh, Trond, and Eriksen, Knut E., *Den hemmelige krigen. Overvåking i Norge 1914–1997*, Vols I–II (Cappelen, Oslo, 1998).

Blindheim, Svein, *Offiser i krig og fred* (Det Norske Samlaget, Oslo, 1981).

Bower, Tom, *The Perfect English Spy: Sir Dick White and the Secret War 1935–90* (Heinemann, London, 1995).

Christensen, Christian, *Det hemmelige Norge* (Atheneum, Oslo 1983).

Christensen, Christian, *Vår hemmelige beredskap. Historien om MM* (Cappelen, Oslo, 1988).

Darling, Arthur B., *The Central Intelligence Agency: An Instrument of Government, to 1950* (Pennsylvania State University Press, Philadelphia, PA, 1990).

Gleditsch, Nils Petter, and Wilkes, Owen, *Onkel Sams kaniner. Teknisk etterretning i Norge* (Pax, Oslo, 1981).

Haarstad, Gunnar, *I hemmelig tjeneste. Etterretning og overvåking i krig og fred* (Aschehoug, Oslo, 1988).

Herman, Michael, *Intelligence Power in Peace and War* (Cambridge University Press, Cambridge, 1996).

Isungset, Odd, and Jentoft, Morten, *Verkebyllen* (Tiden, Oslo, 1995).

Jacobsen, Alf R., and Mørk, Egil, *Svartkammeret. Den innerste hemmeligheten* (Cappelen, Oslo,1989).

Jacobsen, Alf R., *Mistenksomhetens pris: Krigen om de hemmelige tjenester* (Aschehoug, Oslo, 1995).

Johannessen, Folke Hauger, *Erindringer 1948–1973* (Norse, Oslo, 1998).

Mangold, Tom, *Cold Warrior. James Jesus Angleton: The CIA's Master Spy Hunter* (Simon & Schuster, London, 1991).

MccGwire, Michael, *Military Objectives in Soviet Foreign Policy* (Brookings, Washington, DC, 1987).

Meyer, Johan Kr., *NATOs kritikere: Den sikkerhetspolitiske opposisjon 1949–1961*. IFS, *Forsvarsstudier*, 3 (1989).

Njølstad, Olav, and Wicken, Olav, *Kunnskap som våpen: Forsvarets forskningsinstitutt 1946–1975* (TANO Aschehoug, Oslo, 1997).

Nordahl, Konrad, *Dagbøker*, Bd. I (1950–55) and II (1956–1975), (Tiden, Oslo, 1991–92).

Powers, Thomas, *The Man Who Kept the Secrets: Richard Helms and the CIA* (Alfred A. Knopf, New York, 1979).

Richelson, Jeffrey T., and Ball, Desmond, *The Ties That Bind: Intelligence Cooperation between the UKUSA Countries* (Allen & Unwin, Boston, MA, 1985).

Riste, Olav, *Weserübung: Det perfekte strategiske overfall?* IFS, *Forsvarsstudier*, 4 (1990).

Riste, Olav (ed.), *Western Society: The Formative Years* (Norwegian University Press, Oslo, 1985).

Sørdahl, Roger W., *U-1. Et amerikansk spionasjeprosjekt i Norge* (Cappelen, Oslo, 1985).

Tamnes, Rolf, *The United States and the Cold War in the High North* (Ad Notam, Oslo, 1991).

Tamnes, Rolf, 'Norges hemmelige tjenester under den kalde krigen. Et sammenlignende internasjonalt perspektiv', *IFS Info*, 5 (1992).

Tamnes, Rolf, *Oljealder. 1965–1995* (Universitetsforlaget, Oslo, 1998).

Tofte, Ørnulf, *Spaneren: Overvåking for rikets sikkerhet* (Gyldandal, Oslo, 1987).

Westerfield, H. Bradford, *Inside the CIA's Private World: Declassified Articles from the Agency's Internal Journal 1955–1992* (Yale University Press, New Haven, CT, 1995).

Zaloga, Steven J., *Soviet Air Defense Missiles* (Jane's Information Group, London, 1989).

Index

Aas, Sverre, 194
Acoustint (acoustic intelligence), nuclear weapons tests, 192, 193, 200, 201–2, 207–8; submarines, 164–88, 291
air forces: Norwegian (RNoAF), 15, 21, 25, 61–4, 95, 102, 115–43, 155–6, 159, 160, 170, 182, 227; United Kingdom (RAF), 21, 44, 64–6, 67, 68, 95, 102,124, 128, 227; United States (USAF), 66–74, 102, 109, 123, 124–7, 136, 138–42, 154–5, 159–60, 193, 195, 197, 203, 206, 208–9
Åkenenes, Oddmund, 186
Alexander, A. V., 24
Alexander, Lord, 124
Andersen, Andreas, 78, 89, 126, 129, 195, 263–5
Andersen, Robert E., 86
Andøya, 70, 164–84
Angleton, James, 274–7
ARGUS (communications network), 49
Auditor-General's Office (Riksrevisjonen), 235–6, 238–9, 241
Ausland, John, 243

BARHAUG (Elint station), 108, 110; air force establishment of, 131, 133, 134, 139–40, 141–2, 244; taken over by NIS, 152, 153, 155–6, 158, 160, 161–2
Beck, Louis, 104
Berg, Johan (Chief of Intelligence 1966–70), 80, 177, 221, 233, 260, 277; becomes Chief of Intelligence, 284; and Andøya projects, 178, 179, 183, 184; organisational changes, 257–8, 271; and Stay Behind, 53–4

Berg, Ole (Chief of Defence Staff), 10, 18, 24, 26, 262–5
Bernard, Richard L., 216
BLUE MIX (Stay Behind reception and repatriation network), 42, 45, 46, 49, 53
border crossings (agents), 56–61
Borten, Per (Prime Minister 1965–71), 246–7
Bryhn, Asbjørn (Chief of Security Police 1947–66), 15, 17, 28, 30, 59, 274; and Lygren affair, 274–8
Brynildsen, Jon Krag (head of Comint section), 7–9, 91, 95–8, 102, 117, 132, 194
Buzzard, Anthony Wass, 62

Cabinet Defence and Security Committee, 32, 133, 142, 167, 195, 198, 199, 201, 208, 216, 254; and aerial reconnaissance, 62, 67, 70; and Comint, 103–9; concerned about Russian reactions, 108–9, 151–2, 244–7
Central Intelligence Agency (CIA), 35, 50, 60, 88, 96, 101, 102–3, 115, 123–4, 143, 147, 153, 213, 216; and U-2, 67, 70, 73, 74; and shipping agents, 79–80; Oslo station, 86–7, 92, 95, 101, 103, 126, 227; and NORUSA, 90; intelligence estimates, 191, 205, 214; and Lygren affair, 274–5
Chiles, Griffin, 85–6
CIA, *see* Central Intelligence Agency
Comint (communications intelligence), 84–5, 128, 291; TORKEL as first

station, 8–10, 21, 23, 25, 84;
NORUSA agreement, 85–92; further
expansion, 95–112; and nuclear tests,
199–200, 204–5
Control Committee, 10, 94, 106, 108–9,
183, 235, 237; reorganisation, 238–40,
241
Co-ordination Committee: early
establishment of, 15, 23, 60, 62, 66,
77, 88, 89, 129–30, 135, 250, 254, 274;
and Finland operations, 56–7, 58–9;
reorganisation, 263–4, 284–5, 294
CORONA (US satellite project), 214,
220
Crocker, J. Allan, 196, 198
cryptography, 3–4, 23, 92–5, 291–2

Dahl, Arne D., 9, 23
Defence Council, 13, 15, 24, 28–9, 38, 39
Defence High Command, wartime, 2–7,
18; recreated, 287
Defence Staff, 13, 15, 41,67, 70, 99–100,
103, 108, 111, 120, 125–6, 143, 161,
176, 186, 196, 197, 238–40, 276;
relations with Intelligence Staff, 7, 26,
236–7, 239, 249, 257–8, 264–6;
intervenes in RNoAF–NIS dispute,
132–41
DELFINUS, *see* shipping agents
Denmark, 11, 46, 49, 226
Dulles, Allen, 66, 74, 88

Egge, Bjørn, 153
Eisenhower, D. D., 71, 73, 214
Ekeland, Arne, 55
Elint (electronic intelligence), 69, 84,
99–101, 115–43; NIS takes over,
146–62
Evang, Vilhelm (Chief of Intelligence
1946–66): made Intelligence Chief,
6–7; early plans, 10, 11, 13, 15–18, 21,
23; involvement in security and
surveillance, 17–18, 25–6, 30, 32,
46–8; resists NATO's involvement in
SB, 43, 46–8; and Finland operations,
55–60; and air reconnaissance, 25,
63–4, 65–9; role in U-2 affair, 69–74,
283; wants control of Elint, 103, 121,
123–4, 125, 128, 132–7; his 'national

policy', 43–8, 68–9, 78, 89, 107, 109,
133, 143, 173–4, 195–7, 207, 213, 228,
231–2, 254–5, 273, 290–1; supports
Acoustint plans, 172, 201–3, 207–8;
proposes Telint station, 215–16;
difficult relations with military, 256,
266–8, 273, 277–83; and Lygren
affair, 274–7, 280; forced to resign,
283–4; and *passim*

Falchenberg, Dag, 11, 86, 95, 96, 97, 98,
120
Fauske, 87–91, 110, 216–18, 220
Finland, 15, 24–5, 51–2, 55–60, 64, 251,
253
France, 16, 43, 45

GCHQ (UK Government
Communications Headquarters),
95–6, 227–8
Gerhardsen, Einar (Prime Minister
1945–51 and 1955–65), 13, 216; and
surveillance of communists, 14, 28;
suspects NIS involvement in
surveillance, 32; approves intelligence
activities, 70, 104, 193, 195, 204, 245–6
Gerhardsen, Werna, 32
Germany (Federal Republic of), 226, 229
Golitsyn, Anatolyi, 274–5
Great Britain, *see* United Kingdom
Gundersen, Hans B., 178, 187
Gundersen, Herman F. Zeiner, 178–9,
257–8, 276, 282
Gundersen, Oscar C. (Justice Minister),
15, 28, 65, 245–6, 275

Haarstad, Gunnar, 279
Haavik, Gunvor Galtung, 277
Handal, Nils (Defence Minister
1954–61), 67, 69, 70, 99, 156, 173,
198, 199, 201, 238; supports extension
of Comint, 103–4; inspects
intelligence stations, 151–2; proposes
BRIDGE project, 167
Harlem, Gudmund (Defence Minister
1961–65), 216, 222, 244, 246, 268,
281–2, 294; approves extending
Comint, 108–9; and monitoring of
nuclear tests, 203, 204, 207–8

Hauge, Jens Christian (Defence Minister 1945–52), 14, 15, 24, 27, 28, 38, 39, 193–4, 235, 250, 270, 294; and Stay Behind, 16–20, 34–7, 40
Hauge, Sven, 181
Haugland, Jens, 195
Haugland, Knut, 96, 121–37 *passim*, 141
HEKLA (Air Force Elint/Radint station, Vardø), 108, 110, 129, 130–1, 137–42, 152, 153, 158–62, 218
Hellerslien, Erling, 86, 95, 96, 203
Helms, Richard, 161
Herman, Michael, 119, 225, 232
Heyerdahl, Lars R., 135, 229, 277
Himle, Erik, 109, 245; State Secretary, Ministry of Defence, 69, 104, 142, 151–2, 201, 203, 295; Permanent Secretary, Ministry of Defence, 177, 183–4, 243–4
Holberg, Karl, 141
Huizenga, John H., 293
Humint (human intelligence), *see* border crossings, and shipping agents

intelligence co-operation, 225–33, 288–9; as 'sets of professional bargains', 225, 232–3, 288–9; balance between collection and analysis, 90–1, 96–8, 107, 199–200, 204–5, 213, 216, 218, 289–91; national control of activities, 77–8, 100, 133, 136, 139, 142–3, 173–4, 179, 193, 197, 295–6
Israel, 230–1

Jacobsen, Ernst, 147–8
Jensen, Erling, 87
Johannessen, Folke Hauger (Chief of Defence), 53, 108, 175, 178, 183, 186; values Andøya project, 184; wants control of Intelligence Staff, 268–71; and Lygren affair, 275, 277, 279; doubts about Evang, 280–4
Johansen, Trond, 172, 233, 277, 294
Johnsen, Einar Tufte, 71, 125, 140
JUPITER (protection of industry), 15, 17, 18

Kaldager, Christian R., 232, 269, 278, 280, 282

Kekkonen, Urho, 57, 59
KGB, 110–11, 274–5, 277
Khrushchev, Nikita, 67–8, 71, 76, 202
Kola Peninsula, intelligence target, 22, 60, 65, 66, 68, 76–7, 94, 96, 101–3, 130, 147; Soviet build-up, 115–16, 129, 165, 185, 199, 219
Krogh, Christian Fredrik von, 238–9
Kruse, Erling, 135, 161
Kval, Knut Willy, 95

Lange, Halvard (Foreign Minister 1946–65), 38, 39, 71, 73, 193, 195, 246, 283
Langhelle, Nils (Defence Minister 1952–54), 56, 62, 230, 262
Lerheim, Andreas, 5, 274
Lie, Trygve, 5, 245
Lied, Finn, 134, 209
Lien, Jens, 34
LINDUS (Stay Behind intelligence network), 39, 41–2, 45, 51, 53
Loehnis, Sir Clive, 228
Løken, Harald, 108
Lund, Alfred Roscher, 1–6
Lund, Arne G., 222, 295
Lütken, Hans T.H., 235
Lygren, Ingeborg, 274–80

Martell, Charles B., 179–80
Martens, Kaj, 5, 11
Matthews, H. Freeman, 89, 126
Mellbye, J.C. (in Mellbye Commission of Inquiry), 279–85
merchant navy, 74–81; in Far East, 77–9
METRO (Elint/Comint station Korpfjell), 108, 141, 149–58, 160
Meyer, Alf Martens, 78, 102, 194, 201, 203, 217; organises Elint, 139, 142–3, 146–7, 150, 151, 153
MI6 (UK secret intelligence service), 2, 10, 20, 228
Mikoyan, Anastas I., 73
Military Affairs Committee, *see* Storting
Ministry of Defence, 1, 2, 6, 10, 98, 136, 146, 160, 167, 196, 236–7, 264, 271, 294
Ministry of Foreign Affairs, 4, 294
Mohr, Wilhelm, 143, 180, 232

Møller, Fredrik, 193, 195
Motzfeldt, Birger F., 131–2, 136

NABBEN (RNoAF Elint station,
  Kirkenes), 108, 134, 137–42, 152,
  158–9
National Security Agency, 20, 90, 93, 98,
  102, 103, 123, 124, 213, 216; interest
  in Norwegian Comint, 85, 92, 95, 97,
  227; intelligence targets, 106–7
NATO, 35, 99, 100, 107, 123, 125, 155,
  171, 222, 245, 249, 258–9; Norway
  joins, 24, 27; interest in electronic
  warfare, 119–21, 129; Norway seeks
  influence on threat assessments,
  231–2, 252–5; and Stay Behind,
  42–54; 'Retardation' planning, 48–54
navies: Norwegian (RNoN), 15, 76,
  167–83, 185–8, 289; United Kingdom
  (RN), 62, 175–6, 178, 227, 228, 289;
  United States (USN), 166–84, 232,
  289
NDRE, *see* Norwegian Defence Research
  Establishment
Netherlands, 16, 46, 231
Nielsen, Sivert, 89, 126, 130, 133, 136,
  196–7, 295
Nødtvedt, Henrik, 170
Nordlie, Jens H., 20, 35, 37, 40
NORUSA (Norwegian–US intelligence
  co-operation agreement): 1952
  informal arrangement, 86–90; 1954
  agreement, 91–2, 96–8, 227;
  extension, 102–5, 108–10, 240–2, 244,
  245; NORUSA II, 161–2
Norwegian Defence Research
  Establishment, 134, 146–8, 158,
  166–70, 174, 179, 181, 184, 188, 193,
  195–7, 209
Novaya Zemlya: air reconnaissance of, 65,
  70; boat operation to, 148; nuclear test
  site, 195, 197–200, 203–5
NSA, *see* National Security Agency

Øen, Bjarne, 48, 141, 173
Ollestad, Sven, 233

Palm, Thede, 77, 226
Pavlov, Gregoriy F., 31, 58

Photint (photographic intelligence), 21,
  23, 25, 61–83
PINE FOREST (Karasjok Acoustint,
  etc., station), 109, 208–9
POLAR REIN (Kirkenes Seismint etc.,
  station), 109, 205–9
Porter, Robert (Bob), 172–3
Poulden, Edward (Teddy), 95–6, 129
Powers, Gary, 71–4, 116

Radint (radar intelligence), 72, 108, 110,
  119–20, 130–1, 152, 153, 157, 159
Ramm, Fredrik, 198
Rasmussen, Adolf Harbitz, 46
Reiss-Andersen, Helge, 142, 152, 156–7,
  161, 217
Ringvold, Hans, 41
Robertsen, Lars W., 121
ROC (Stay Behind sabotage network),
  19–21, 34–41, 46, 51, 53
Rowlett, Frank B., 90
Royal Air Force, *see* air forces
Royal Norwegian Air Force, *see* air forces
Ruge, Carl, 276, 284

SATURN (Stay Behind intelligence
  network), 15, 16–17, 18, 34, 41
security, 3–4, 11, 14–15, 17–18, 25–6,
  28–30, 288; part of remit of
  Intelligence Staff, 7, 25, 26, 265;
  civil/military 'turf battles', 30, 226,
  274–7; separate Security Staff
  established, 268–9, 274, 280, 284
Security Police, 14, 17, 25, 28, 29, 31, 32,
  40, 111, 256; conflicts with NIS, 30,
  274–7; and Lygren affair, 274–7
Seismint (seismic intelligence), 108,
  192–3, 195–6, 206, 207, 209
shipping agents, 15, 74–83, 148, 158, 240
Sigint (signals intelligence), 15, 62, 72,
  84, 102, 106, 117, 137, 161, 212, 214,
  246–7, 291; boat operations, 147–9;
  and nuclear tests, 199; and ABM
  systems, 219; increasing
  specialisation, 233; *see also* Comint,
  Elint, Telint
Sire, Thor, 235–6, 238–9, 240–1
Skau, Hallfred, 22, 25, 55, 58, 88
Sørenssen, Aimar, 179–81

Soviet Union, 22, 23, 26, 40, 55, 64, 69, 71, 74, 76, 129, 140, 152, 289, 291; perceived threat from, 14, 24–5, 52, 222, 252–5, 258–60; agents of, 31, 111; target areas for NIS, 9, 21, 56, 57, 60, 61–3, 84–9, 90–2, 96, 101–2, 110, 115–16, 130, 147–8, 150, 154–5; protests against Western intelligence activity, 57, 58, 65–6, 68, 71, 73, 296; submarines, 101, 104, 106, 156–7, 164–87; nuclear weapons, 106–7, 191–209

Stay Behind (occupation preparedness network), 15–21, 29, 30, 34–53, 227, 233, 237, 240, 247, 288; *see also* BLUE MIX, LINDUS, ROC

Stordahl, Nils, 5, 93, 292

Storting (Norwegian Parliament), 10, 29, 71, 98, 235, 237–9, 247, 288; Military Affairs Committee, 104, 236, 237, 239, 240, 242, 246, 247, 264, 271

Stuart, Harold, 20

Svalbard (Spitsbergen), 11, 21, 70, 110–11, 148, 221–3

Svensen, Henrik, 104, 248

Sweden, 7–8, 51, 77, 86, 96, 150, 226–7, 253

Taylor, Rufus L., 172, 174

Telint (telemetric intelligence), 212–13, 291; CODHOOK station, 216–20

Thon, Asbjørn, 122, 127, 130

Thorsen, Bjarne, 111, 148

Tidemand, Otto Grieg (Defence Minister 1965–70), 179, 186, 209, 242, 246, 273, 279–80, 284

Tordella, Louis, 85–6, 90, 106, 107, 213

TORKEL (first Comint operation), 8–10, 21, 23, 25, 84, 226

Torp, Oscar (Prime Minister 1951–55), 56, 62

Torp, Reidar (Chief of Intelligence 1970–75), 187, 232, 258–9, 295

U-2, 66–74, 151, 177, 201, 214, 283, 296

United Kingdom, 10–11, 16–17, 20–1, 24, 64, 166, 169, 175–6, 203, 204, 206, 227–8; and Stay Behind, 16–17, 34–7, 46, 53–4; and Sigint, 68, 95–6, 116–17, 123, 124–5, 128, 130, 135; *see also under* air forces and navies

United States of America, 11, 14, 20, 77–9, 80–1; and Stay Behind, 35–7, 53–4, 60; and Sigint, 85–109, 121–44, 147–8, 153–6, 159–62; and monitoring of nuclear tests, 191–210; and telemetry 212–21; financing of NIS, 240–6; *see also under* air forces and navies

URANUS (intelligence mission to Spitsbergen), 15, 21

Vadsø, 88–91, 108, 110

Vardø, 9, 108, 128, 131, 140

Waage, Jakob Andreas, 125–6, 135–6

Welsh, William (Bill), 78

White, Sir Dick, 228

Willis, Frances, 196–7

Yugoslavia, 229–30

Zorin, Valerian A., 65, 68